MARK WAID FIONA STAPLES
ANNIE WU VERONICA FISH

ARCHIE®

VOLUME ONE

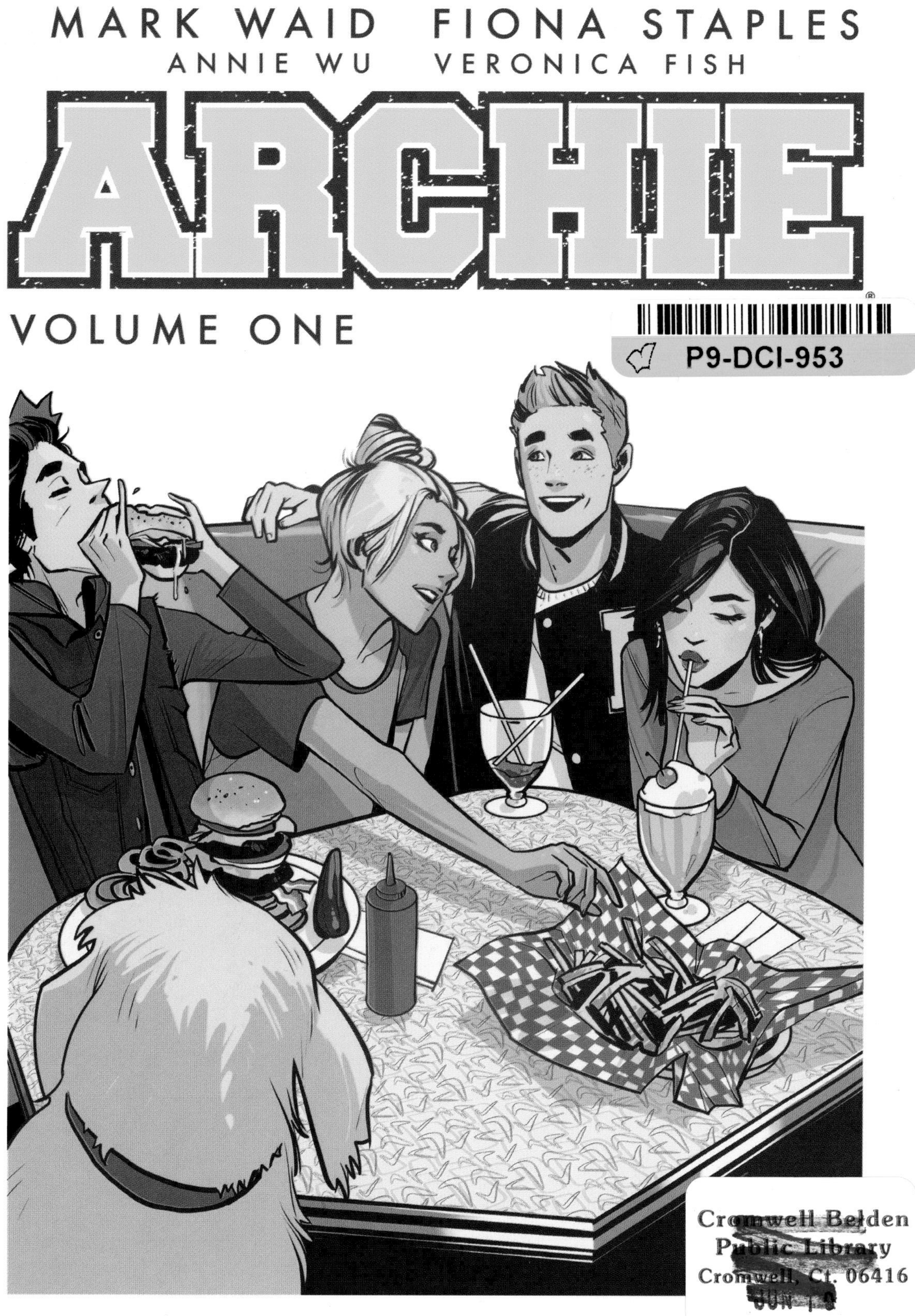

THE NEW RIVERDALE

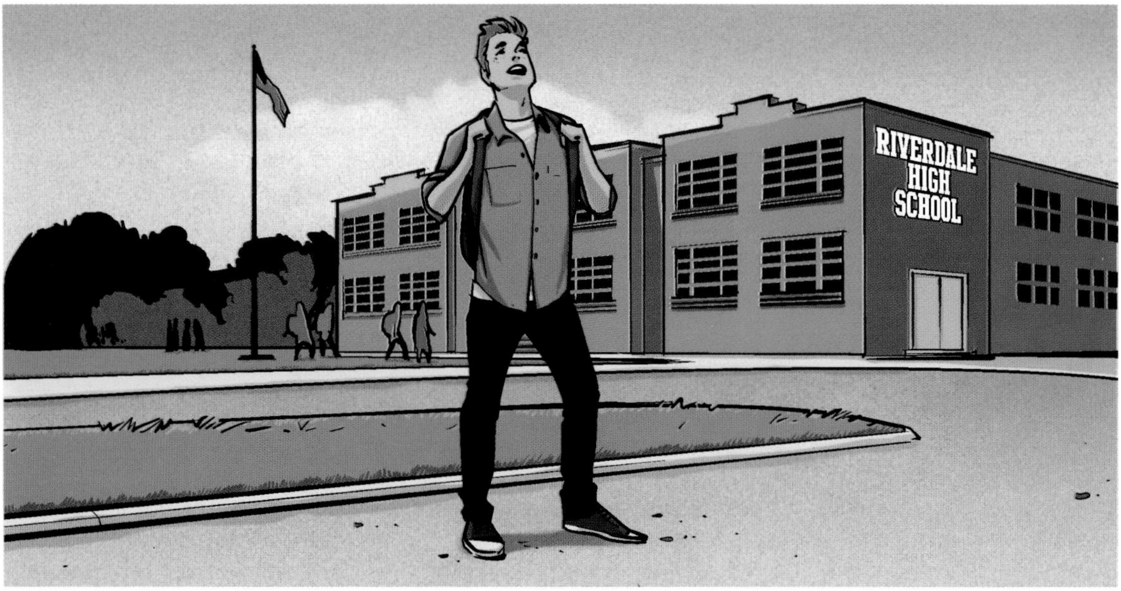
RIVERDALE
HIGH
SCHOOL

STORY BY
MARK WAID

ART BY
FIONA STAPLES (ISSUES 1-3)
ANNIE WU (ISSUE 4)
VERONICA FISH (ISSUES 5-6)

COLORING BY
ANDRE SZYMANOWICZ
WITH JEN VAUGHN

LETTERING BY
JACK MORELLI

PUBLISHER
JON GOLDWATER

EDITOR
MIKE PELLERITO

INTRODUCING THE NEW

ARCHIE®

by FIONA STAPLES

High school is weird. When I was 17 I was a band geek, had hair not unlike Sheila Wu's, was becoming a regular at the comic book store in the mall, and was trying to cull enough anime fanart from my portfolio to apply to Art College. I was in the eye-opening phase between "shy, fearful kid" and "somewhat functional adult." I'd occasionally pick up an old Archie comic out of my vast collection and see nothing that reflected my own experience of school, dating or what people look like in bikinis.

...And it was incredibly endearing! Archie and the gang would never graduate and go to university or get boring full-time jobs. They'd never even had to go through puberty— they just went from being li'l to being teens. Awesome! I didn't expect Archie to be realistic any more than I expected *B.C.* to be historically accurate. They were cute characters, expertly drafted, getting into funny or charmingly bizarre situations. The publisher's commitment to consistency and suspended time made Riverdale iconic. I always thought it would be criminal to disrupt such a comforting tradition, and I still kind of thought that when Archie President Mike Pellerito called me and said they were rebooting the series, and they wanted me to draw it.

"A redesigned Archie? No one wants that!" I thought. "If you change the art style, he won't be Archie anymore, he'll just be some guy with red hair. Oh God, I would be the artist that ruined Archie."

Still, this job offer was clearly a big deal and I wasn't going to turn it down until I knew for sure that it was going to be a terrible disaster. I learned that Mark Waid was going to be writing it, which, hey, was very promising. We scheduled a phone call to talk about what Archie means to us and what we'd want a reboot to look like. Mark opened with, "First of all, there's nothing wrong with Archie."

By the end of our conversation, I was on board. I realized that Mark was a huge fan of these characters, and if I could be as open-minded as the guys at Archie Comics themselves were, we might actually make a pretty good comic. And when Mark sent me the script for #1, any last doubts I had were wiped out and replaced with wild excitement. Archie and Betty have a past, and the future is uncertain! Jughead has known some real troubles, and is canny and wise! I felt that the story's new intricacies just enhanced what the characters had always been. "Wow," I thought. "Anyone could draw this and it would still be Archie!"

I put that theory to the test and drew the gang in my own style. Having grown up on a steady diet of Archie digests, artists like Harry Lucey and Samm Schwartz have always informed my work, and I tried to imbue the characters with at least some of the personality (or "bounce," as Mark calls it) that those masters did. There's a bit more detail and complexity in their world now, but I hope this version of Archie still feels like an old friend! Thanks for picking it up.

ISSUE ONE

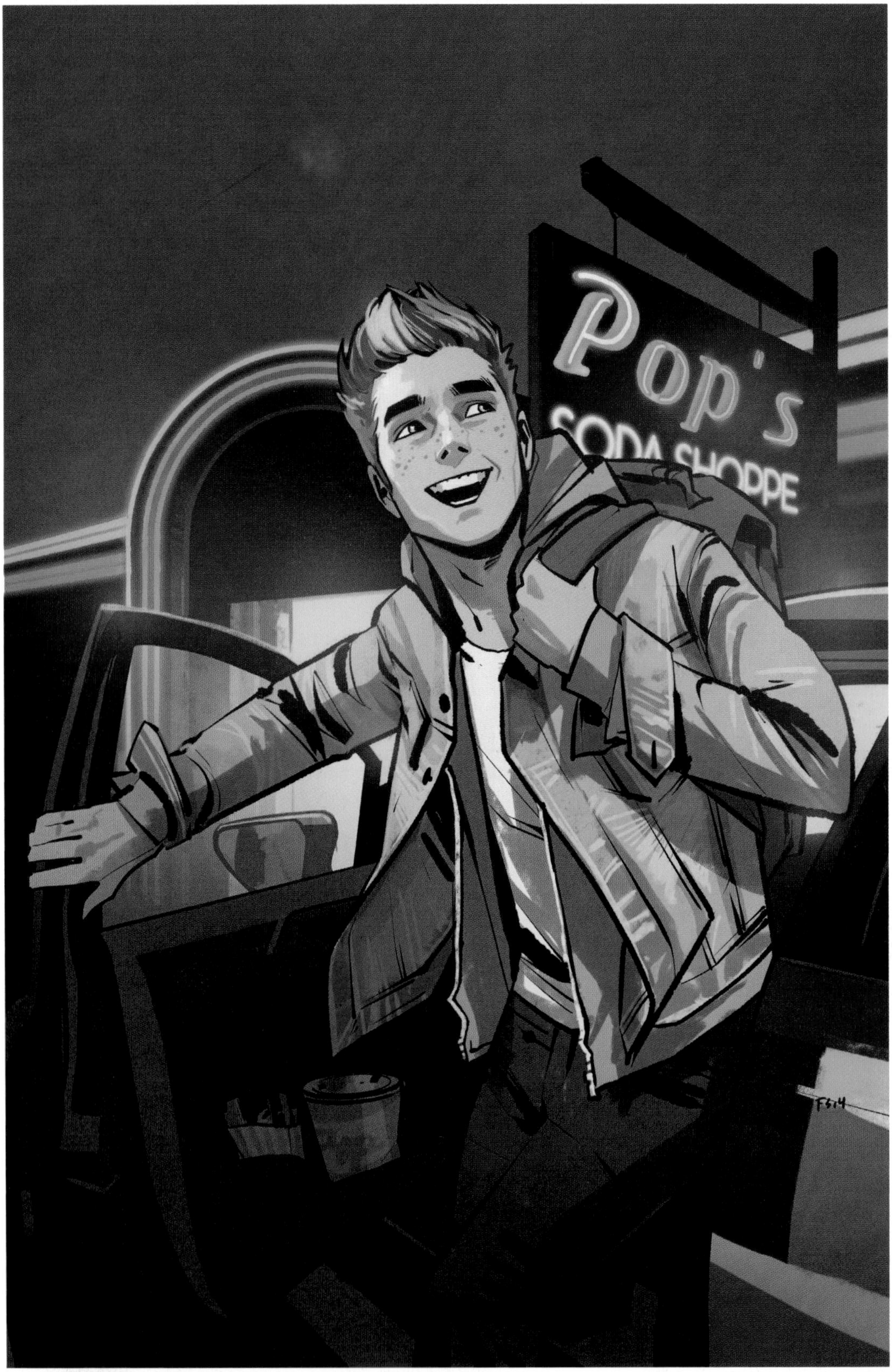
Pop's
SODA SHOPPE

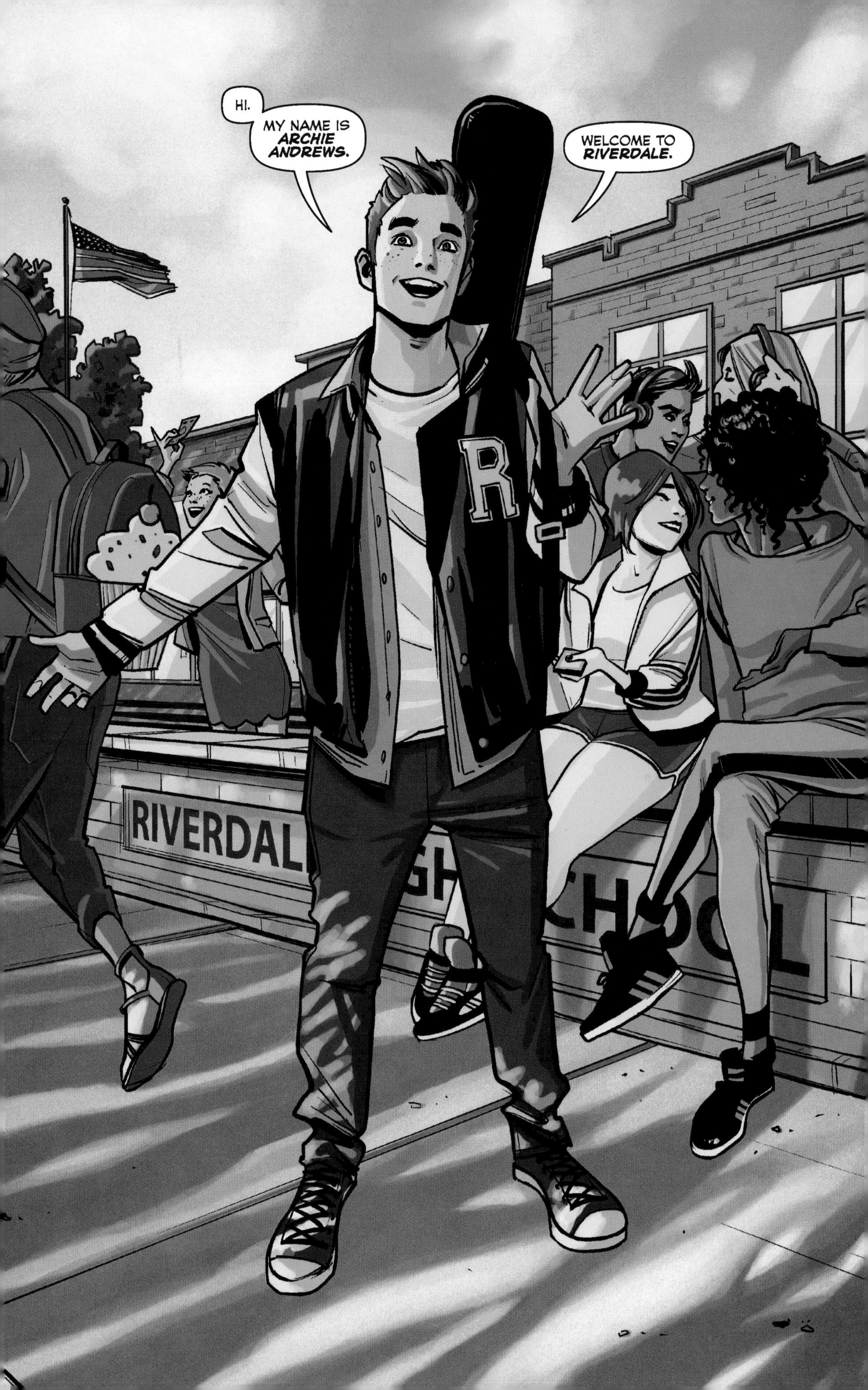
HI.
MY NAME IS ARCHIE ANDREWS.
WELCOME TO RIVERDALE.

CHAPTER ONE: There is this Girl

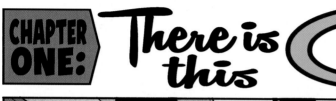

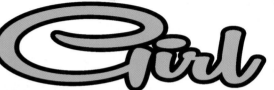

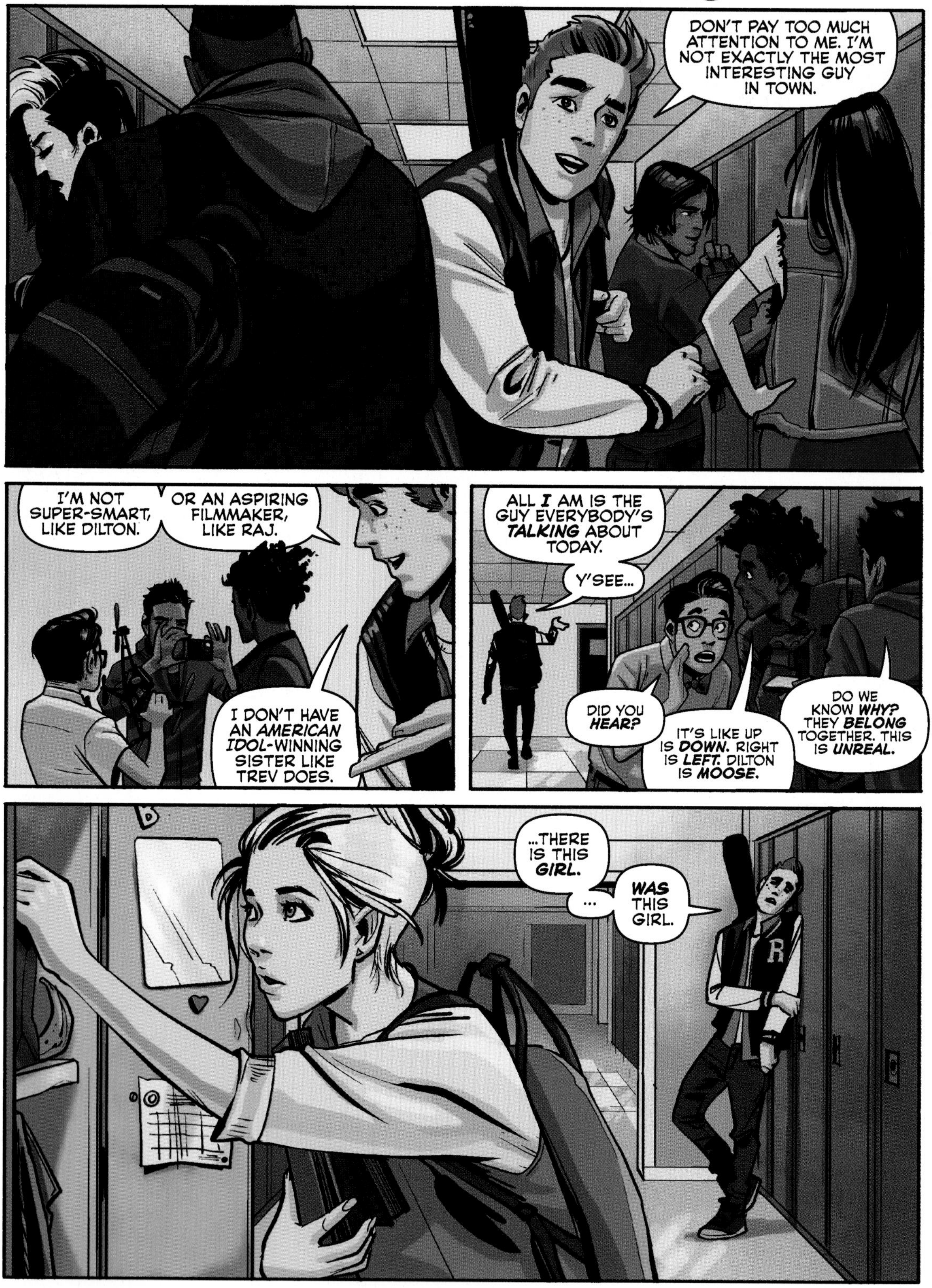
DON'T PAY TOO MUCH ATTENTION TO ME. I'M NOT EXACTLY THE MOST INTERESTING GUY IN TOWN.
I'M NOT SUPER-SMART, LIKE DILTON.
OR AN ASPIRING FILMMAKER, LIKE RAJ.
I DON'T HAVE AN *AMERICAN IDOL*-WINNING SISTER LIKE TREV DOES.
ALL ***I*** AM IS THE GUY EVERYBODY'S ***TALKING*** ABOUT TODAY.
Y'SEE...
DID YOU ***HEAR?***
IT'S LIKE UP IS ***DOWN.*** RIGHT IS ***LEFT.*** DILTON IS ***MOOSE.***
DO WE KNOW ***WHY?*** THEY ***BELONG*** TOGETHER. THIS IS ***UNREAL.***
...THERE IS THIS ***GIRL.***
...
WAS THIS GIRL.

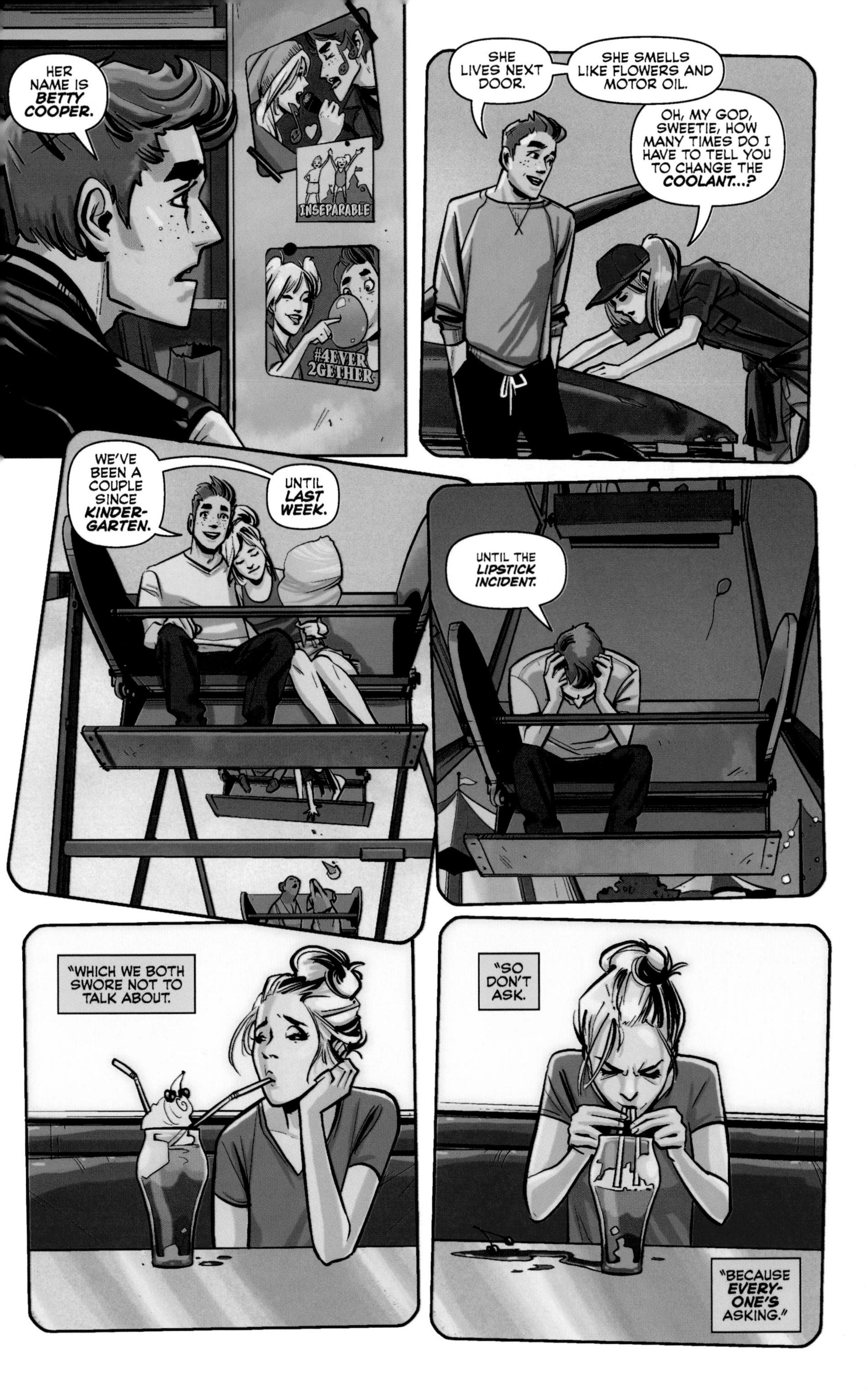
HER NAME IS BETTY COOPER.
INSEPARABLE
#4EVER 2GETHER
SHE LIVES NEXT DOOR.
SHE SMELLS LIKE FLOWERS AND MOTOR OIL.
OH, MY GOD, SWEETIE, HOW MANY TIMES DO I HAVE TO TELL YOU TO CHANGE THE COOLANT...?
WE'VE BEEN A COUPLE SINCE KINDER-GARTEN.
UNTIL LAST WEEK.
UNTIL THE LIPSTICK INCIDENT.
"WHICH WE BOTH SWORE NOT TO TALK ABOUT.
"SO DON'T ASK.
"BECAUSE EVERY-ONE'S ASKING."

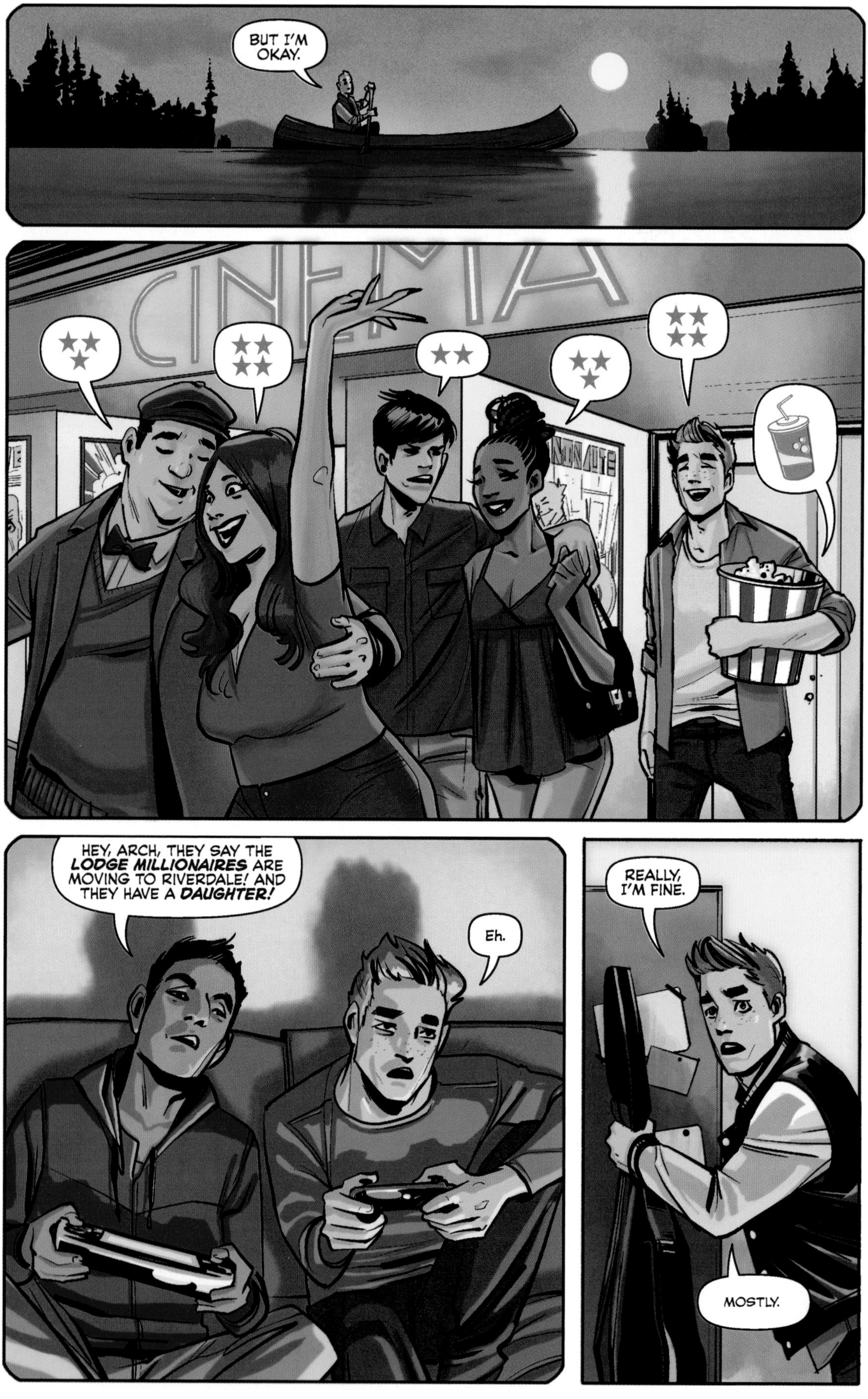
BUT I'M OKAY.
CINEMA
HEY, ARCH, THEY SAY THE **LODGE MILLIONAIRES** ARE MOVING TO RIVERDALE! AND THEY HAVE A **DAUGHTER!**
Eh.
REALLY, I'M FINE.
MOSTLY.

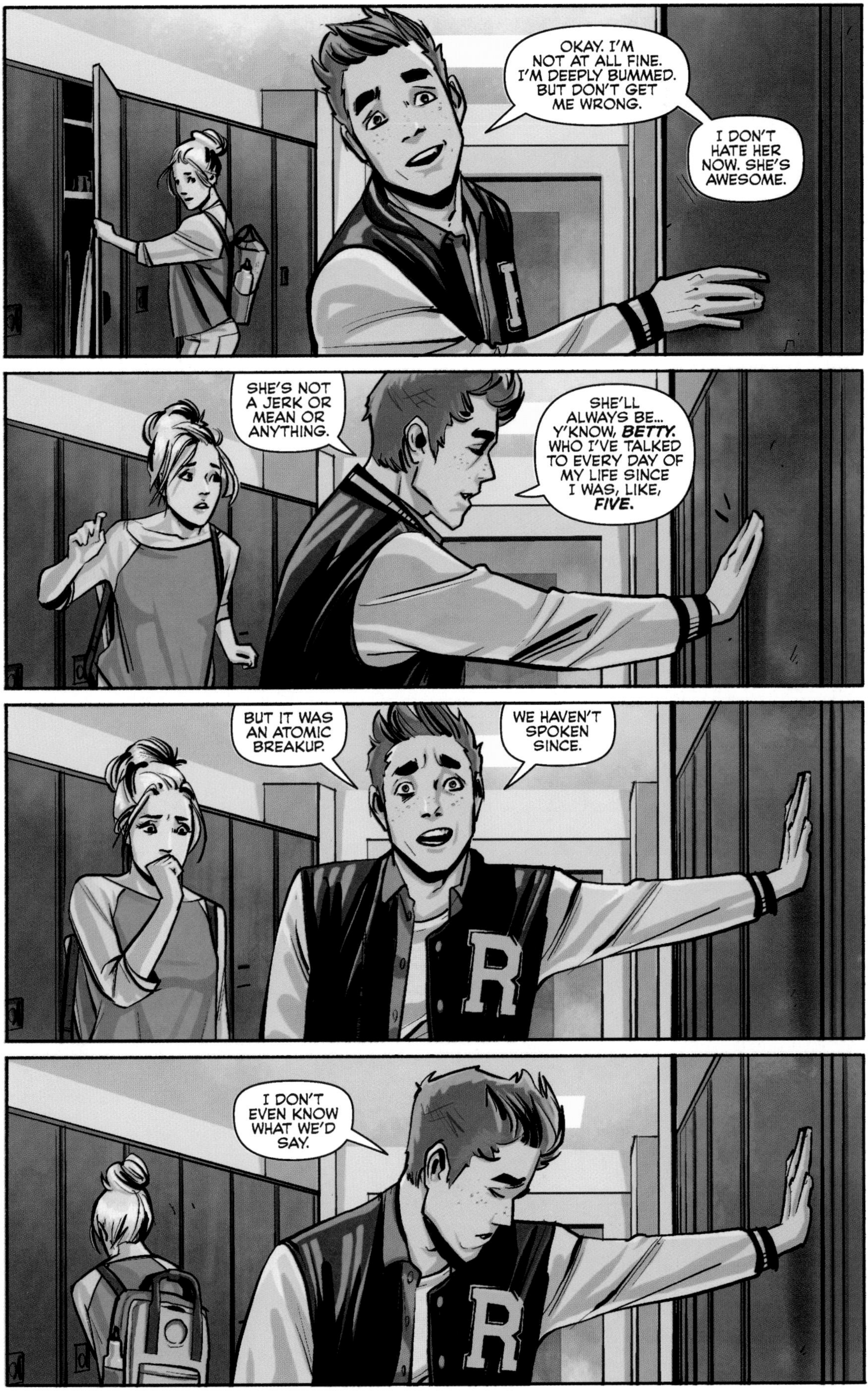
OKAY. I'M NOT AT ALL FINE. I'M DEEPLY BUMMED. BUT DON'T GET ME WRONG.
I DON'T HATE HER NOW. SHE'S AWESOME.
SHE'S NOT A JERK OR MEAN OR ANYTHING.
SHE'LL ALWAYS BE... Y'KNOW, **BETTY.** WHO I'VE TALKED TO EVERY DAY OF MY LIFE SINCE I WAS, LIKE, **FIVE.**
BUT IT WAS AN ATOMIC BREAKUP.
WE HAVEN'T SPOKEN SINCE.
I DON'T EVEN KNOW WHAT WE'D SAY.

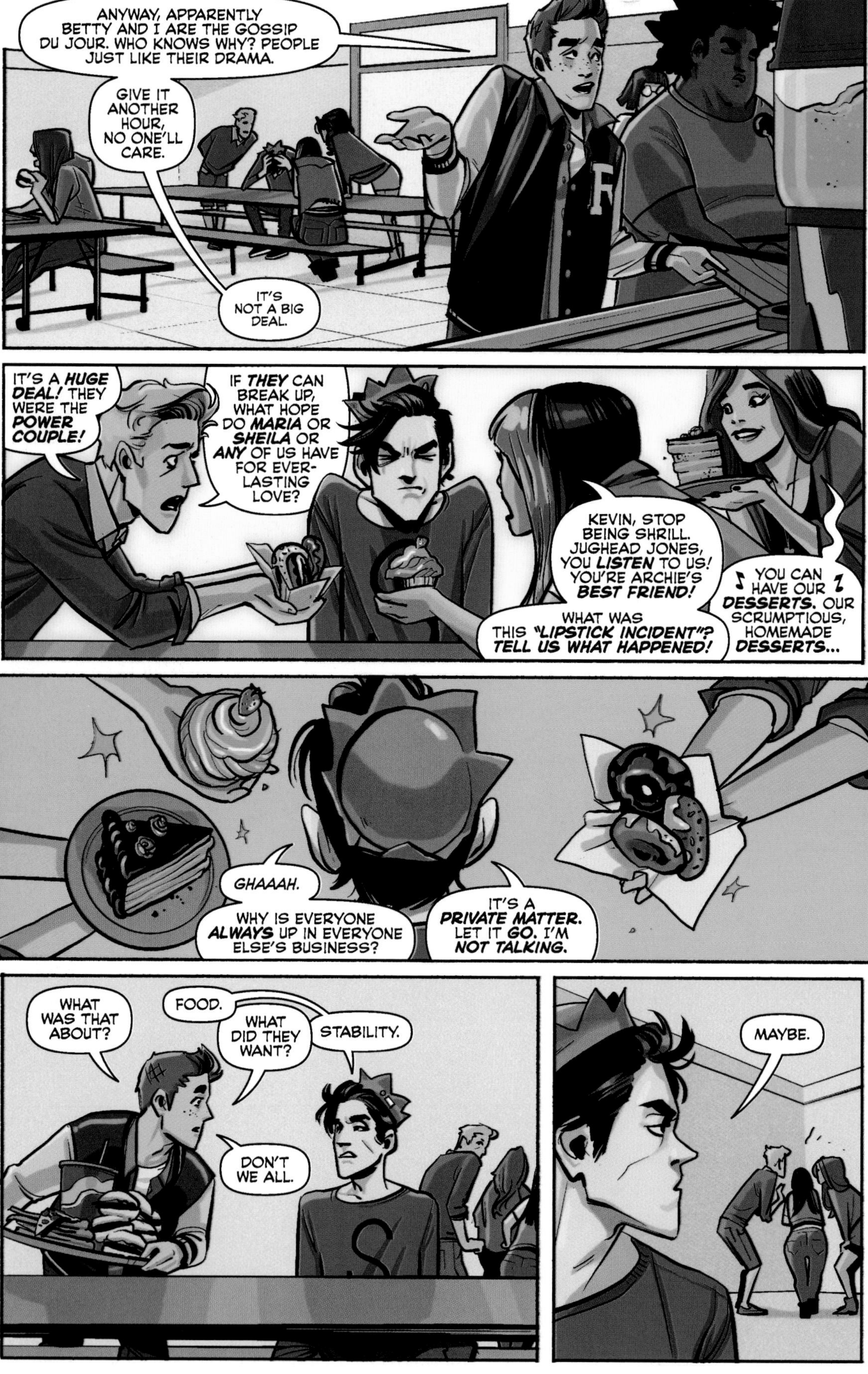
ANYWAY, APPARENTLY BETTY AND I ARE THE GOSSIP DU JOUR. WHO KNOWS WHY? PEOPLE JUST LIKE THEIR DRAMA.
GIVE IT ANOTHER HOUR, NO ONE'LL CARE.
IT'S NOT A BIG DEAL.
IT'S A HUGE DEAL! THEY WERE THE POWER COUPLE!
IF THEY CAN BREAK UP, WHAT HOPE DO MARIA OR SHEILA OR ANY OF US HAVE FOR EVER-LASTING LOVE?
KEVIN, STOP BEING SHRILL. JUGHEAD JONES, YOU LISTEN TO US! YOU'RE ARCHIE'S BEST FRIEND!
WHAT WAS THIS "LIPSTICK INCIDENT"? TELL US WHAT HAPPENED!
YOU CAN HAVE OUR DESSERTS. OUR SCRUMPTIOUS, HOMEMADE DESSERTS...
GHAAAH.
WHY IS EVERYONE ALWAYS UP IN EVERYONE ELSE'S BUSINESS?
IT'S A PRIVATE MATTER. LET IT GO. I'M NOT TALKING.
WHAT WAS THAT ABOUT?
FOOD.
WHAT DID THEY WANT?
STABILITY.
DON'T WE ALL.
MAYBE.

CHAPTER TWO: I Be A Genius

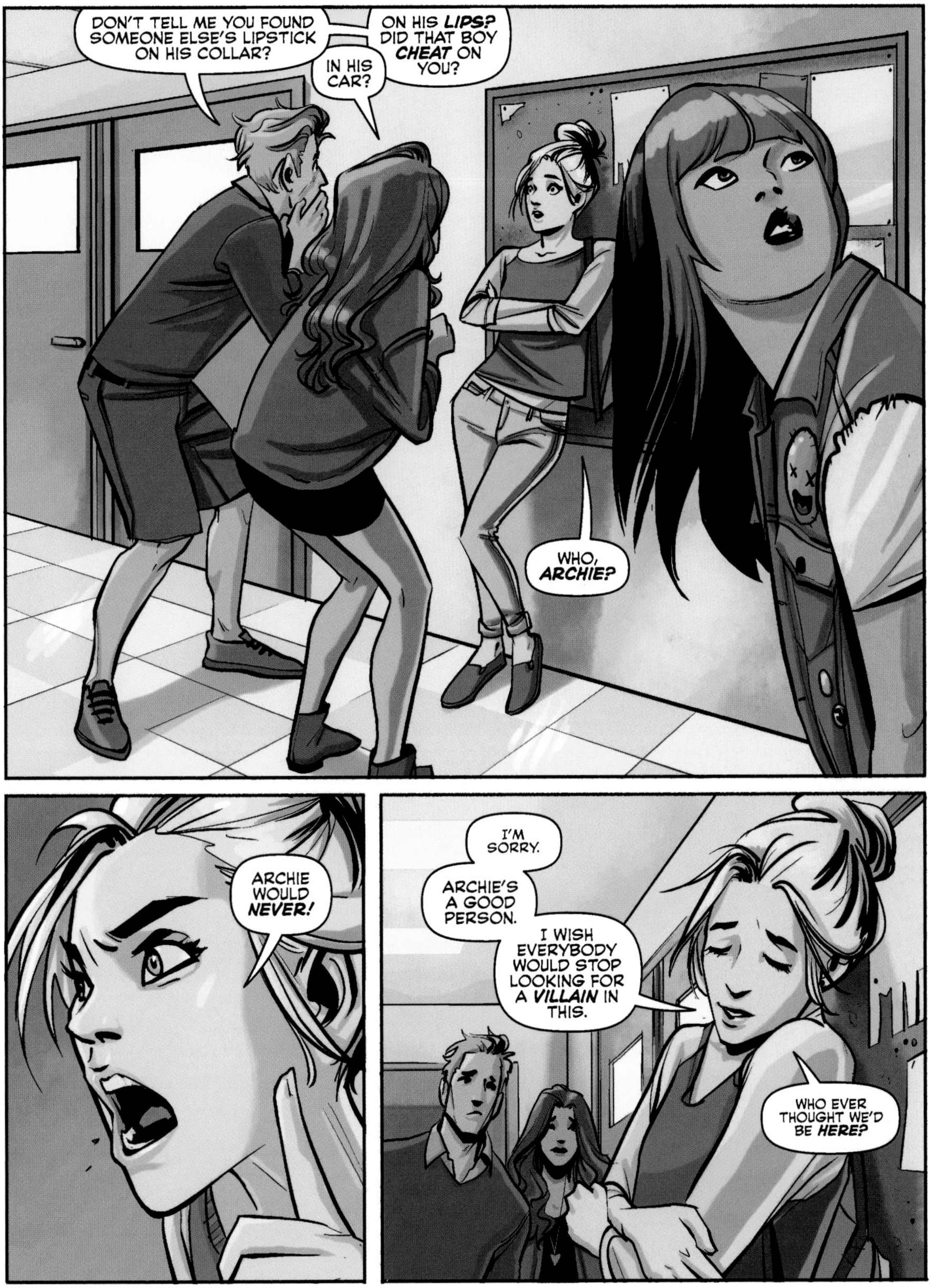
DON'T TELL ME YOU FOUND SOMEONE ELSE'S LIPSTICK ON HIS COLLAR?
IN HIS CAR?
ON HIS *LIPS?* DID THAT BOY *CHEAT* ON YOU?
WHO, *ARCHIE?*
ARCHIE WOULD *NEVER!*
I'M SORRY.
ARCHIE'S A GOOD PERSON.
I WISH EVERYBODY WOULD STOP LOOKING FOR A *VILLAIN* IN THIS.
WHO EVER THOUGHT WE'D BE *HERE?*

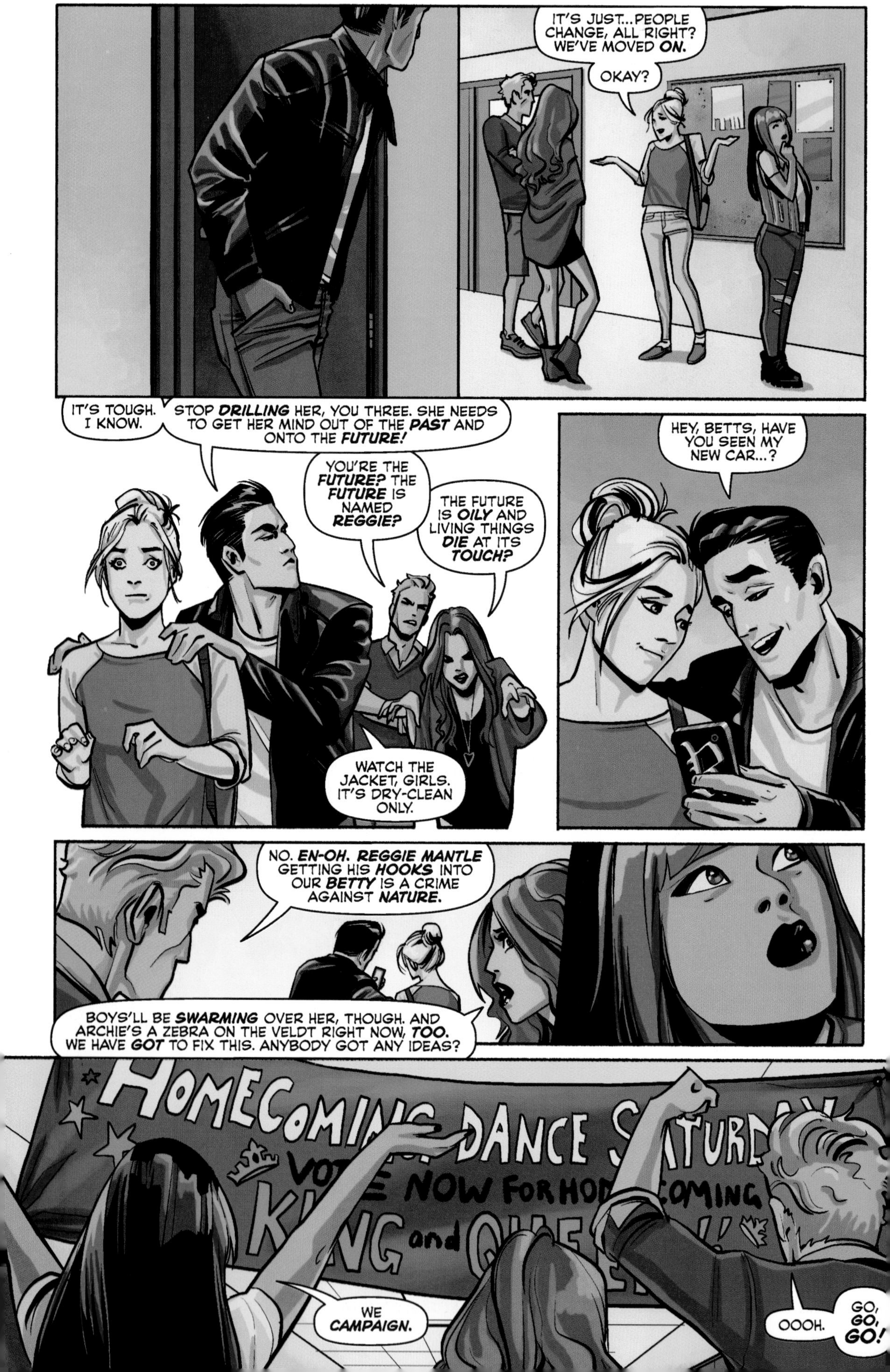

IT'S JUST...PEOPLE CHANGE, ALL RIGHT? WE'VE MOVED ON.
OKAY?
IT'S TOUGH. I KNOW.
STOP DRILLING HER, YOU THREE. SHE NEEDS TO GET HER MIND OUT OF THE PAST AND ONTO THE FUTURE!
YOU'RE THE FUTURE? THE FUTURE IS NAMED REGGIE?
THE FUTURE IS OILY AND LIVING THINGS DIE AT ITS TOUCH?
WATCH THE JACKET, GIRLS. IT'S DRY-CLEAN ONLY.
HEY, BETTS, HAVE YOU SEEN MY NEW CAR...?
NO. EN-OH. REGGIE MANTLE GETTING HIS HOOKS INTO OUR BETTY IS A CRIME AGAINST NATURE.
BOYS'LL BE SWARMING OVER HER, THOUGH. AND ARCHIE'S A ZEBRA ON THE VELDT RIGHT NOW, TOO. WE HAVE GOT TO FIX THIS. ANYBODY GOT ANY IDEAS?
HOMECOMING DANCE SATURDAY
NOW FOR HO COMING
WE CAMPAIGN.
OOOH.
GO, GO, GO!

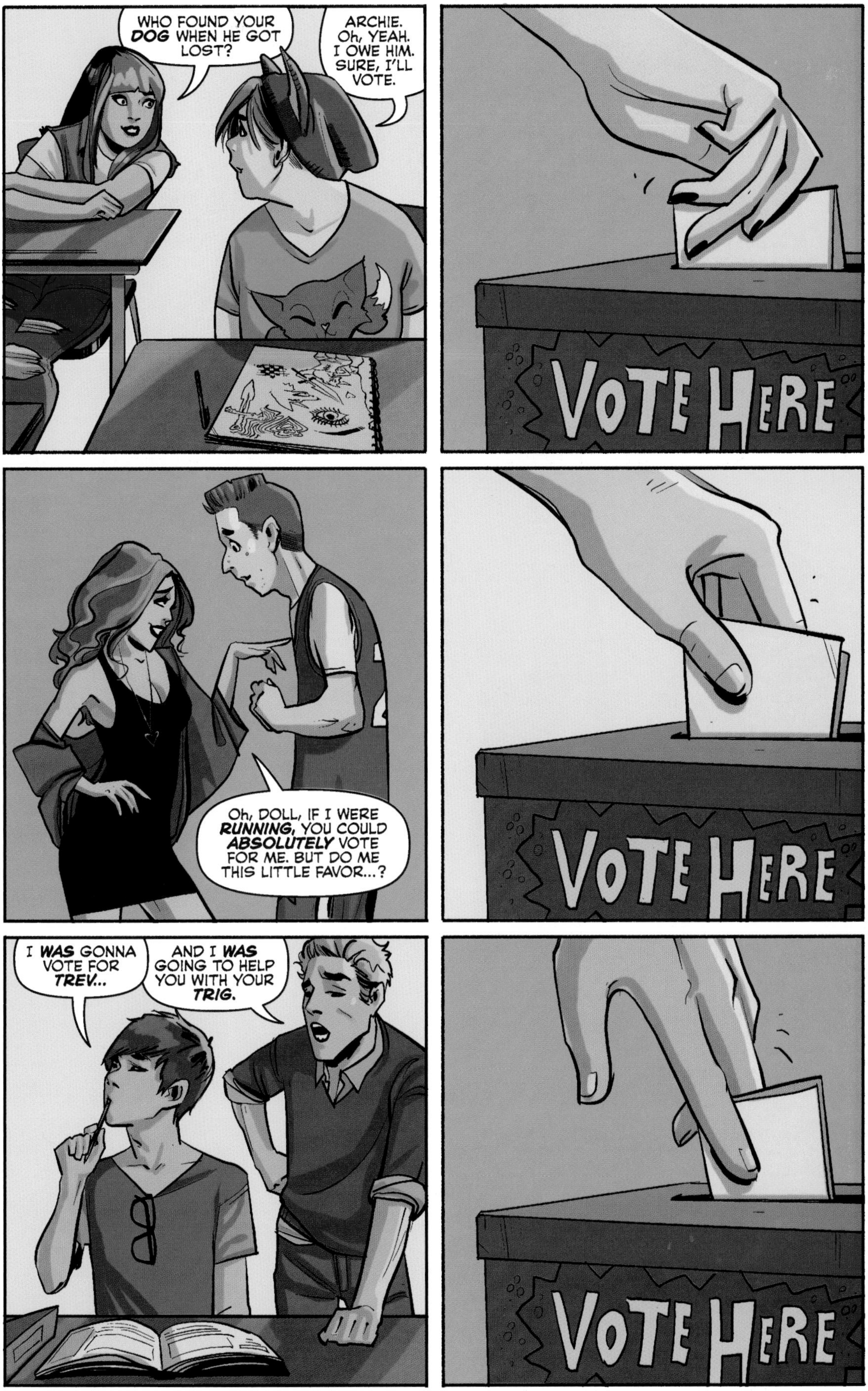
WHO FOUND YOUR **DOG** WHEN HE GOT LOST?
ARCHIE. Oh, YEAH. I OWE HIM. SURE, I'LL VOTE.
VOTE HERE
Oh, DOLL, IF I WERE **RUNNING,** YOU COULD **ABSOLUTELY** VOTE FOR ME. BUT DO ME THIS LITTLE FAVOR...?
VOTE HERE
I **WAS** GONNA VOTE FOR **TREV...**
AND I **WAS** GOING TO HELP YOU WITH YOUR **TRIG.**
VOTE HERE

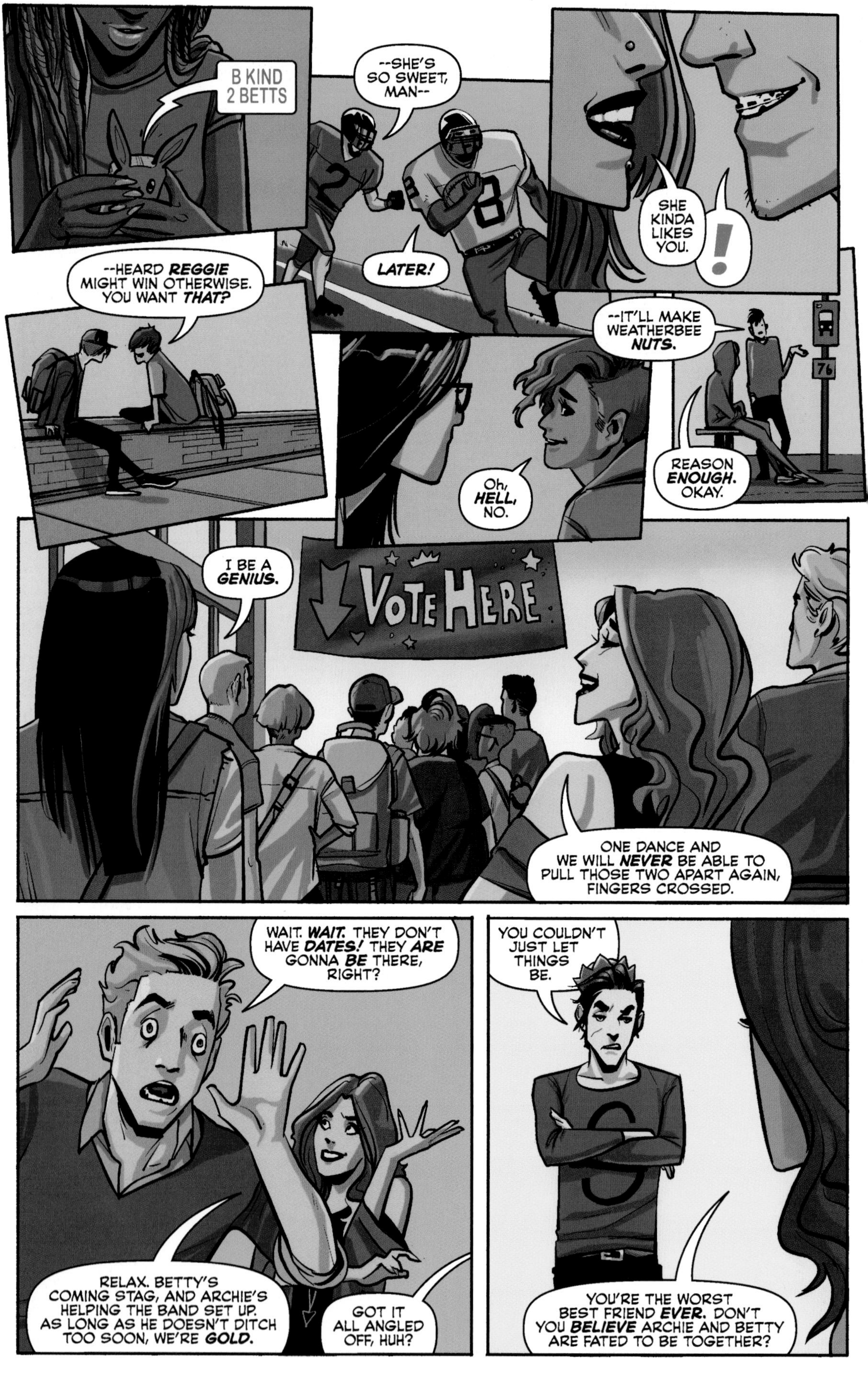
B KIND 2 BETTS
--SHE'S SO SWEET, MAN--
LATER!
SHE KINDA LIKES YOU.
!
--HEARD REGGIE MIGHT WIN OTHERWISE. YOU WANT THAT?
Oh, HELL, NO.
--IT'LL MAKE WEATHERBEE NUTS.
REASON ENOUGH. OKAY.
I BE A GENIUS.
VOTE HERE
ONE DANCE AND WE WILL NEVER BE ABLE TO PULL THOSE TWO APART AGAIN, FINGERS CROSSED.
WAIT. WAIT. THEY DON'T HAVE DATES! THEY ARE GONNA BE THERE, RIGHT?
RELAX. BETTY'S COMING STAG, AND ARCHIE'S HELPING THE BAND SET UP. AS LONG AS HE DOESN'T DITCH TOO SOON, WE'RE GOLD.
GOT IT ALL ANGLED OFF, HUH?
YOU COULDN'T JUST LET THINGS BE.
YOU'RE THE WORST BEST FRIEND EVER. DON'T YOU BELIEVE ARCHIE AND BETTY ARE FATED TO BE TOGETHER?

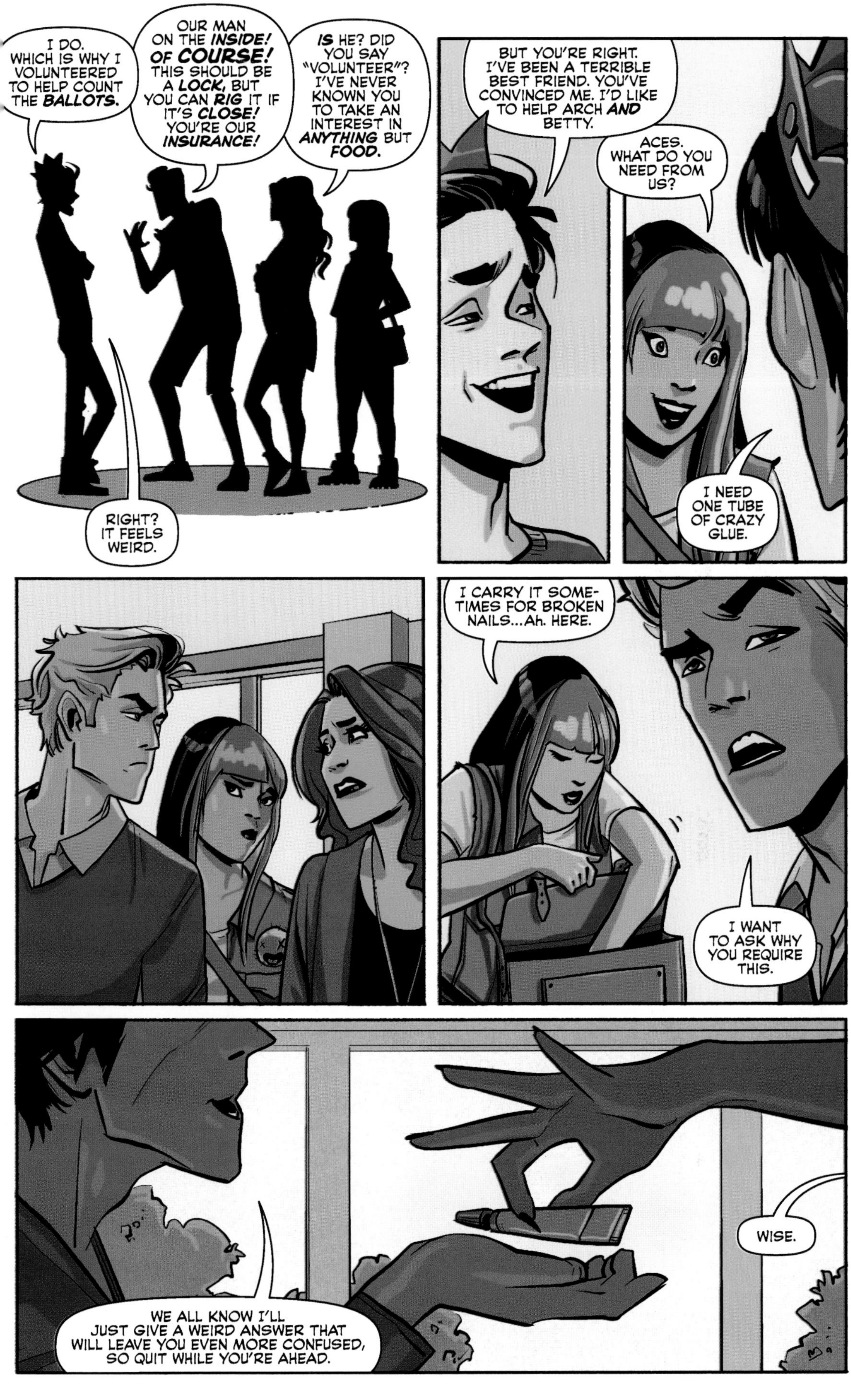
I DO. WHICH IS WHY I VOLUNTEERED TO HELP COUNT THE BALLOTS.
OUR MAN ON THE INSIDE! OF COURSE! THIS SHOULD BE A LOCK, BUT YOU CAN RIG IT IF IT'S CLOSE! YOU'RE OUR INSURANCE!
IS HE? DID YOU SAY "VOLUNTEER"? I'VE NEVER KNOWN YOU TO TAKE AN INTEREST IN ANYTHING BUT FOOD.
RIGHT? IT FEELS WEIRD.
BUT YOU'RE RIGHT. I'VE BEEN A TERRIBLE BEST FRIEND. YOU'VE CONVINCED ME. I'D LIKE TO HELP ARCH AND BETTY.
ACES. WHAT DO YOU NEED FROM US?
I NEED ONE TUBE OF CRAZY GLUE.
I CARRY IT SOMETIMES FOR BROKEN NAILS...Ah. HERE.
I WANT TO ASK WHY YOU REQUIRE THIS.
WE ALL KNOW I'LL JUST GIVE A WEIRD ANSWER THAT WILL LEAVE YOU EVEN MORE CONFUSED, SO QUIT WHILE YOU'RE AHEAD.
WISE.

CHAPTER THREE:

THAT'S MY DAD.

HE TAUGHT ME EVERYTHING I KNOW ABOUT HIS THREE PASSIONS: HOME REPAIR, BOWLING, AND THE GUITAR.

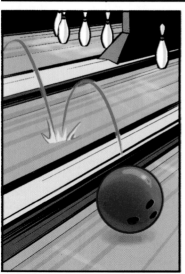

THANK GOD THAT ONE STUCK, OR WE'D HAVE *NOTHING* IN COMMON.

HEY, *ANGUS YOUNG*, HAND OVER THE AXE.

ARE YOU PLAYING TONIGHT? IN *PUBLIC*, FINALLY? CAN I COME?

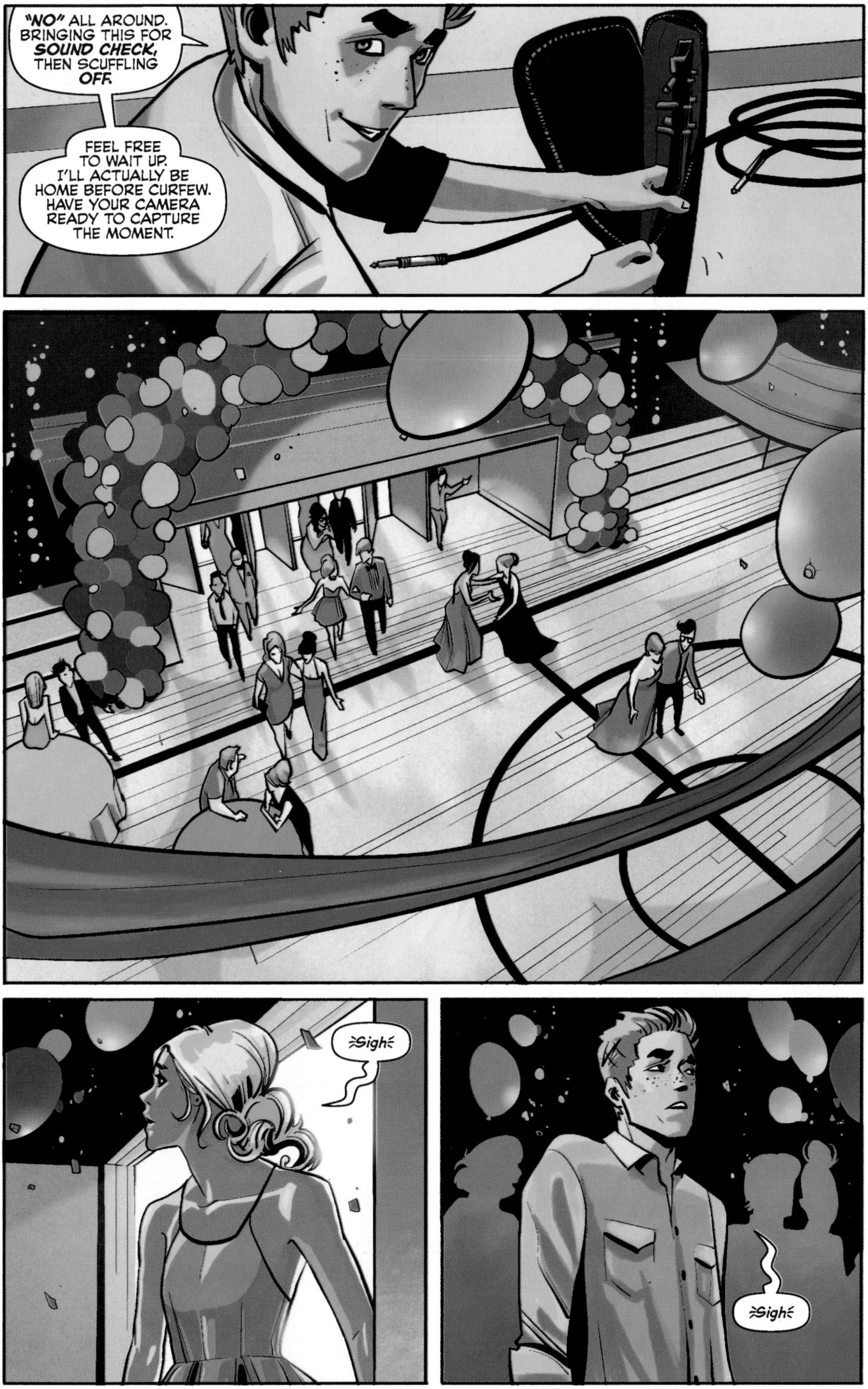
"NO" ALL AROUND. BRINGING THIS FOR SOUND CHECK, THEN SCUFFLING OFF.
FEEL FREE TO WAIT UP. I'LL ACTUALLY BE HOME BEFORE CURFEW. HAVE YOUR CAMERA READY TO CAPTURE THE MOMENT.
Sigh
Sigh

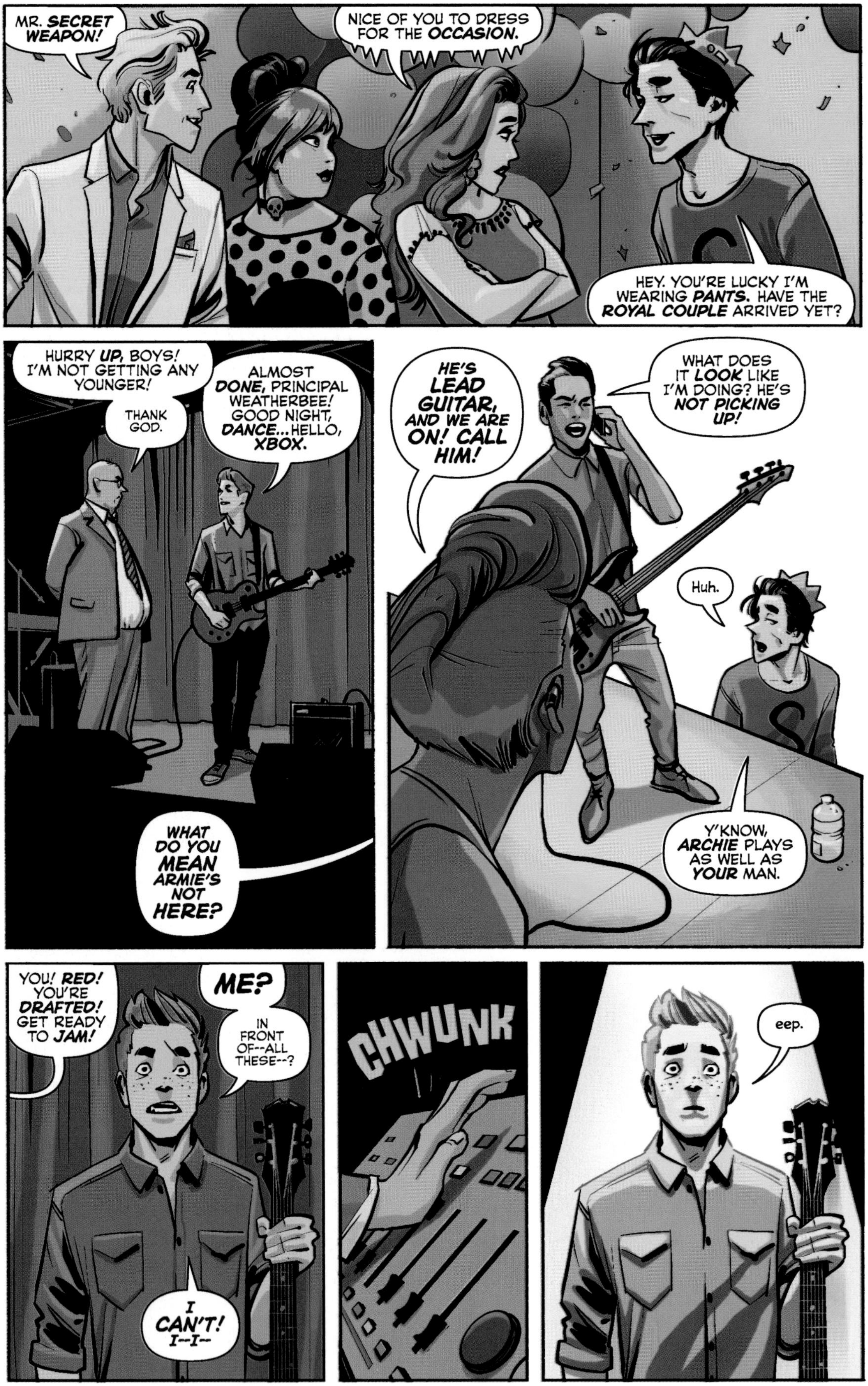
MR. SECRET WEAPON!
NICE OF YOU TO DRESS FOR THE OCCASION.
HEY. YOU'RE LUCKY I'M WEARING PANTS. HAVE THE ROYAL COUPLE ARRIVED YET?
HURRY UP, BOYS! I'M NOT GETTING ANY YOUNGER!
THANK GOD.
ALMOST DONE, PRINCIPAL WEATHERBEE! GOOD NIGHT, DANCE...HELLO, XBOX.
WHAT DO YOU MEAN ARMIE'S NOT HERE?
HE'S LEAD GUITAR, AND WE ARE ON! CALL HIM!
WHAT DOES IT LOOK LIKE I'M DOING? HE'S NOT PICKING UP!
Huh.
Y'KNOW, ARCHIE PLAYS AS WELL AS YOUR MAN.
YOU! RED! YOU'RE DRAFTED! GET READY TO JAM!
ME?
IN FRONT OF--ALL THESE--?
I CAN'T! I--I--
CHWUNK
eep.

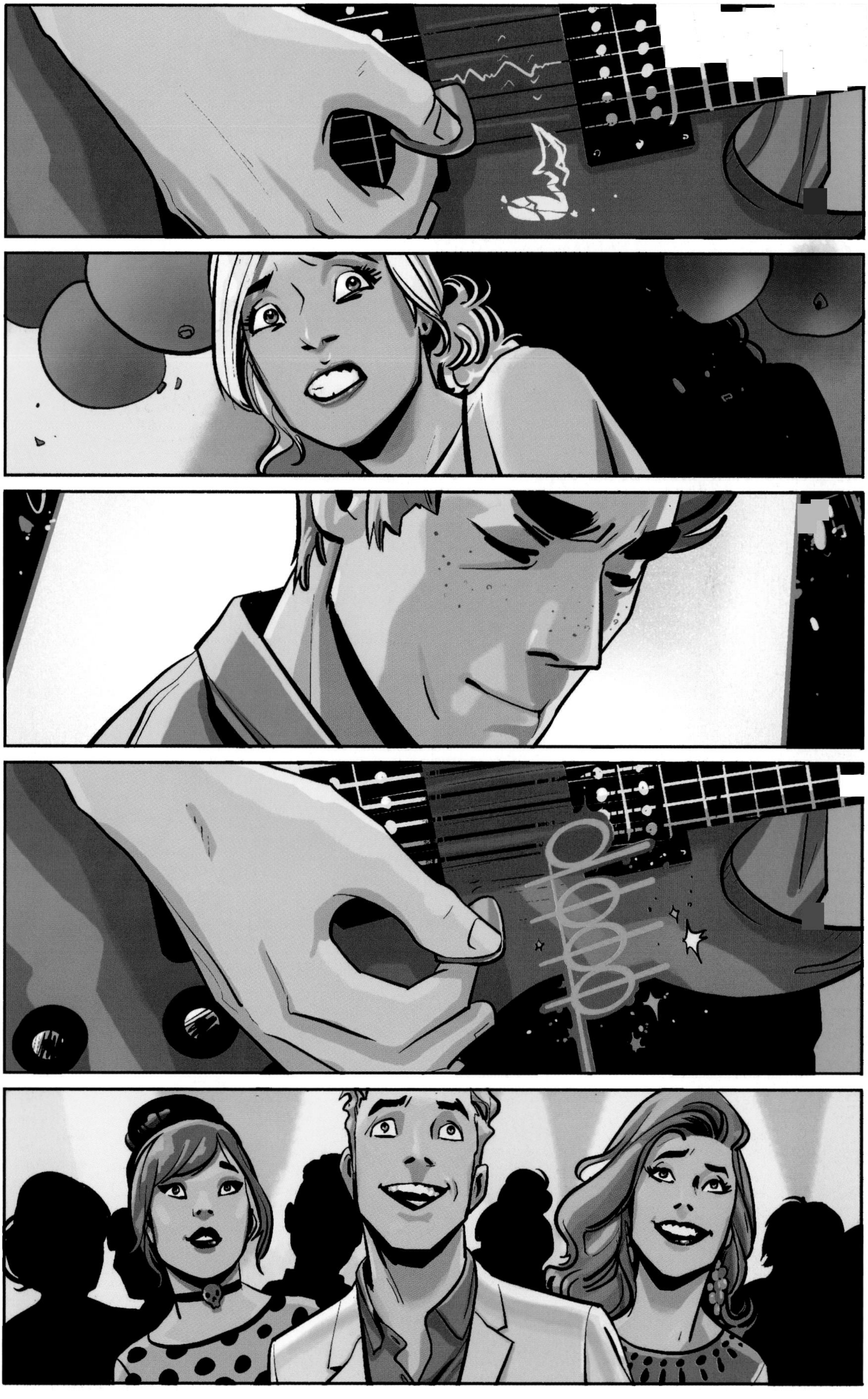

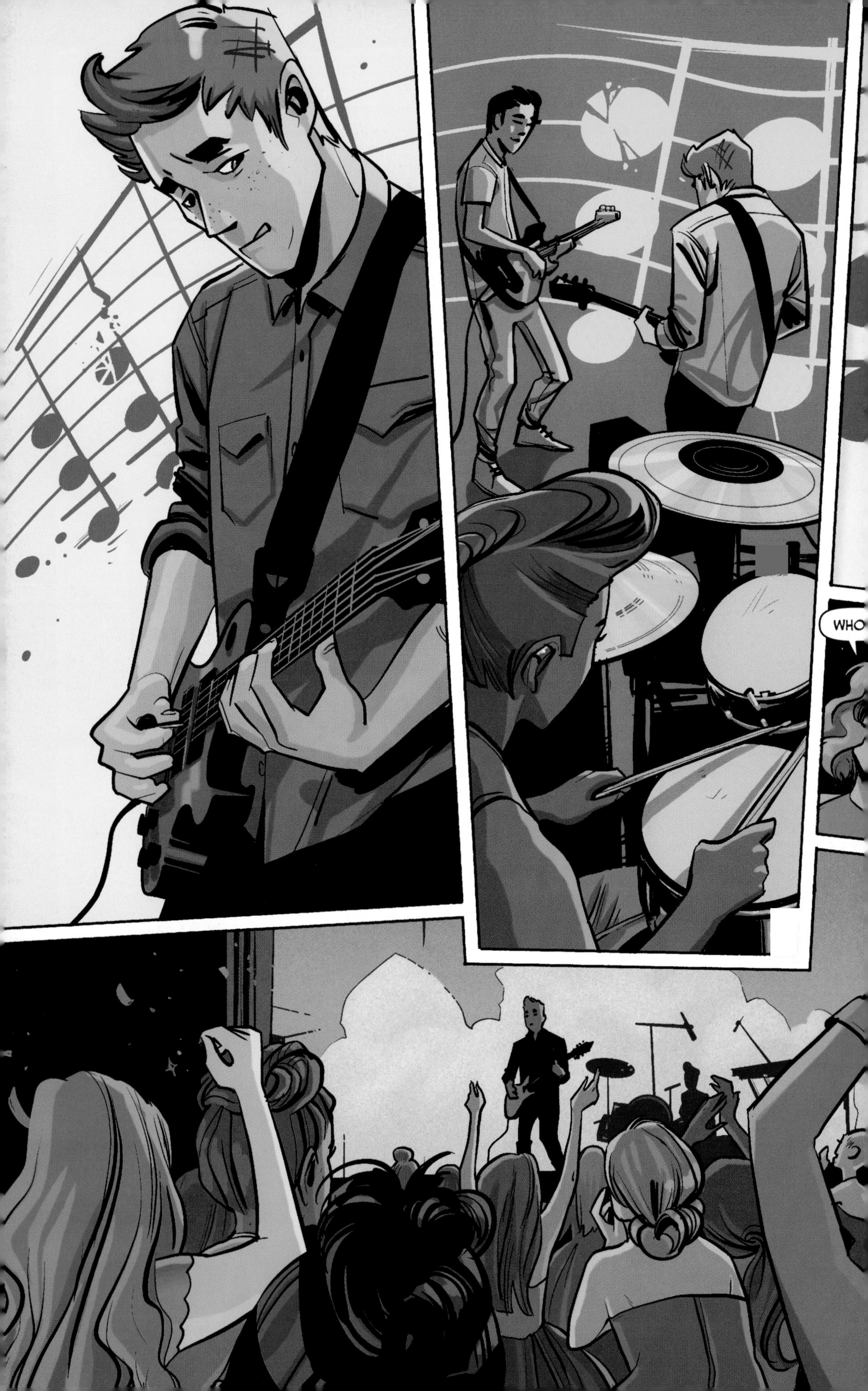
WHO

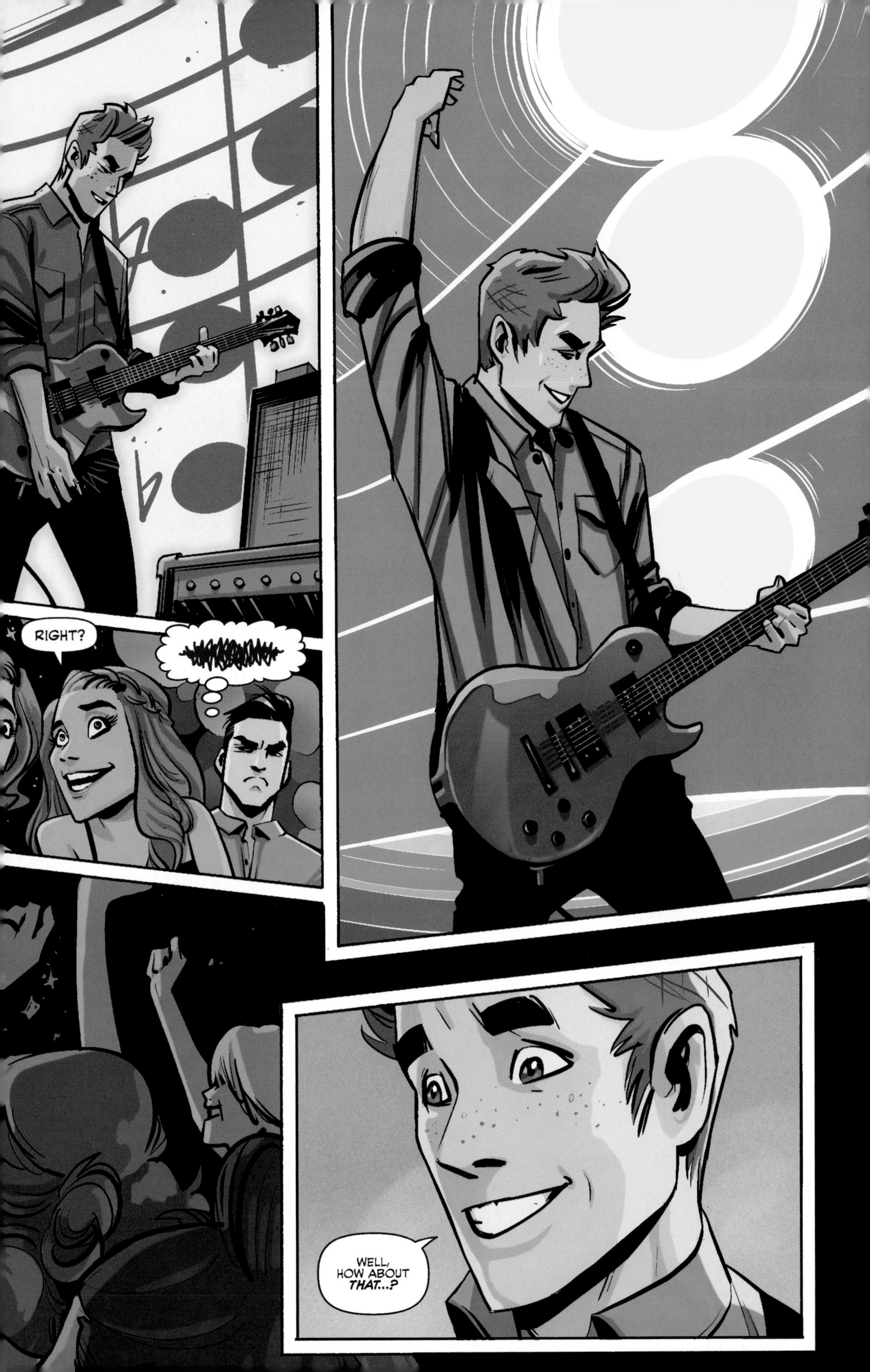
RIGHT?
WELL, HOW ABOUT THAT...?

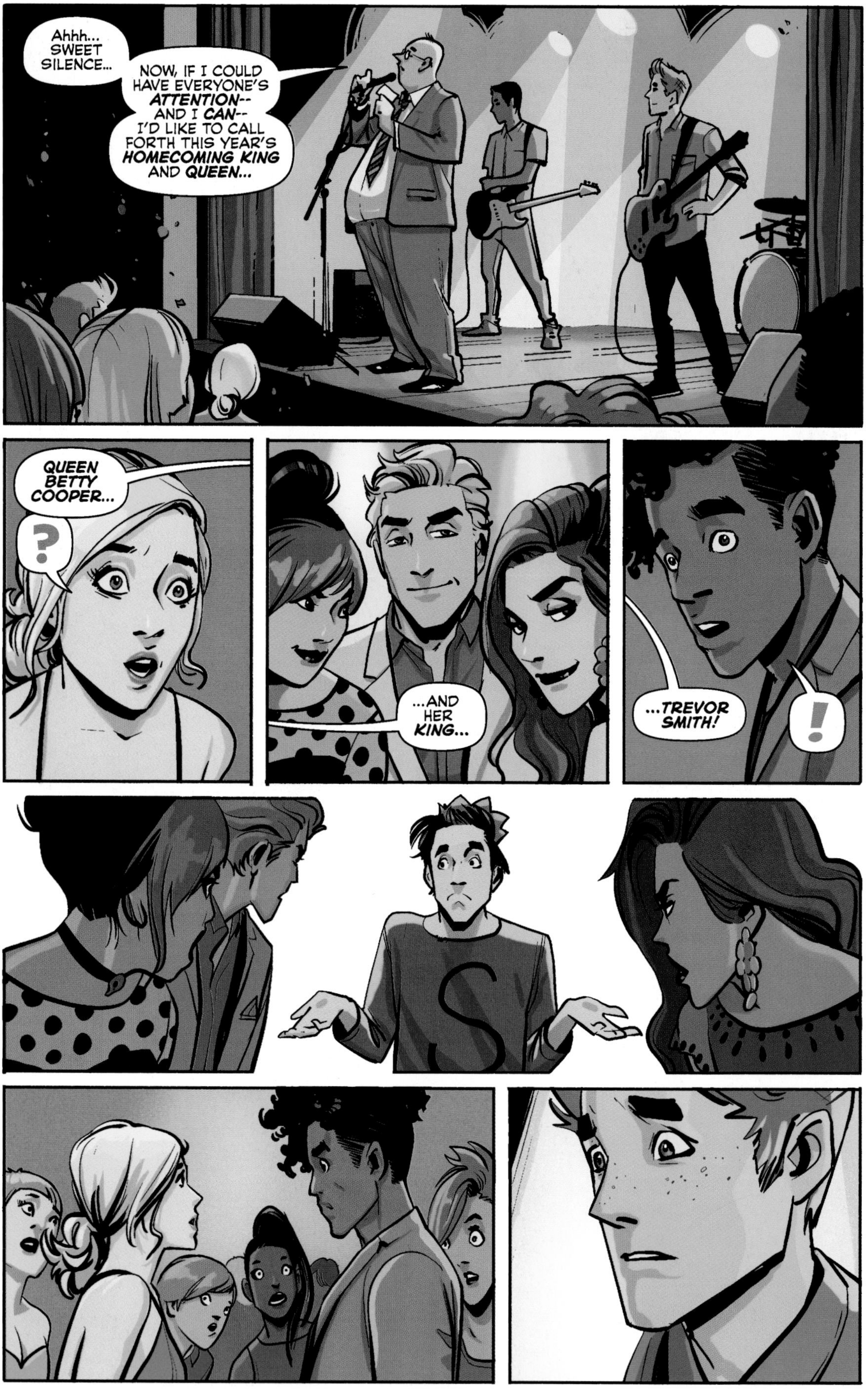

Ahhh... SWEET SILENCE...
NOW, IF I COULD HAVE EVERYONE'S ATTENTION-- AND I CAN-- I'D LIKE TO CALL FORTH THIS YEAR'S HOMECOMING KING AND QUEEN...
QUEEN BETTY COOPER...
?
...AND HER KING...
...TREVOR SMITH!
!

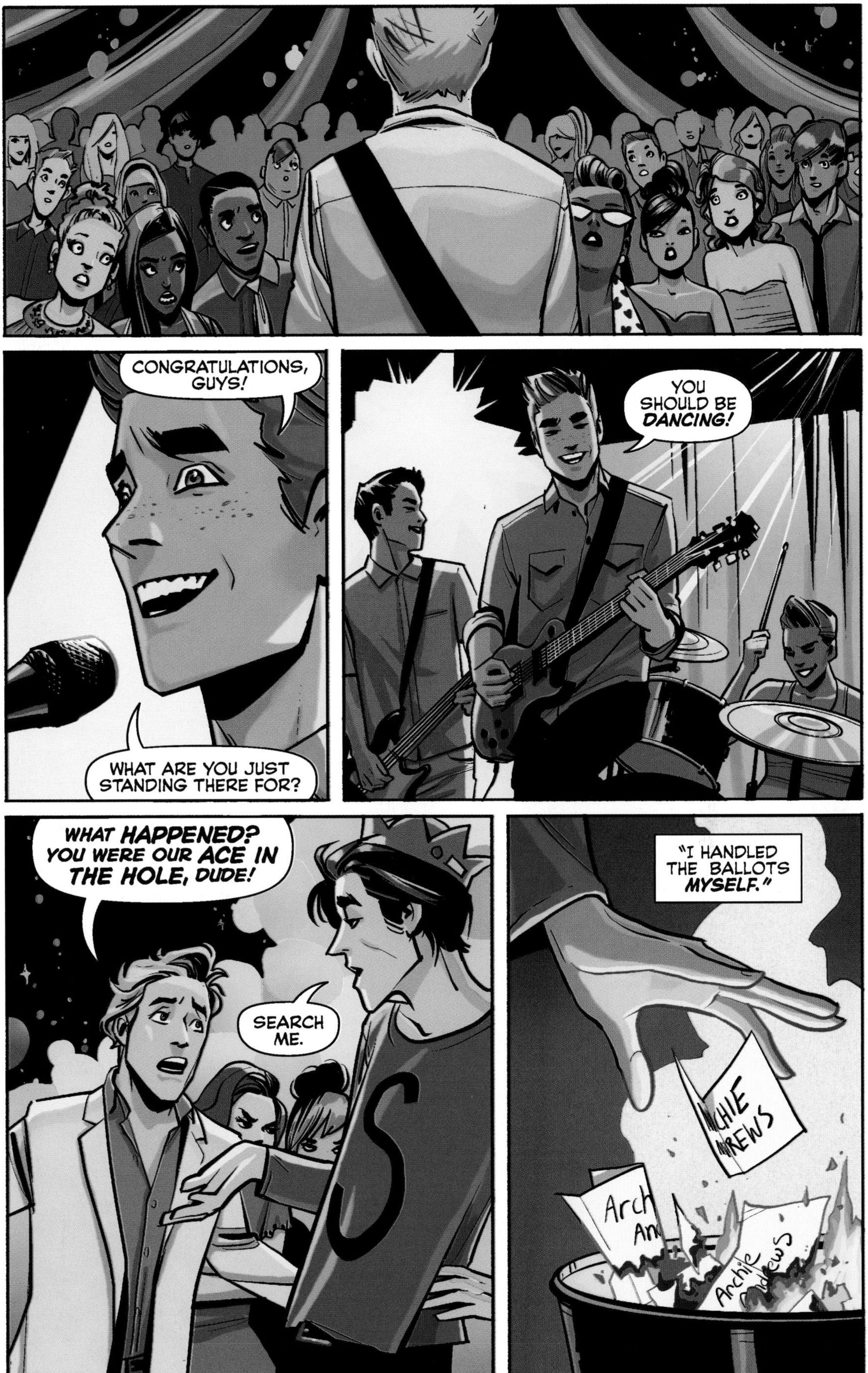
CONGRATULATIONS, GUYS!
WHAT ARE YOU JUST STANDING THERE FOR?
YOU SHOULD BE DANCING!
WHAT HAPPENED? YOU WERE OUR ACE IN THE HOLE, DUDE!
SEARCH ME.
"I HANDLED THE BALLOTS MYSELF."
ARCHIE ANDREWS
Archie
Archie Andrews

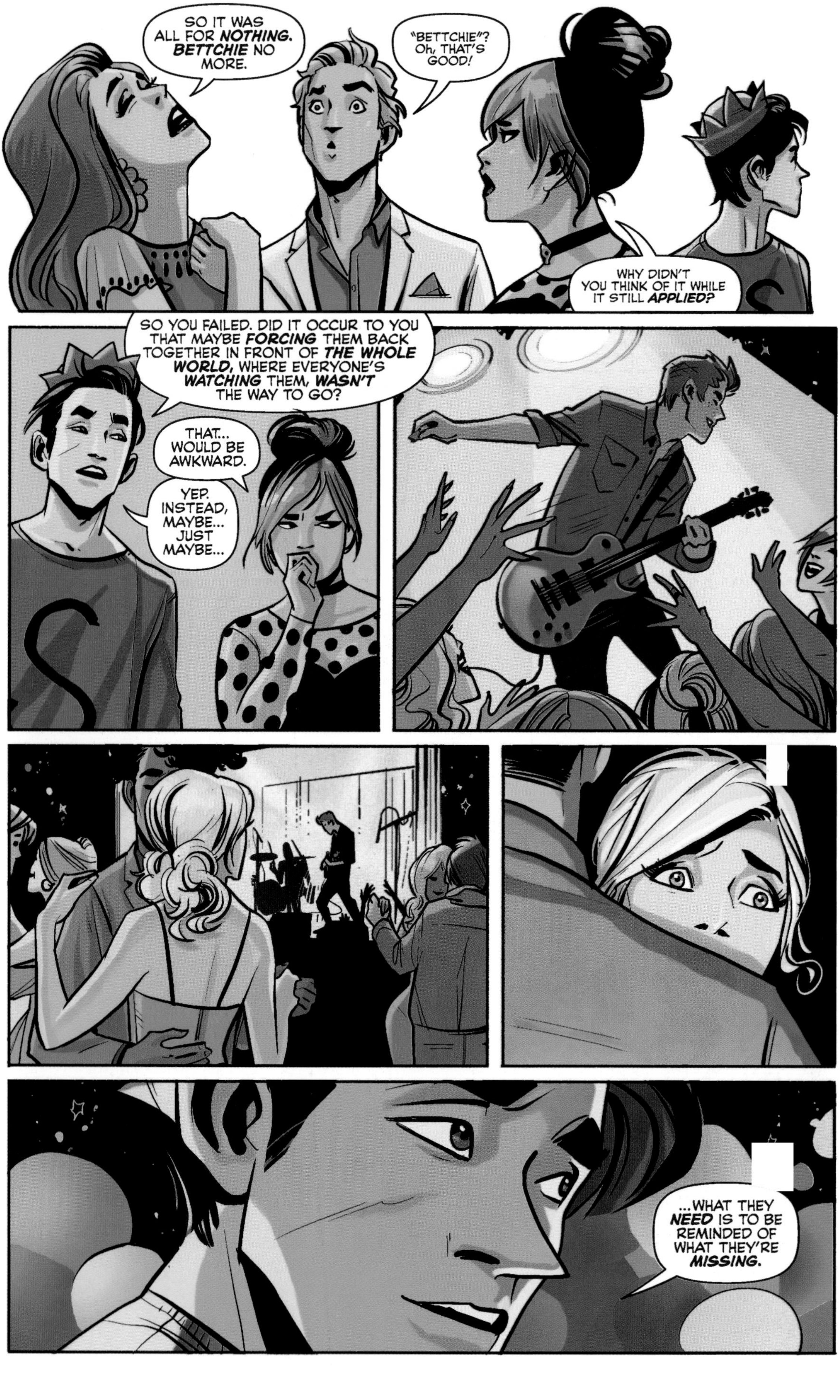
SO IT WAS ALL FOR NOTHING. BETTCHIE NO MORE.
"BETTCHIE"? Oh, THAT'S GOOD!
WHY DIDN'T YOU THINK OF IT WHILE IT STILL APPLIED?
SO YOU FAILED. DID IT OCCUR TO YOU THAT MAYBE FORCING THEM BACK TOGETHER IN FRONT OF THE WHOLE WORLD, WHERE EVERYONE'S WATCHING THEM, WASN'T THE WAY TO GO?
THAT... WOULD BE AWKWARD.
YEP. INSTEAD, MAYBE... JUST MAYBE...
...WHAT THEY NEED IS TO BE REMINDED OF WHAT THEY'RE MISSING.

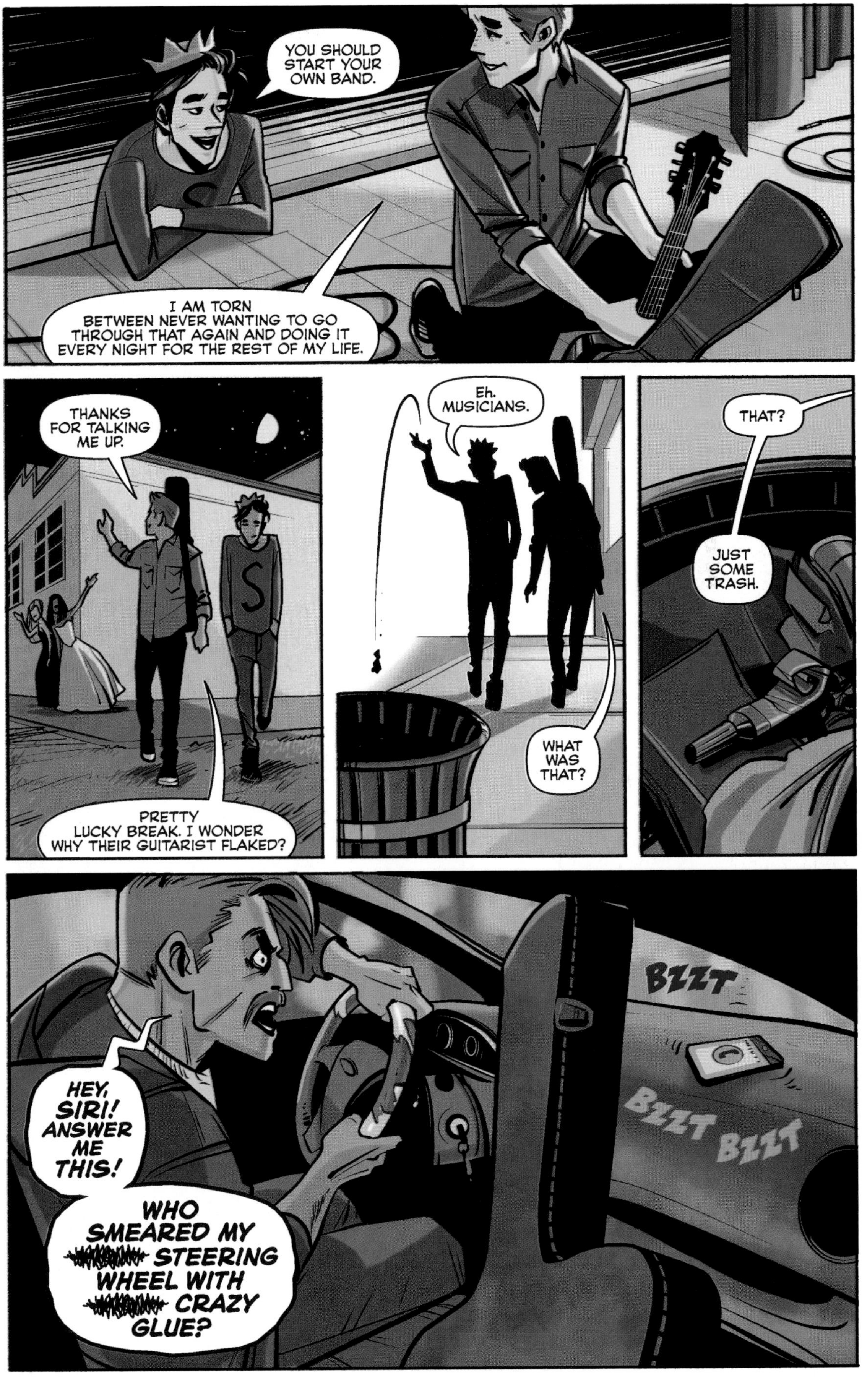
YOU SHOULD START YOUR OWN BAND.
I AM TORN BETWEEN NEVER WANTING TO GO THROUGH THAT AGAIN AND DOING IT EVERY NIGHT FOR THE REST OF MY LIFE.
THANKS FOR TALKING ME UP.
PRETTY LUCKY BREAK. I WONDER WHY THEIR GUITARIST FLAKED?
Eh. MUSICIANS.
WHAT WAS THAT?
THAT?
JUST SOME TRASH.
BZZT
HEY, SIRI! ANSWER ME THIS!
WHO SMEARED MY STEERING WHEEL WITH CRAZY GLUE?
BZZT BZZT

BURGERS AT *POP'S*. YOU'RE BUYING.

GONNA PASS. I'M STILL A LITTLE DOWN. PLUS, MY DAD STILL THINKS I'M COMING HOME LATE, AND IT'S ALWAYS BEST TO KEEP HIM OFF BALANCE.

MAÑANA, BUD.

YOU, TOO.

THANKS FOR STOPPING BY.

HOPE YOU ENJOYED YOUR STAY. SEE YOU NEXT TIME AROUND.

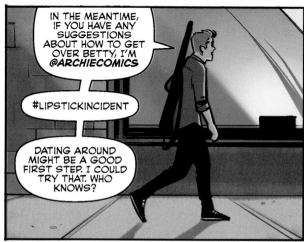

IN THE MEANTIME, IF YOU HAVE ANY SUGGESTIONS ABOUT HOW TO GET OVER BETTY, I'M @ARCHIECOMICS

#LIPSTICKINCIDENT

DATING AROUND MIGHT BE A GOOD FIRST STEP. I COULD TRY THAT. WHO KNOWS?

COMING SOON TO TRANSFORM RIVERDALE:

LODGE INDUSTRIES

CHANGING YOUR TOWN FROM THE GROUND UP!

MAYBE THERE'S SOME AMAZING NEW GIRL JUST AROUND THE CORNER...

TO BE CONTINUED...

ISSUE TWO

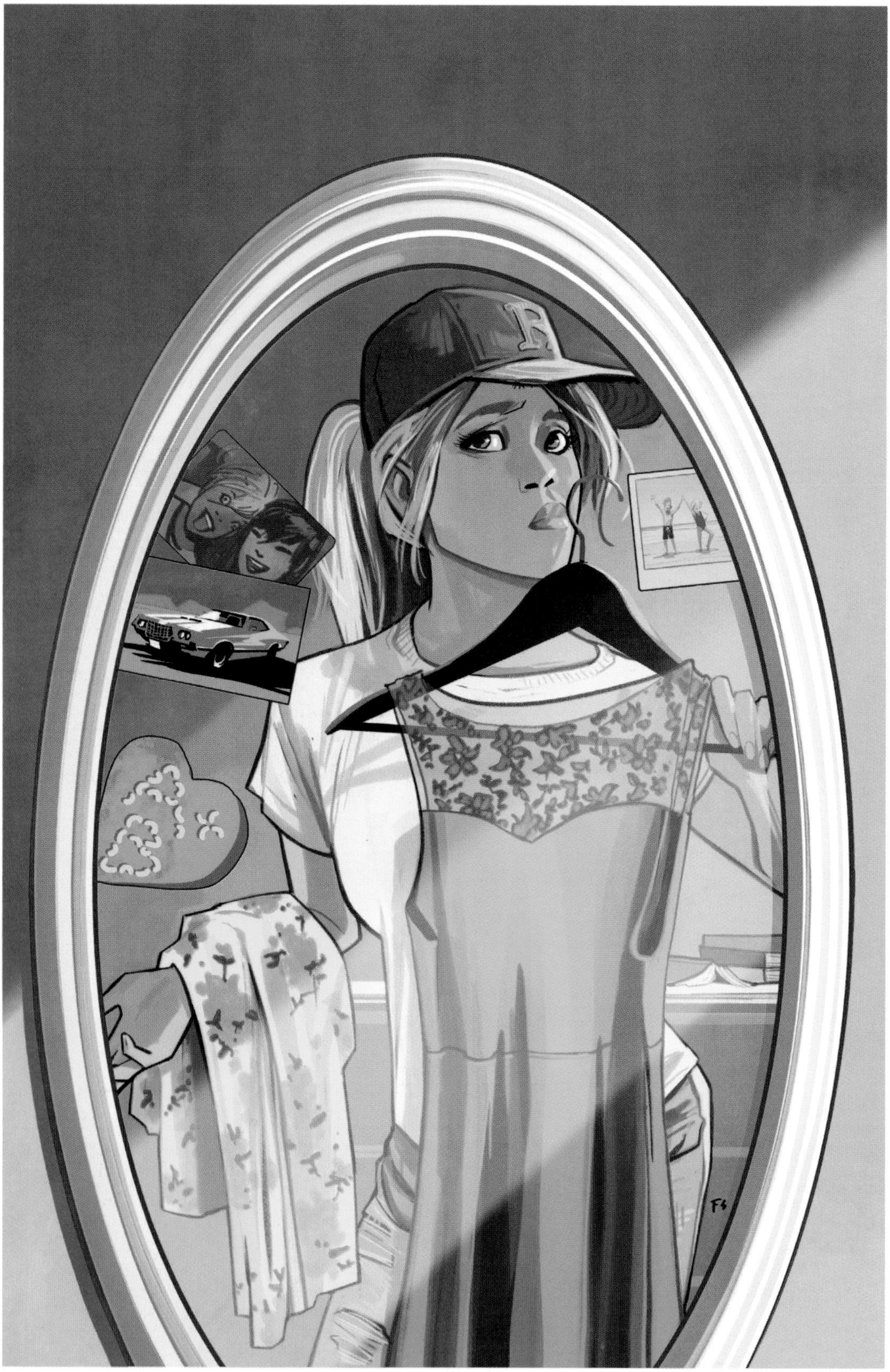

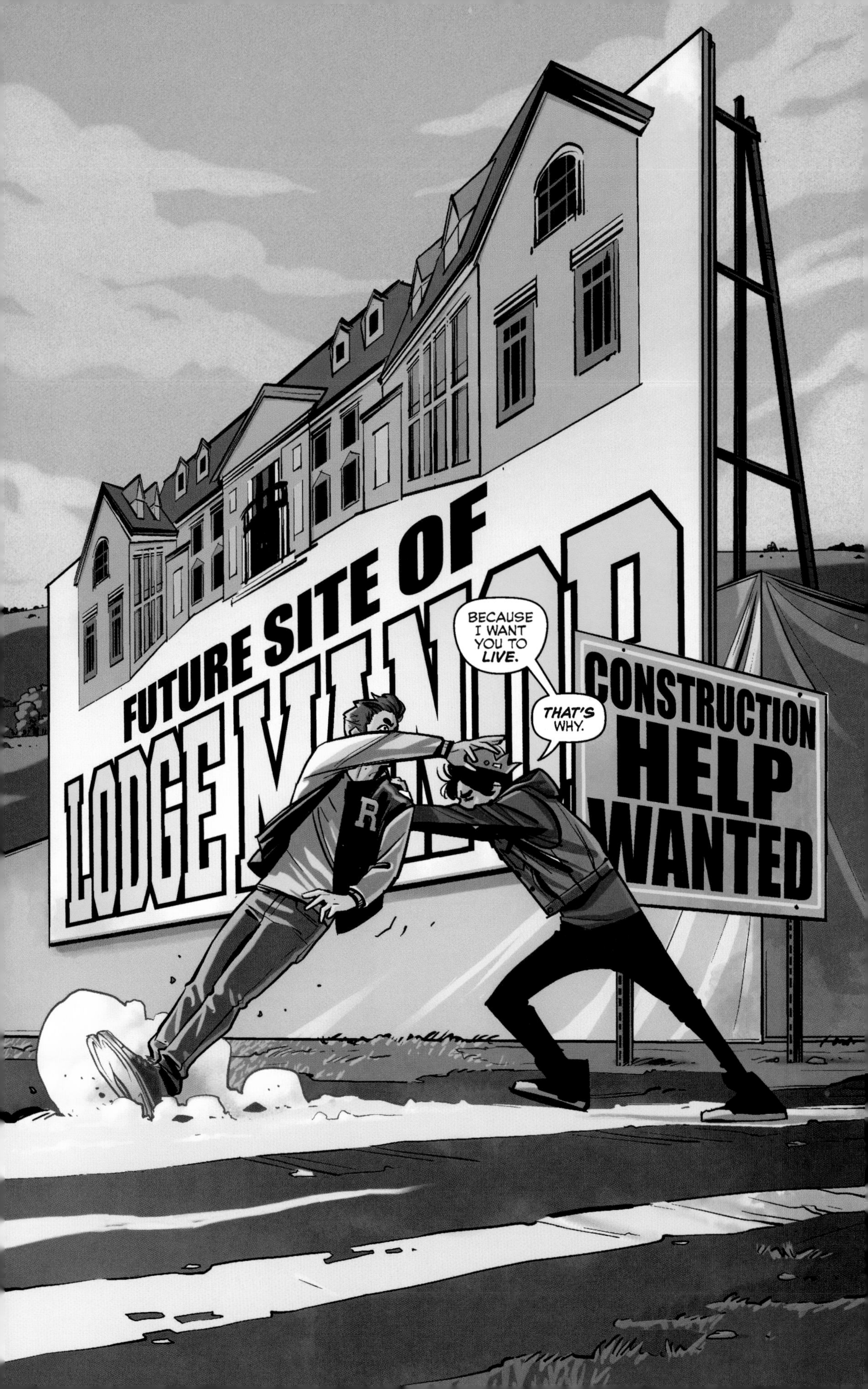
FUTURE SITE OF
LODGE MANOR
BECAUSE I WANT YOU TO *LIVE*.
THAT'S WHY.
CONSTRUCTION
HELP
WANTED

CHAPTER ONE: IT'S BETTER THAN "FORSYTHE"

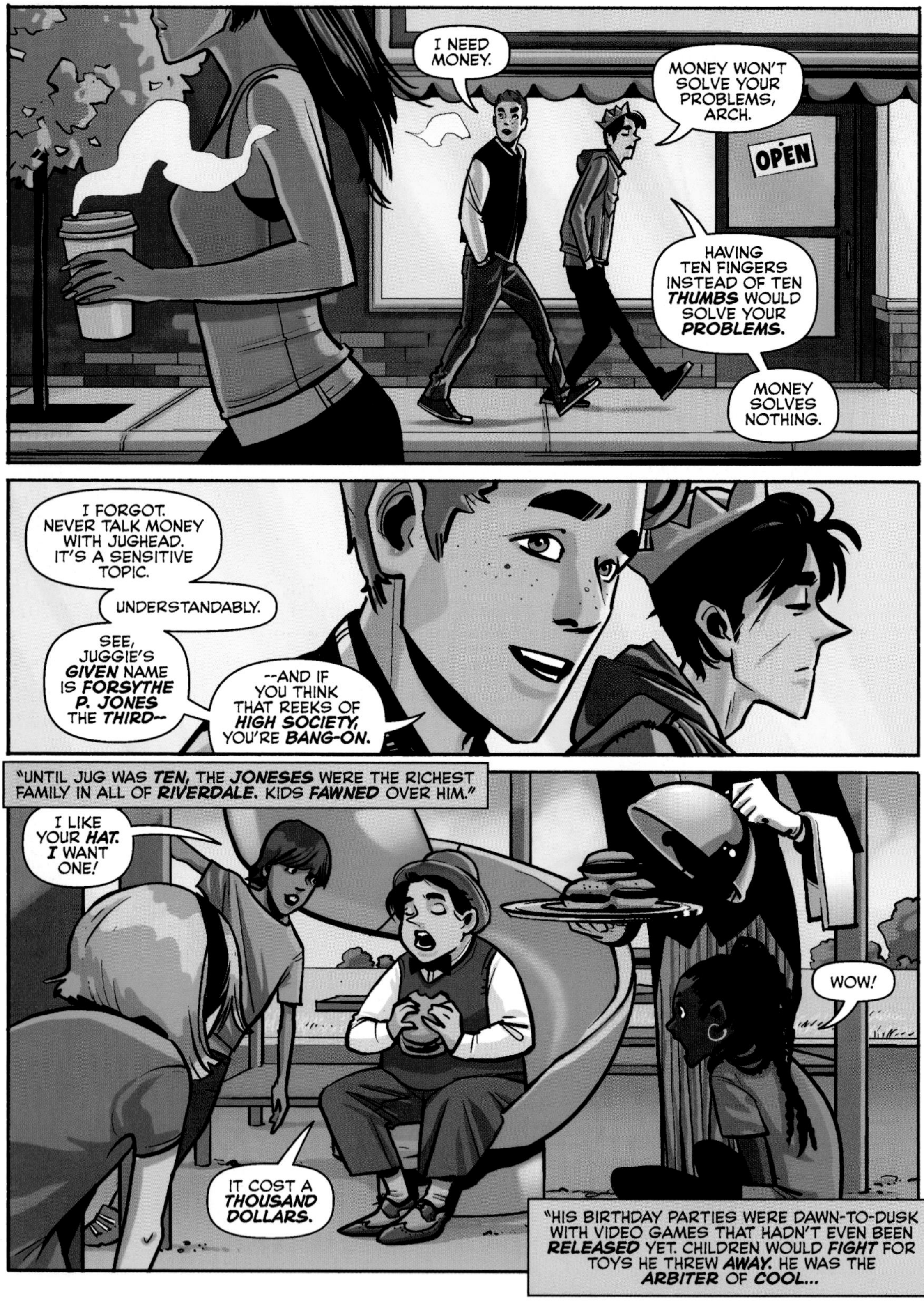

I NEED MONEY.
MONEY WON'T SOLVE YOUR PROBLEMS, ARCH.
OPEN
HAVING TEN FINGERS INSTEAD OF TEN *THUMBS* WOULD SOLVE YOUR *PROBLEMS.*
MONEY SOLVES NOTHING.
I FORGOT. NEVER TALK MONEY WITH JUGHEAD. IT'S A SENSITIVE TOPIC.
UNDERSTANDABLY.
SEE, JUGGIE'S *GIVEN* NAME IS *FORSYTHE P. JONES* THE *THIRD*--
--AND IF YOU THINK THAT REEKS OF *HIGH SOCIETY,* YOU'RE *BANG-ON.*
"UNTIL JUG WAS *TEN,* THE *JONESES* WERE THE RICHEST FAMILY IN ALL OF *RIVERDALE.* KIDS *FAWNED* OVER HIM."
I LIKE YOUR *HAT. I* WANT ONE!
WOW!
IT COST A *THOUSAND DOLLARS.*
"HIS BIRTHDAY PARTIES WERE DAWN-TO-DUSK WITH VIDEO GAMES THAT HADN'T EVEN BEEN *RELEASED* YET. CHILDREN WOULD *FIGHT* FOR TOYS HE THREW *AWAY.* HE WAS THE *ARBITER* OF *COOL...*

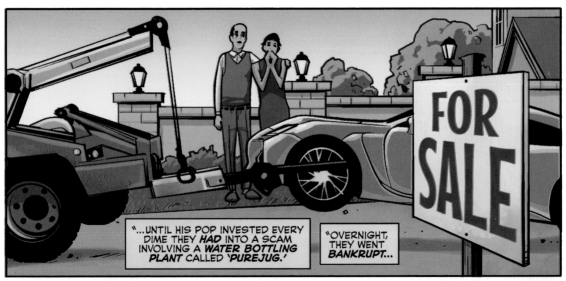

"...UNTIL HIS POP INVESTED EVERY DIME THEY *HAD* INTO A SCAM INVOLVING A *WATER BOTTLING PLANT* CALLED '*PUREJUG.*'"

"OVERNIGHT, THEY WENT *BANKRUPT...*"

"...AND LI'L *FORSYTHE* GOT A NICKNAME-- AND A *LIFE-LESSON*--THAT ENDURES TO THIS DAY."

I LIKE YOUR *SHIRT!* DID IT COST A *THOUSAND DOLLARS?*

AH HA HA HA HA!

HEY, "*JUGHEAD*"! WHY YOU HANGING OUT *HERE?* YOUR *PILOT* RUN OUTTA *HELICOPTER FUEL?*

HA HA HA HA!

IF YOU'RE GOING TO SURVIVE IN THIS WORLD, HERE'S WHAT YOU NEED TO KNOW:

YOU ARE WHO YOU ARE, NOT WHAT PEOPLE *THINK* YOU ARE.

BE STRAIGHT. BE WEIRD. BE WHAT-EVER. JUST BE WHAT YOU *WANNA* BE. AND IF PEOPLE DON'T LIKE IT...

...THAT'S WHAT THE "*S*" STANDS FOR?

THAT'S WHAT THE "*S*" STANDS FOR.

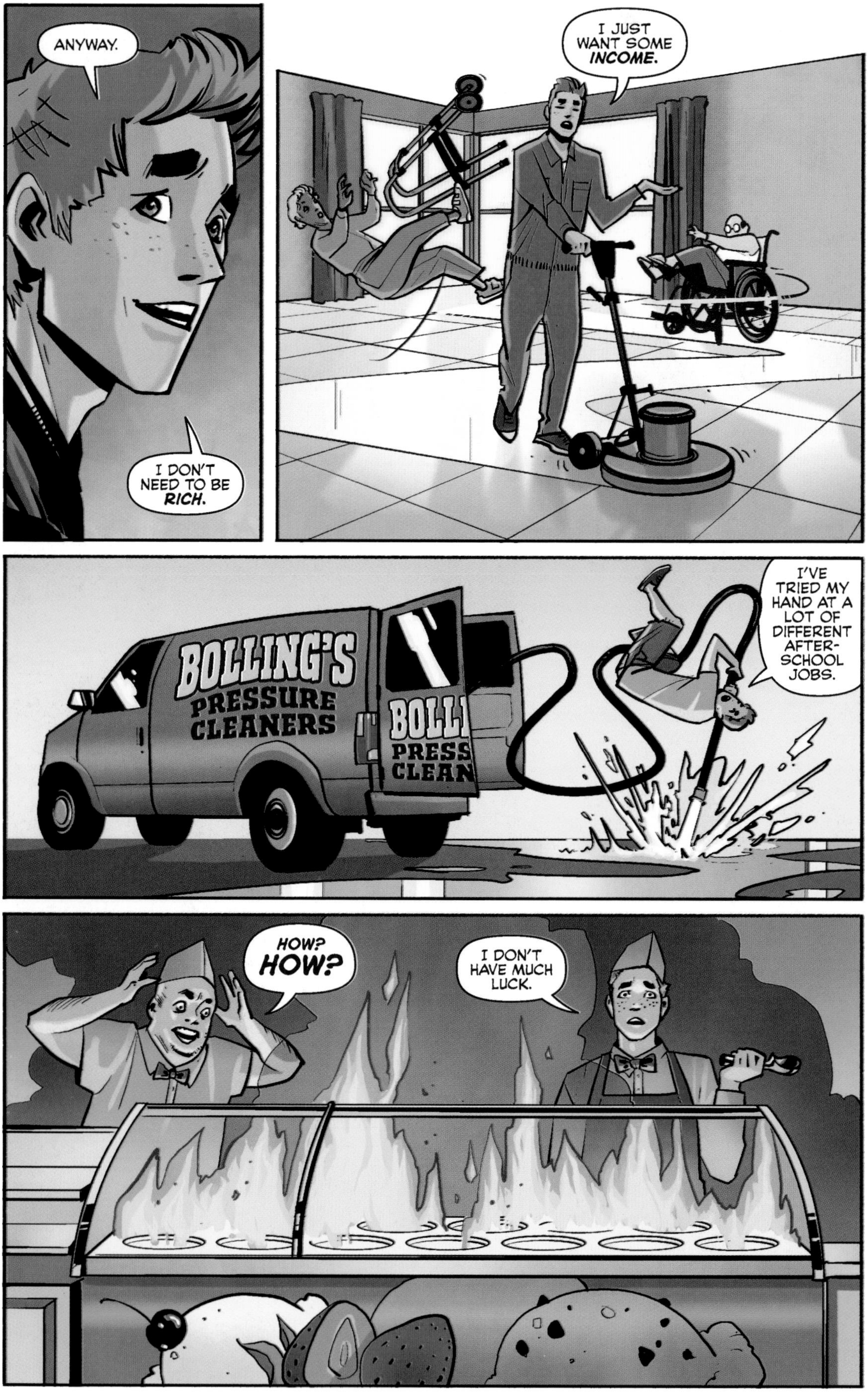
ANYWAY.
I DON'T NEED TO BE *RICH*.
I JUST WANT SOME *INCOME*.
BOLLING'S PRESSURE CLEANERS
I'VE TRIED MY HAND AT A LOT OF DIFFERENT AFTER-SCHOOL JOBS.
HOW? *HOW?*
I DON'T HAVE MUCH LUCK.

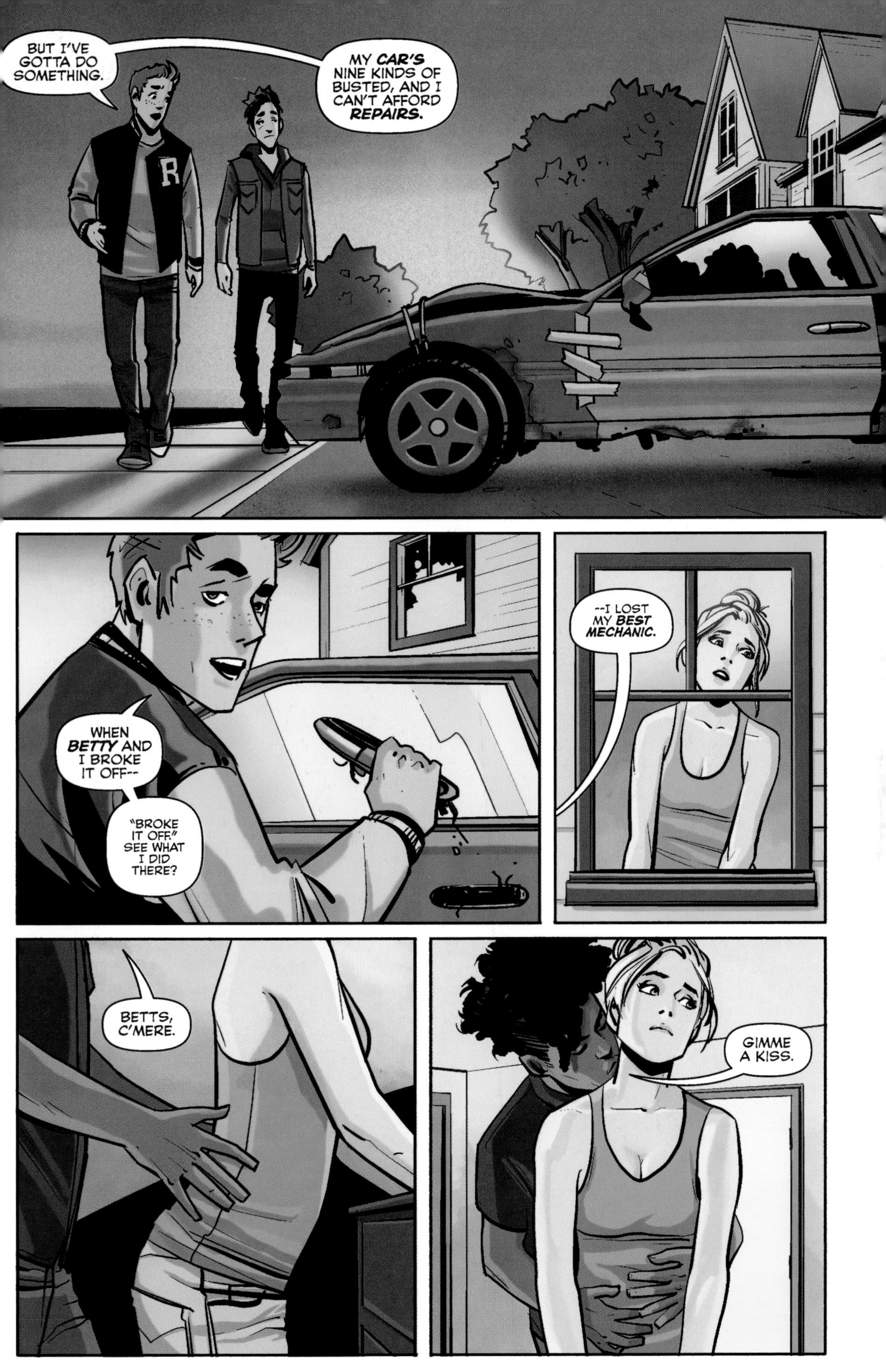
BUT I'VE GOTTA DO SOMETHING.
MY CAR'S NINE KINDS OF BUSTED, AND I CAN'T AFFORD REPAIRS.
WHEN BETTY AND I BROKE IT OFF--
"BROKE IT OFF." SEE WHAT I DID THERE?
--I LOST MY BEST MECHANIC.
BETTS, C'MERE.
GIMME A KISS.

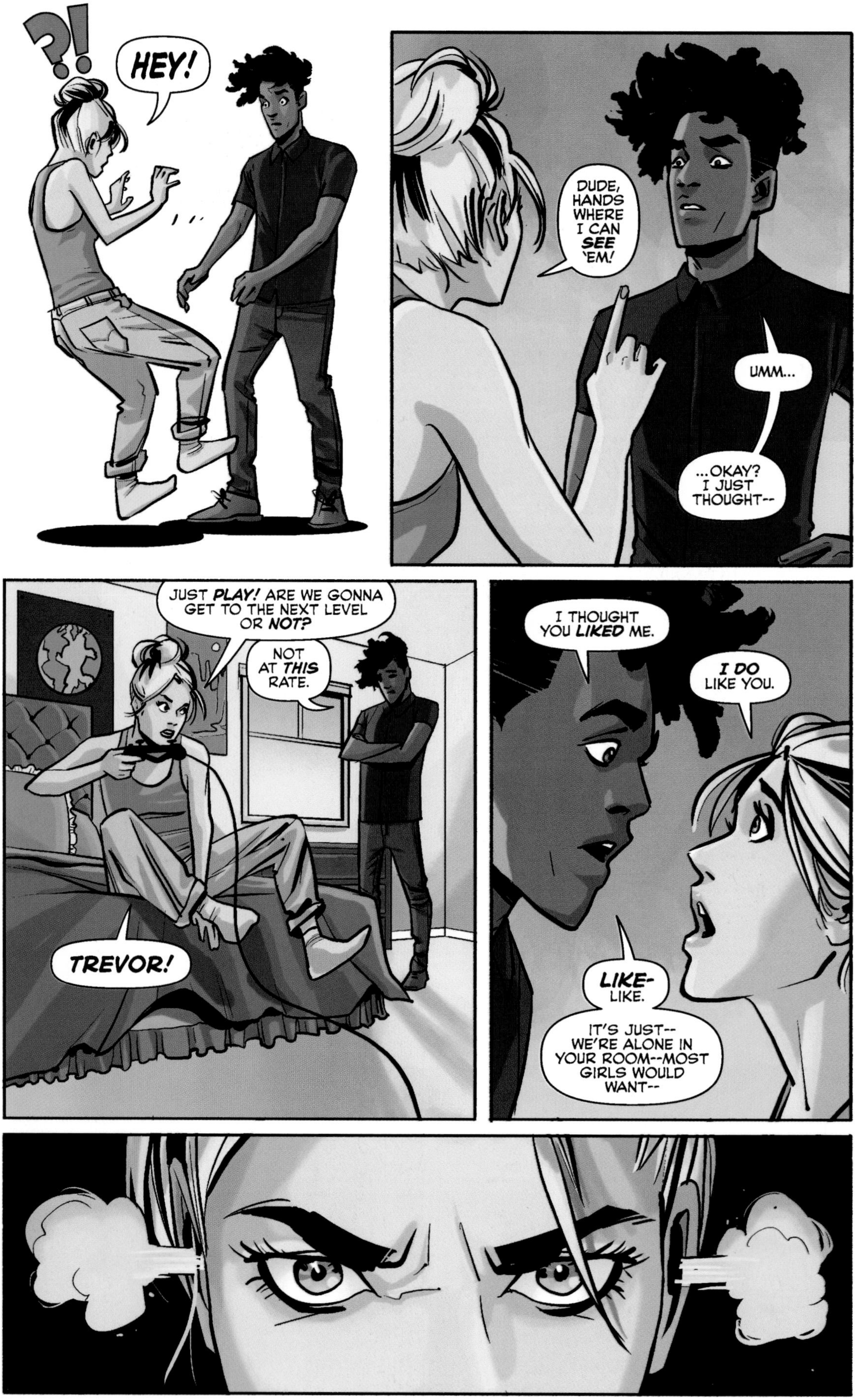
?!
HEY!
DUDE, HANDS WHERE I CAN SEE 'EM!
UMM...
...OKAY? I JUST THOUGHT--
JUST PLAY! ARE WE GONNA GET TO THE NEXT LEVEL OR NOT?
NOT AT THIS RATE.
TREVOR!
I THOUGHT YOU LIKED ME.
I DO LIKE YOU.
LIKE-LIKE.
IT'S JUST-- WE'RE ALONE IN YOUR ROOM--MOST GIRLS WOULD WANT--

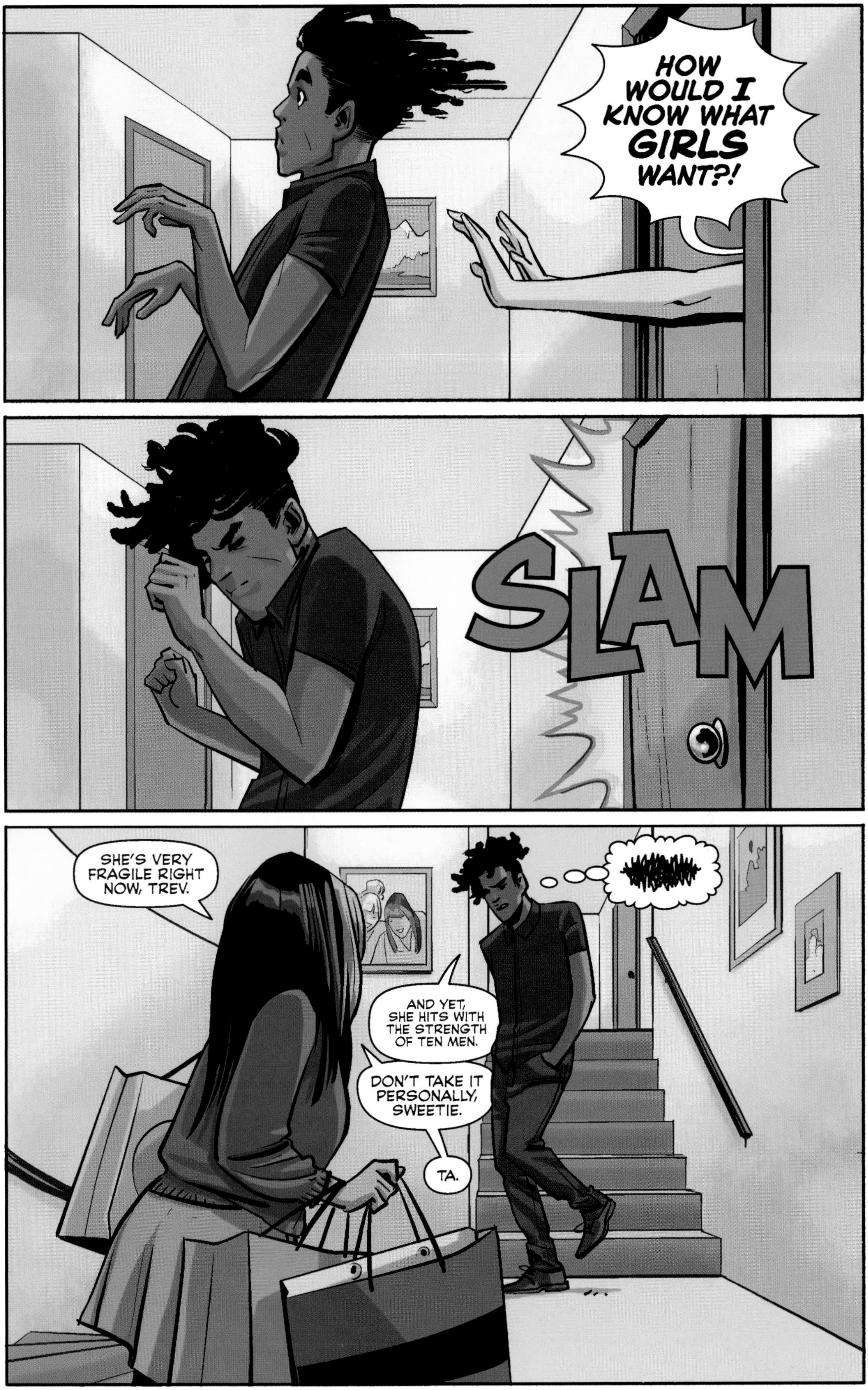
HOW WOULD I KNOW WHAT GIRLS WANT?!
SLAM
SHE'S VERY FRAGILE RIGHT NOW, TREV.
AND YET, SHE HITS WITH THE STRENGTH OF TEN MEN.
DON'T TAKE IT PERSONALLY, SWEETIE.
TA.

CHAPTER TWO: ONE OF THE GUYS

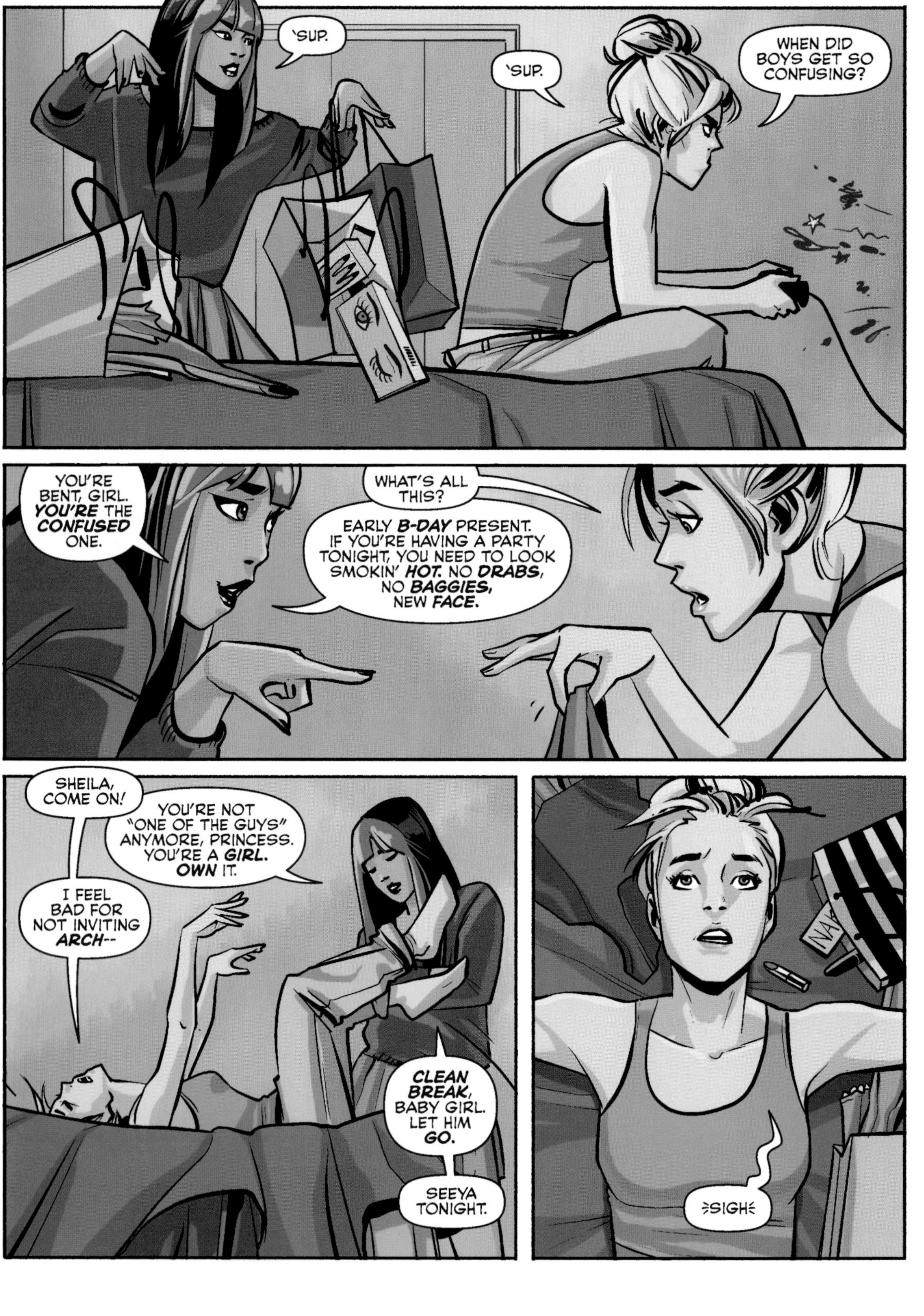

'SUP.
'SUP.
WHEN DID BOYS GET SO CONFUSING?
YOU'RE BENT, GIRL. YOU'RE THE CONFUSED ONE.
WHAT'S ALL THIS?
EARLY B-DAY PRESENT. IF YOU'RE HAVING A PARTY TONIGHT, YOU NEED TO LOOK SMOKIN' HOT. NO DRABS, NO BAGGIES, NEW FACE.
SHEILA, COME ON!
YOU'RE NOT "ONE OF THE GUYS" ANYMORE, PRINCESS. YOU'RE A GIRL. OWN IT.
I FEEL BAD FOR NOT INVITING ARCH--
CLEAN BREAK, BABY GIRL. LET HIM GO.
SEEYA TONIGHT.
SIGH

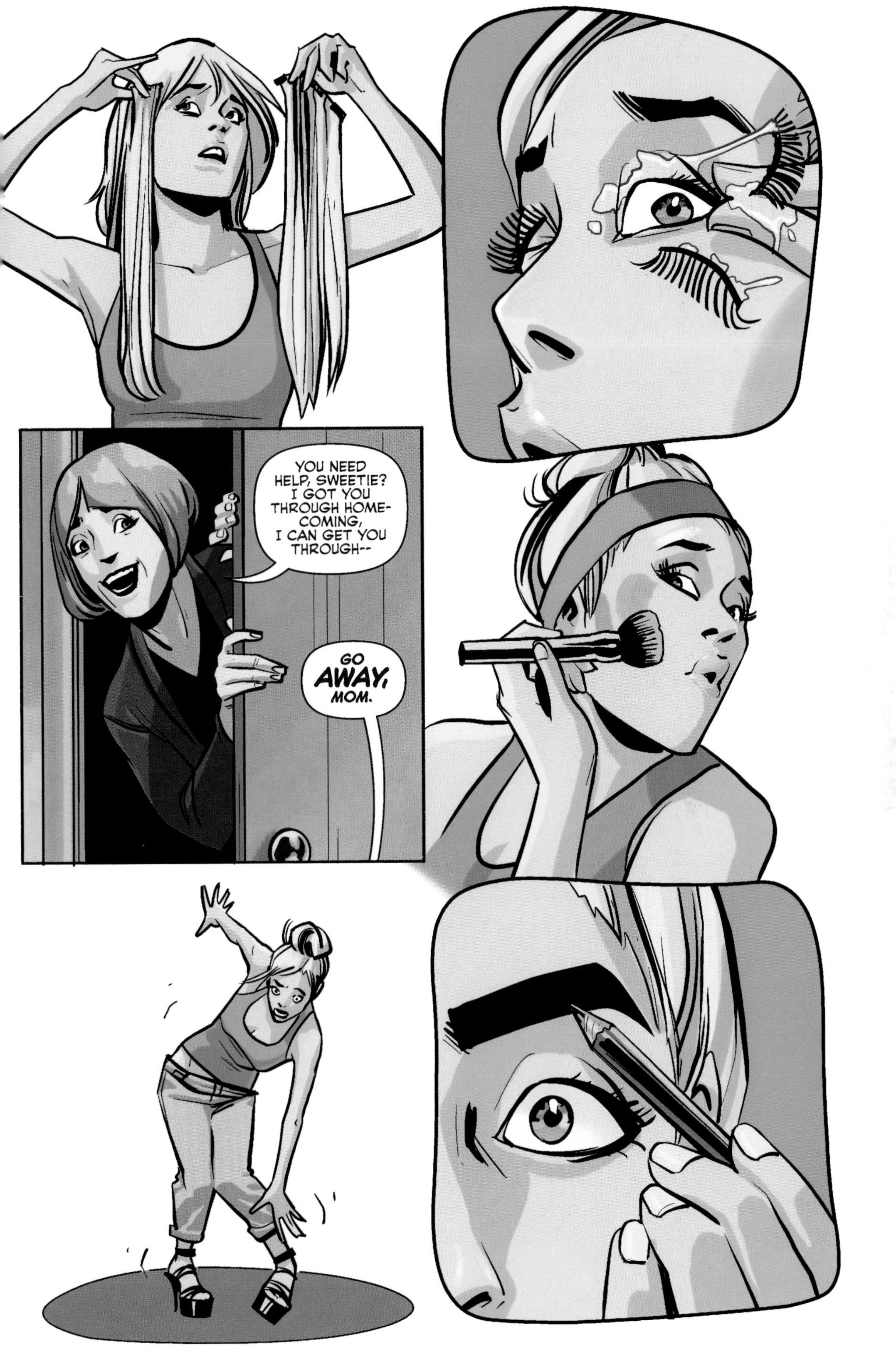

YOU NEED HELP, SWEETIE? I GOT YOU THROUGH HOME-COMING, I CAN GET YOU THROUGH--
GO AWAY, MOM.

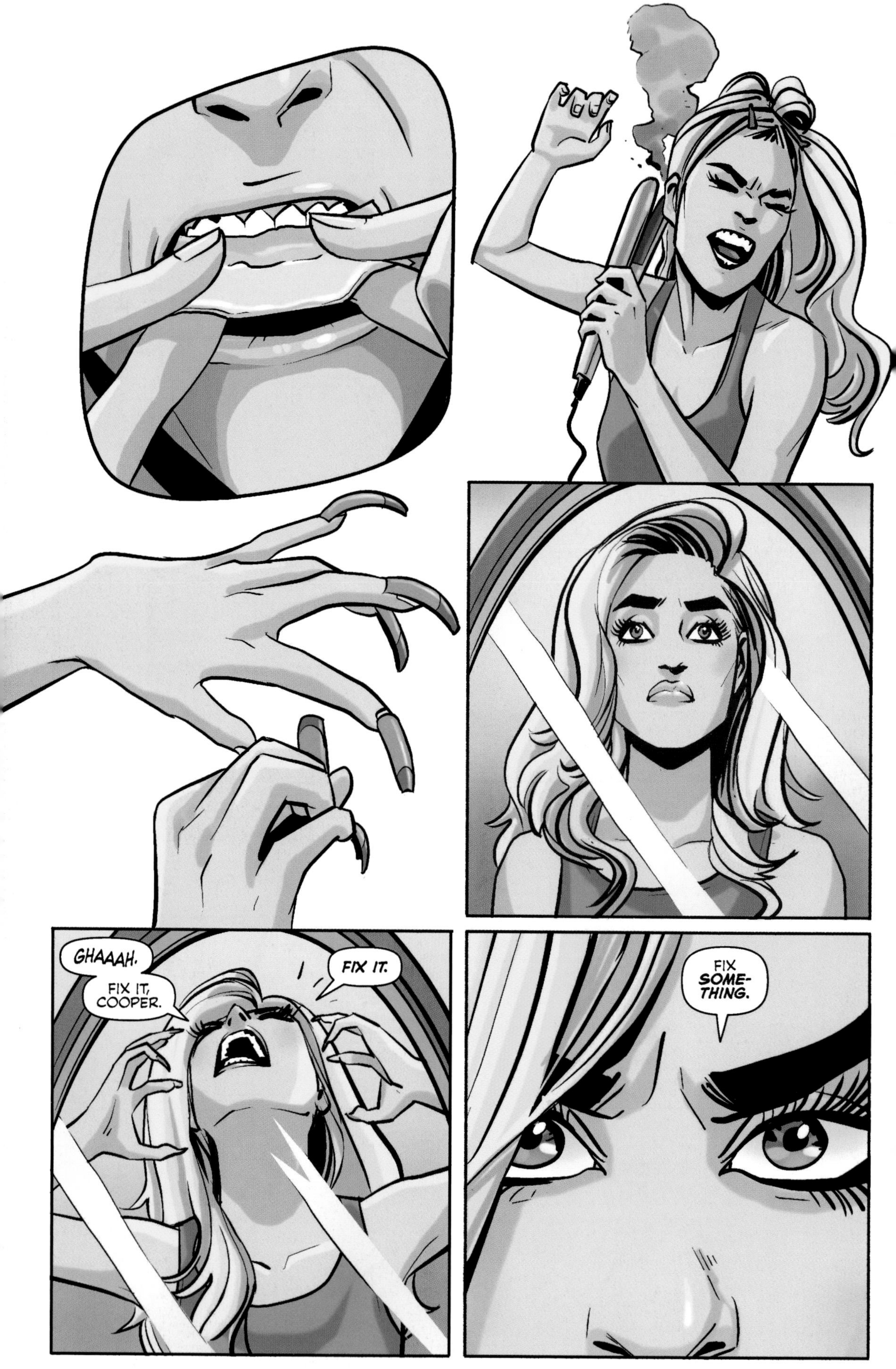
GHAAAH.
FIX IT, COOPER.
FIX IT.
FIX SOMETHING.

CHAPTER THREE: CAKEWALK

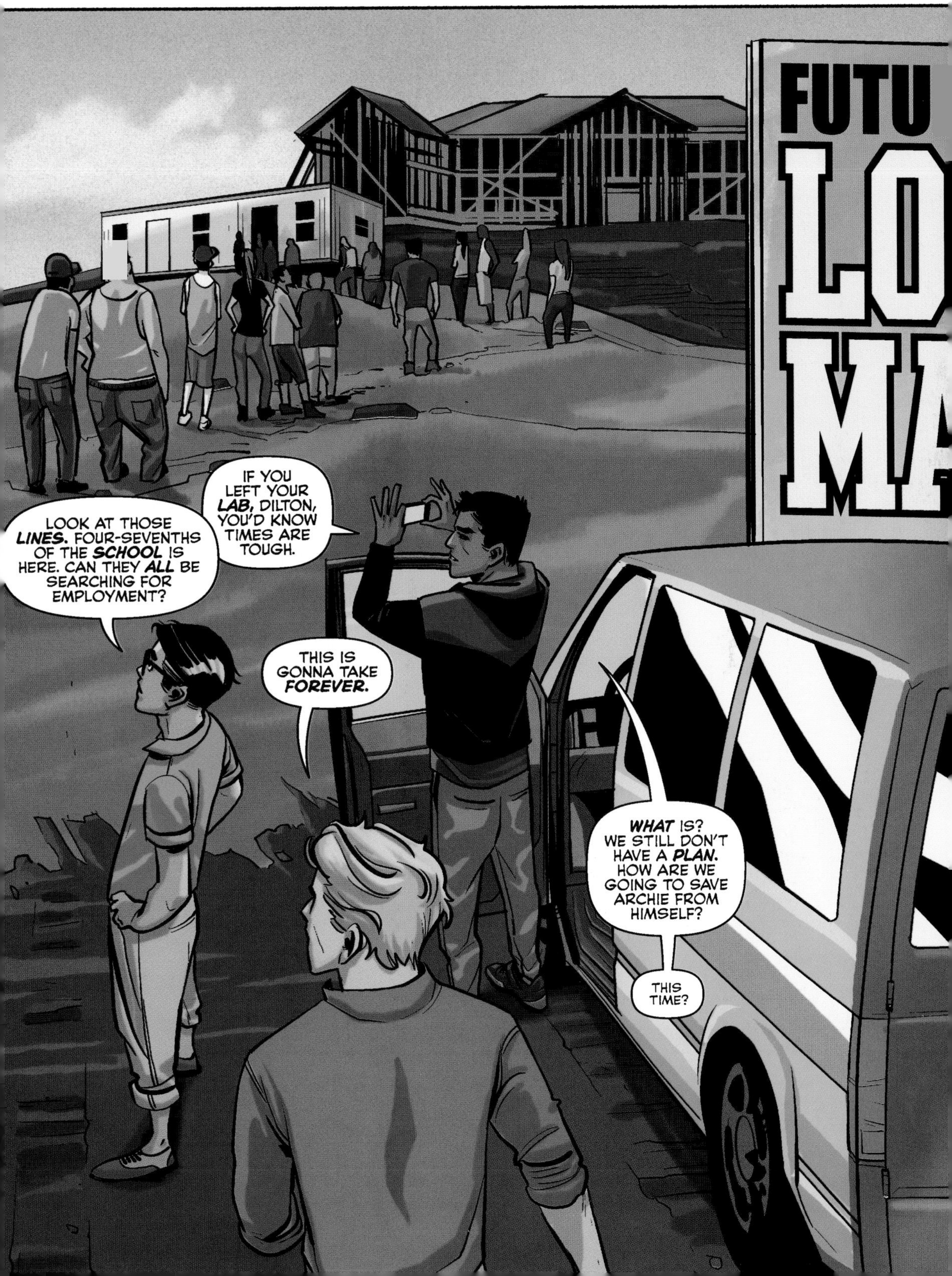
LOOK AT THOSE LINES. FOUR-SEVENTHS OF THE SCHOOL IS HERE. CAN THEY ALL BE SEARCHING FOR EMPLOYMENT?
IF YOU LEFT YOUR LAB, DILTON, YOU'D KNOW TIMES ARE TOUGH.
THIS IS GONNA TAKE FOREVER.
WHAT IS? WE STILL DON'T HAVE A PLAN. HOW ARE WE GOING TO SAVE ARCHIE FROM HIMSELF?
THIS TIME?

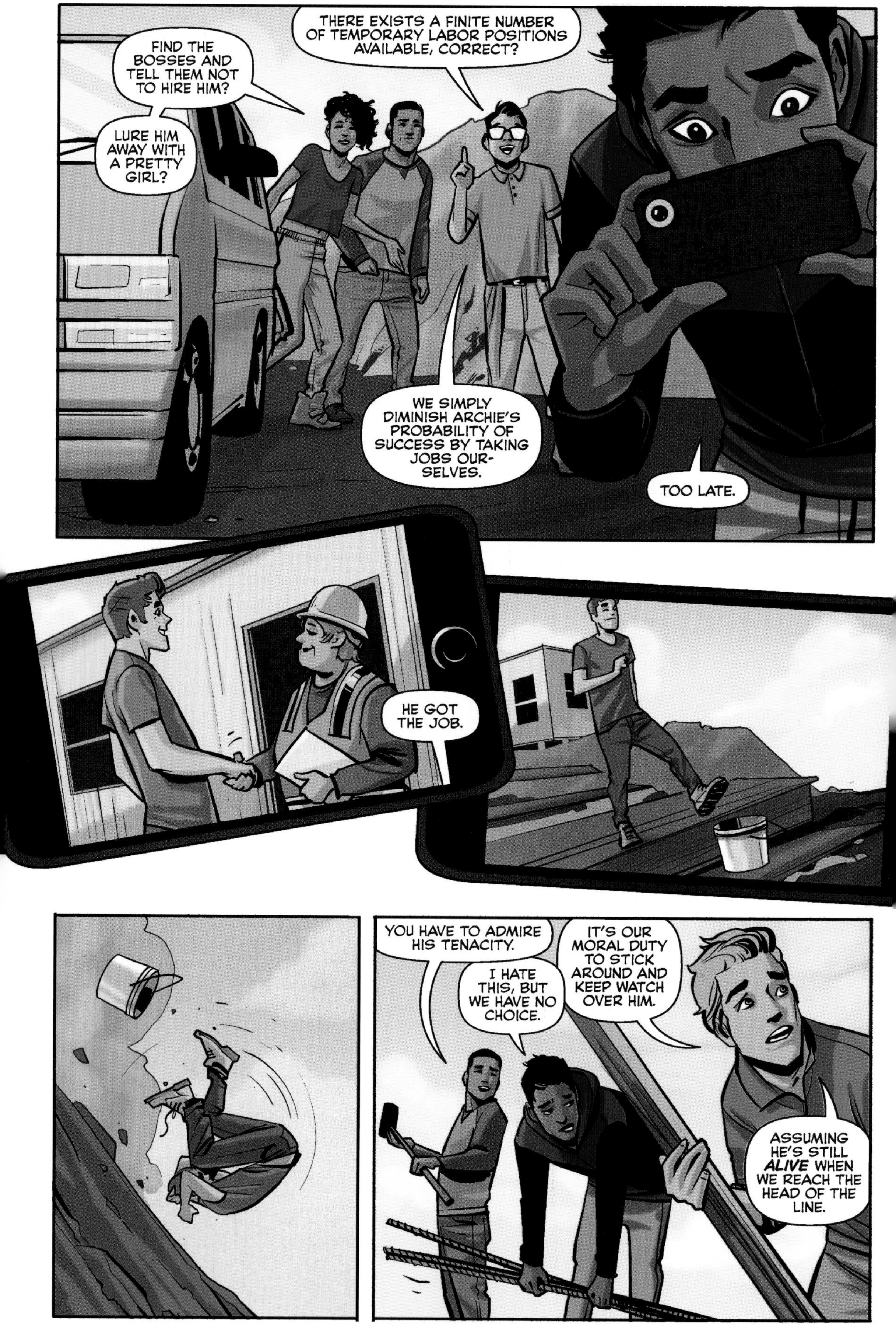
FIND THE BOSSES AND TELL THEM NOT TO HIRE HIM?
LURE HIM AWAY WITH A PRETTY GIRL?
THERE EXISTS A FINITE NUMBER OF TEMPORARY LABOR POSITIONS AVAILABLE, CORRECT?
WE SIMPLY DIMINISH ARCHIE'S PROBABILITY OF SUCCESS BY TAKING JOBS OUR-SELVES.
TOO LATE.
HE GOT THE JOB.
YOU HAVE TO ADMIRE HIS TENACITY.
I HATE THIS, BUT WE HAVE NO CHOICE.
IT'S OUR MORAL DUTY TO STICK AROUND AND KEEP WATCH OVER HIM.
ASSUMING HE'S STILL *ALIVE* WHEN WE REACH THE HEAD OF THE LINE.

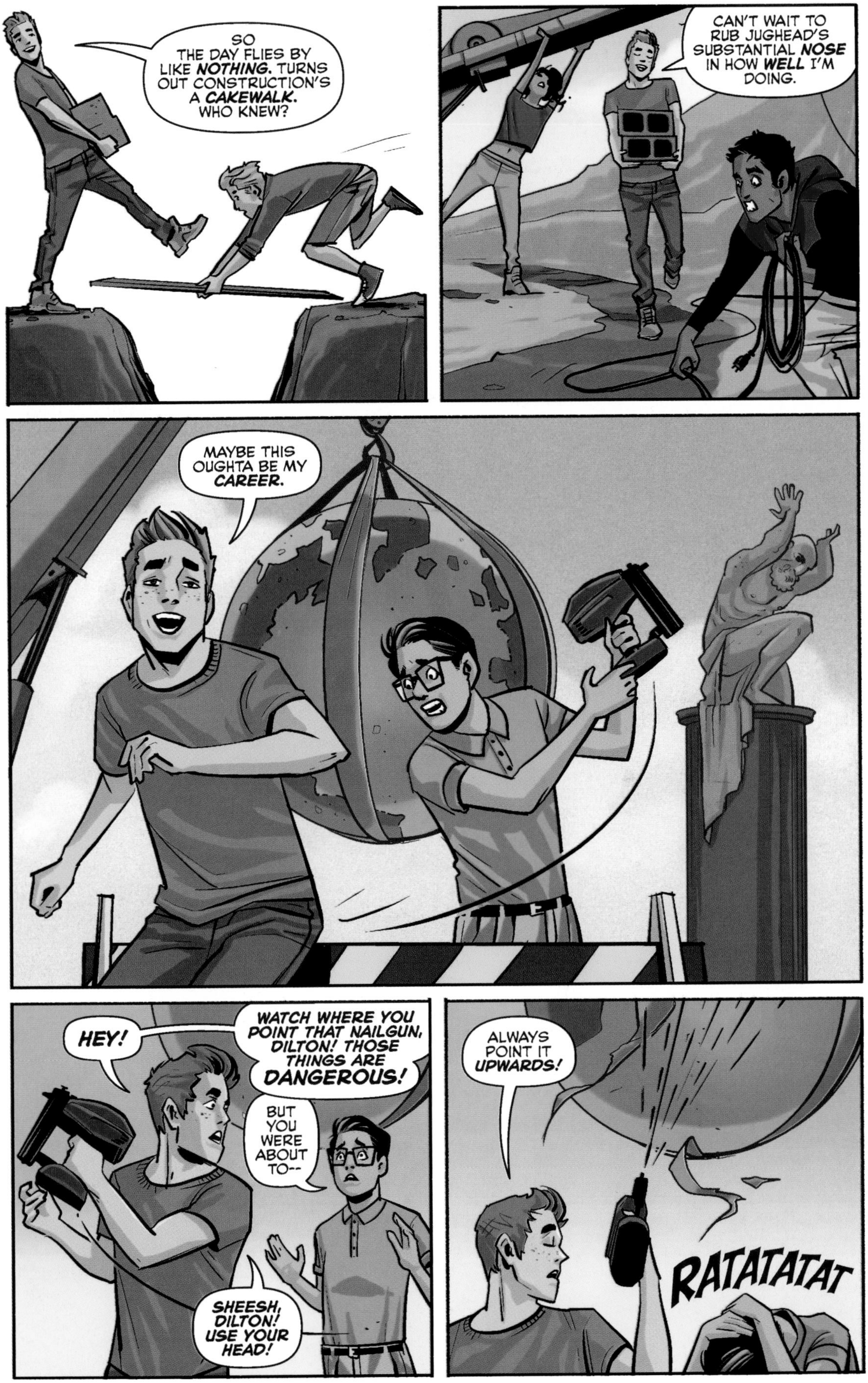

SO THE DAY FLIES BY LIKE NOTHING. TURNS OUT CONSTRUCTION'S A CAKEWALK. WHO KNEW?
CAN'T WAIT TO RUB JUGHEAD'S SUBSTANTIAL NOSE IN HOW WELL I'M DOING.
MAYBE THIS OUGHTA BE MY CAREER.
HEY!
WATCH WHERE YOU POINT THAT NAILGUN, DILTON! THOSE THINGS ARE DANGEROUS!
BUT YOU WERE ABOUT TO--
SHEESH, DILTON! USE YOUR HEAD!
ALWAYS POINT IT UPWARDS!
RATATATAT

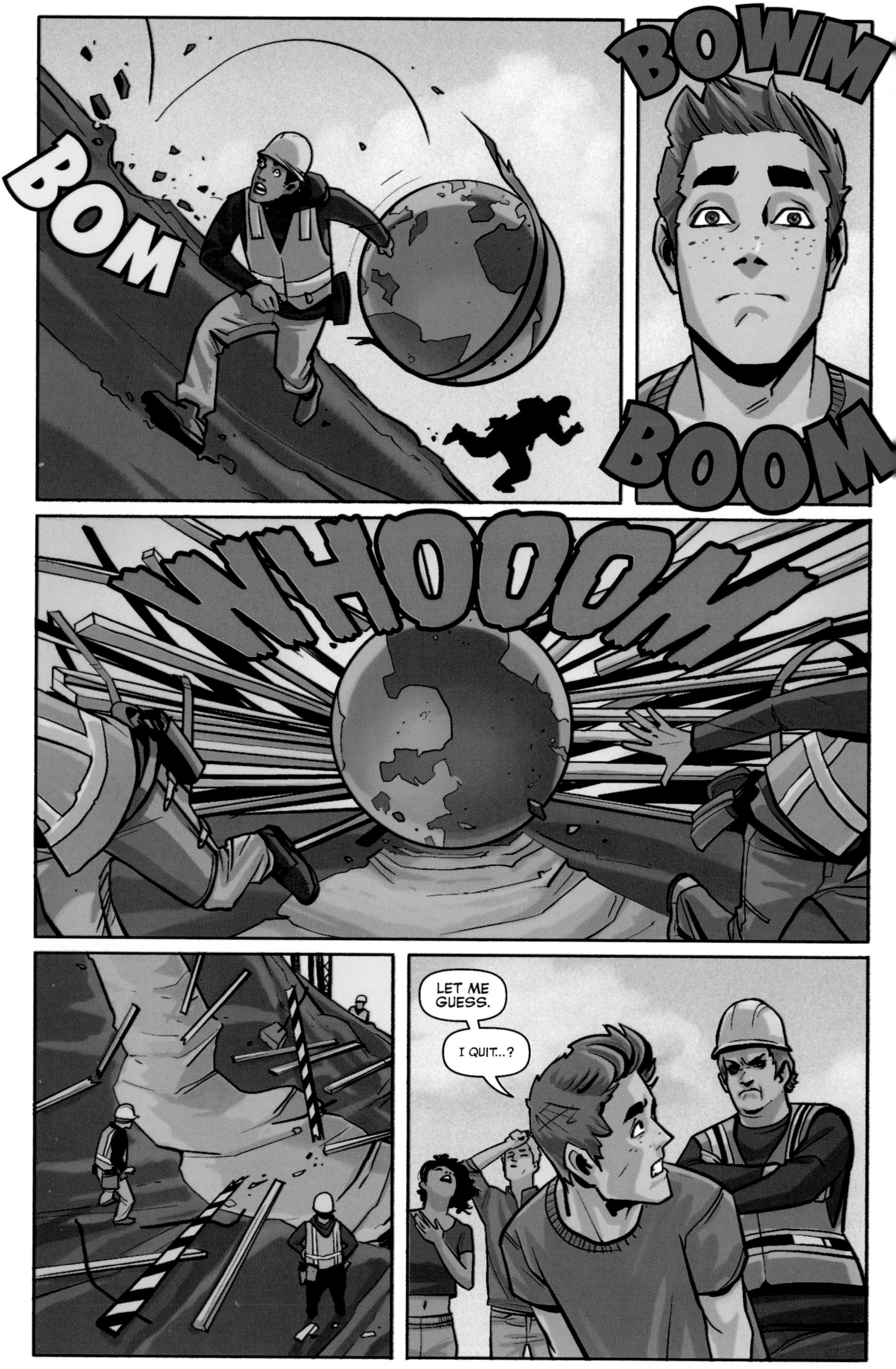
BOM
BOWM
BOOM
WHOOOM
LET ME GUESS.
I QUIT...?

CHAPTER FOUR: NOT MY SPECIAL TALENT

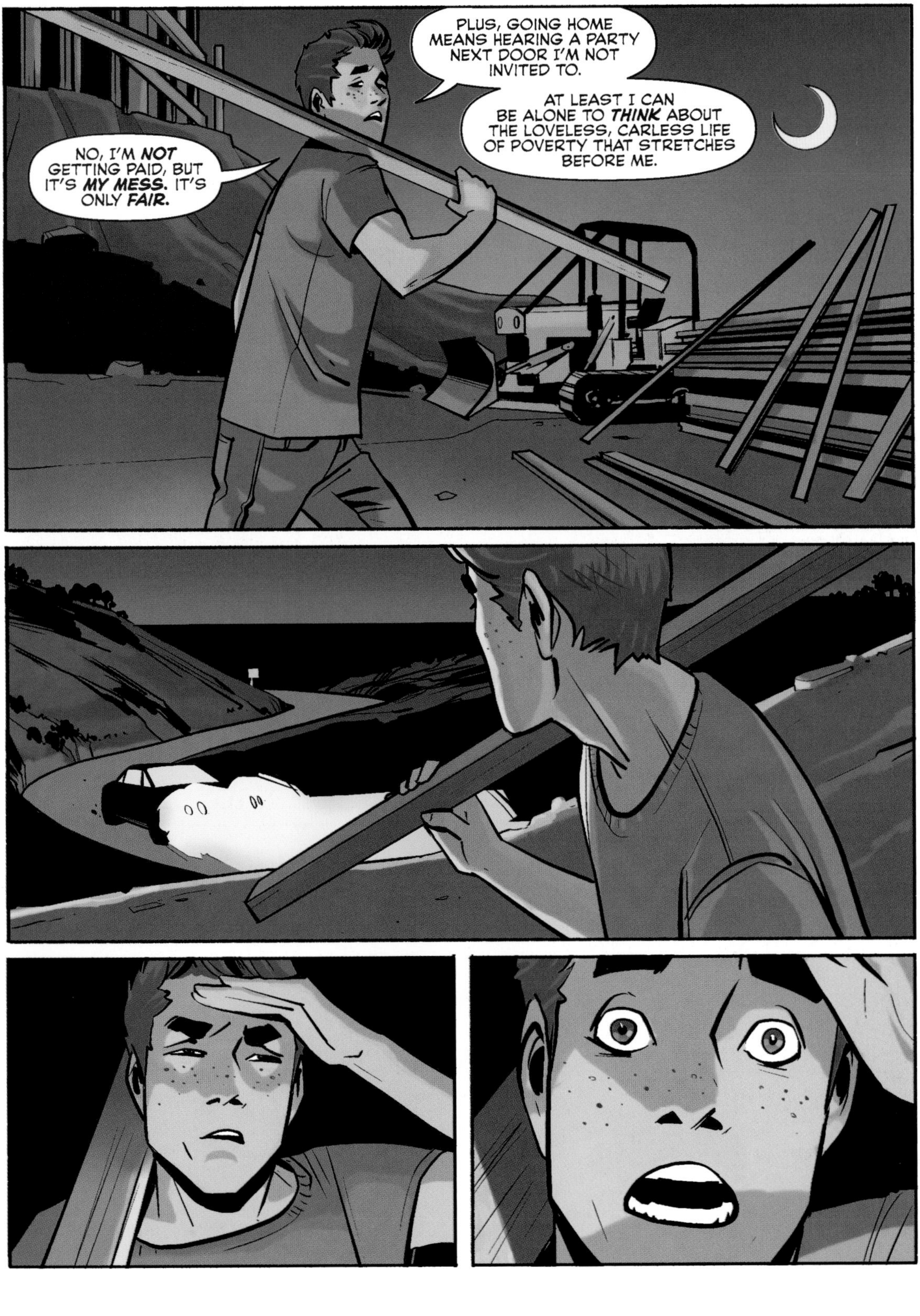

NO, I'M **NOT** GETTING PAID, BUT IT'S ***MY MESS.*** IT'S ONLY **FAIR.**
PLUS, GOING HOME MEANS HEARING A PARTY NEXT DOOR I'M NOT INVITED TO.
AT LEAST I CAN BE ALONE TO ***THINK*** ABOUT THE LOVELESS, CARLESS LIFE OF POVERTY THAT STRETCHES BEFORE ME.

WOW.

LOVE AT FIRST SIGHT.

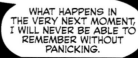

TIME STOPS, THEN LURCHES VIOLENTLY FORWARD, THEN COLLAPSES, SMELLING OF ELECTRICAL FIRE. NOT UNLIKE MY CAR.

WHAT HAPPENS IN THE VERY NEXT MOMENT, I WILL NEVER BE ABLE TO REMEMBER WITHOUT PANICKING.

CHOKK

HURRM

AAH!

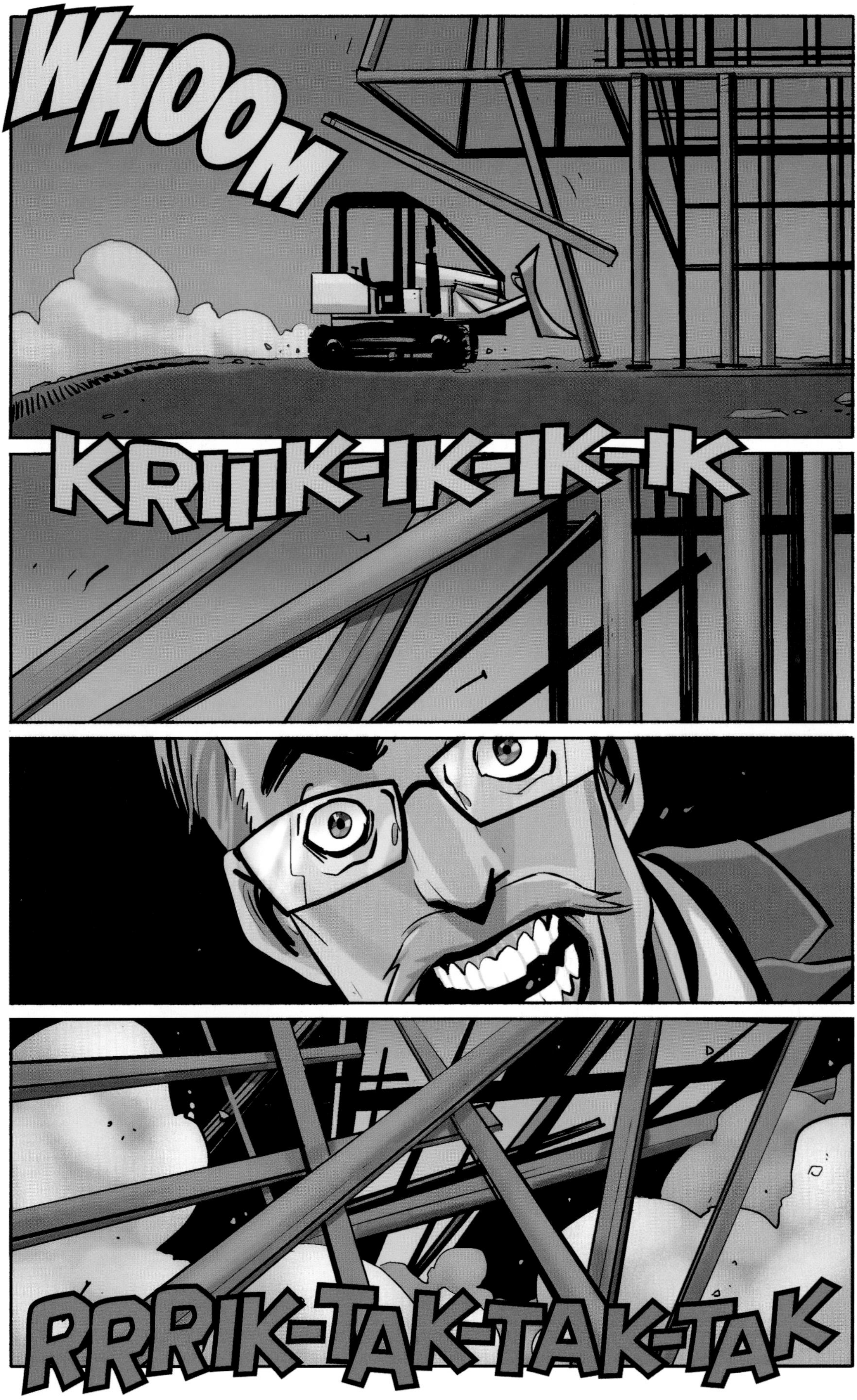
WHOOM
KRIIIK-IK-IK-IK
RRRIK-TAK-TAK-TAK

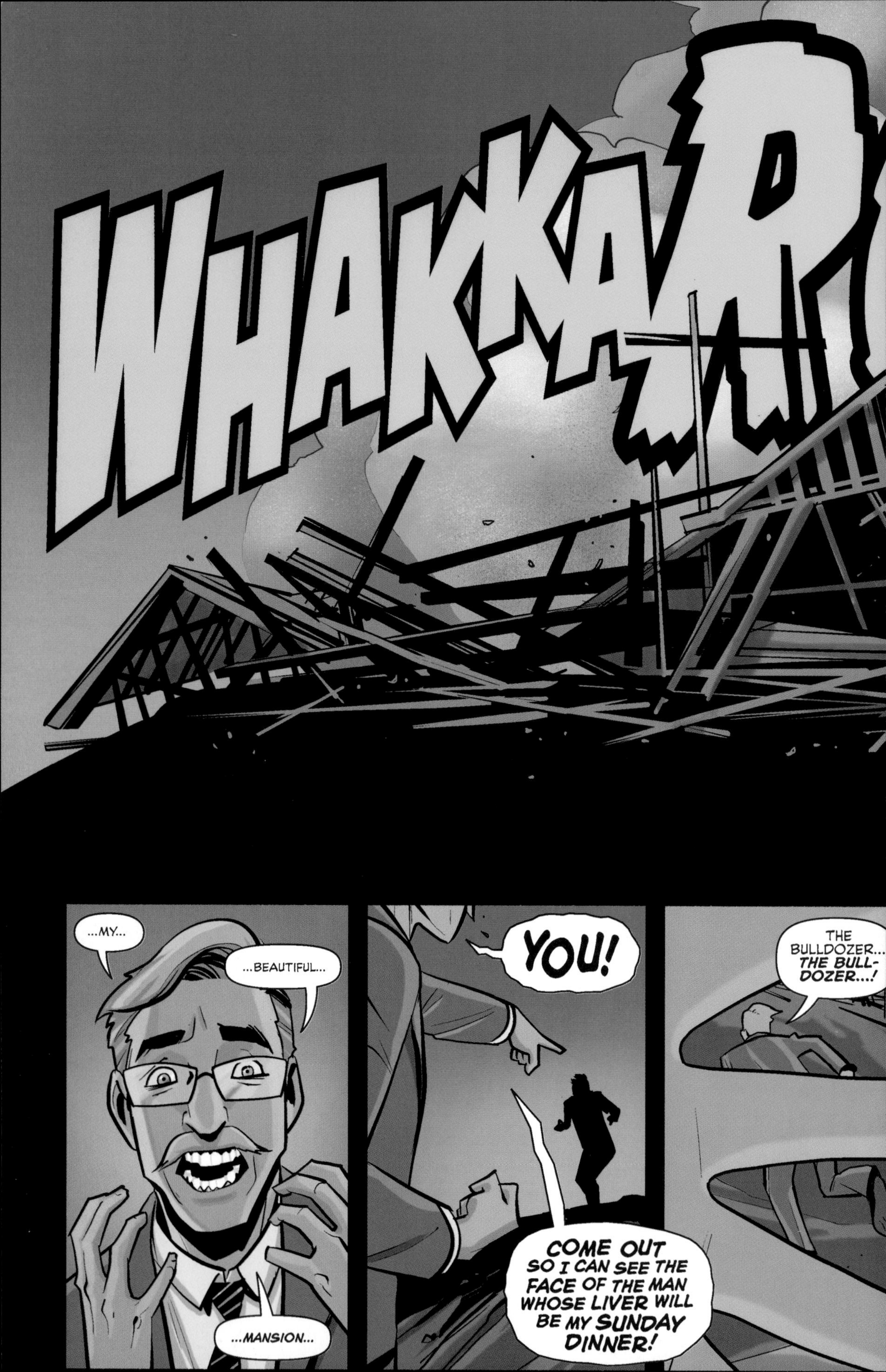

WHAKKA
...MY...
...BEAUTIFUL...
...MANSION...
YOU!
COME OUT SO I CAN SEE THE FACE OF THE MAN WHOSE LIVER WILL BE MY SUNDAY DINNER!
THE BULLDOZER... THE BULL-DOZER...!

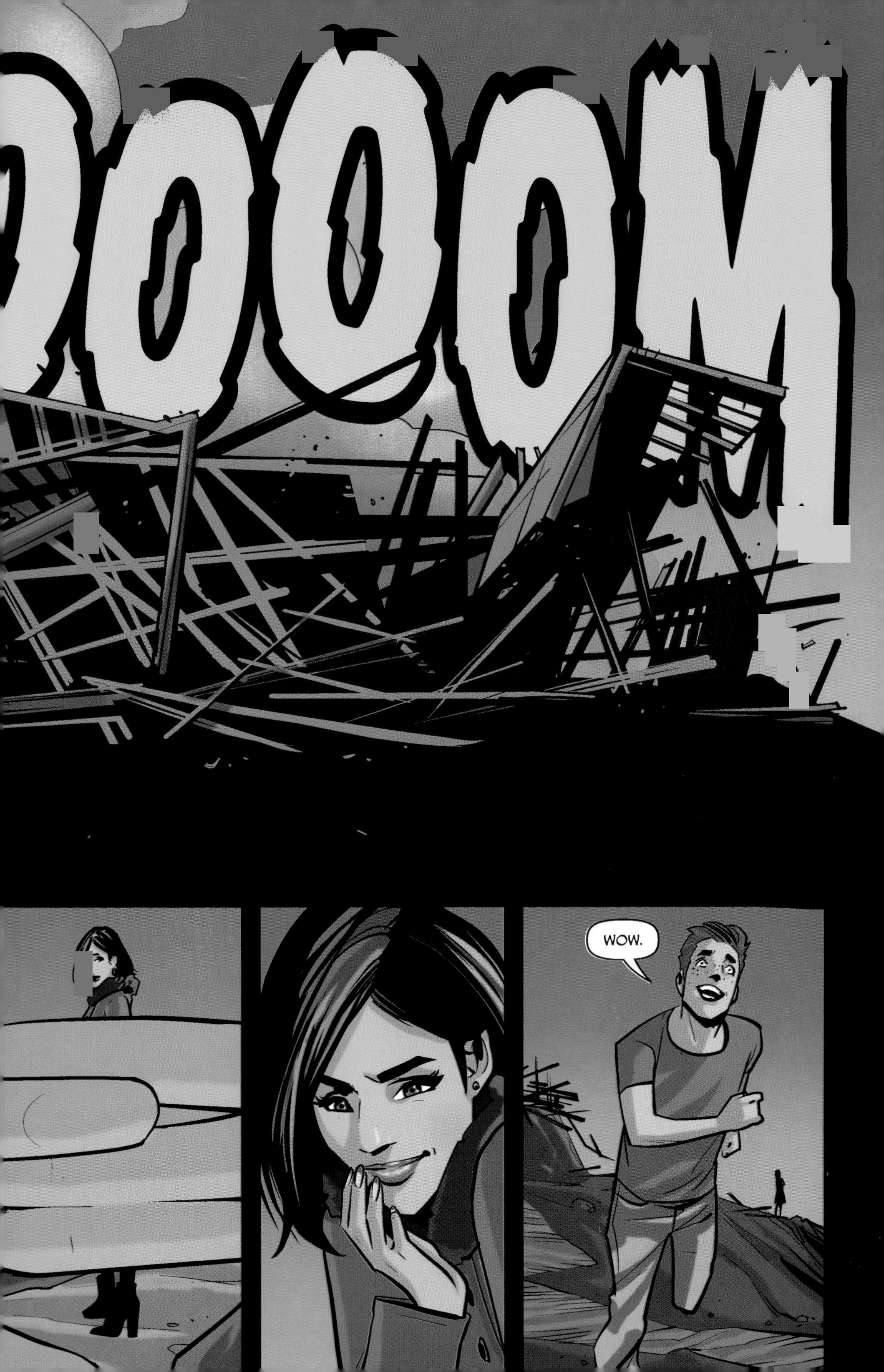
OOOOM
WOW.

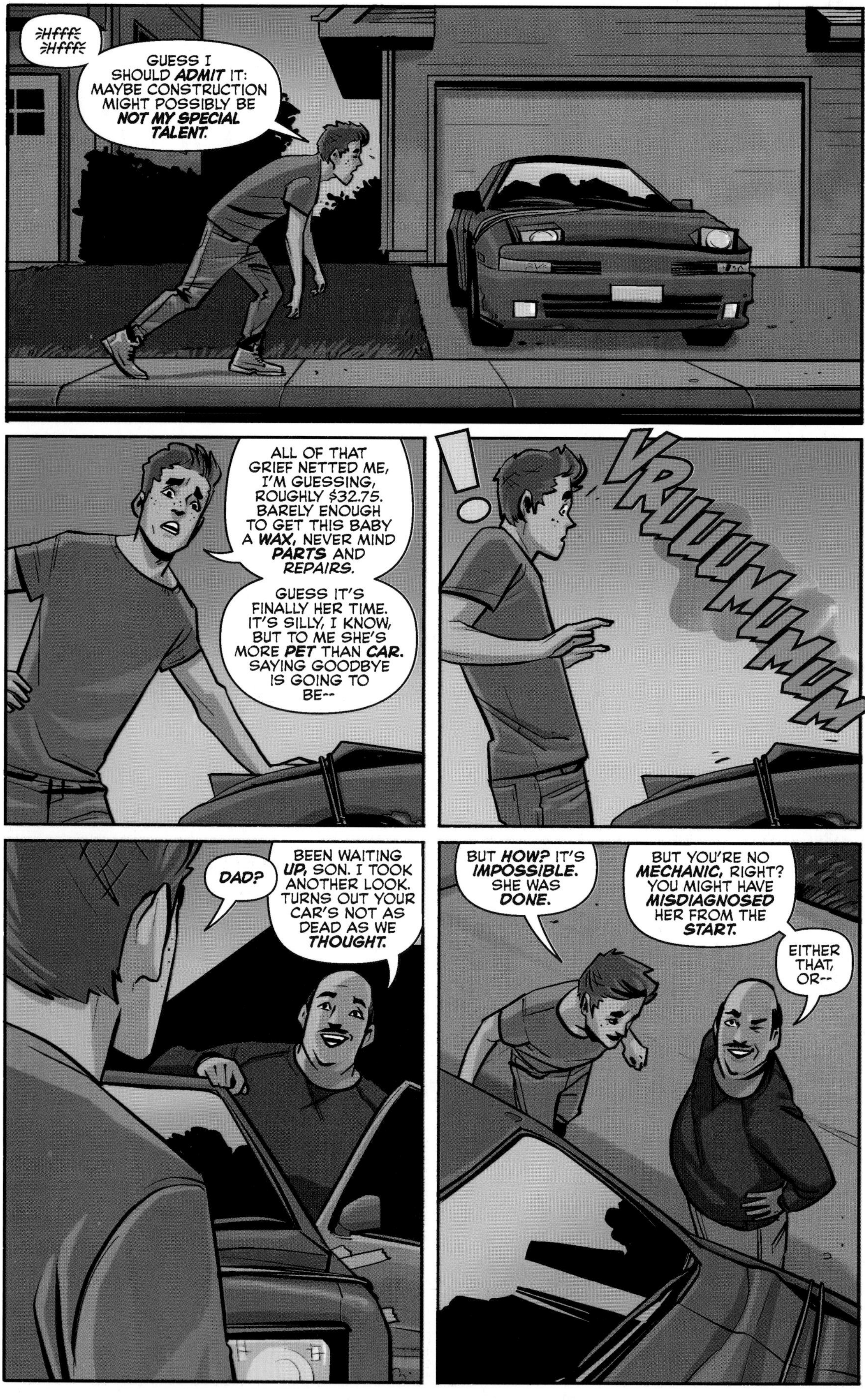

HFFF HFFF
GUESS I SHOULD ADMIT IT: MAYBE CONSTRUCTION MIGHT POSSIBLY BE NOT MY SPECIAL TALENT.
ALL OF THAT GRIEF NETTED ME, I'M GUESSING, ROUGHLY $32.75. BARELY ENOUGH TO GET THIS BABY A WAX, NEVER MIND PARTS AND REPAIRS.
GUESS IT'S FINALLY HER TIME. IT'S SILLY, I KNOW, BUT TO ME SHE'S MORE PET THAN CAR. SAYING GOODBYE IS GOING TO BE--
!
VRUUUMUMUMUM
DAD?
BEEN WAITING UP, SON. I TOOK ANOTHER LOOK. TURNS OUT YOUR CAR'S NOT AS DEAD AS WE THOUGHT.
BUT HOW? IT'S IMPOSSIBLE. SHE WAS DONE.
BUT YOU'RE NO MECHANIC, RIGHT? YOU MIGHT HAVE MISDIAGNOSED HER FROM THE START.
EITHER THAT, OR--

--SOMEBODY UP THERE LIKES YOU.

SHOWTIME, GIRL! DOWNSTAIRS, NOW!

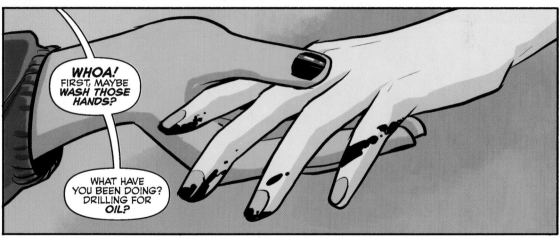

WHOA! FIRST, MAYBE WASH THOSE HANDS?

WHAT HAVE YOU BEEN DOING? DRILLING FOR OIL?

--REG, YOU HEAR ABOUT THE LODGE HOUSE COLLAPSING--?

THAT WASN'T YOU, WAS IT...?

Pfft. MANTLE WORSHIPS AT THE ALTAR OF BILLIONAIRES. HE WOULDN'T TAKE THE CHANCE OF MAKING AN ENEMY OUT OF ONE.

'SPECIALLY IF DAUGHTER BILLIONAIRE IS AS HOT AS SHE'S RUMORED TO BE. WHAT'S HER NAME? RONNIE? SOMETHING LIKE THAT?

BUUUT RONNIE'S A BOY'S NAME...

Oh, MOOSE, YOU ARE ADORBS.

WE'LL FIND OUT. I HEAR SHE STARTS SCHOOL NEXT--

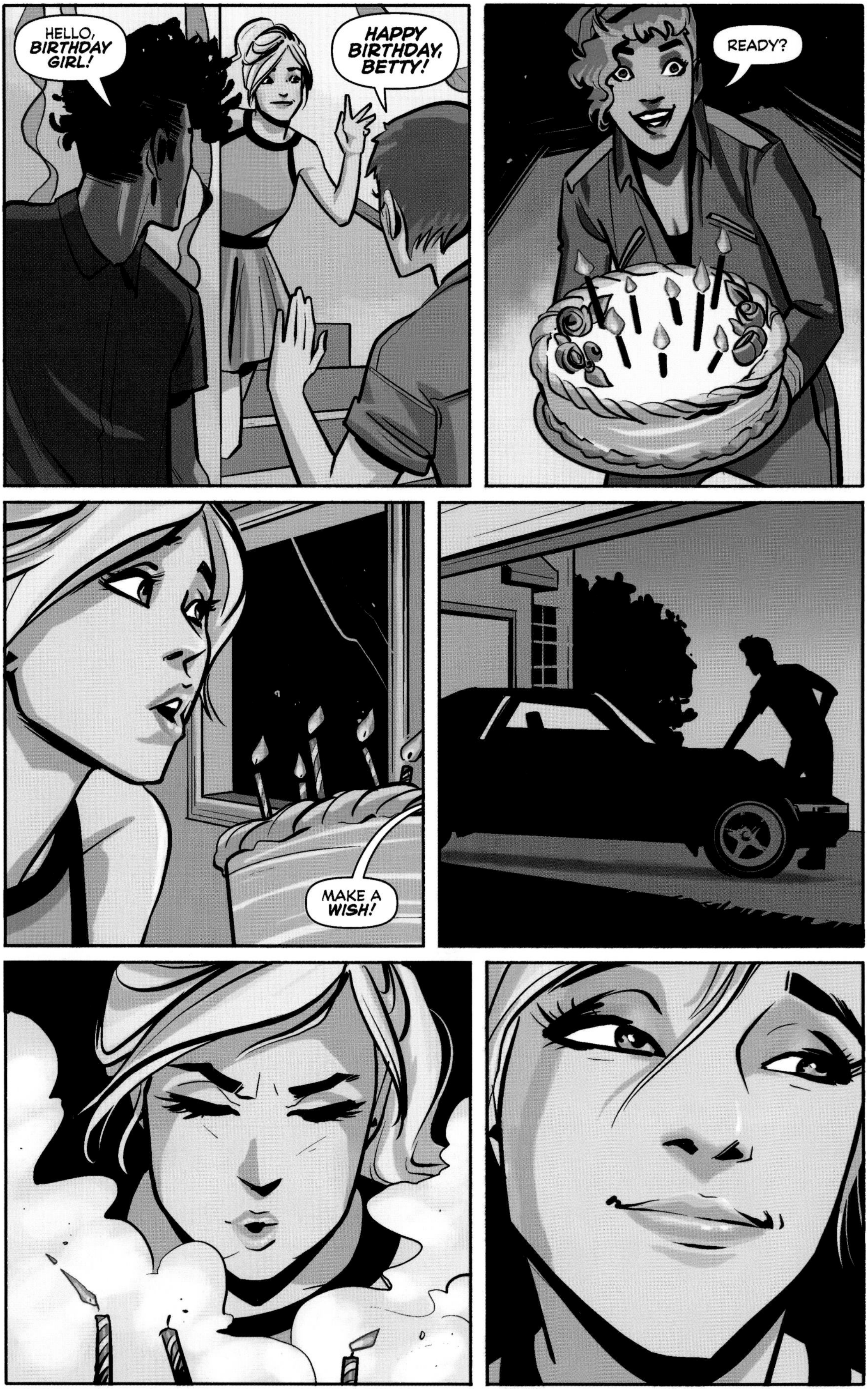
HELLO, BIRTHDAY GIRL!
HAPPY BIRTHDAY, BETTY!
READY?
MAKE A WISH!

TO BE CONTINUED...

ISSUE THREE

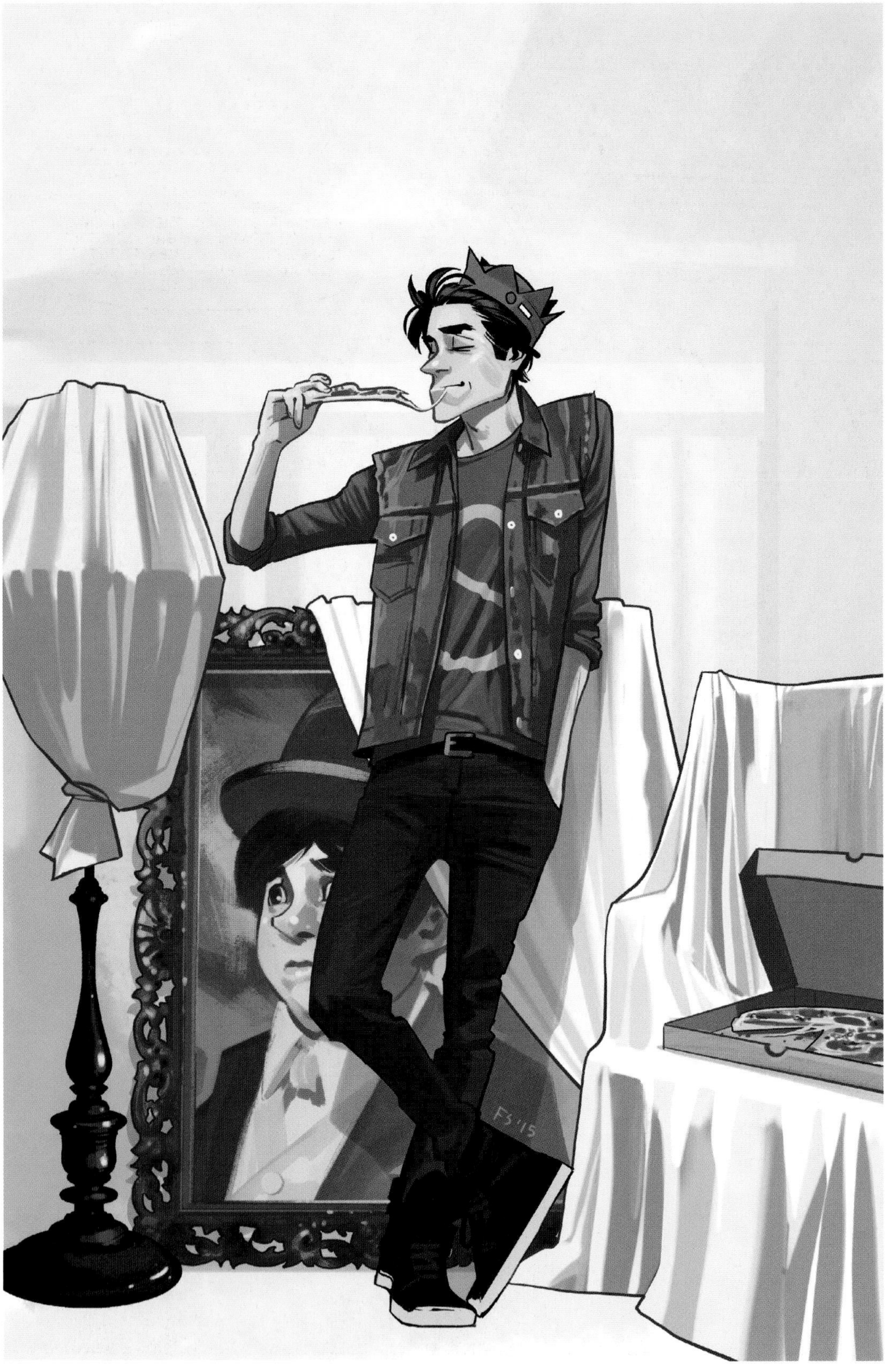
FS '15

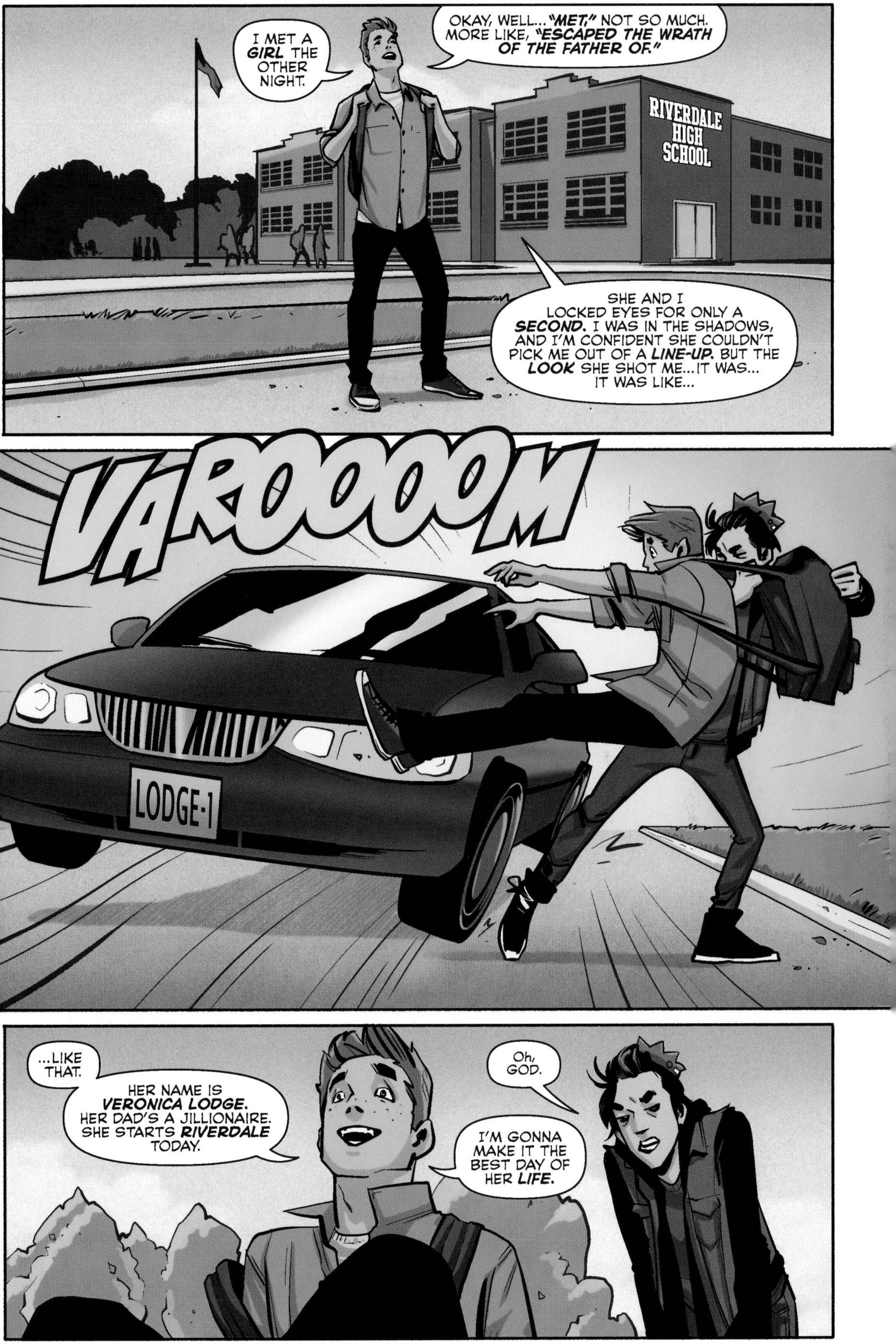
I MET A GIRL THE OTHER NIGHT.
OKAY, WELL... "MET," NOT SO MUCH. MORE LIKE, "ESCAPED THE WRATH OF THE FATHER OF."
RIVERDALE HIGH SCHOOL
SHE AND I LOCKED EYES FOR ONLY A SECOND. I WAS IN THE SHADOWS, AND I'M CONFIDENT SHE COULDN'T PICK ME OUT OF A LINE-UP. BUT THE LOOK SHE SHOT ME...IT WAS... IT WAS LIKE...
VAROOOOM
LODGE-1
...LIKE THAT.
HER NAME IS VERONICA LODGE. HER DAD'S A JILLIONAIRE. SHE STARTS RIVERDALE TODAY.
Oh, GOD.
I'M GONNA MAKE IT THE BEST DAY OF HER LIFE.

CHAPTER ONE: NICE Purse, ANDREWS

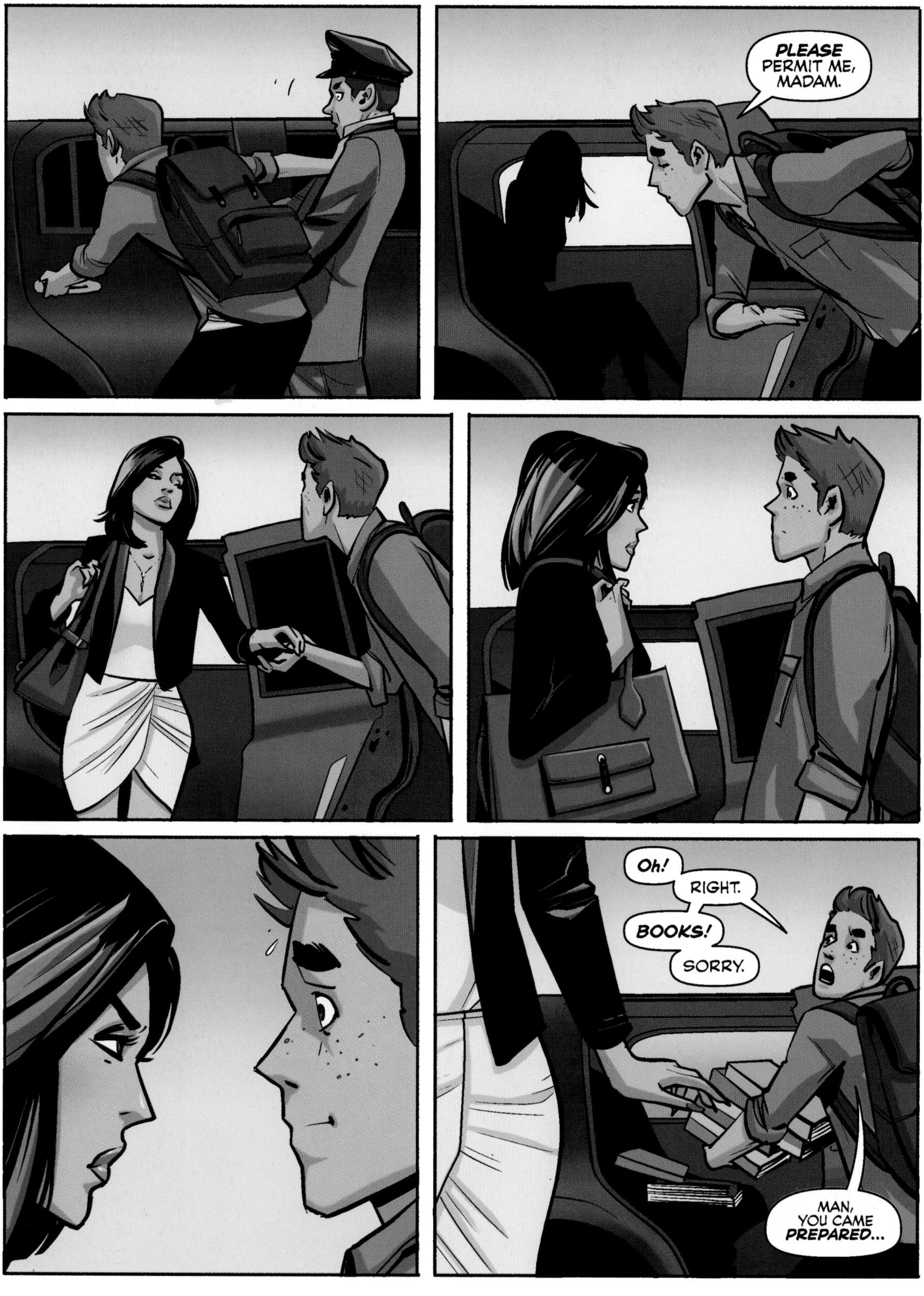

PLEASE PERMIT ME, MADAM.
Oh!
RIGHT.
BOOKS!
SORRY.
MAN, YOU CAME PREPARED...

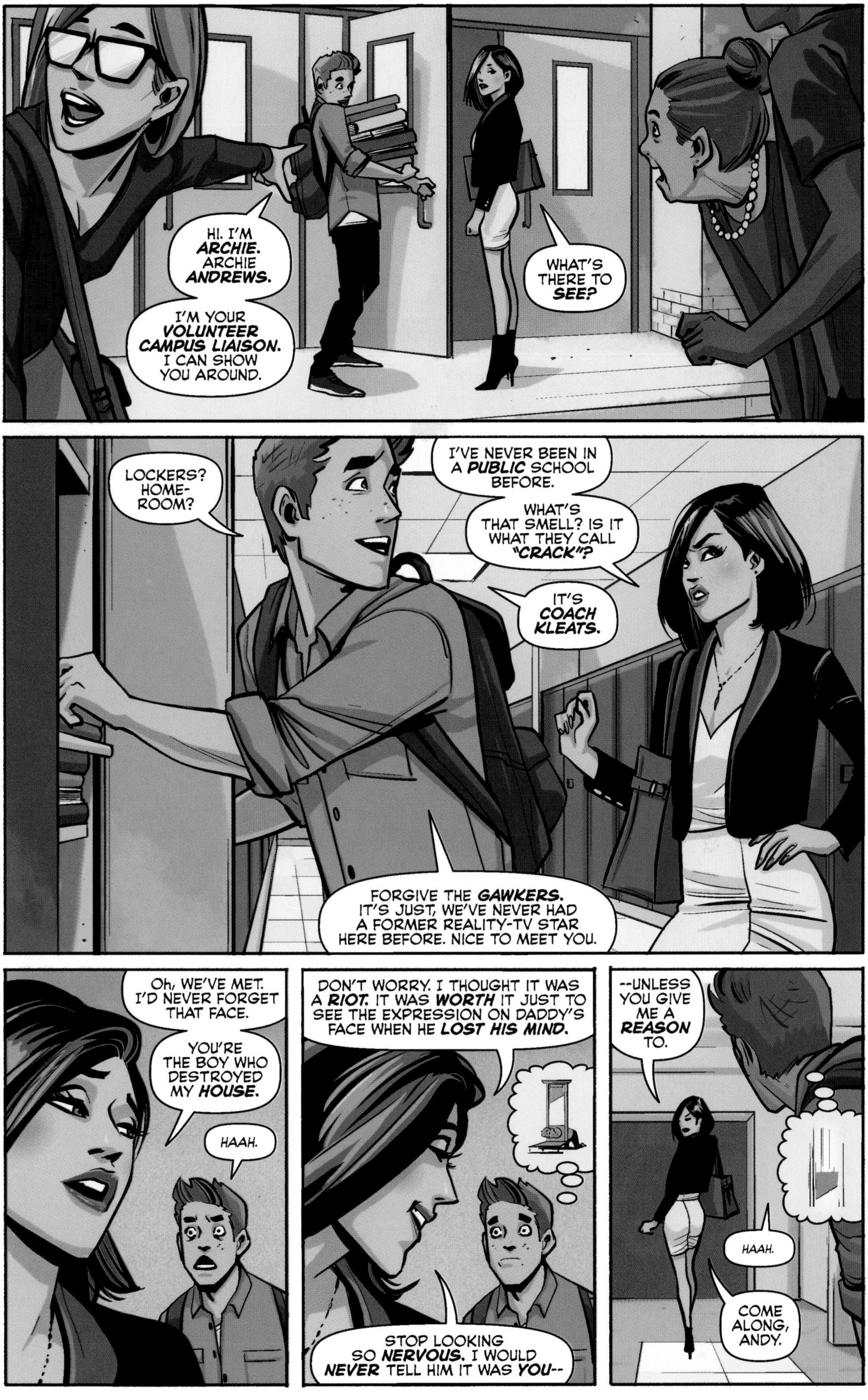
HI. I'M **ARCHIE.** ARCHIE **ANDREWS.**
I'M YOUR **VOLUNTEER CAMPUS LIAISON.** I CAN SHOW YOU AROUND.
WHAT'S THERE TO **SEE?**
LOCKERS? HOME-ROOM?
I'VE NEVER BEEN IN A **PUBLIC** SCHOOL BEFORE.
WHAT'S THAT SMELL? IS IT WHAT THEY CALL **"CRACK"?**
IT'S **COACH KLEATS.**
FORGIVE THE **GAWKERS.** IT'S JUST, WE'VE NEVER HAD A FORMER REALITY-TV STAR HERE BEFORE. NICE TO MEET YOU.
Oh, WE'VE MET. I'D NEVER FORGET THAT FACE.
YOU'RE THE BOY WHO DESTROYED MY **HOUSE.**
HAAH.
DON'T WORRY. I THOUGHT IT WAS A **RIOT.** IT WAS **WORTH** IT JUST TO SEE THE EXPRESSION ON DADDY'S FACE WHEN HE **LOST HIS MIND.**
STOP LOOKING SO **NERVOUS.** I WOULD **NEVER** TELL HIM IT WAS **YOU--**
--UNLESS YOU GIVE ME A **REASON** TO.
HAAH.
COME ALONG, ANDY.

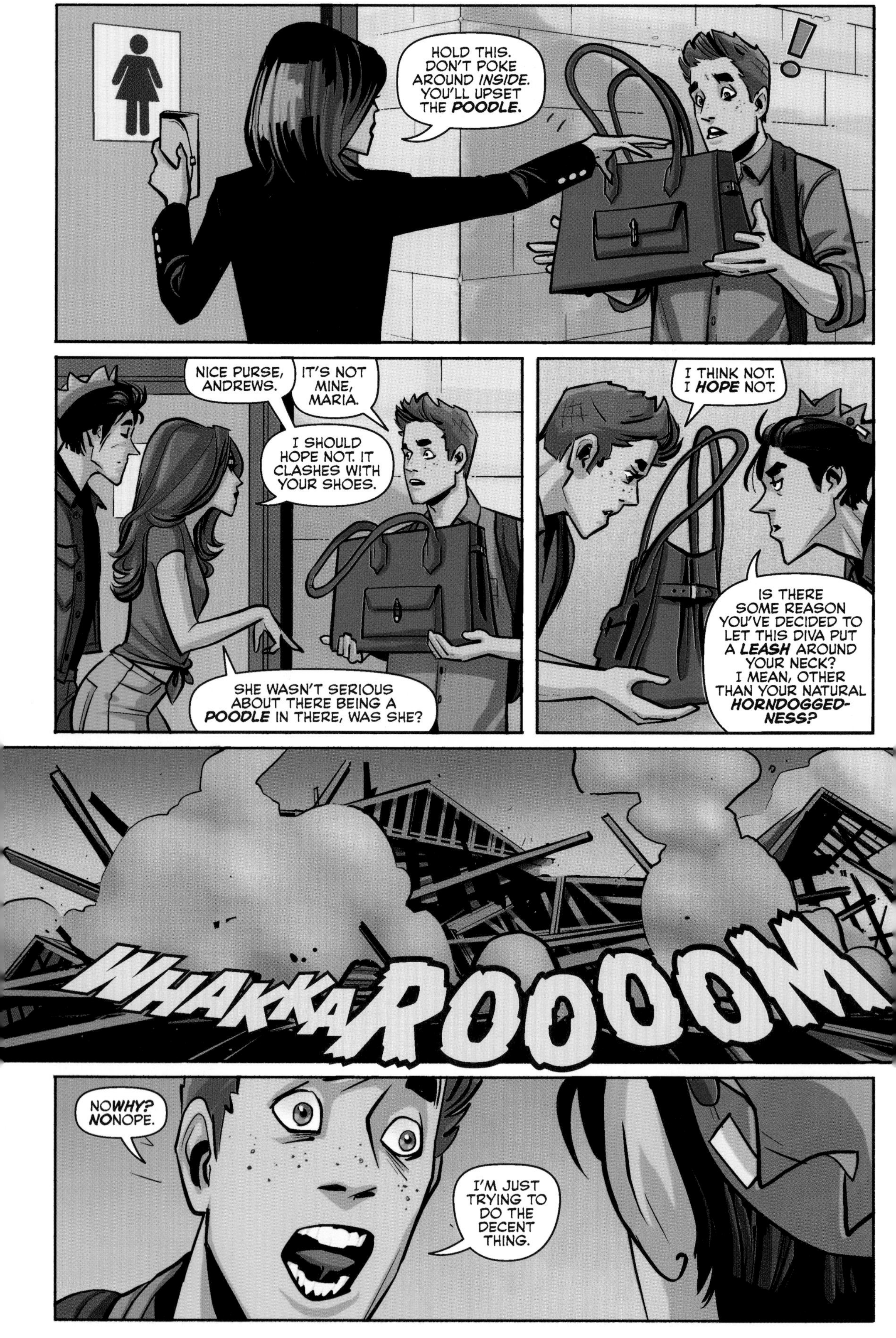
HOLD THIS. DON'T POKE AROUND *INSIDE*. YOU'LL UPSET THE ***POODLE***.
!
NICE PURSE, ANDREWS.
IT'S NOT MINE, MARIA.
I SHOULD HOPE NOT. IT CLASHES WITH YOUR SHOES.
SHE WASN'T SERIOUS ABOUT THERE BEING A ***POODLE*** IN THERE, WAS SHE?
I THINK NOT. I ***HOPE*** NOT.
IS THERE SOME REASON YOU'VE DECIDED TO LET THIS DIVA PUT A ***LEASH*** AROUND YOUR NECK? I MEAN, OTHER THAN YOUR NATURAL ***HORNDOGGED-NESS?***
WHAKKAROOOOOM
NO***WHY? NO***NOPE.
I'M JUST TRYING TO DO THE DECENT THING.

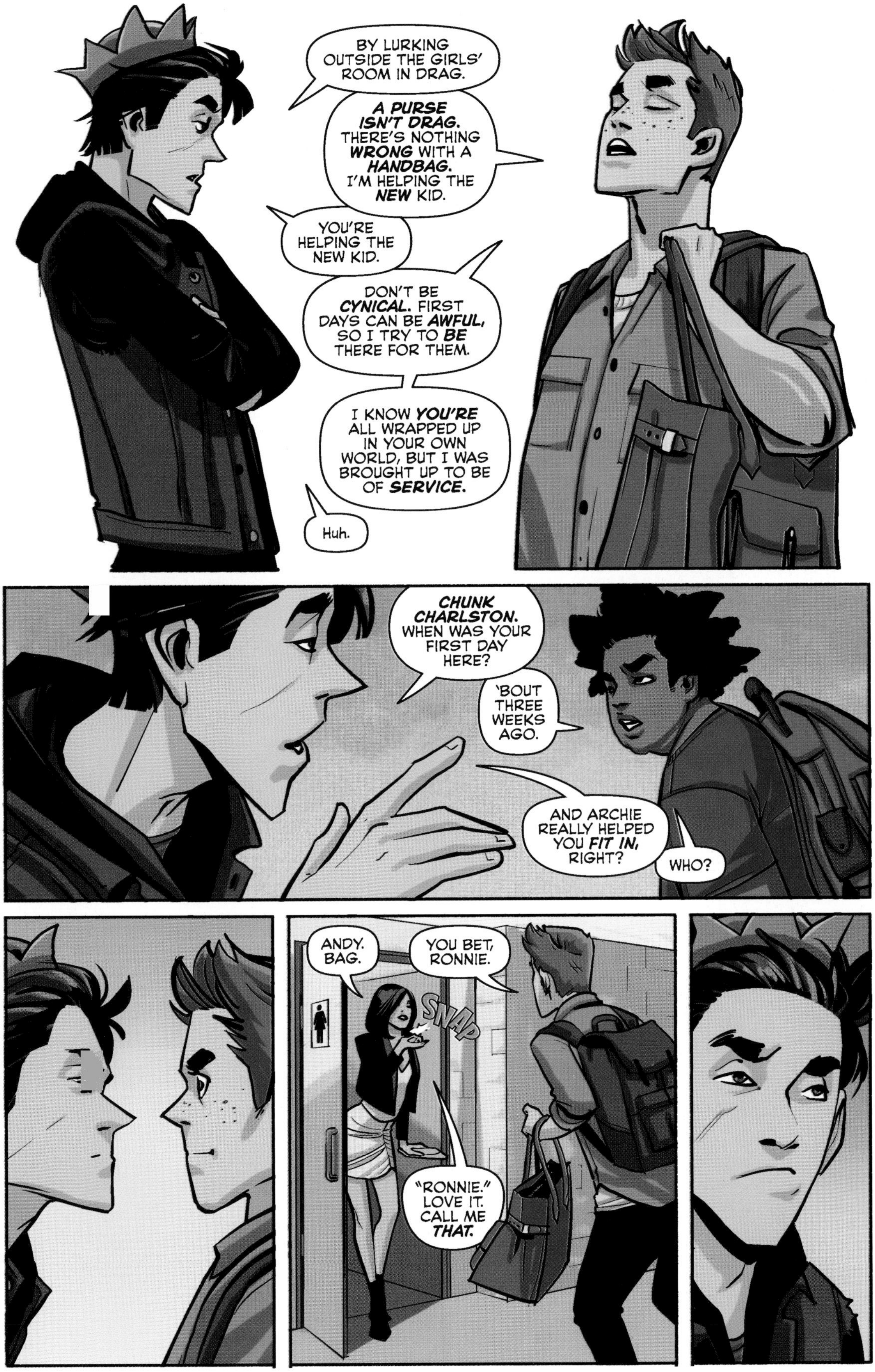
BY LURKING OUTSIDE THE GIRLS' ROOM IN DRAG.
A PURSE ISN'T DRAG. THERE'S NOTHING WRONG WITH A HANDBAG. I'M HELPING THE NEW KID.
YOU'RE HELPING THE NEW KID.
DON'T BE CYNICAL. FIRST DAYS CAN BE AWFUL, SO I TRY TO BE THERE FOR THEM.
I KNOW YOU'RE ALL WRAPPED UP IN YOUR OWN WORLD, BUT I WAS BROUGHT UP TO BE OF SERVICE.
Huh.
CHUNK CHARLSTON. WHEN WAS YOUR FIRST DAY HERE?
'BOUT THREE WEEKS AGO.
AND ARCHIE REALLY HELPED YOU FIT IN, RIGHT?
WHO?
ANDY. BAG.
YOU BET, RONNIE.
SNAP
"RONNIE." LOVE IT. CALL ME THAT.

CHAPTER TWO: THEN Taylor SANG TO Katie

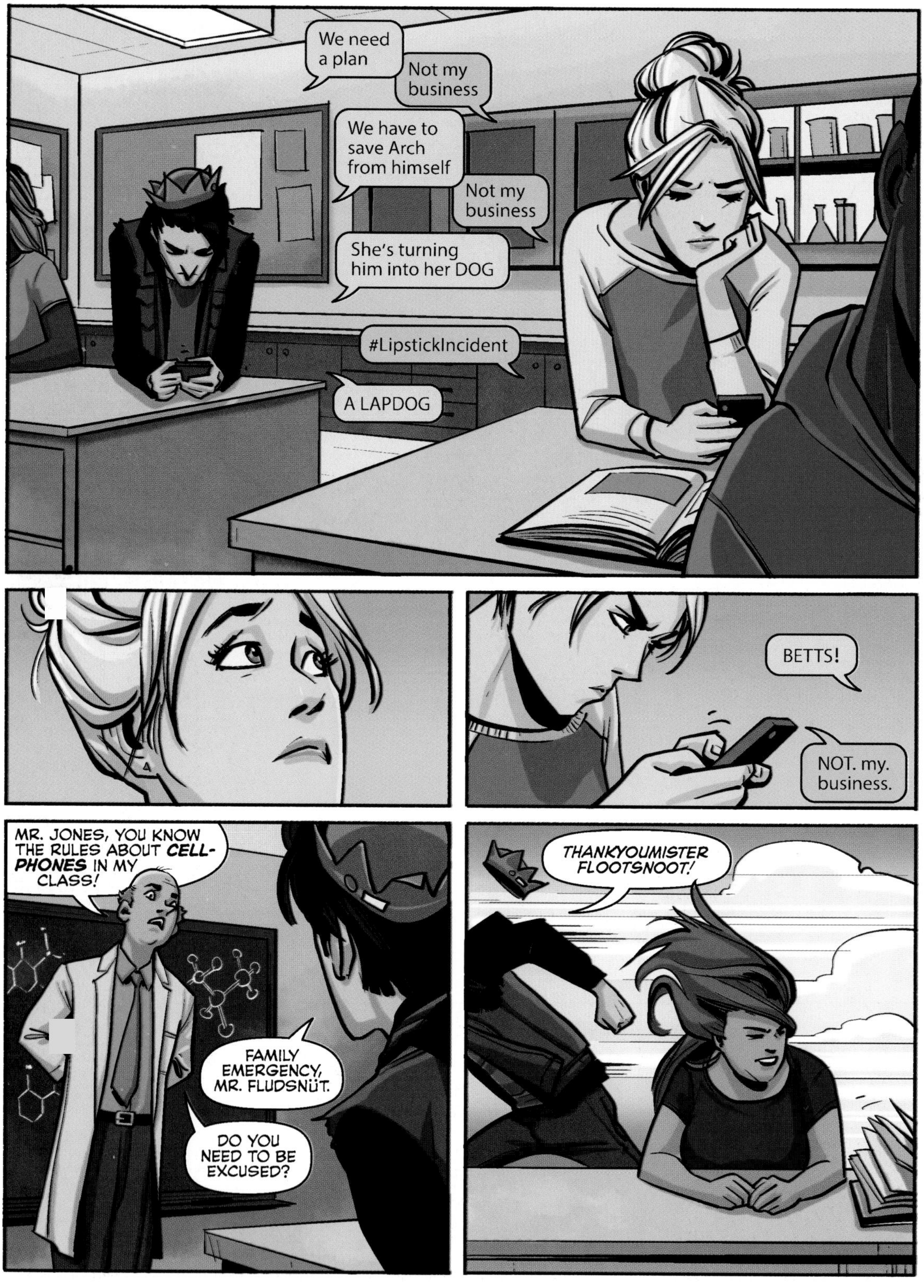
We need a plan
Not my business
We have to save Arch from himself
Not my business
She's turning him into her DOG
#LipstickIncident
A LAPDOG
BETTS!
NOT. my. business.
MR. JONES, YOU KNOW THE RULES ABOUT **CELL-PHONES** IN MY CLASS!
FAMILY EMERGENCY, MR. FLUDSNÜT.
DO YOU NEED TO BE EXCUSED?
THANKYOUMISTER FLOOTSNOOT!

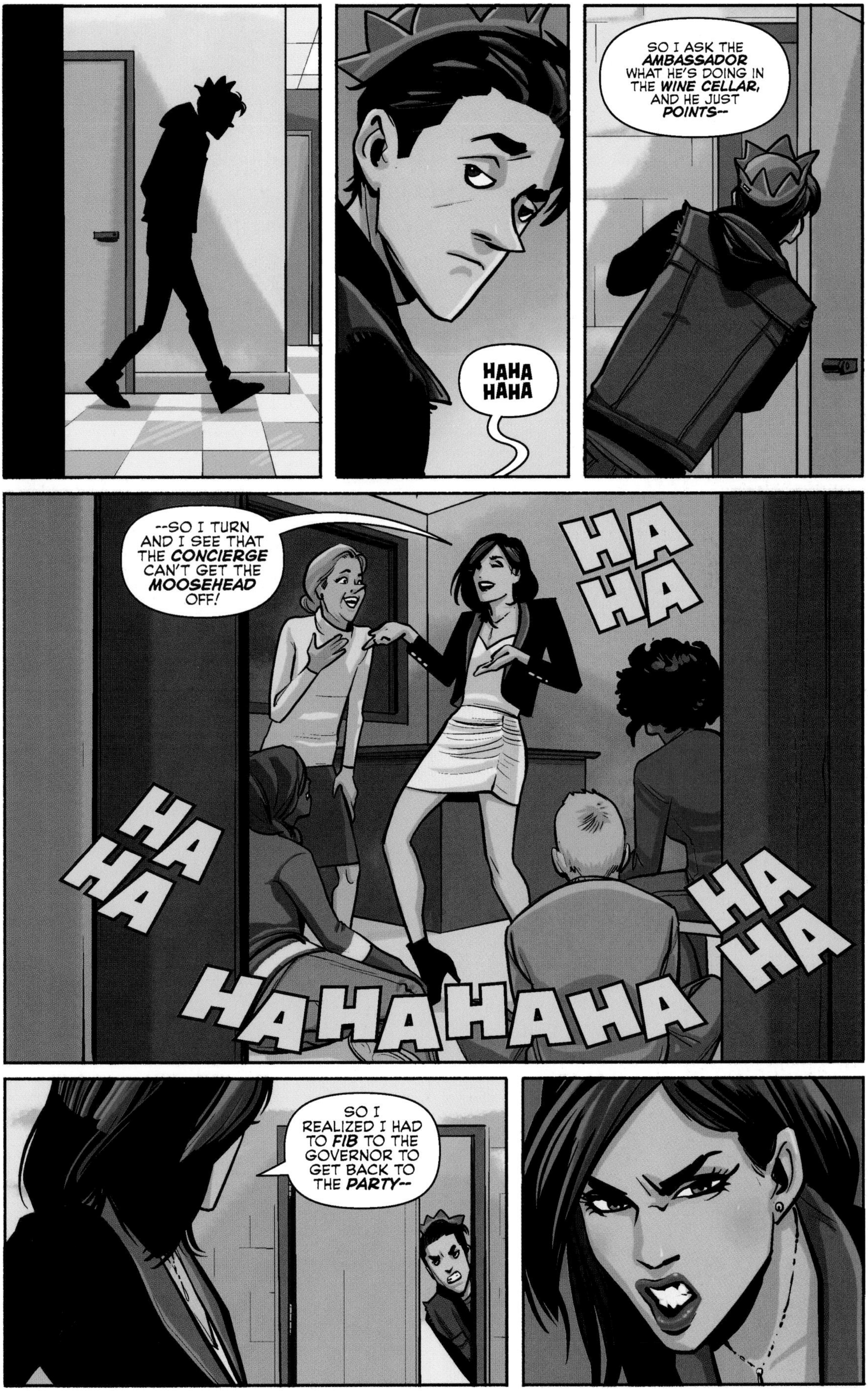
HAHA HAHA
SO I ASK THE AMBASSADOR WHAT HE'S DOING IN THE WINE CELLAR, AND HE JUST POINTS--
--SO I TURN AND I SEE THAT THE CONCIERGE CAN'T GET THE MOOSEHEAD OFF!
HA HA HA
HA HA
HA HA
HAHAHAHAHAHA
SO I REALIZED I HAD TO FIB TO THE GOVERNOR TO GET BACK TO THE PARTY--

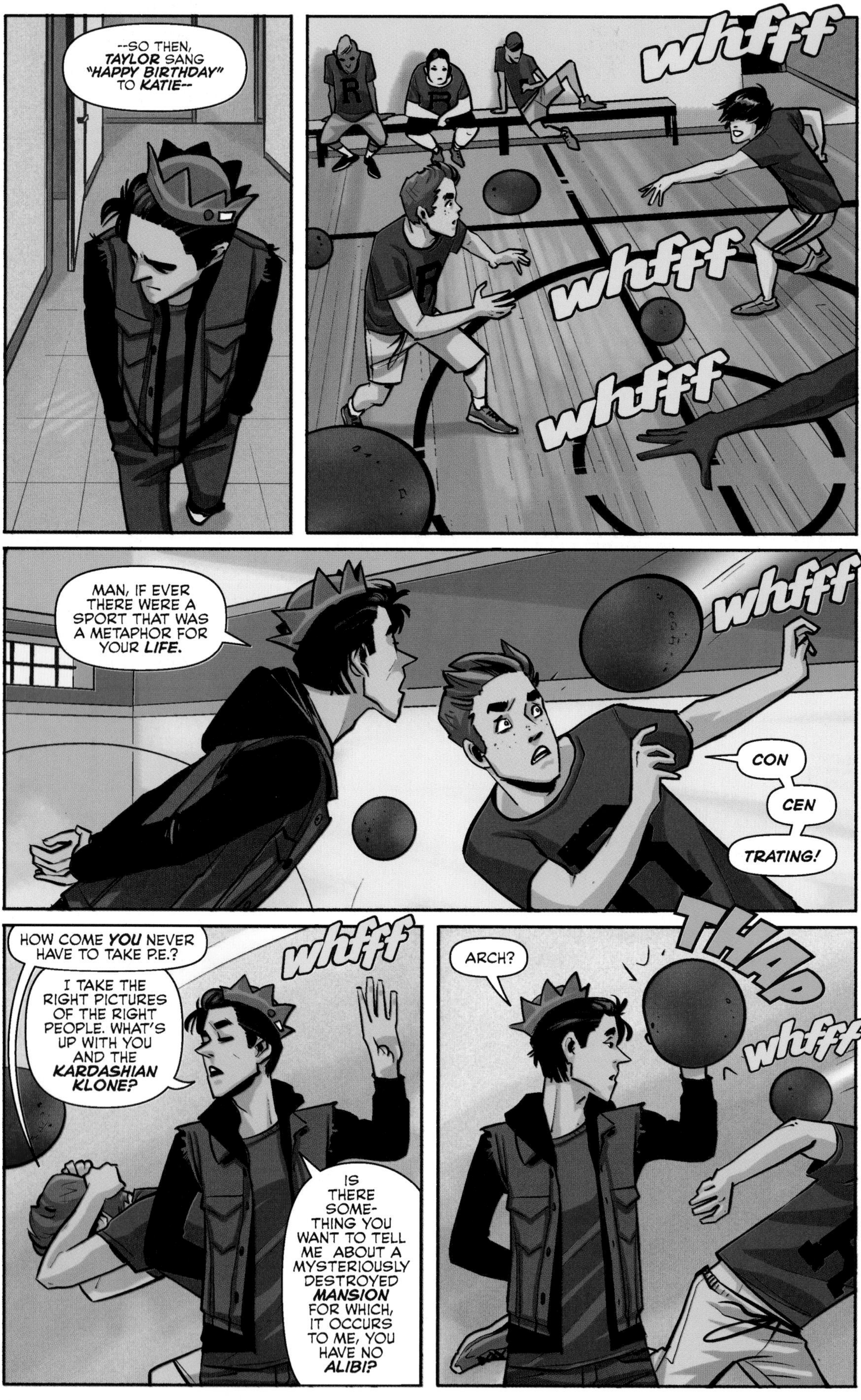
--SO THEN, TAYLOR SANG "HAPPY BIRTHDAY" TO KATIE--
whfff
whfff
whfff
MAN, IF EVER THERE WERE A SPORT THAT WAS A METAPHOR FOR YOUR LIFE.
whfff
CON
CEN
TRATING!
HOW COME YOU NEVER HAVE TO TAKE P.E.?
whfff
I TAKE THE RIGHT PICTURES OF THE RIGHT PEOPLE. WHAT'S UP WITH YOU AND THE KARDASHIAN KLONE?
IS THERE SOME-THING YOU WANT TO TELL ME ABOUT A MYSTERIOUSLY DESTROYED MANSION FOR WHICH, IT OCCURS TO ME, YOU HAVE NO ALIBI?
ARCH?
THAP
whfff

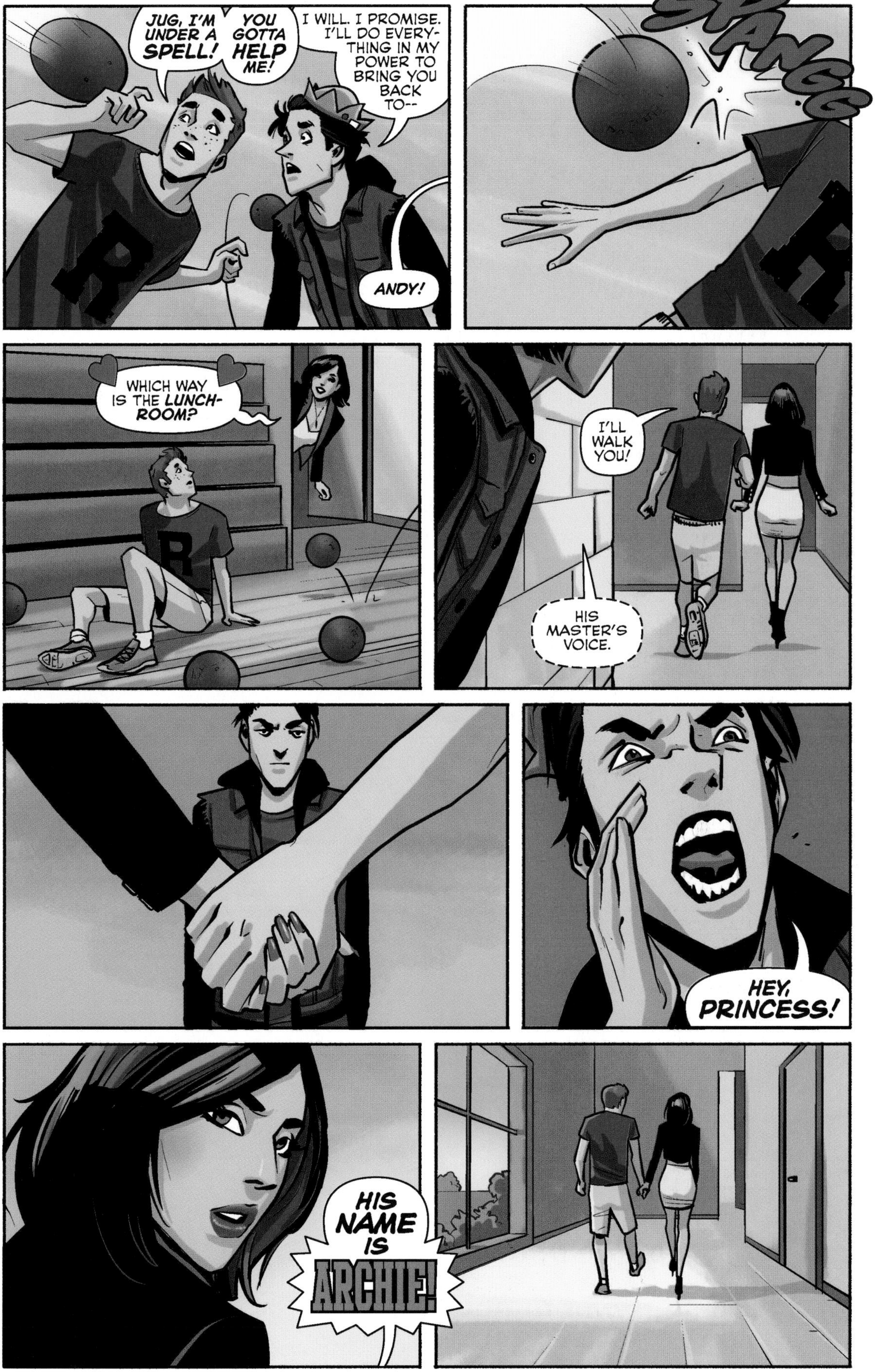
JUG, I'M UNDER A SPELL!
YOU GOTTA HELP ME!
I WILL. I PROMISE. I'LL DO EVERY-THING IN MY POWER TO BRING YOU BACK TO--
ANDY!
SPANGG
WHICH WAY IS THE LUNCH-ROOM?
I'LL WALK YOU!
HIS MASTER'S VOICE.
HEY, PRINCESS!
HIS NAME IS ARCHIE!

CHAPTER THREE: WHO'S YOUR Chef?

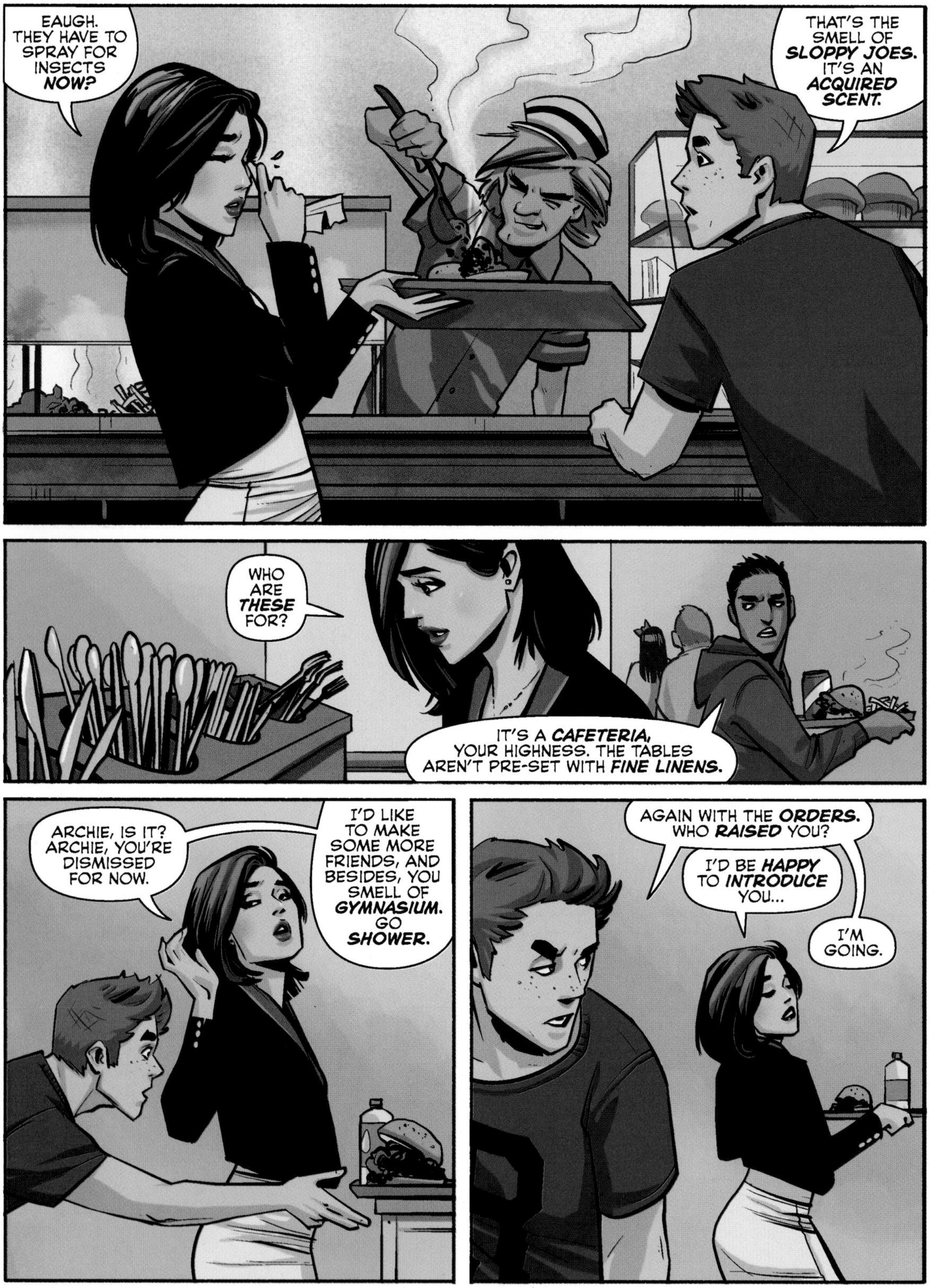
EAUGH. THEY HAVE TO SPRAY FOR INSECTS NOW?
THAT'S THE SMELL OF SLOPPY JOES. IT'S AN ACQUIRED SCENT.
WHO ARE THESE FOR?
IT'S A CAFETERIA, YOUR HIGHNESS. THE TABLES AREN'T PRE-SET WITH FINE LINENS.
ARCHIE, IS IT? ARCHIE, YOU'RE DISMISSED FOR NOW.
I'D LIKE TO MAKE SOME MORE FRIENDS, AND BESIDES, YOU SMELL OF GYMNASIUM. GO SHOWER.
AGAIN WITH THE ORDERS. WHO RAISED YOU?
I'D BE HAPPY TO INTRODUCE YOU...
I'M GOING.

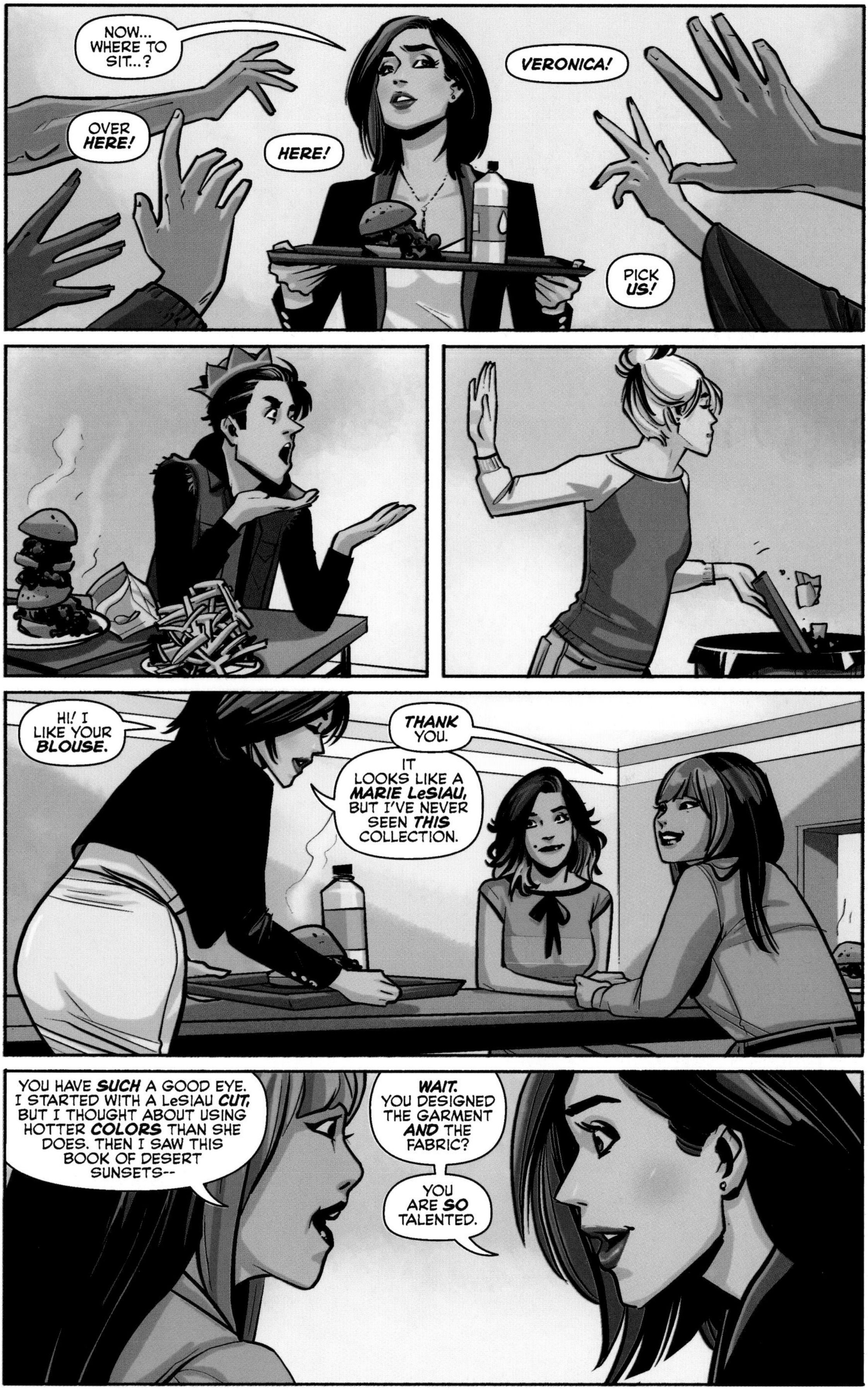
NOW... WHERE TO SIT...?
VERONICA!
OVER HERE!
HERE!
PICK US!
HI! I LIKE YOUR BLOUSE.
THANK YOU.
IT LOOKS LIKE A MARIE LeSIAU, BUT I'VE NEVER SEEN THIS COLLECTION.
YOU HAVE SUCH A GOOD EYE. I STARTED WITH A LeSIAU CUT, BUT I THOUGHT ABOUT USING HOTTER COLORS THAN SHE DOES. THEN I SAW THIS BOOK OF DESERT SUNSETS--
WAIT. YOU DESIGNED THE GARMENT AND THE FABRIC?
YOU ARE SO TALENTED.

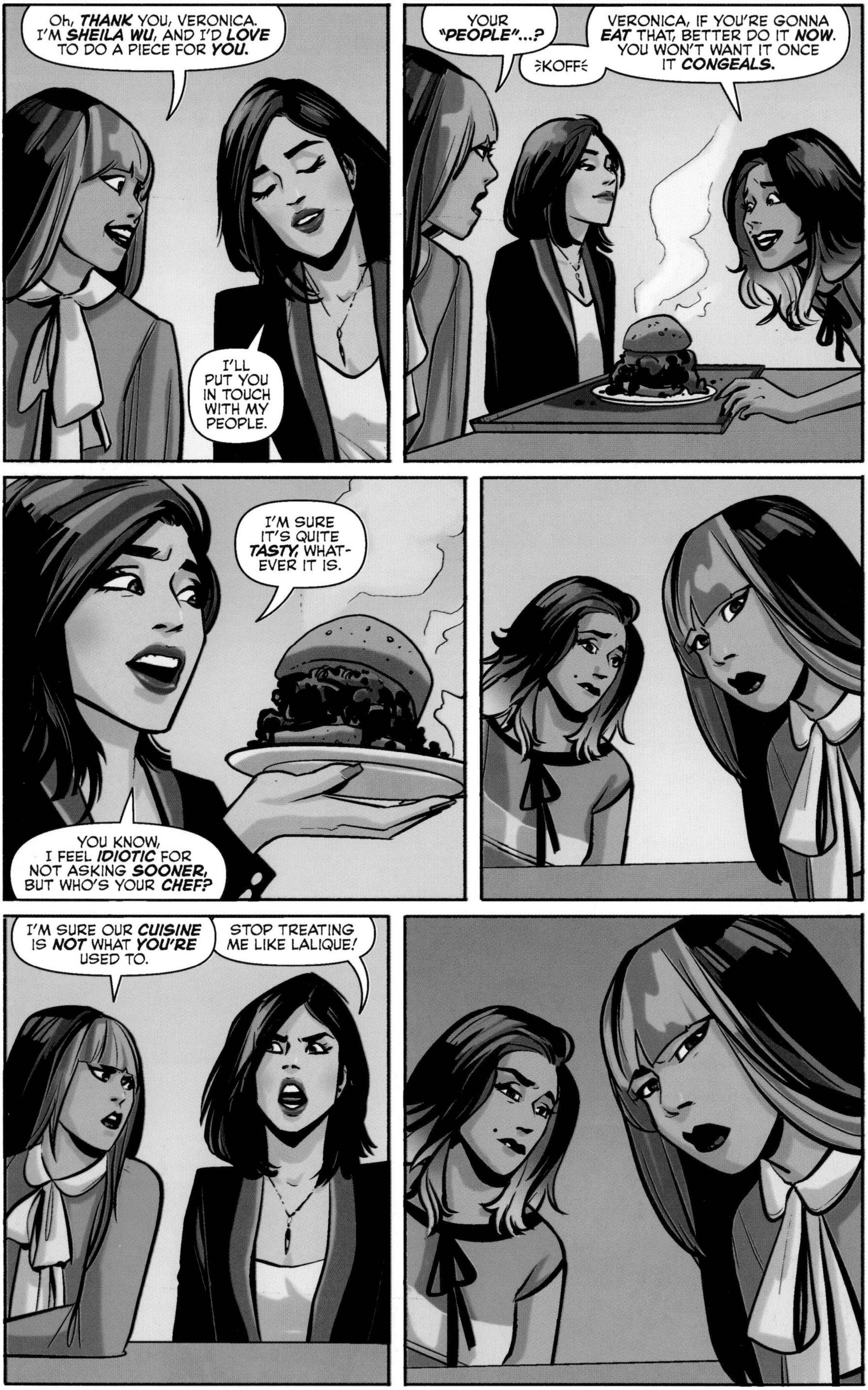
Oh, THANK YOU, VERONICA. I'M SHEILA WU, AND I'D LOVE TO DO A PIECE FOR YOU.
I'LL PUT YOU IN TOUCH WITH MY PEOPLE.
YOUR "PEOPLE"...?
KOFF
VERONICA, IF YOU'RE GONNA EAT THAT, BETTER DO IT NOW. YOU WON'T WANT IT ONCE IT CONGEALS.
I'M SURE IT'S QUITE TASTY, WHATEVER IT IS.
YOU KNOW, I FEEL IDIOTIC FOR NOT ASKING SOONER, BUT WHO'S YOUR CHEF?
I'M SURE OUR CUISINE IS NOT WHAT YOU'RE USED TO.
STOP TREATING ME LIKE LALIQUE!

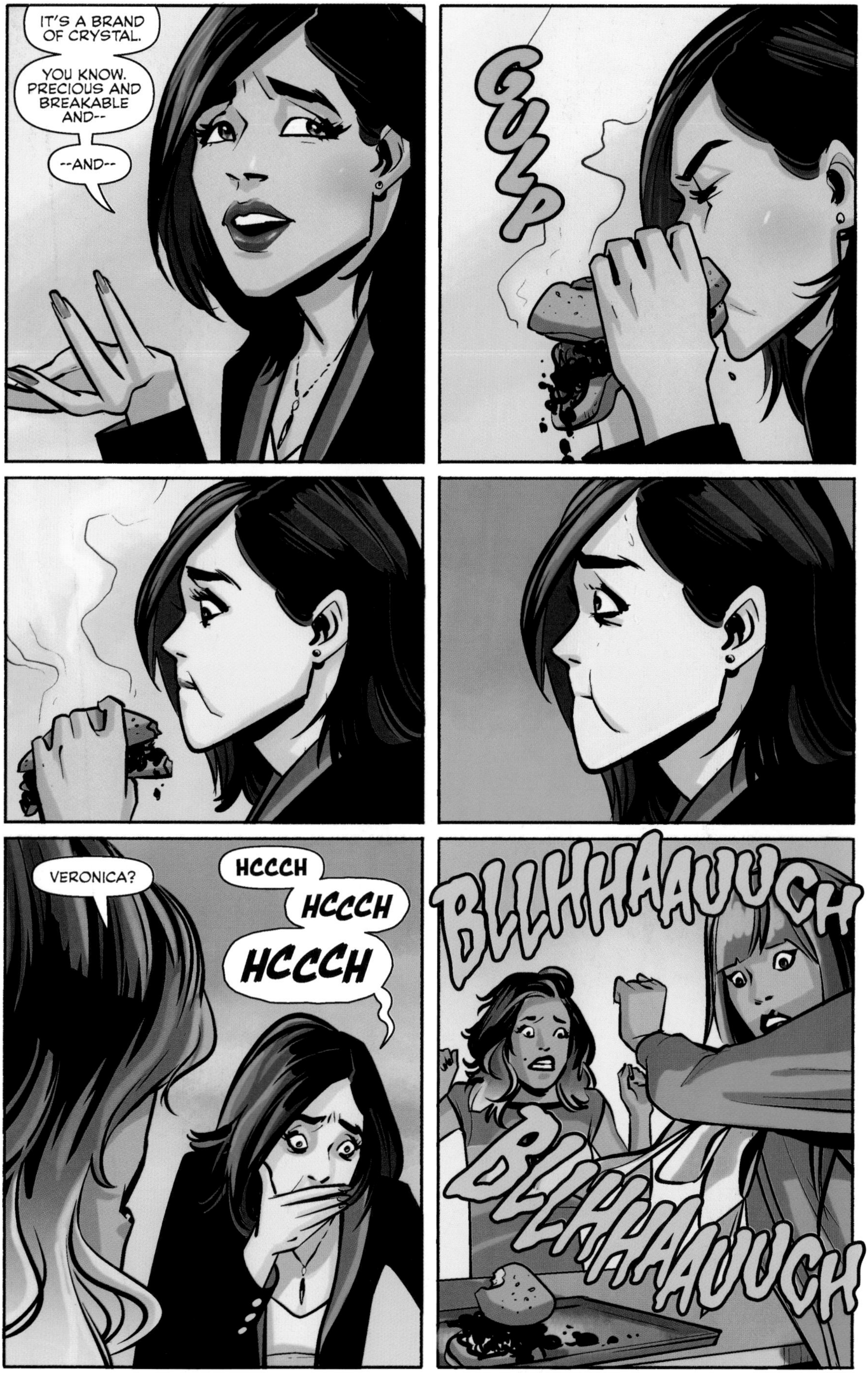
IT'S A BRAND OF CRYSTAL.
YOU KNOW. PRECIOUS AND BREAKABLE AND--
--AND--
GULP
VERONICA?
HCCCH
HCCCH
HCCCH
BLLHHAAUUCH
BLLHHAAUUCH

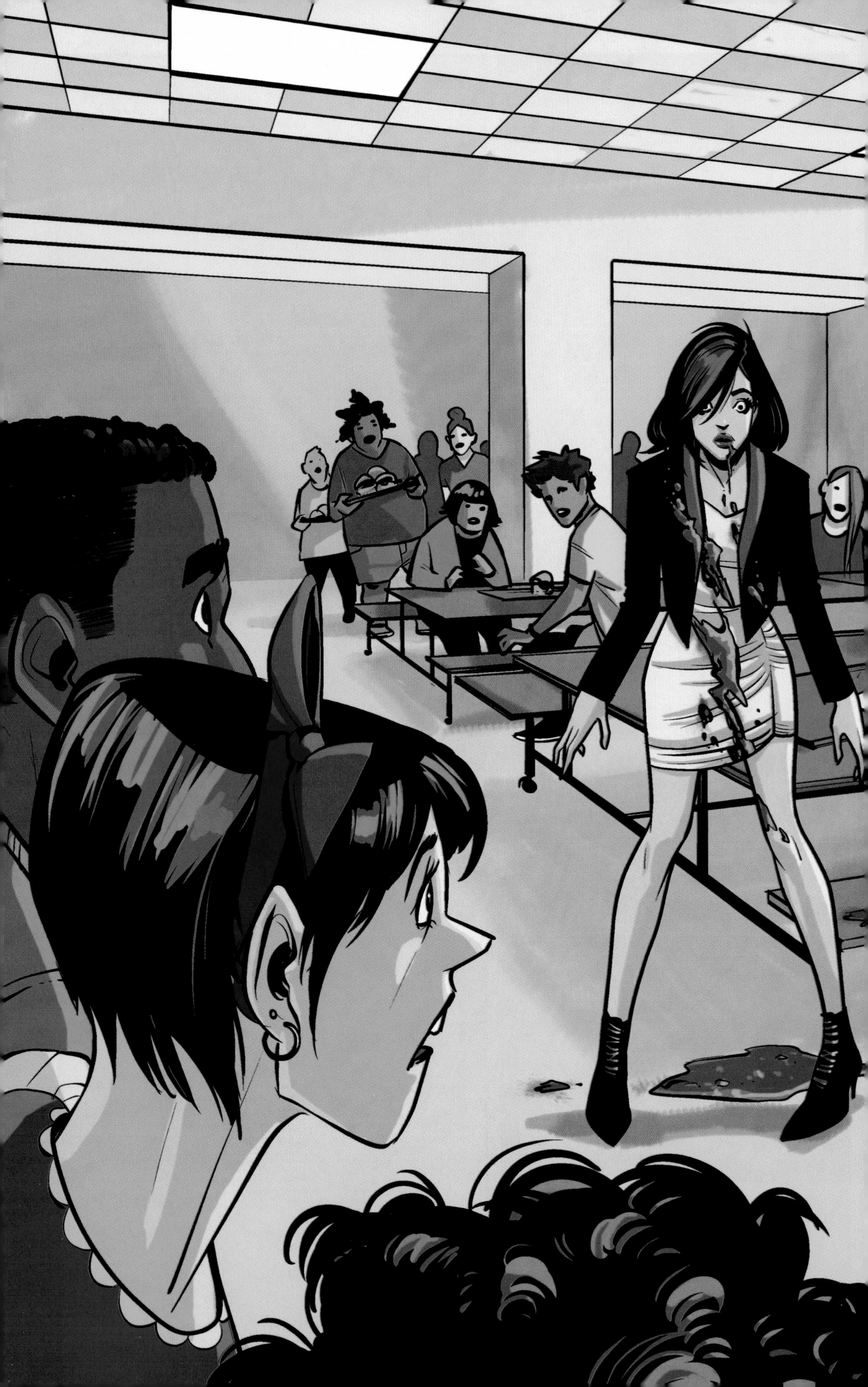

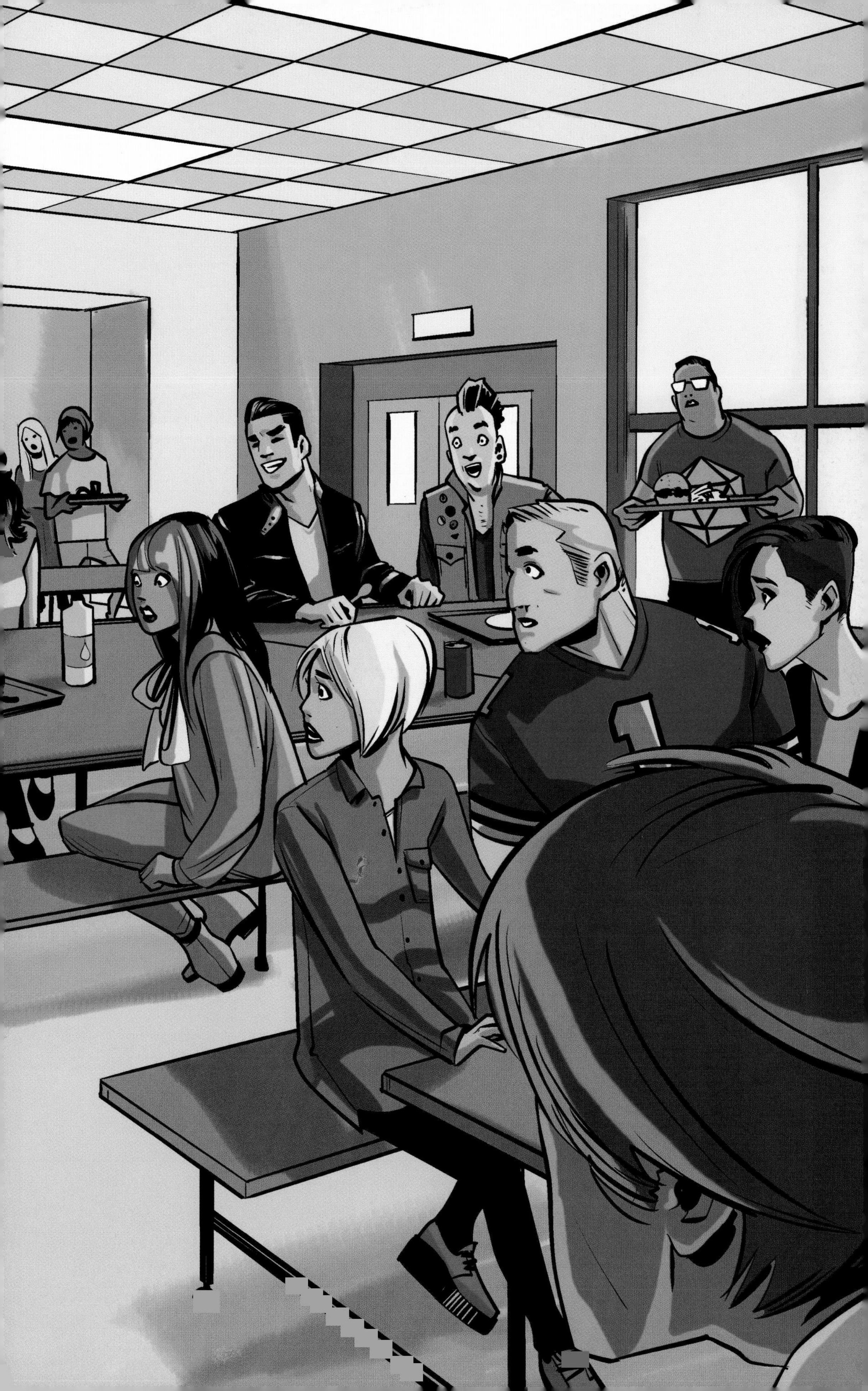

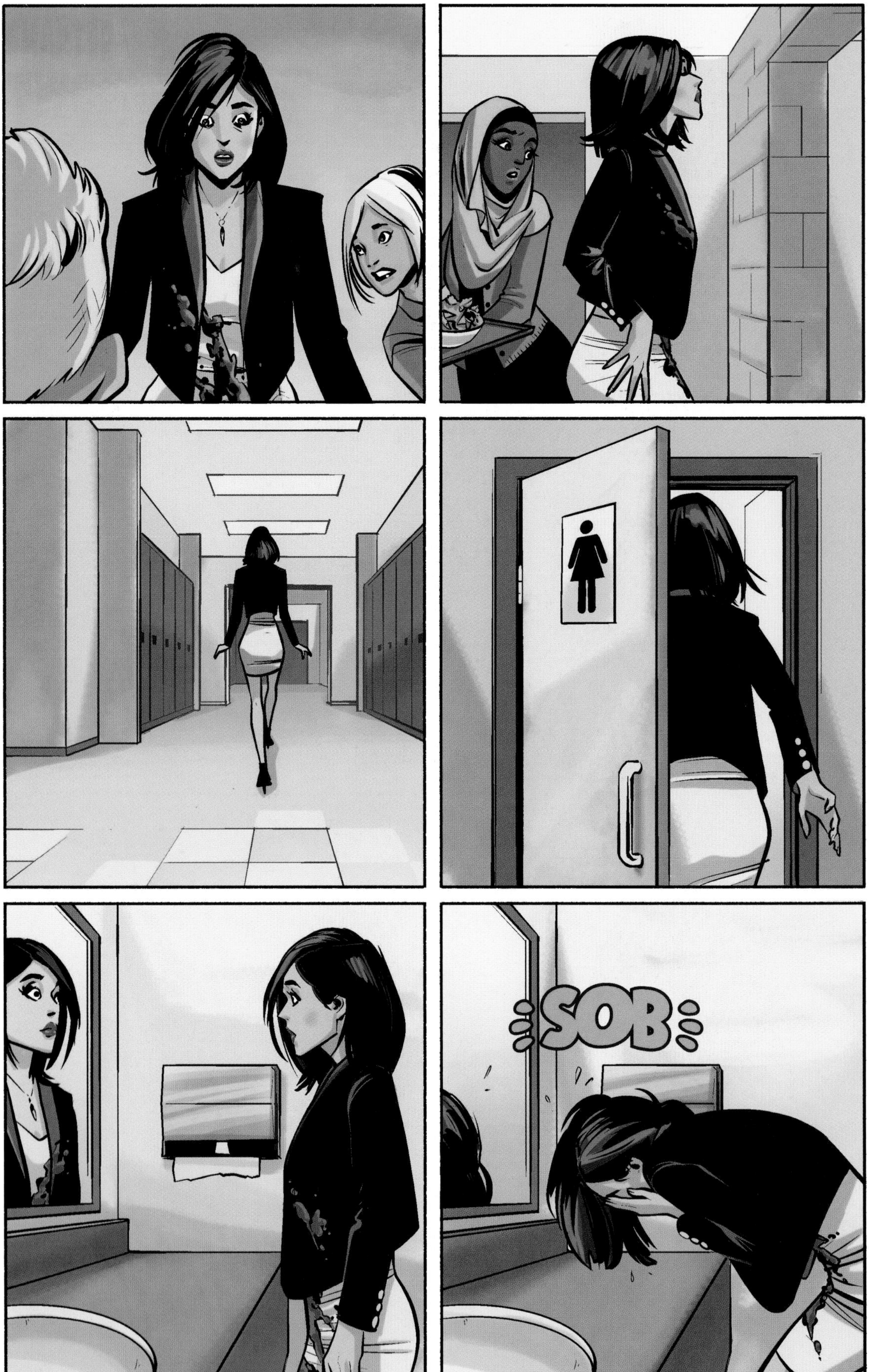
SOB

CHAPTER FOUR: PARADE FLOAT

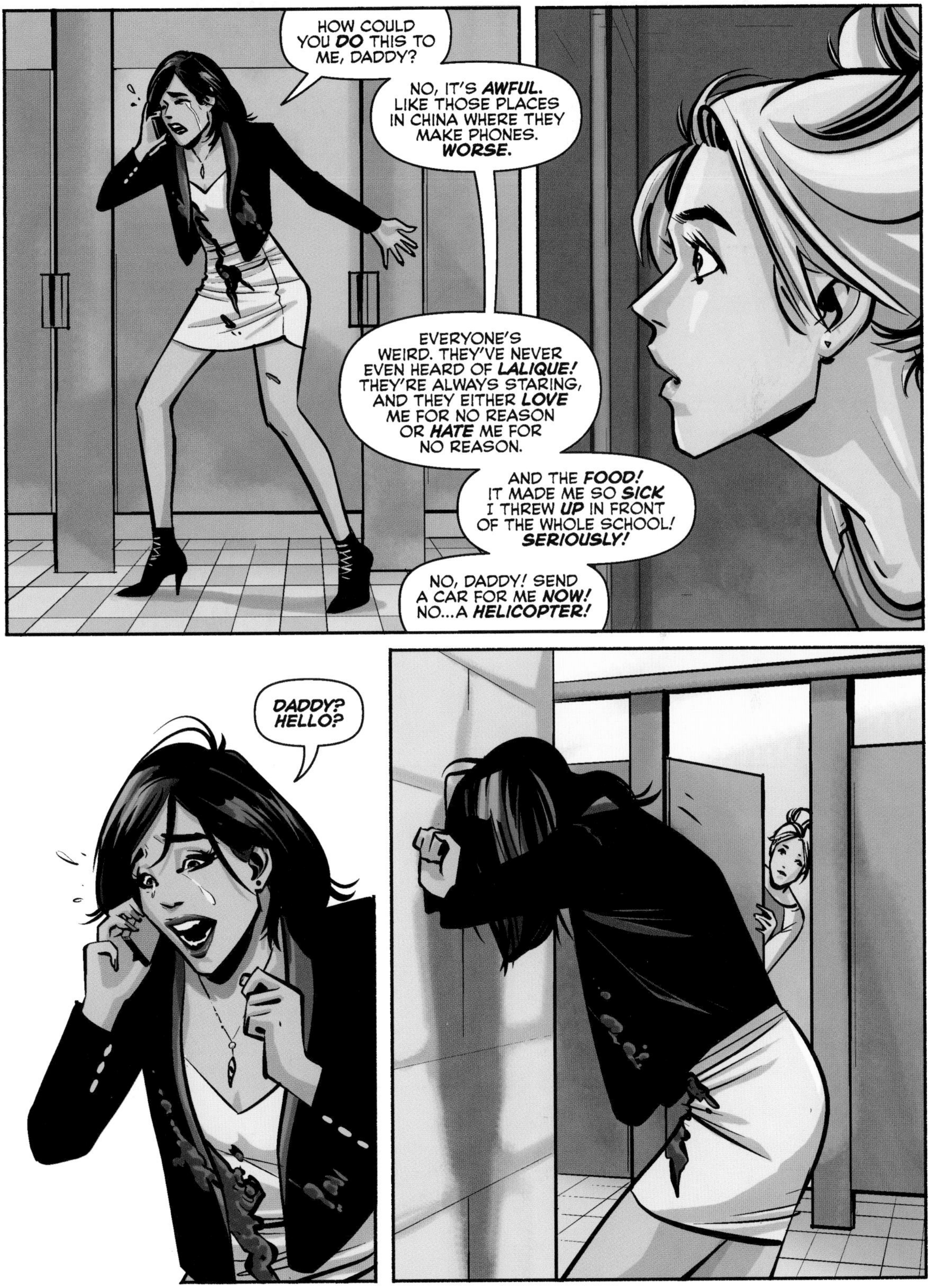
HOW COULD YOU DO THIS TO ME, DADDY?
NO, IT'S AWFUL. LIKE THOSE PLACES IN CHINA WHERE THEY MAKE PHONES. WORSE.
EVERYONE'S WEIRD. THEY'VE NEVER EVEN HEARD OF LALIQUE! THEY'RE ALWAYS STARING, AND THEY EITHER LOVE ME FOR NO REASON OR HATE ME FOR NO REASON.
AND THE FOOD! IT MADE ME SO SICK I THREW UP IN FRONT OF THE WHOLE SCHOOL! SERIOUSLY!
NO, DADDY! SEND A CAR FOR ME NOW! NO...A HELICOPTER!
DADDY? HELLO?

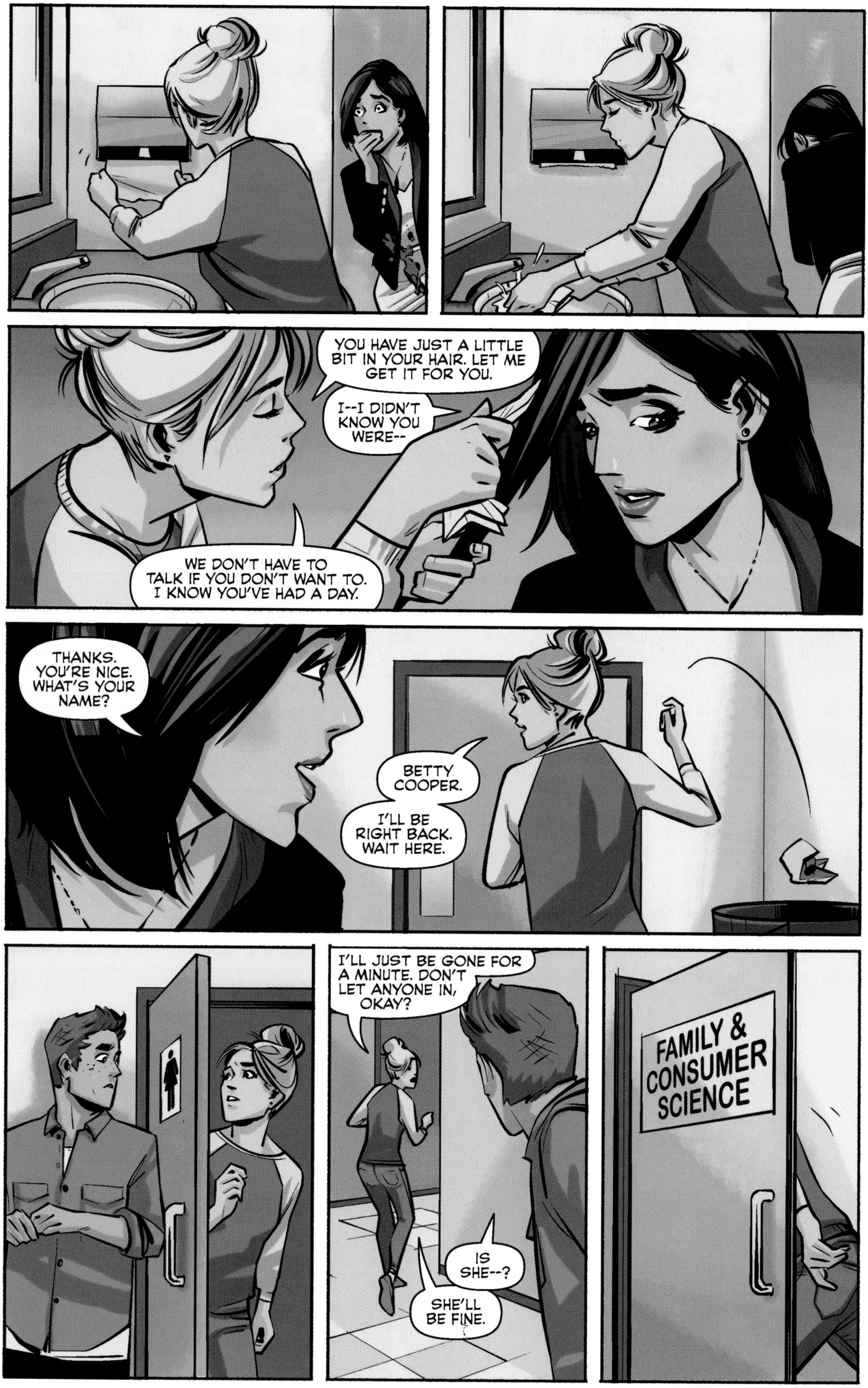
YOU HAVE JUST A LITTLE BIT IN YOUR HAIR. LET ME GET IT FOR YOU.
I--I DIDN'T KNOW YOU WERE--
WE DON'T HAVE TO TALK IF YOU DON'T WANT TO. I KNOW YOU'VE HAD A DAY.
THANKS. YOU'RE NICE. WHAT'S YOUR NAME?
BETTY COOPER.
I'LL BE RIGHT BACK. WAIT HERE.
I'LL JUST BE GONE FOR A MINUTE. DON'T LET ANYONE IN, OKAY?
IS SHE--?
SHE'LL BE FINE.
FAMILY & CONSUMER SCIENCE

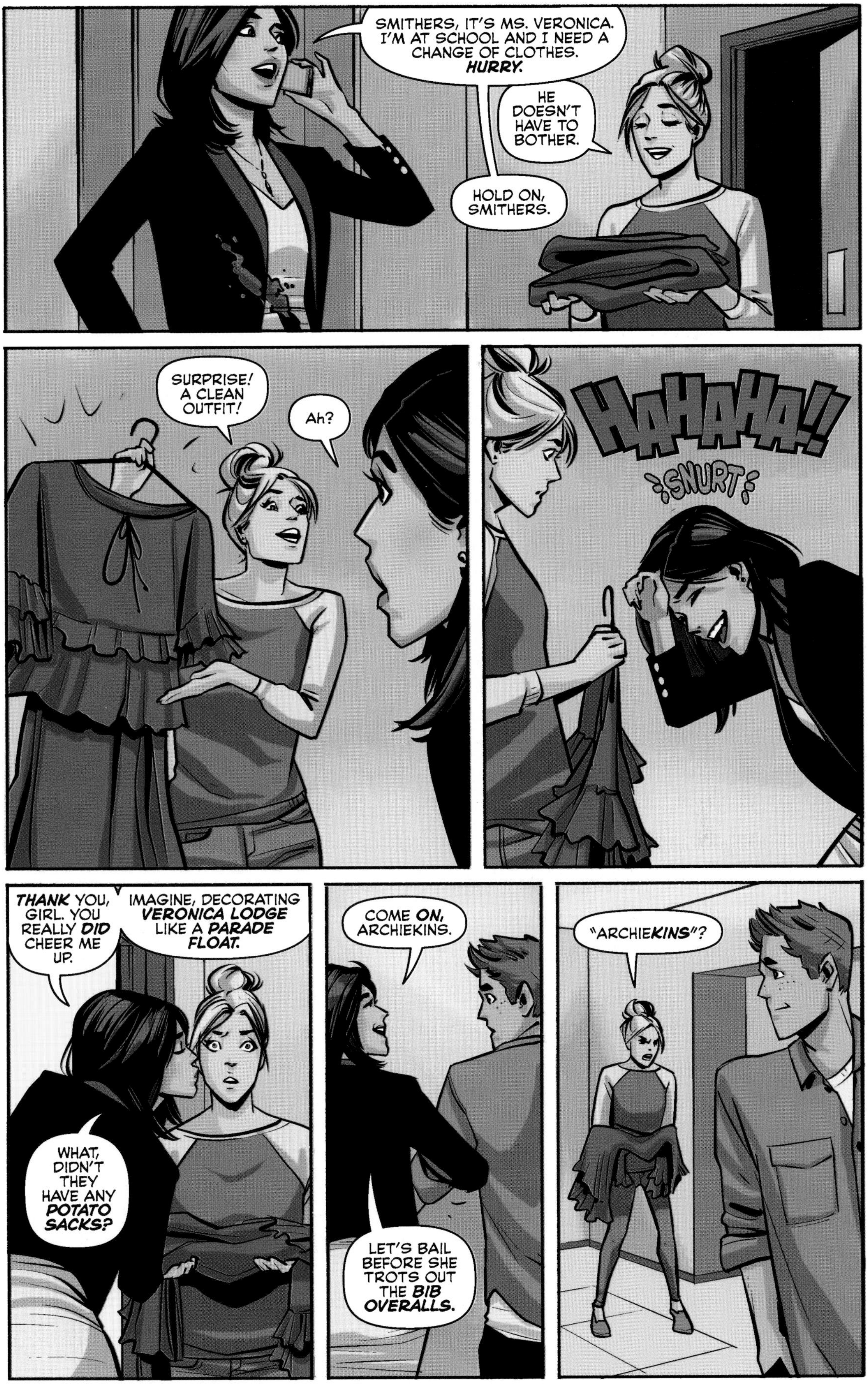
SMITHERS, IT'S MS. VERONICA. I'M AT SCHOOL AND I NEED A CHANGE OF CLOTHES. **HURRY.**
HE DOESN'T HAVE TO BOTHER.
HOLD ON, SMITHERS.
SURPRISE! A CLEAN OUTFIT!
Ah?
HAHAHA!!
SNURT
THANK YOU, GIRL. YOU REALLY **DID** CHEER ME UP.
IMAGINE, DECORATING **VERONICA LODGE** LIKE A **PARADE FLOAT.**
WHAT, DIDN'T THEY HAVE ANY **POTATO SACKS?**
COME **ON,** ARCHIEKINS.
LET'S BAIL BEFORE SHE TROTS OUT THE **BIB OVERALLS.**
"ARCHIE**KINS**"?

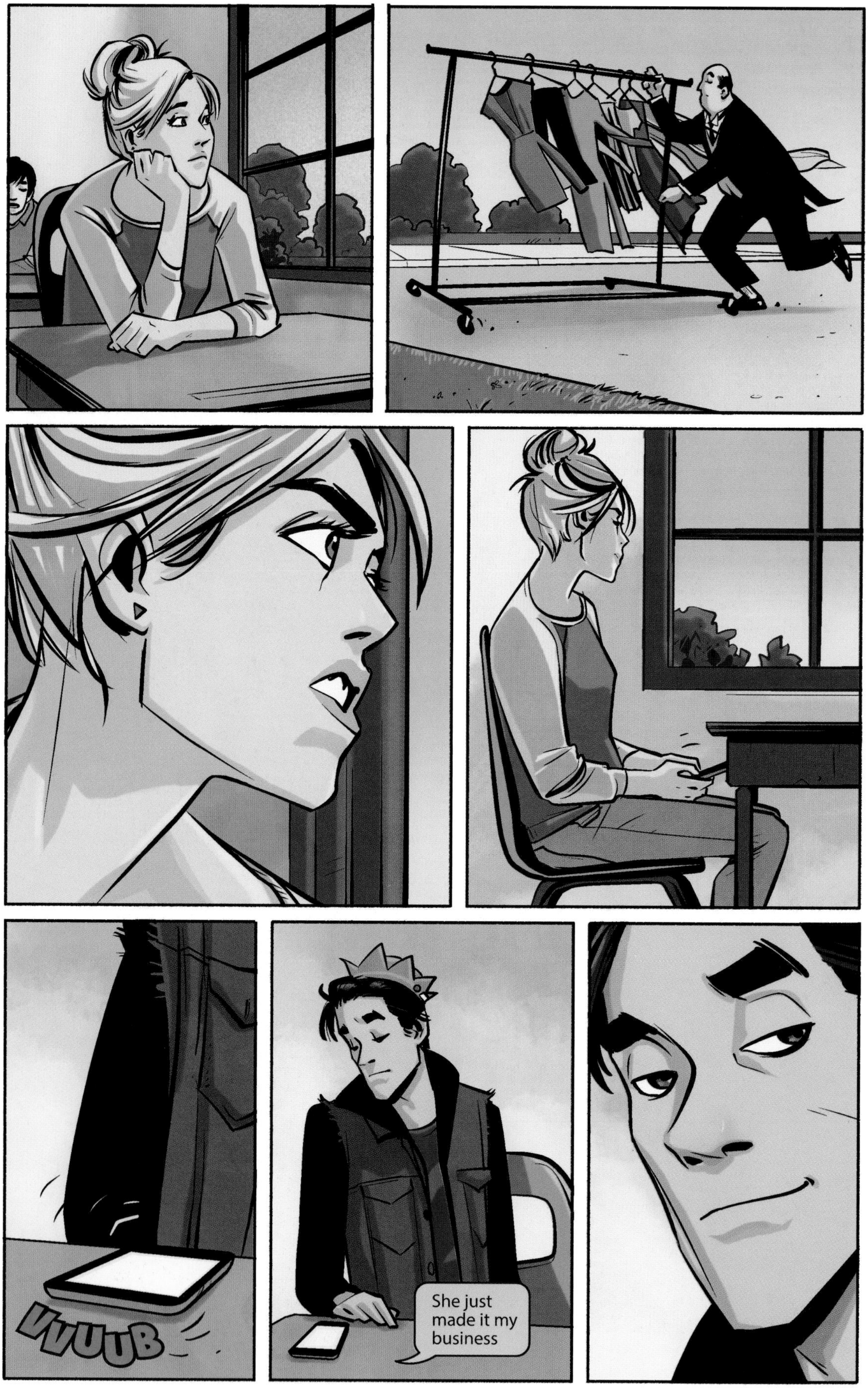
VVUUB
She just made it my business

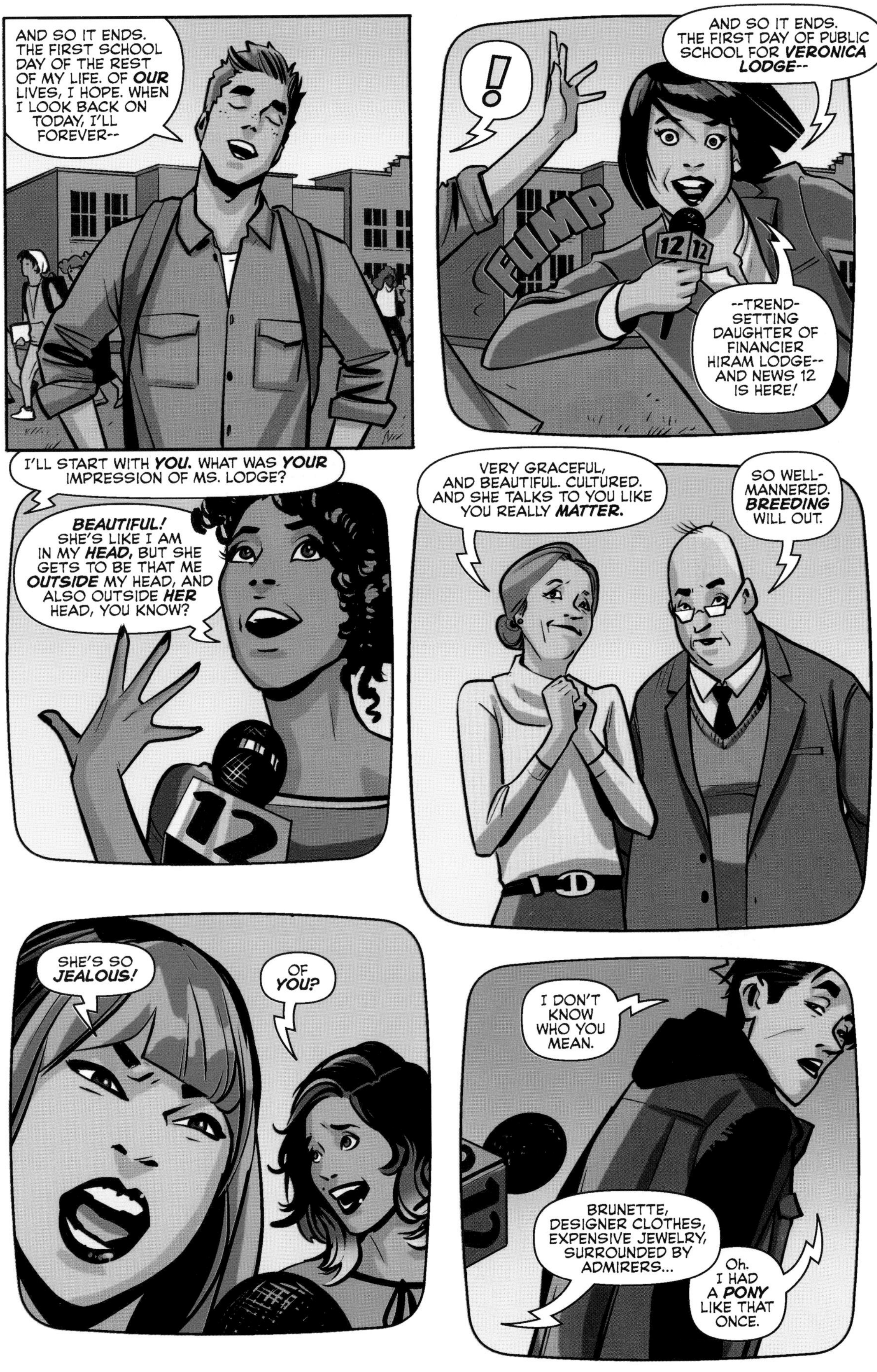
AND SO IT ENDS. THE FIRST SCHOOL DAY OF THE REST OF MY LIFE. OF OUR LIVES, I HOPE. WHEN I LOOK BACK ON TODAY, I'LL FOREVER--
!
AND SO IT ENDS. THE FIRST DAY OF PUBLIC SCHOOL FOR VERONICA LODGE--
FUMP
12 12
--TREND-SETTING DAUGHTER OF FINANCIER HIRAM LODGE--AND NEWS 12 IS HERE!
I'LL START WITH YOU. WHAT WAS YOUR IMPRESSION OF MS. LODGE?
BEAUTIFUL! SHE'S LIKE I AM IN MY HEAD, BUT SHE GETS TO BE THAT ME OUTSIDE MY HEAD, AND ALSO OUTSIDE HER HEAD, YOU KNOW?
VERY GRACEFUL, AND BEAUTIFUL. CULTURED. AND SHE TALKS TO YOU LIKE YOU REALLY MATTER.
SO WELL-MANNERED. BREEDING WILL OUT.
SHE'S SO JEALOUS!
OF YOU?
I DON'T KNOW WHO YOU MEAN.
BRUNETTE, DESIGNER CLOTHES, EXPENSIVE JEWELRY, SURROUNDED BY ADMIRERS...
Oh. I HAD A PONY LIKE THAT ONCE.

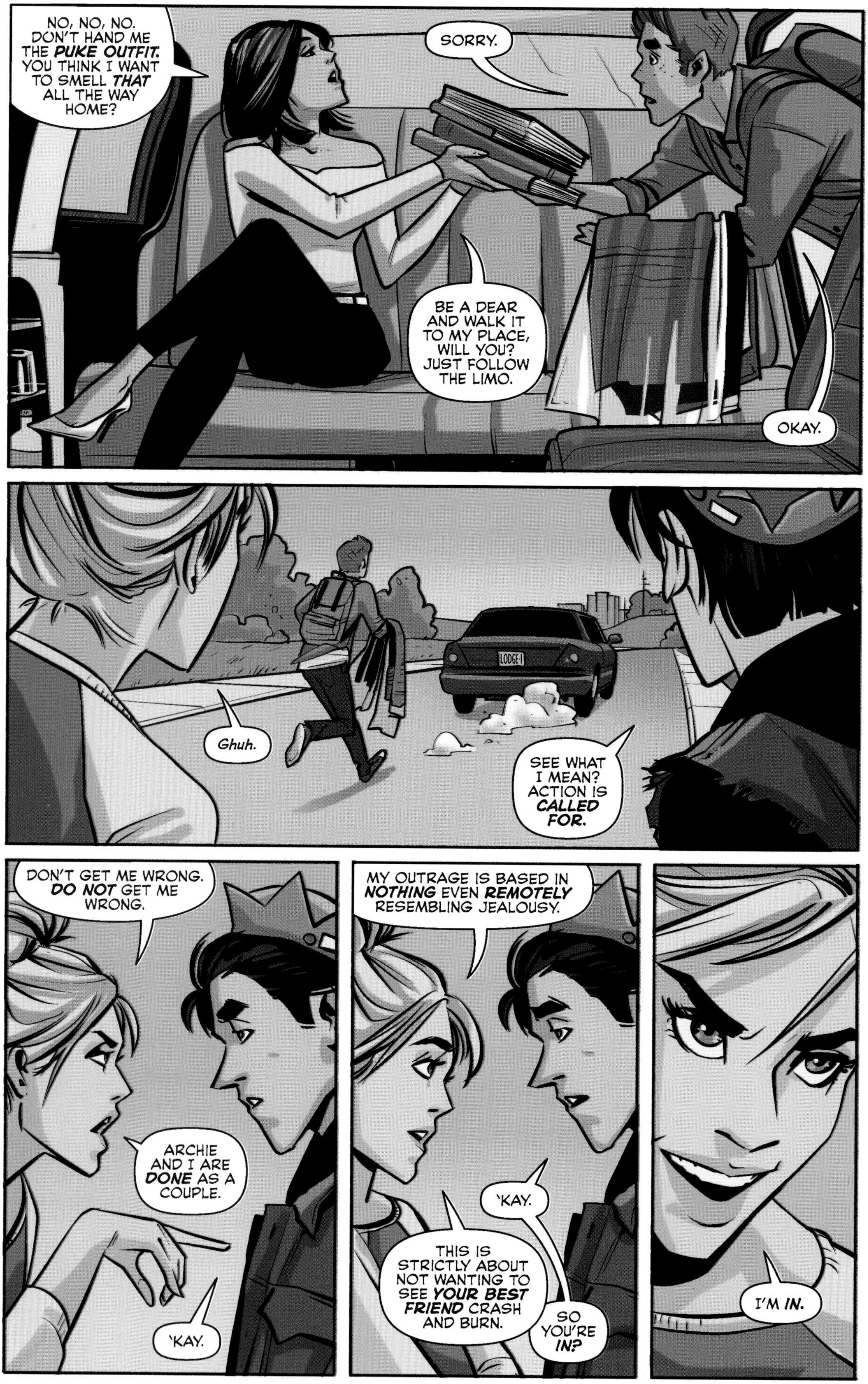

NO, NO, NO. DON'T HAND ME THE **PUKE OUTFIT.** YOU THINK I WANT TO SMELL **THAT** ALL THE WAY HOME?
SORRY.
BE A DEAR AND WALK IT TO MY PLACE, WILL YOU? JUST FOLLOW THE LIMO.
OKAY.
LODGE-1
Ghuh.
SEE WHAT I MEAN? ACTION IS **CALLED FOR.**
DON'T GET ME WRONG. **DO NOT** GET ME WRONG.
ARCHIE AND I ARE **DONE** AS A COUPLE.
'KAY.
MY OUTRAGE IS BASED IN **NOTHING** EVEN **REMOTELY** RESEMBLING JEALOUSY.
THIS IS STRICTLY ABOUT NOT WANTING TO SEE **YOUR BEST FRIEND** CRASH AND BURN.
'KAY.
SO YOU'RE **IN?**
I'M **IN.**

TO BE CONTINUED...

ISSUE FOUR

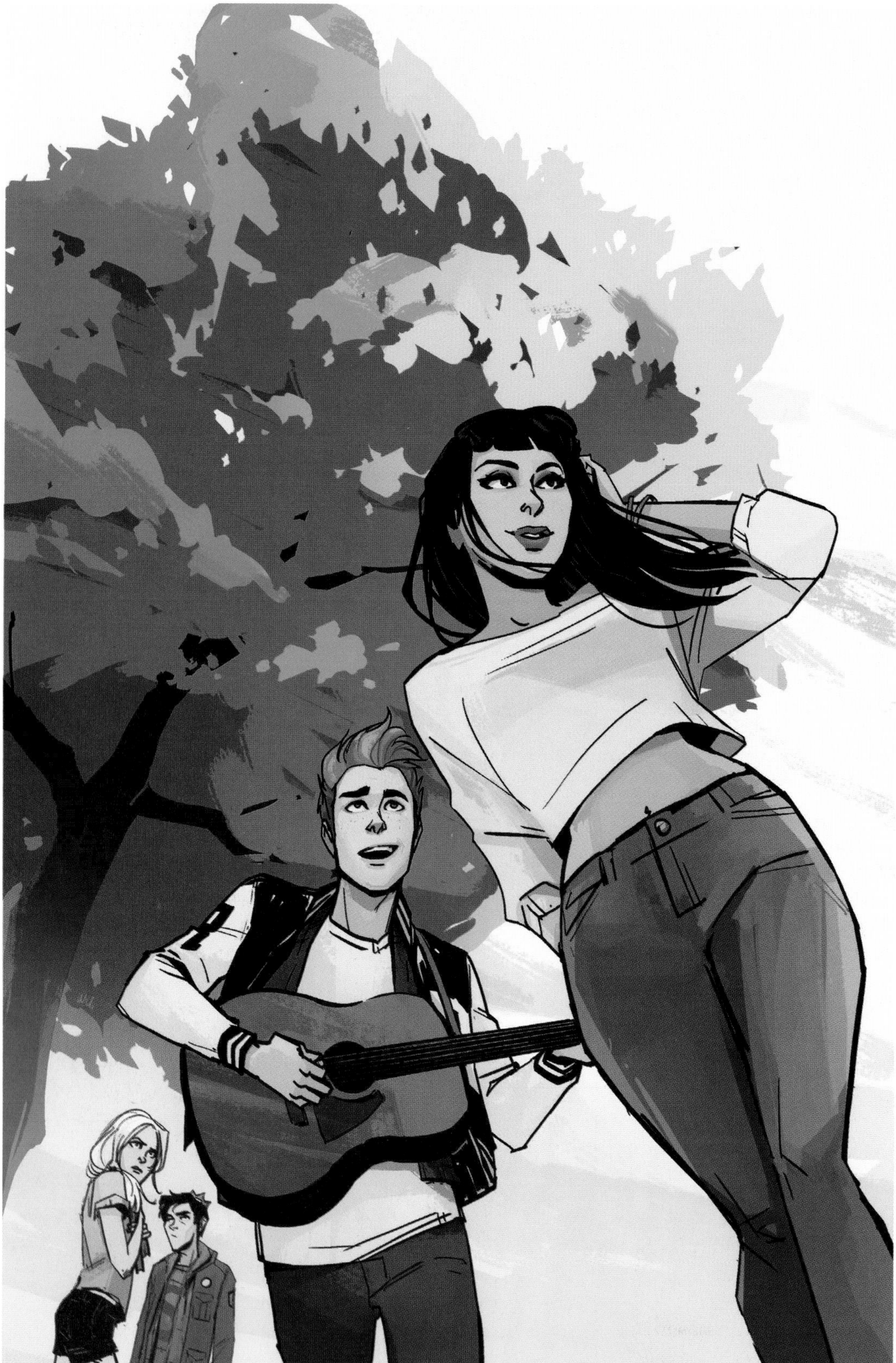

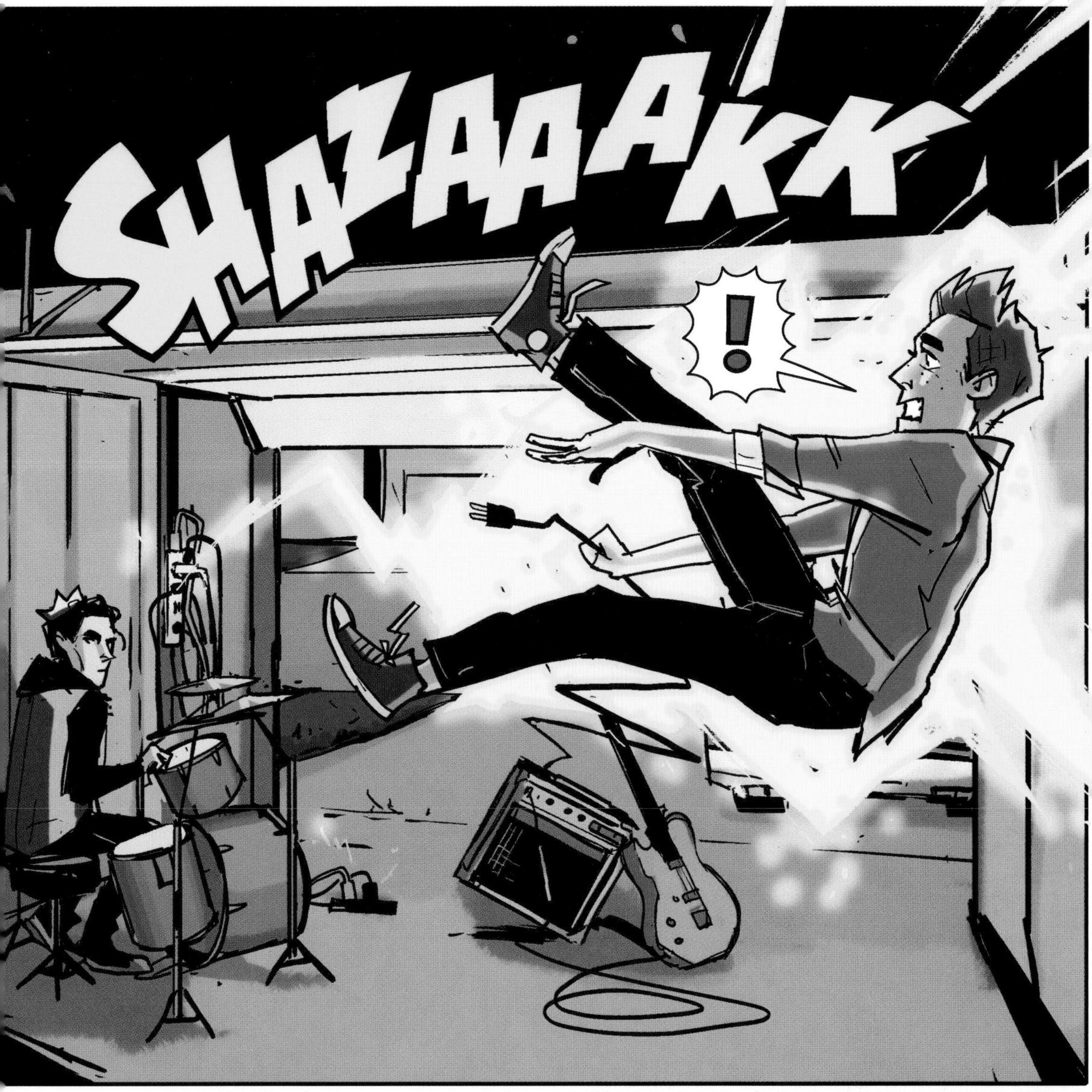
SHAZAAAKK
!

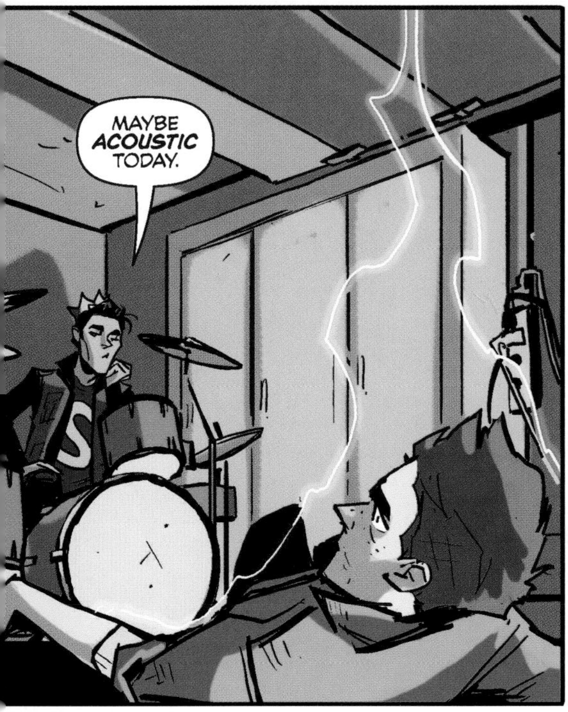
MAYBE ACOUSTIC TODAY.

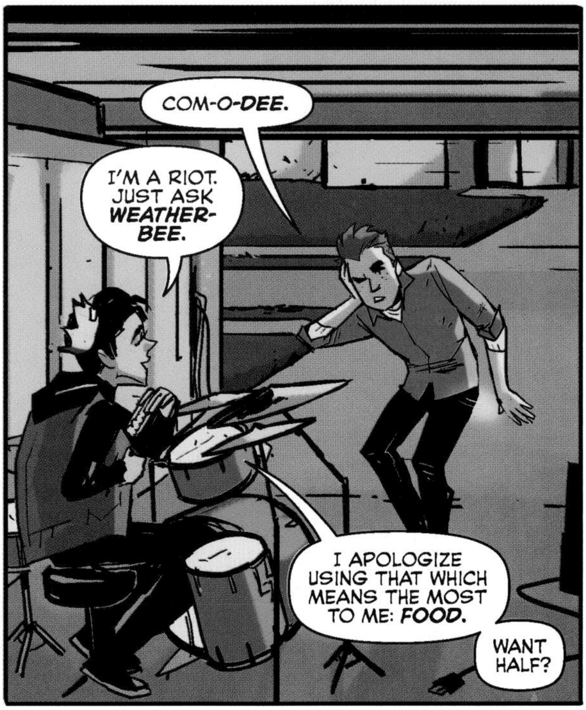
COM-O-DEE.
I'M A RIOT. JUST ASK WEATHER-BEE.
I APOLOGIZE USING THAT WHICH MEANS THE MOST TO ME: FOOD.
WANT HALF?

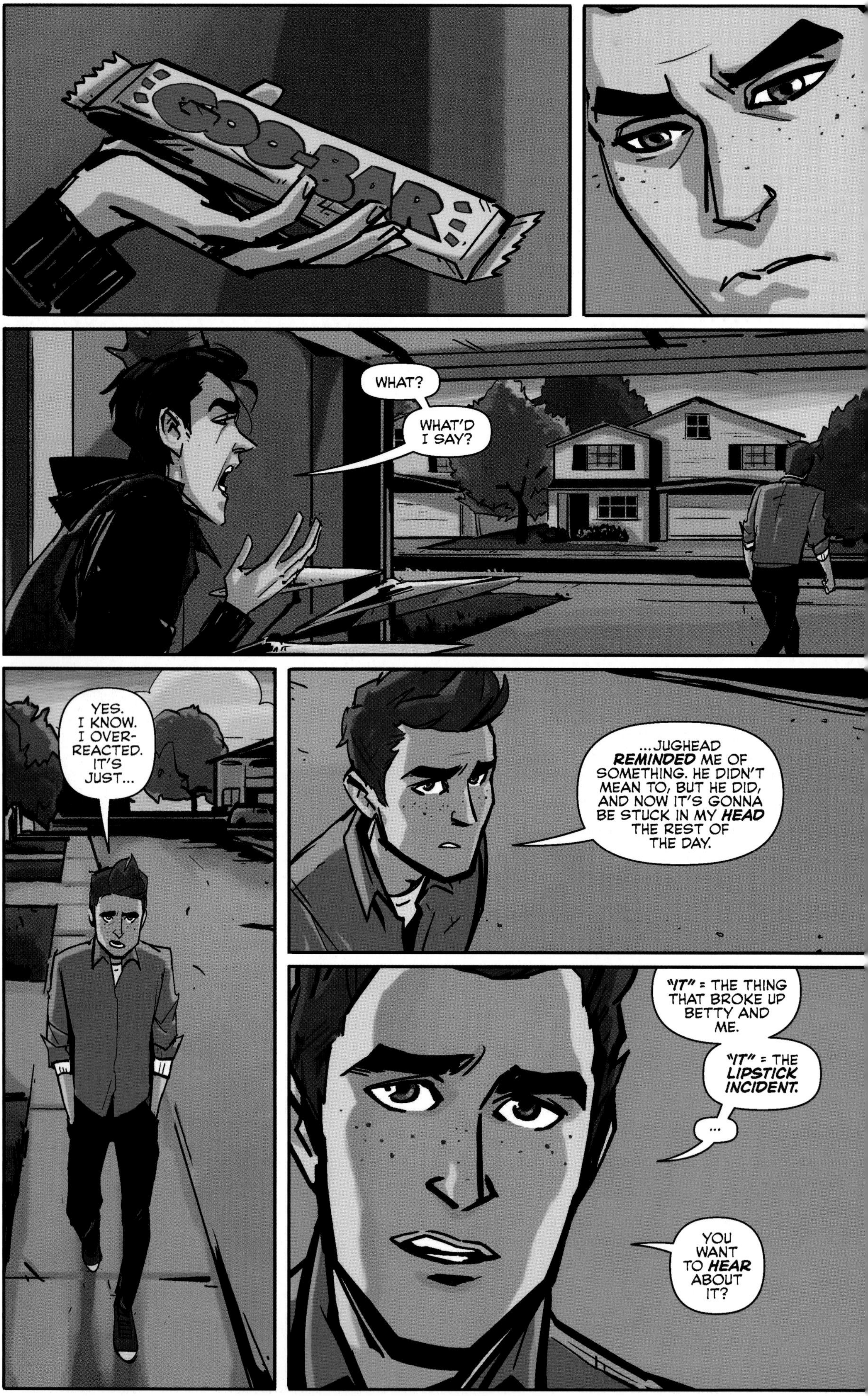
GOO-BAR
WHAT?
WHAT'D I SAY?
YES. I KNOW. I OVER-REACTED. IT'S JUST...
...JUGHEAD REMINDED ME OF SOMETHING. HE DIDN'T MEAN TO, BUT HE DID, AND NOW IT'S GONNA BE STUCK IN MY HEAD THE REST OF THE DAY.
"IT" = THE THING THAT BROKE UP BETTY AND ME.
"IT" = THE LIPSTICK INCIDENT.
...
YOU WANT TO HEAR ABOUT IT?

CHAPTER ONE: YES, OF COURSE WE WANT TO HEAR ABOUT IT. OBVIOUSLY.

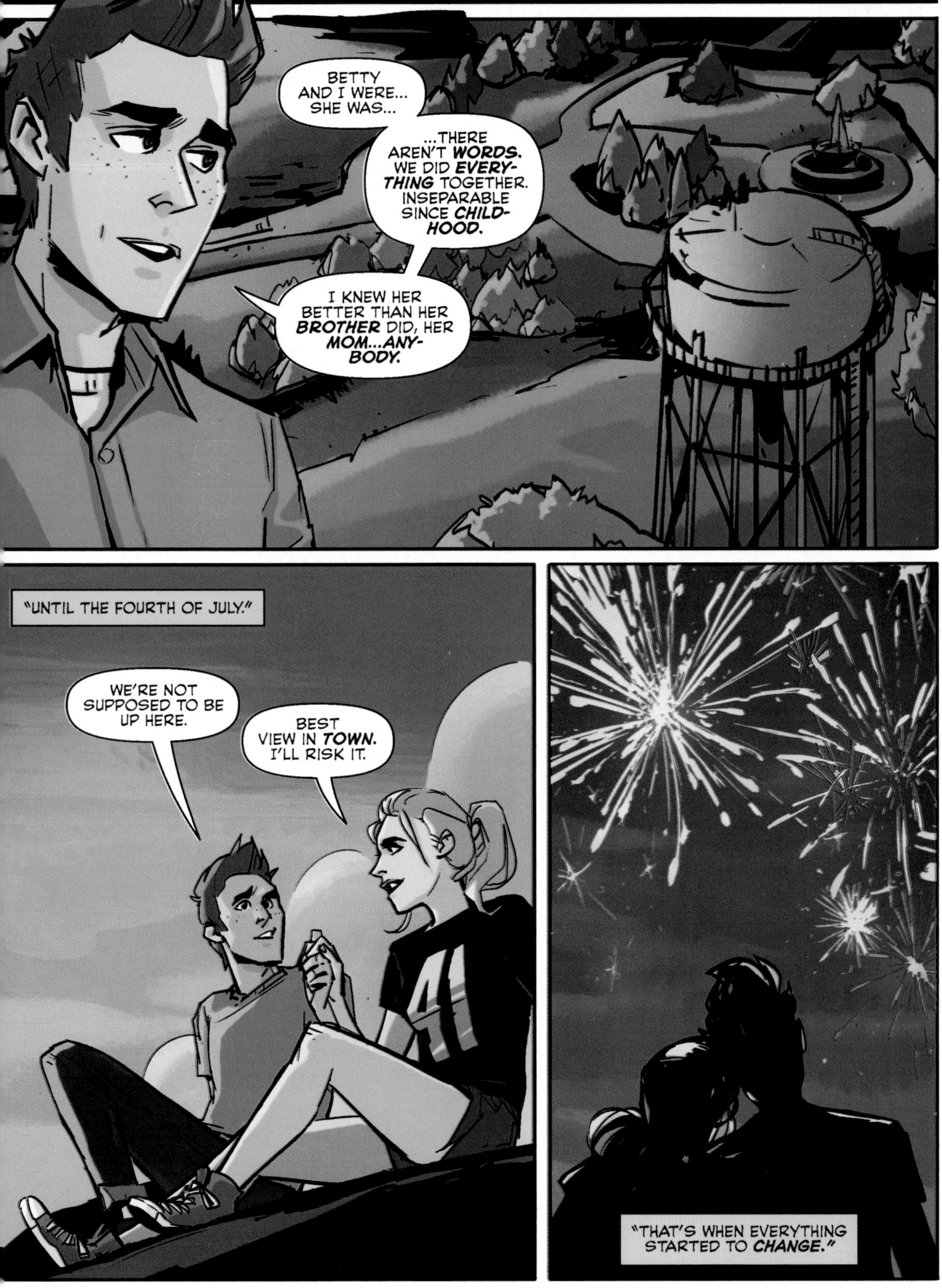

BETTY AND I WERE... SHE WAS...
...THERE AREN'T **WORDS.** WE DID **EVERYTHING** TOGETHER. INSEPARABLE SINCE **CHILDHOOD.**
I KNEW HER BETTER THAN HER **BROTHER** DID, HER **MOM...ANYBODY.**
"UNTIL THE FOURTH OF JULY."
WE'RE NOT SUPPOSED TO BE UP HERE.
BEST VIEW IN **TOWN.** I'LL RISK IT.
"THAT'S WHEN EVERYTHING STARTED TO **CHANGE.**"

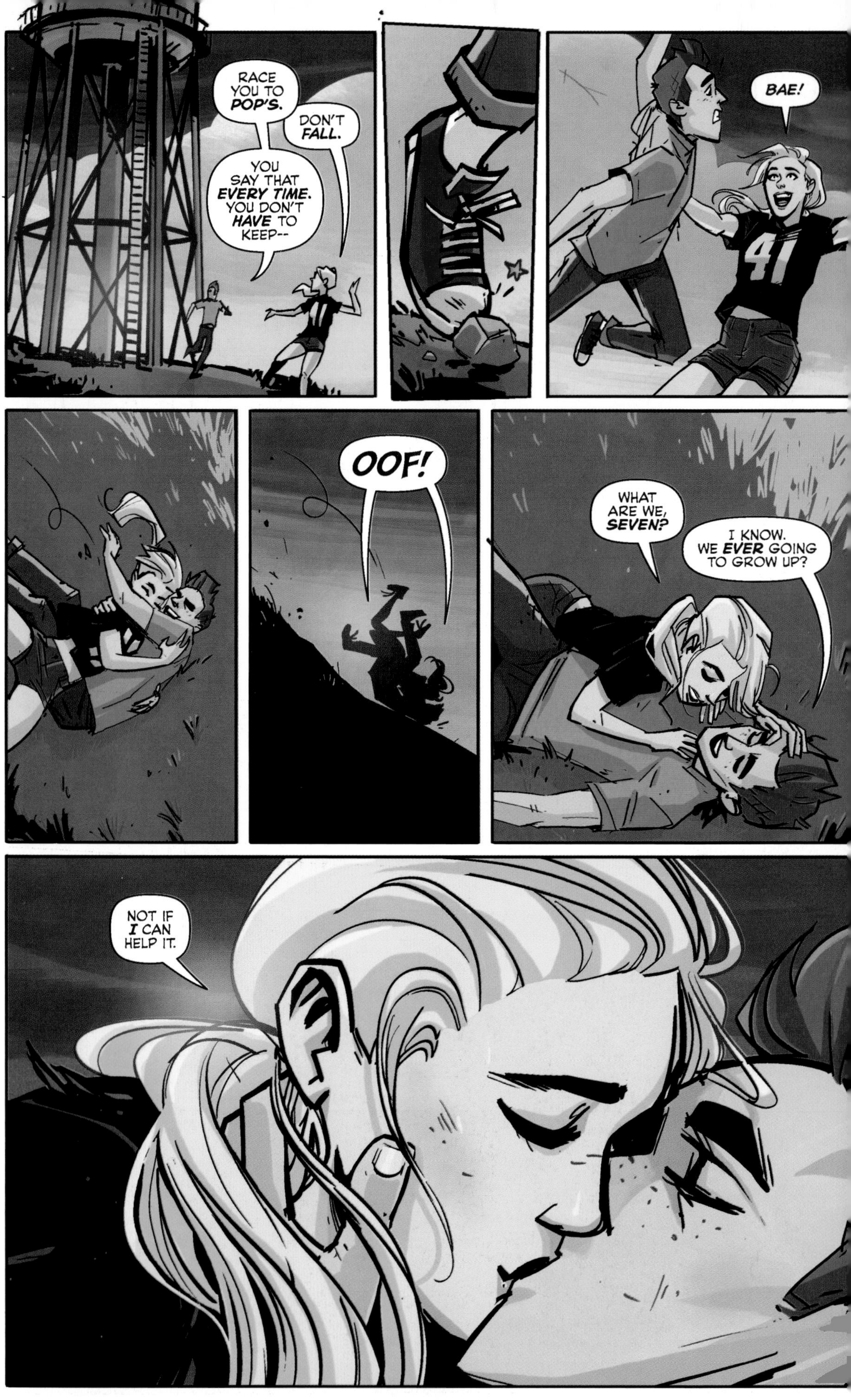
RACE YOU TO POP'S.
DON'T FALL.
YOU SAY THAT EVERY TIME. YOU DON'T HAVE TO KEEP--
BAE!
OOF!
WHAT ARE WE, SEVEN?
I KNOW. WE EVER GOING TO GROW UP?
NOT IF I CAN HELP IT.

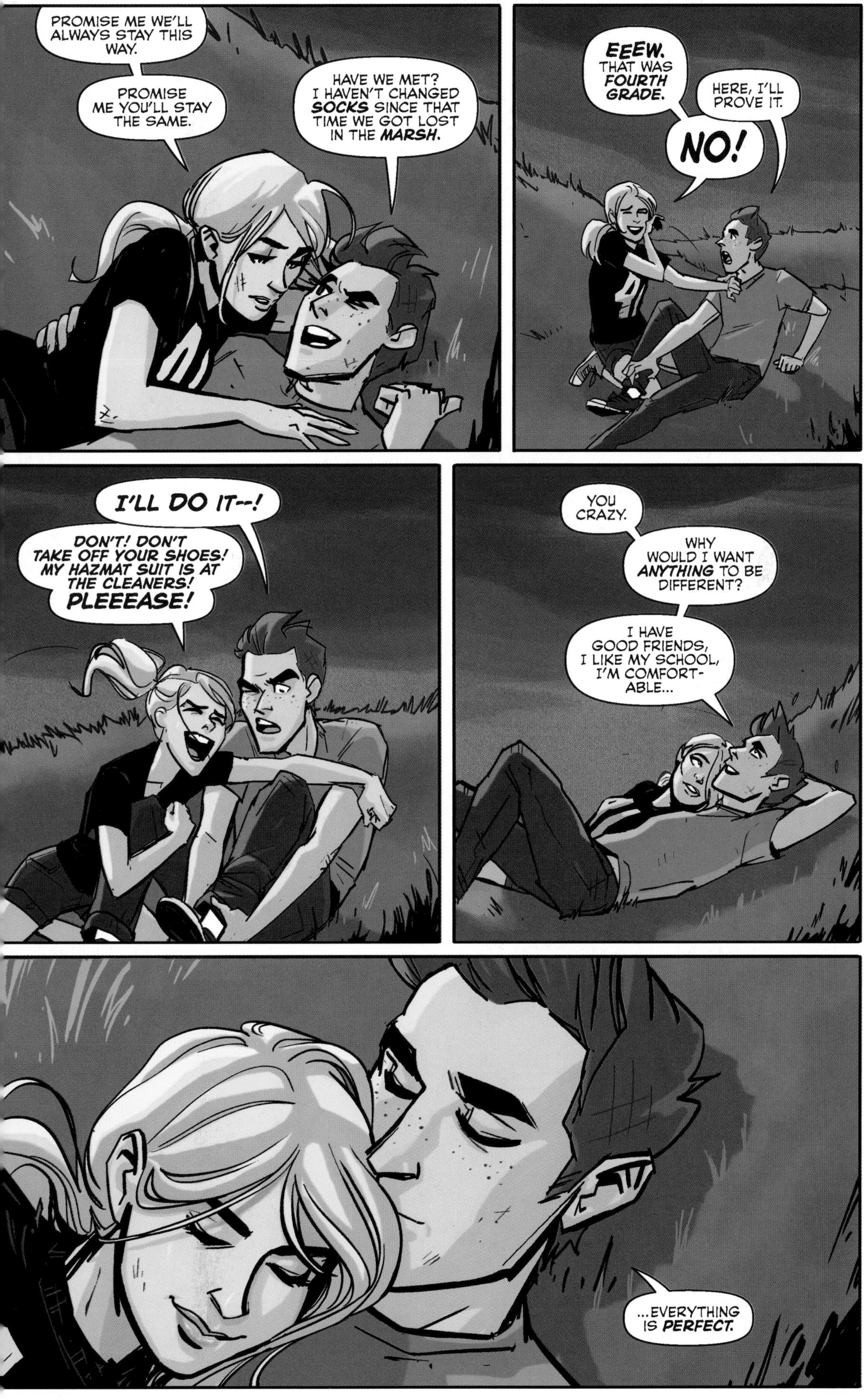
PROMISE ME WE'LL ALWAYS STAY THIS WAY.
PROMISE ME YOU'LL STAY THE SAME.
HAVE WE MET? I HAVEN'T CHANGED **SOCKS** SINCE THAT TIME WE GOT LOST IN THE **MARSH**.
EEEW. THAT WAS **FOURTH GRADE.**
HERE, I'LL PROVE IT.
NO!
I'LL DO IT--!
DON'T! DON'T TAKE OFF YOUR SHOES! MY HAZMAT SUIT IS AT THE CLEANERS! PLEEEASE!
YOU CRAZY.
WHY WOULD I WANT **ANYTHING** TO BE DIFFERENT?
I HAVE GOOD FRIENDS, I LIKE MY SCHOOL, I'M COMFORT-ABLE...
...EVERYTHING IS **PERFECT.**

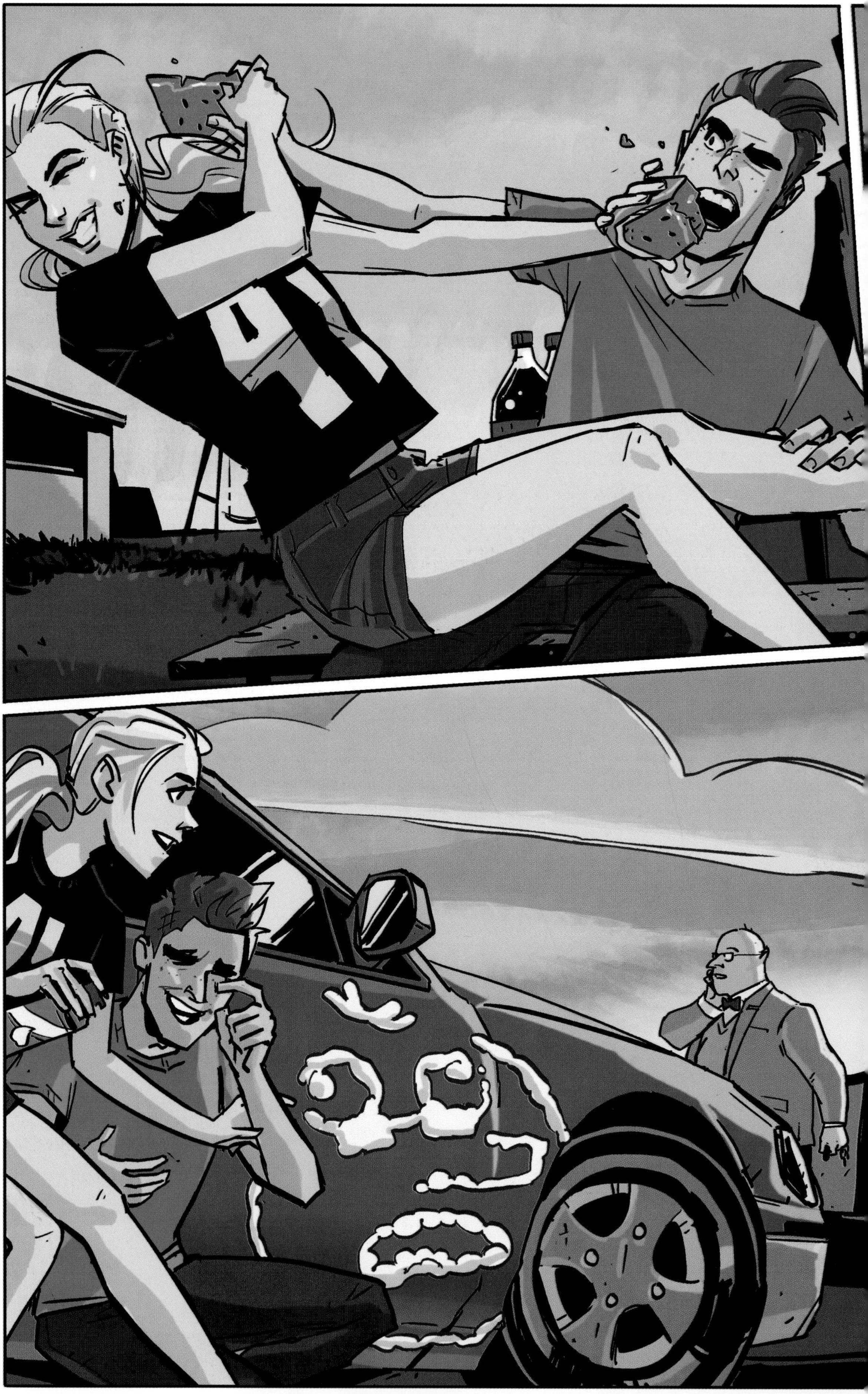

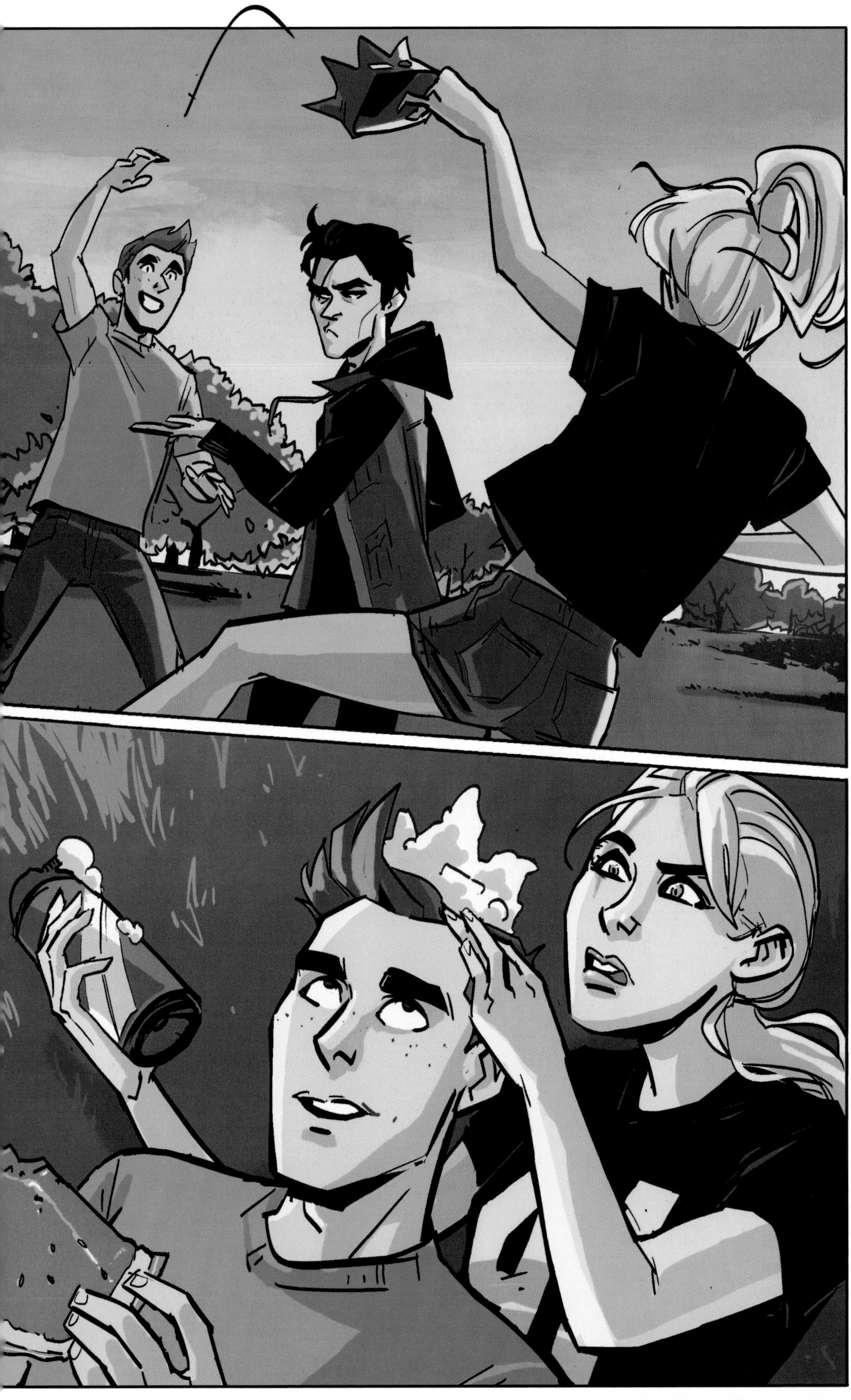

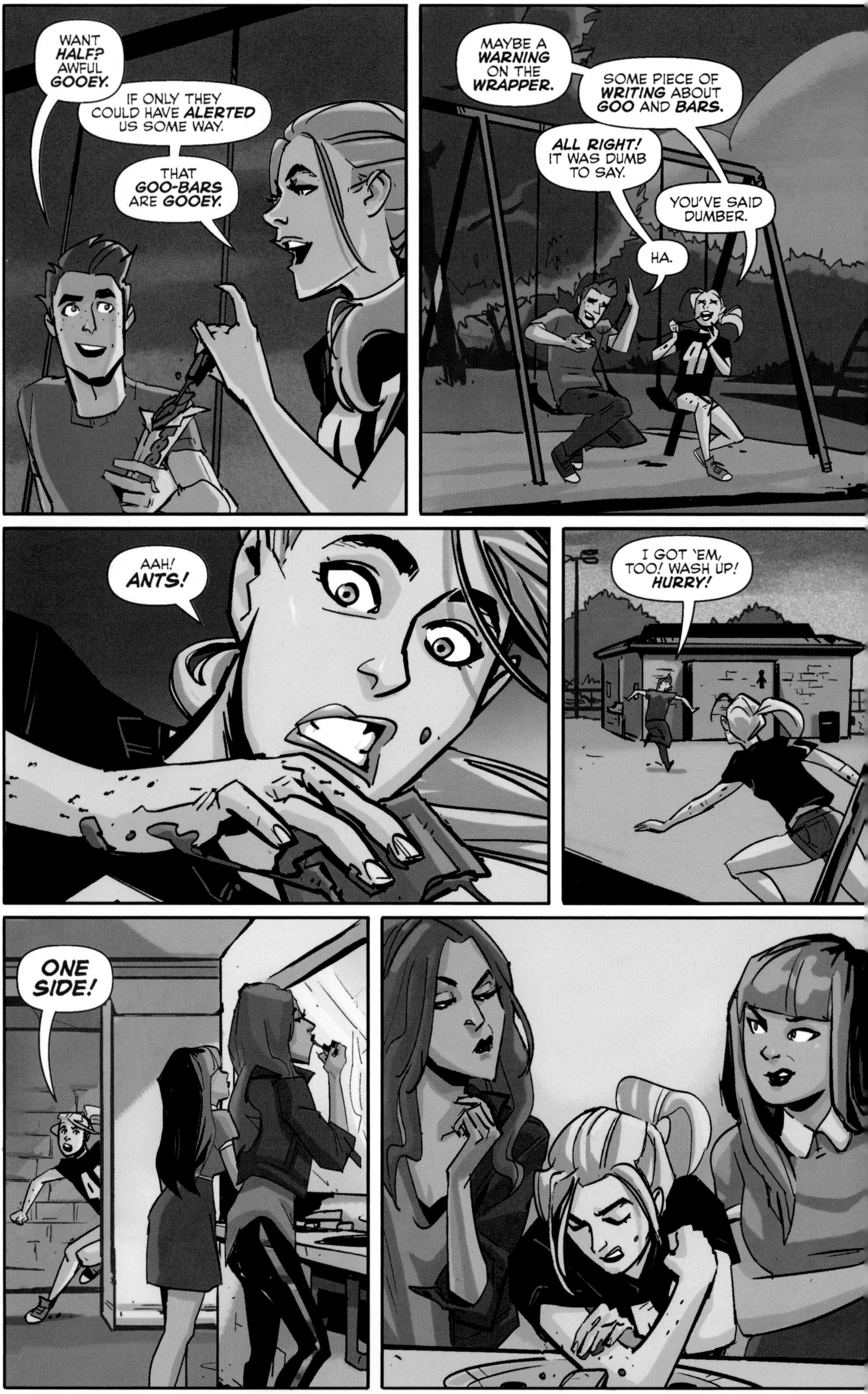
WANT HALF? AWFUL GOOEY.
IF ONLY THEY COULD HAVE ALERTED US SOME WAY.
THAT GOO-BARS ARE GOOEY.
MAYBE A WARNING ON THE WRAPPER.
SOME PIECE OF WRITING ABOUT GOO AND BARS.
ALL RIGHT! IT WAS DUMB TO SAY.
YOU'VE SAID DUMBER.
HA.
AAH! ANTS!
I GOT 'EM, TOO! WASH UP! HURRY!
ONE SIDE!

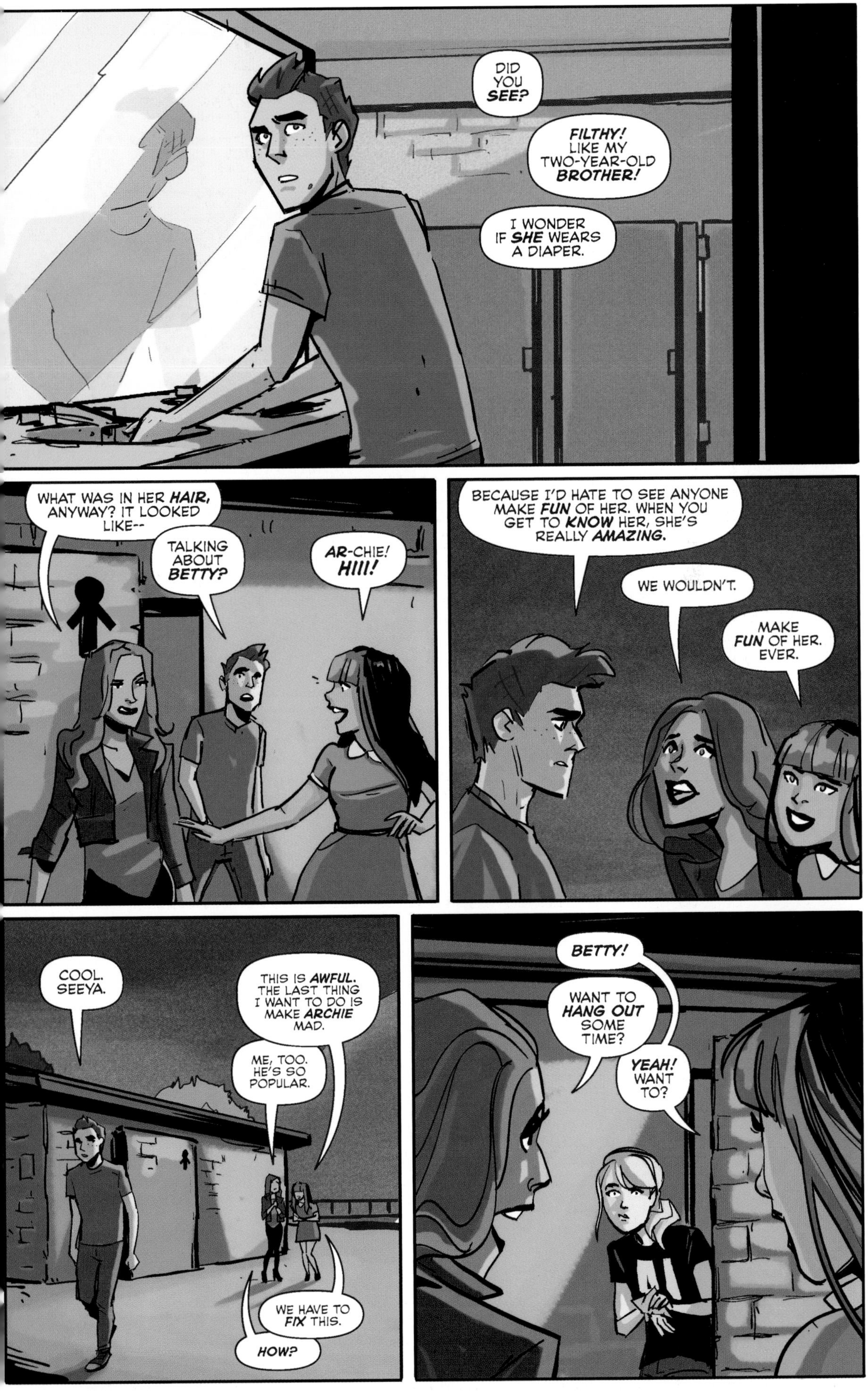
DID YOU SEE?
FILTHY! LIKE MY TWO-YEAR-OLD BROTHER!
I WONDER IF SHE WEARS A DIAPER.
WHAT WAS IN HER HAIR, ANYWAY? IT LOOKED LIKE--
TALKING ABOUT BETTY?
AR-CHIE! HIII!
BECAUSE I'D HATE TO SEE ANYONE MAKE FUN OF HER. WHEN YOU GET TO KNOW HER, SHE'S REALLY AMAZING.
WE WOULDN'T.
MAKE FUN OF HER. EVER.
COOL. SEEYA.
THIS IS AWFUL. THE LAST THING I WANT TO DO IS MAKE ARCHIE MAD.
ME, TOO. HE'S SO POPULAR.
WE HAVE TO FIX THIS.
HOW?
BETTY!
WANT TO HANG OUT SOME TIME?
YEAH! WANT TO?

CHAPTER TWO: Lizzie

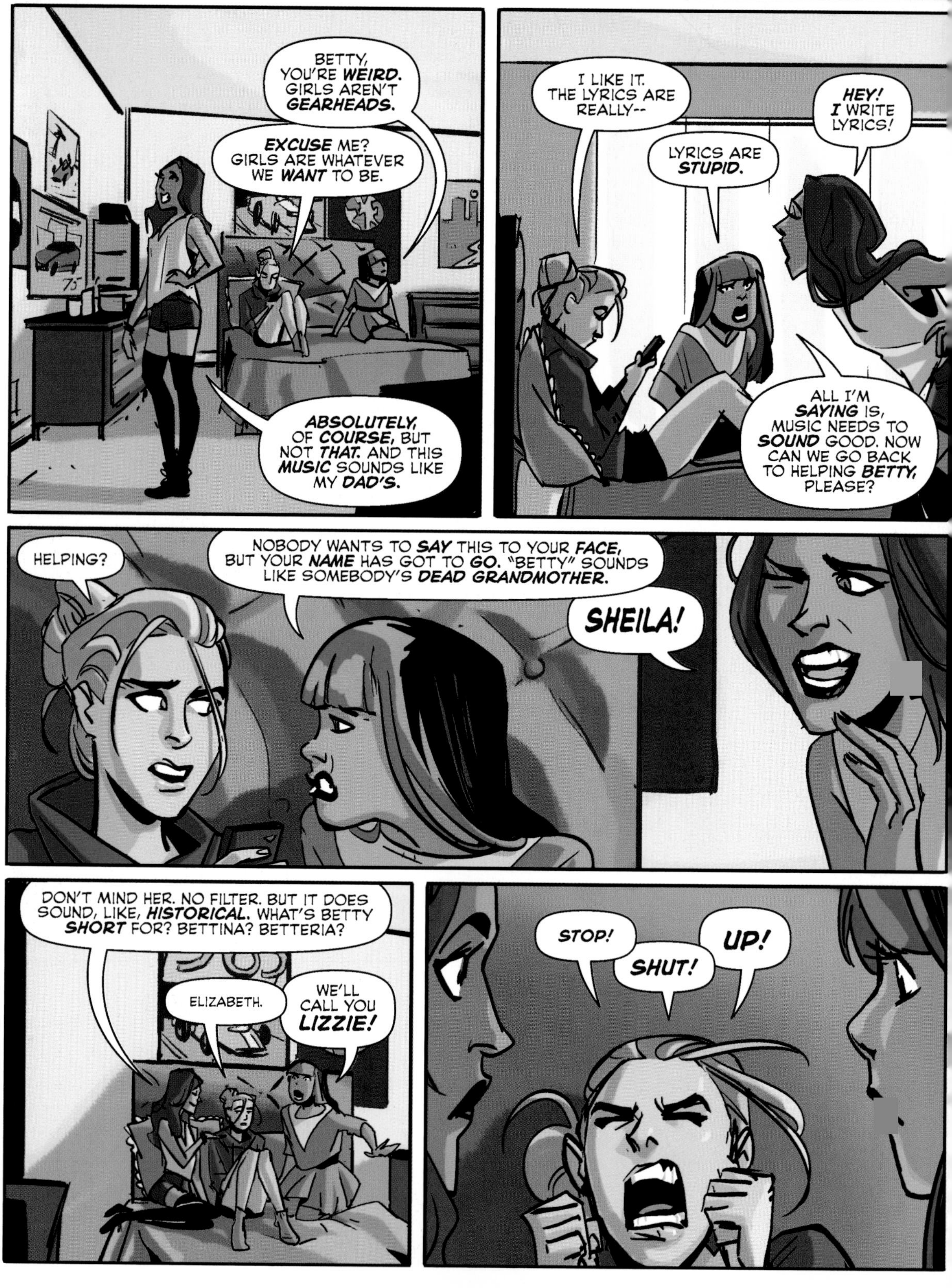
BETTY, YOU'RE WEIRD. GIRLS AREN'T GEARHEADS.
EXCUSE ME? GIRLS ARE WHATEVER WE WANT TO BE.
ABSOLUTELY, OF COURSE, BUT NOT THAT. AND THIS MUSIC SOUNDS LIKE MY DAD'S.
I LIKE IT. THE LYRICS ARE REALLY--
LYRICS ARE STUPID.
HEY! I WRITE LYRICS!
ALL I'M SAYING IS, MUSIC NEEDS TO SOUND GOOD. NOW CAN WE GO BACK TO HELPING BETTY, PLEASE?
HELPING?
NOBODY WANTS TO SAY THIS TO YOUR FACE, BUT YOUR NAME HAS GOT TO GO. "BETTY" SOUNDS LIKE SOMEBODY'S DEAD GRANDMOTHER.
SHEILA!
DON'T MIND HER. NO FILTER. BUT IT DOES SOUND, LIKE, HISTORICAL. WHAT'S BETTY SHORT FOR? BETTINA? BETTERIA?
ELIZABETH.
WE'LL CALL YOU LIZZIE!
STOP!
SHUT!
UP!

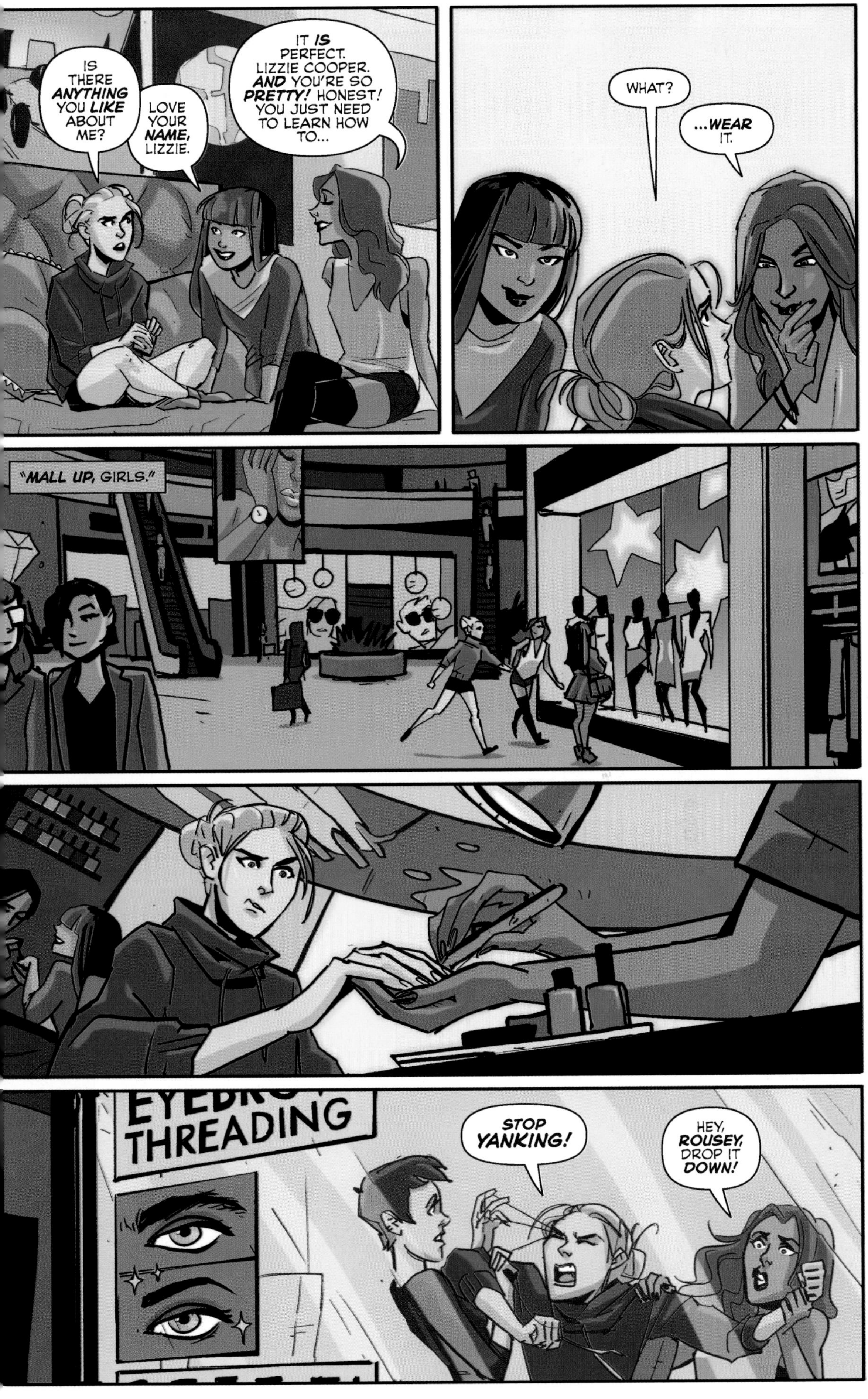
IS THERE ANYTHING YOU LIKE ABOUT ME?
LOVE YOUR NAME, LIZZIE.
IT IS PERFECT. LIZZIE COOPER. AND YOU'RE SO PRETTY! HONEST! YOU JUST NEED TO LEARN HOW TO...
WHAT?
...WEAR IT.
"MALL UP, GIRLS."
EYEBRO THREADING
STOP YANKING!
HEY, ROUSEY, DROP IT DOWN!

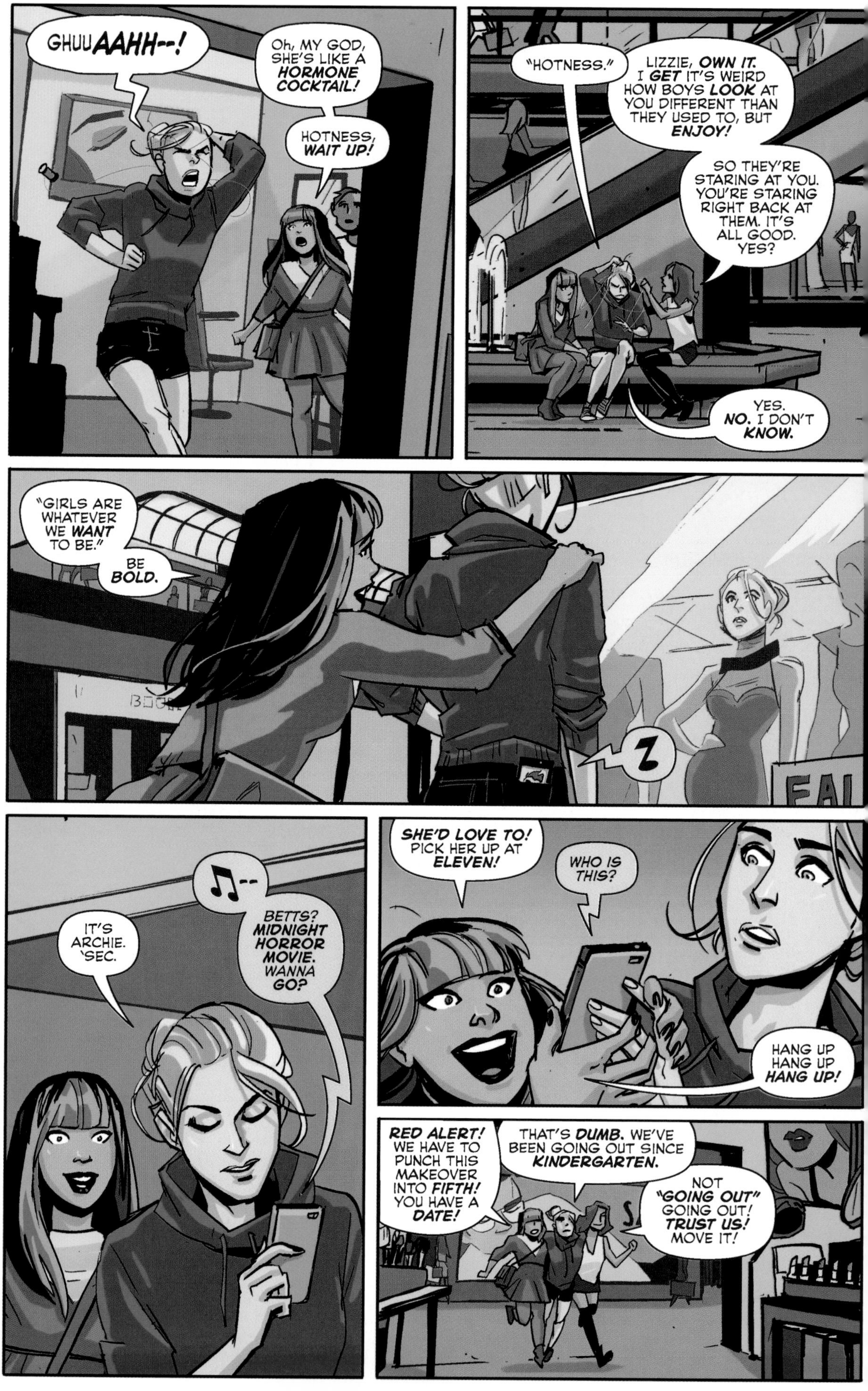
GHUUAAHH--!
Oh, MY GOD, SHE'S LIKE A HORMONE COCKTAIL!
HOTNESS, WAIT UP!
"HOTNESS."
LIZZIE, OWN IT. I GET IT'S WEIRD HOW BOYS LOOK AT YOU DIFFERENT THAN THEY USED TO, BUT ENJOY!
SO THEY'RE STARING AT YOU. YOU'RE STARING RIGHT BACK AT THEM. IT'S ALL GOOD. YES?
YES. NO. I DON'T KNOW.
"GIRLS ARE WHATEVER WE WANT TO BE."
BE BOLD.
IT'S ARCHIE. 'SEC.
BETTS? MIDNIGHT HORROR MOVIE. WANNA GO?
SHE'D LOVE TO! PICK HER UP AT ELEVEN!
WHO IS THIS?
HANG UP HANG UP HANG UP!
RED ALERT! WE HAVE TO PUNCH THIS MAKEOVER INTO FIFTH! YOU HAVE A DATE!
THAT'S DUMB. WE'VE BEEN GOING OUT SINCE KINDERGARTEN.
NOT "GOING OUT" GOING OUT! TRUST US! MOVE IT!

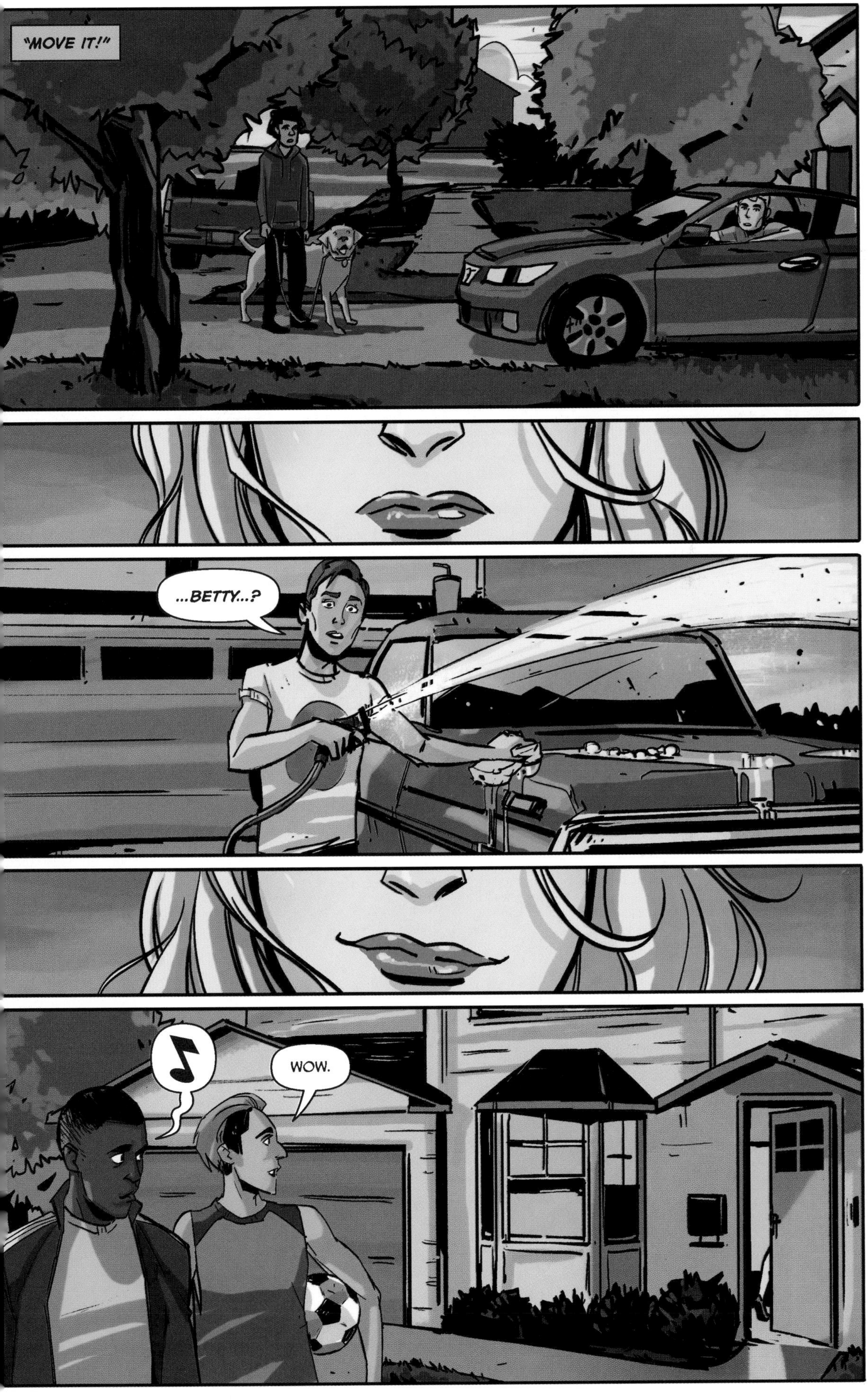
"MOVE IT!"
...BETTY...?
♪
WOW.

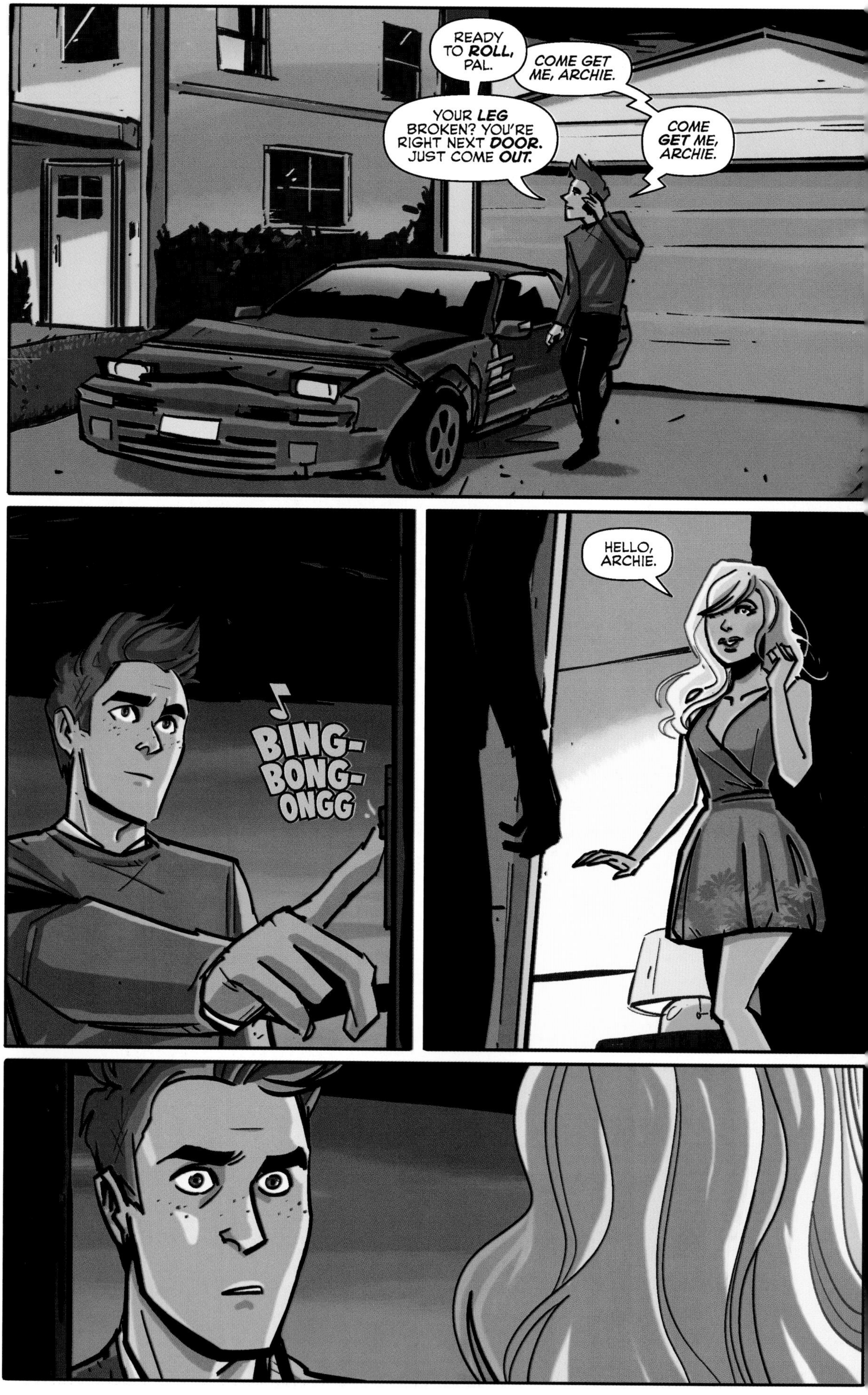
READY TO ROLL, PAL.
COME GET ME, ARCHIE.
YOUR LEG BROKEN? YOU'RE RIGHT NEXT DOOR. JUST COME OUT.
COME GET ME, ARCHIE.
BING-BONG-ONGG
HELLO, ARCHIE.

CHAPTER THREE: #LIPSTICKINCIDENT

SPLIT A GOO-BAR?

NO.

I DON'T WANT TO MESS UP MY DRESS.

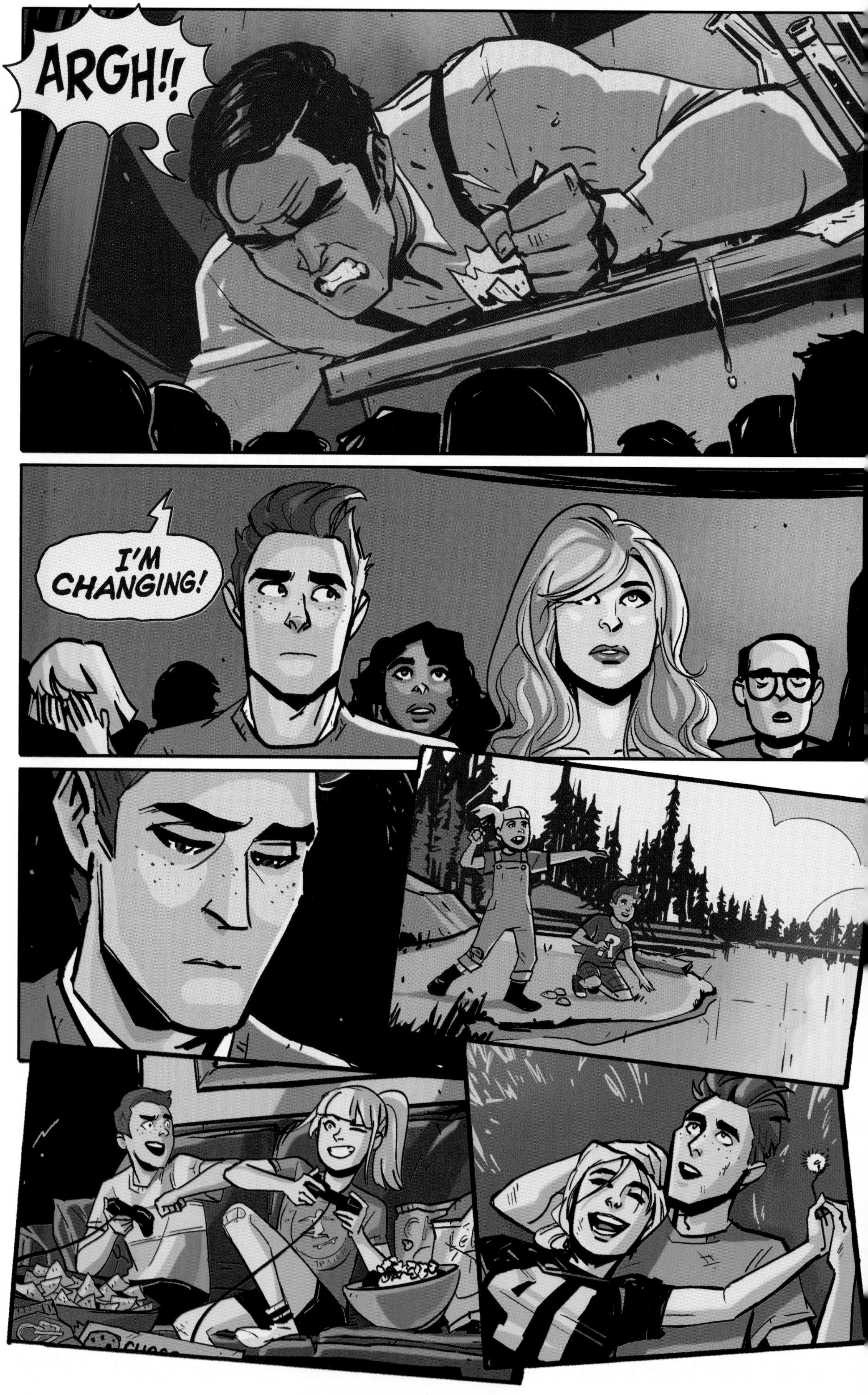
ARGH!!
I'M CHANGING!

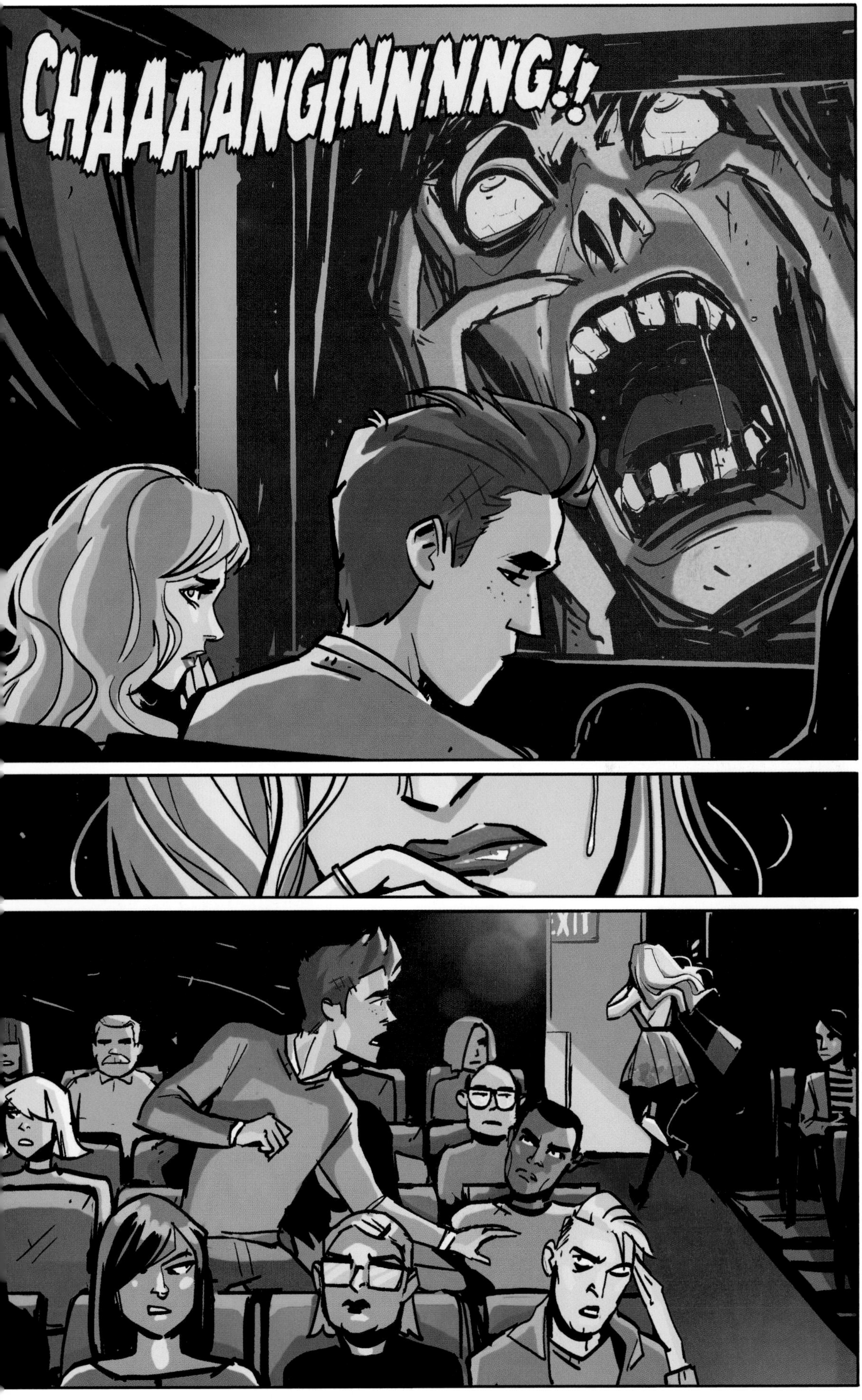
CHAAAANGINNNNG!!
EXIT

CREATURE DOUBLE FEATURE

BETTY, WAIT!

WHY? WHY ARE YOU BEING SO *WEIRD* ALL OF A SUDDEN?

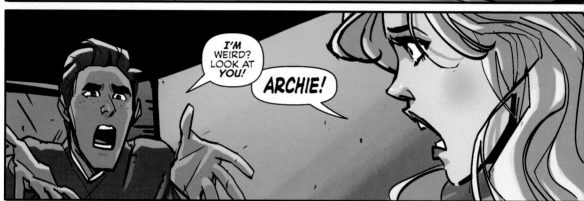

I'M WEIRD? LOOK AT *YOU!*

ARCHIE!

THAT'S NOT WHAT I--

WHAT'S *WRONG* WITH ME?

NOTHING!

I *KNOW* YOU LOOK AT GIRLS DRESSED UP *JUST LIKE THIS!*

SOMETIMES! I DON'T MEAN TO! IT'S JUST THAT *THEY'RE--*

THEY'RE *WHAT?*

WE'RE TALKING ABOUT *YOU,* OKAY?

THIS! *THIS* IS THE CRAP THAT DOESN'T *BELONG* ON YOU! WHERE'S THE BETTY I *KNOW?*

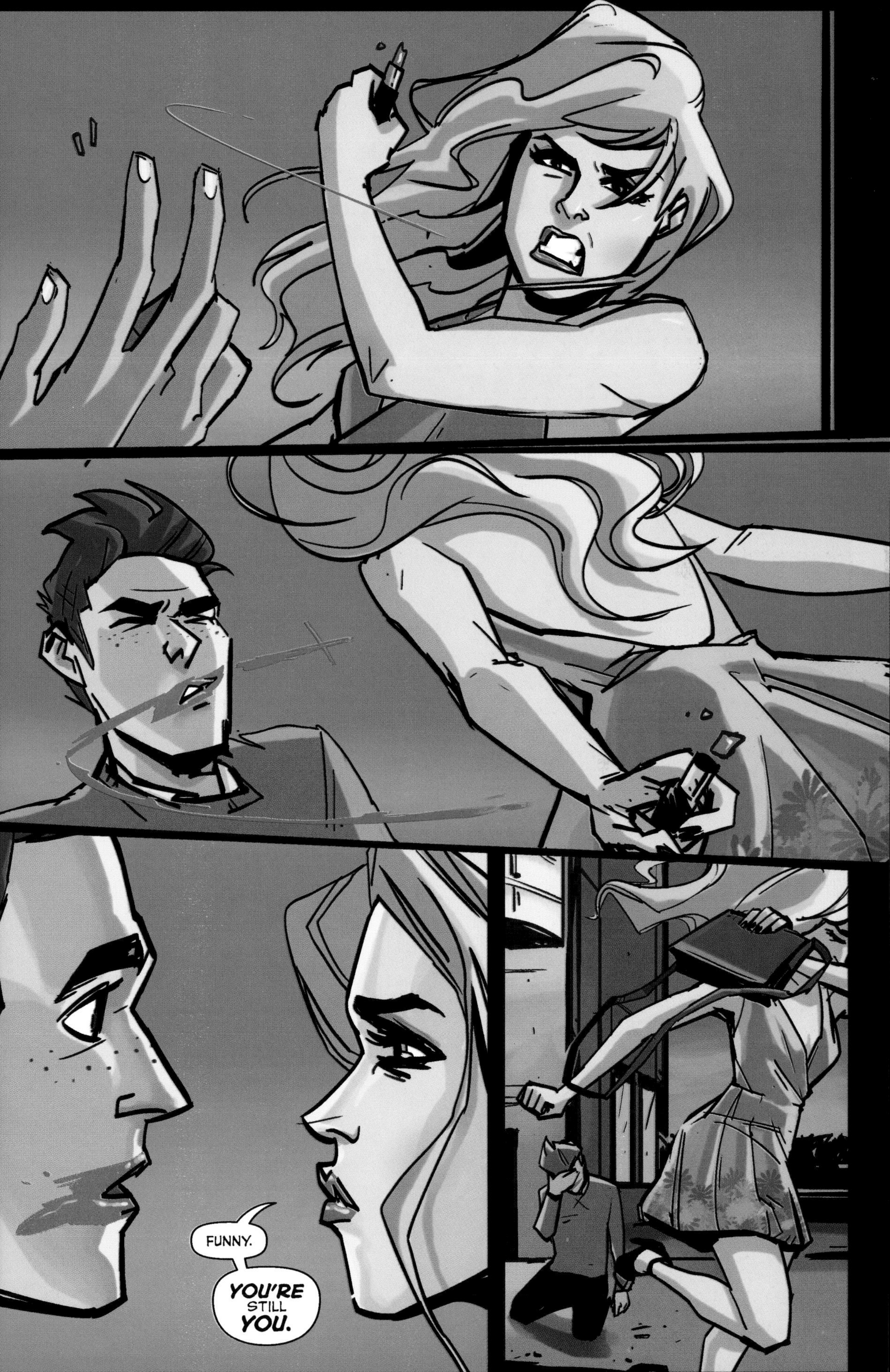
FUNNY.
YOU'RE STILL YOU.

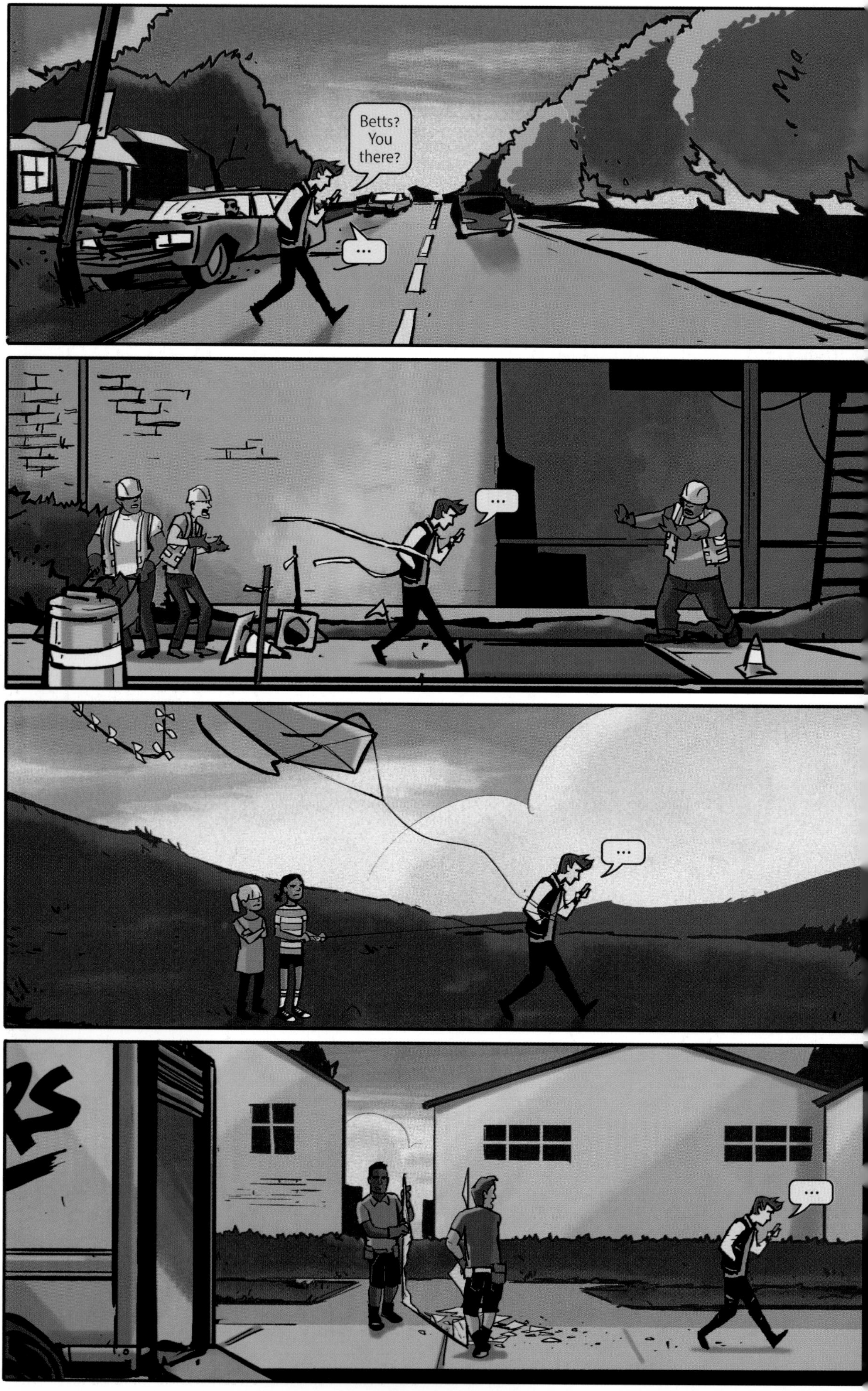
Betts? You there?
...
...
...
...

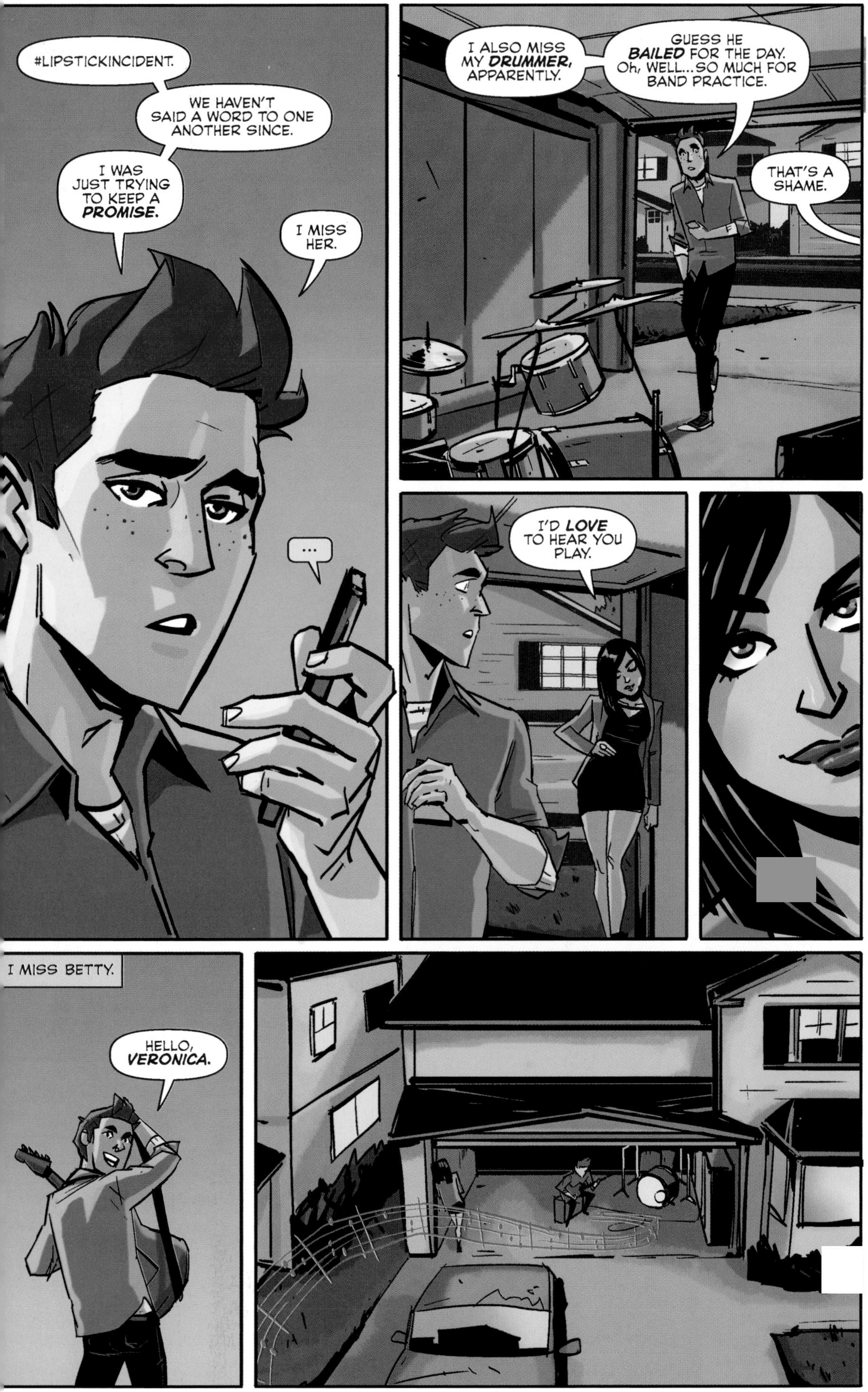
#LIPSTICKINCIDENT.
WE HAVEN'T SAID A WORD TO ONE ANOTHER SINCE.
I WAS JUST TRYING TO KEEP A PROMISE.
I MISS HER.
...
I ALSO MISS MY DRUMMER, APPARENTLY.
GUESS HE BAILED FOR THE DAY. Oh, WELL...SO MUCH FOR BAND PRACTICE.
THAT'S A SHAME.
I'D LOVE TO HEAR YOU PLAY.
I MISS BETTY.
HELLO, VERONICA.

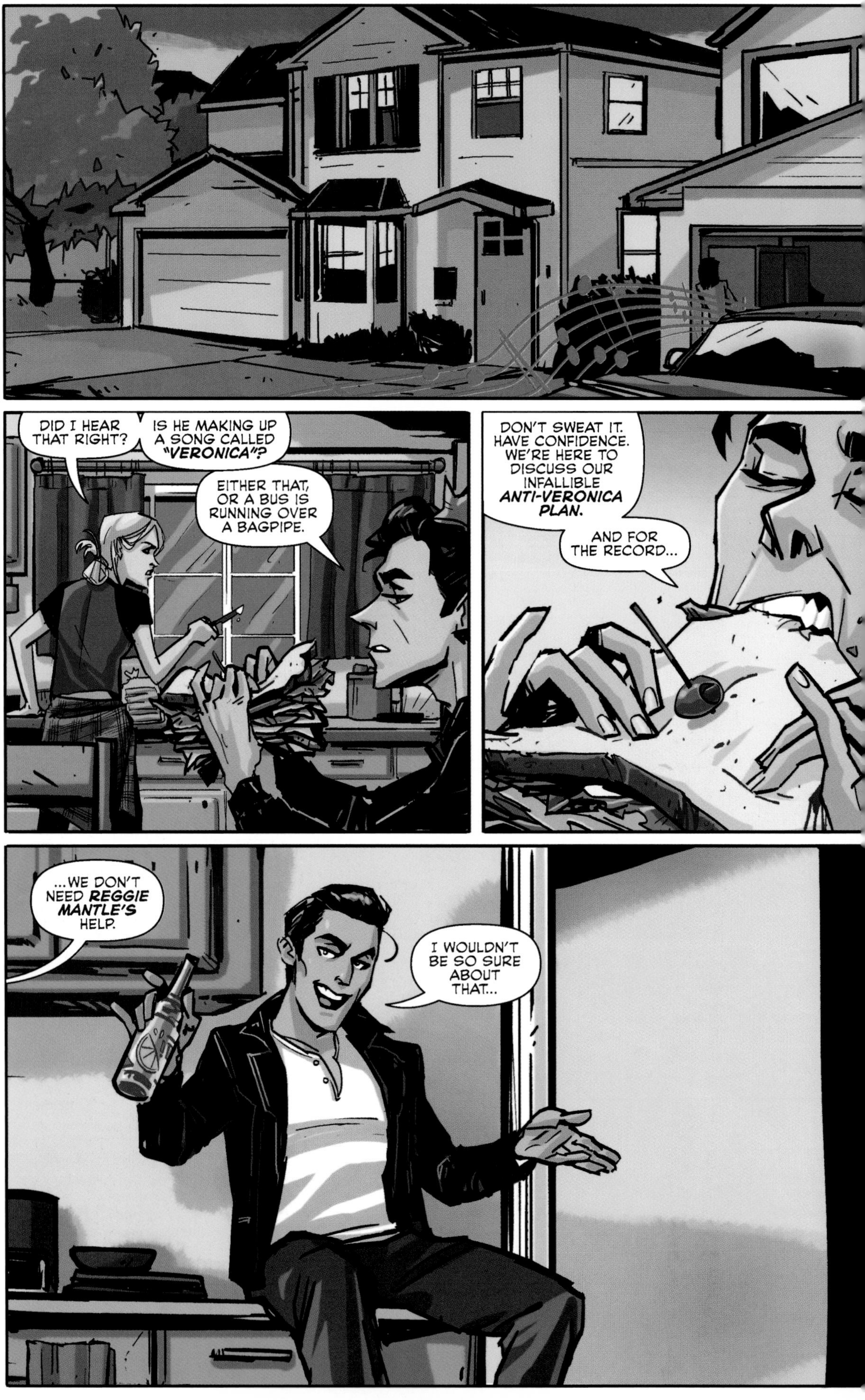
DID I HEAR THAT RIGHT?
IS HE MAKING UP A SONG CALLED "VERONICA"?
EITHER THAT, OR A BUS IS RUNNING OVER A BAGPIPE.
DON'T SWEAT IT. HAVE CONFIDENCE. WE'RE HERE TO DISCUSS OUR INFALLIBLE ANTI-VERONICA PLAN.
AND FOR THE RECORD...
...WE DON'T NEED REGGIE MANTLE'S HELP.
I WOULDN'T BE SO SURE ABOUT THAT...

TO BE CONTINUED...

ISSUE FIVE

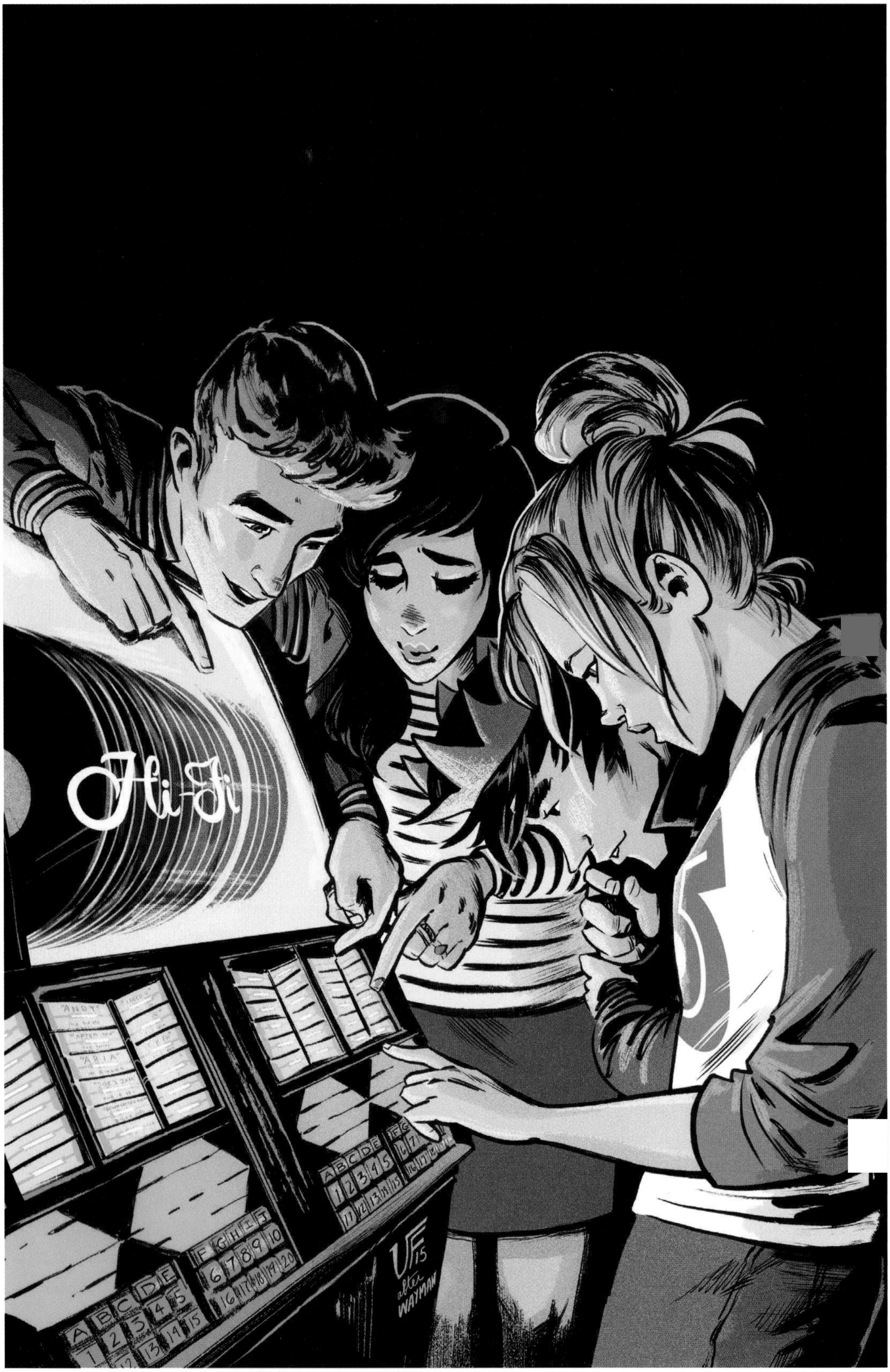
Hi-Fi

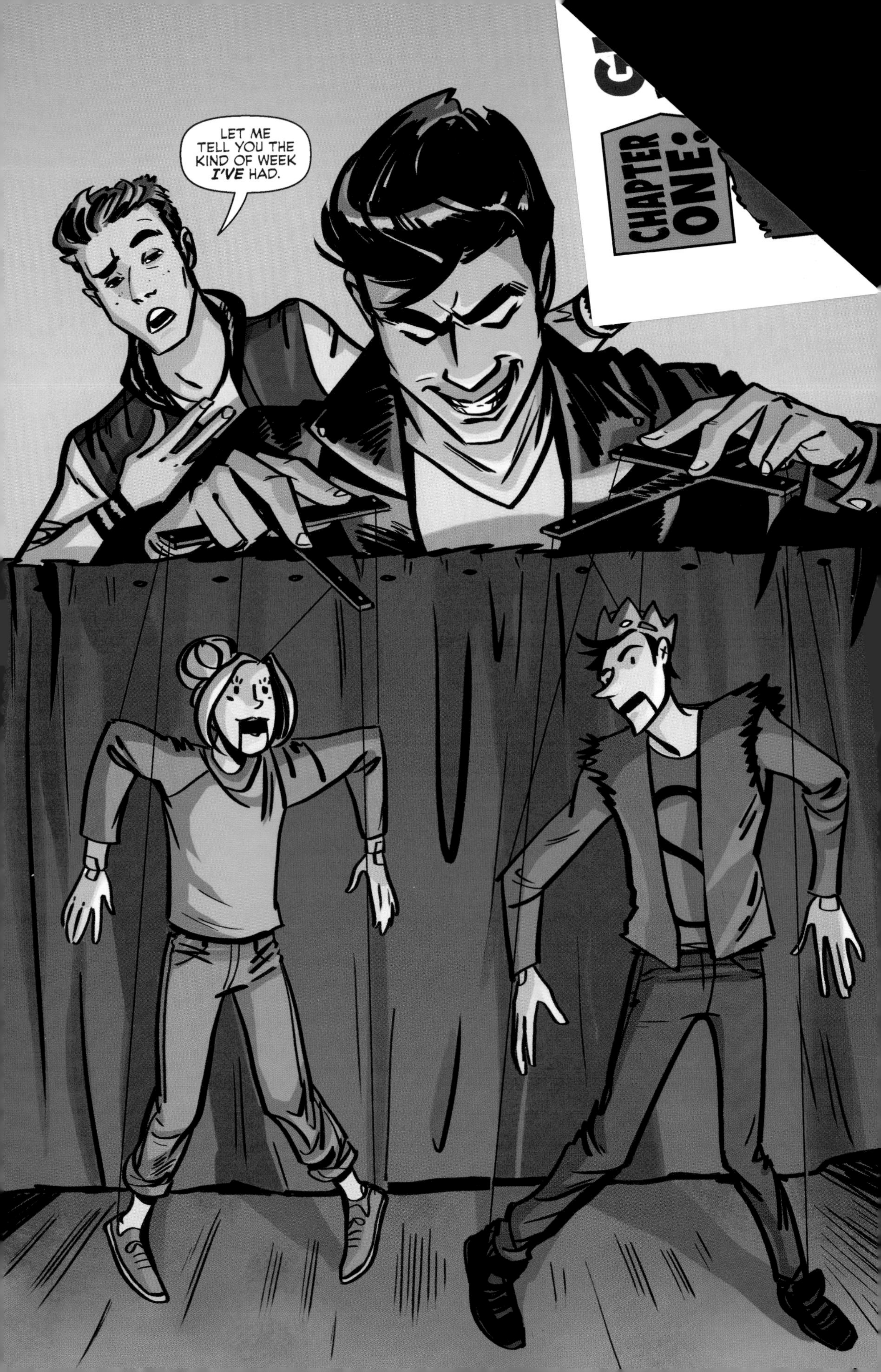
LET ME TELL YOU THE KIND OF WEEK *I'VE* HAD.
CHAPTER ONE:

THIS IS THE JERK I'M ABOUT TO HAVE TO *SAVE* TWO PEOPLE FROM.

BEFORE *VERONICA* CAME TO RIVERDALE AND TOTALLY WRECKED THE CURVE, *REGGIE MANTLE* WAS OUR RICHEST KID.

ALSO THE MOST UNIVERSALLY *REVILED* ONE.

HE'S SELF-CENTERED, SCHEMING AND NASTY. ALL HE LOVES IS *PRANKING* PEOPLE. NOBODY KNOWS OR CARES WHY HE'S SO ROTTEN.

MANTLE'S THE CLOSEST THING RIVERDALE HAS TO A *SUPER-VILLAIN.*

"THE ONLY TIME WE EVER BONDED WAS FOR TWO MINUTES BACK IN FOURTH GRADE, WHEN HE TOLD ME A PRETTY GOOD JOKE THAT IS FOR SOME REASON STICKING WITH ME LATELY.

"GUY WALKS INTO A PET SHOP.

"HE LIVES IN A TINY APARTMENT WITH THIN WALLS, SO HE WANTS SOMETHING

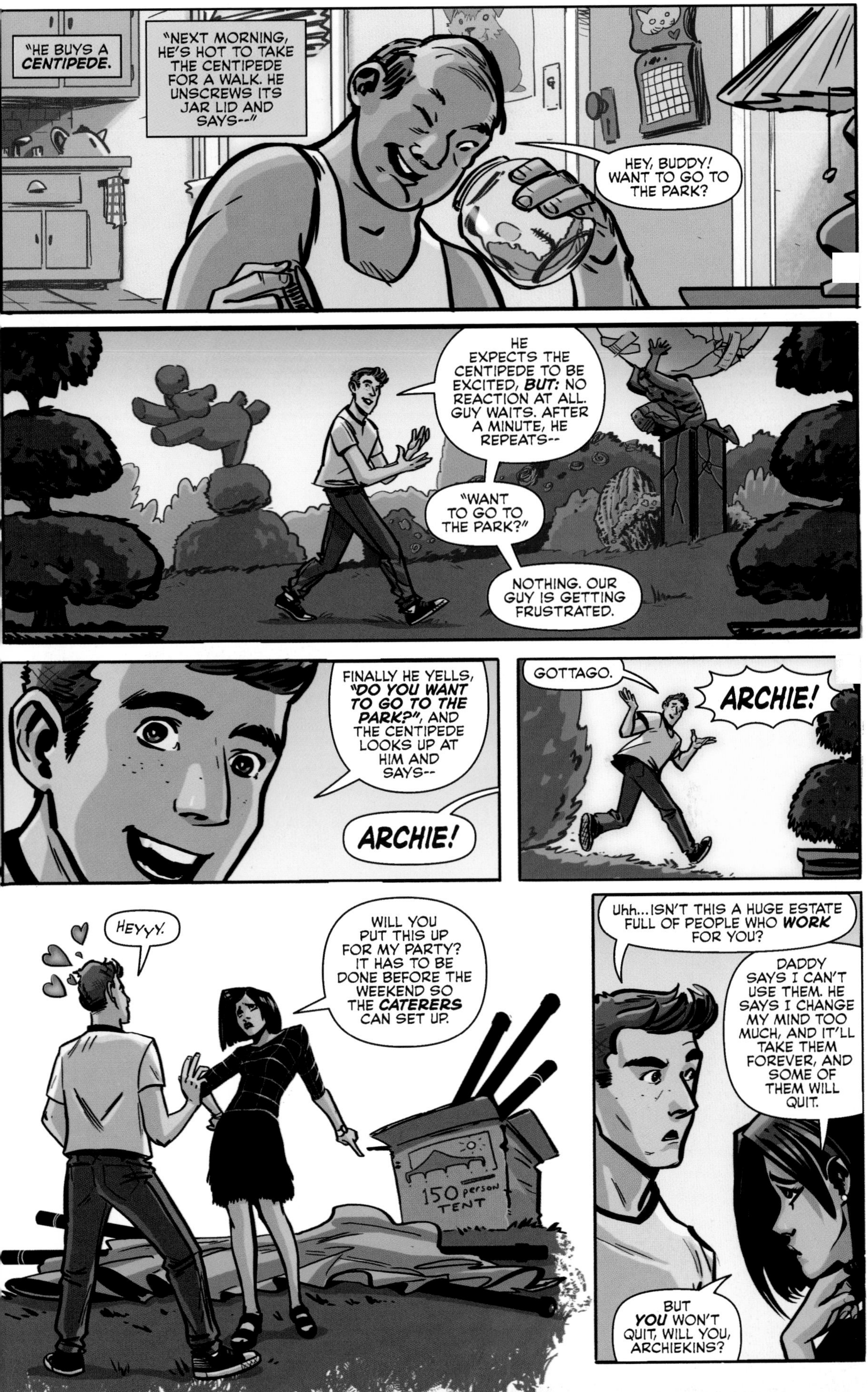
"HE BUYS A *CENTIPEDE.*
"NEXT MORNING, HE'S HOT TO TAKE THE CENTIPEDE FOR A WALK. HE UNSCREWS ITS JAR LID AND SAYS--"
HEY, BUDDY! WANT TO GO TO THE PARK?
HE EXPECTS THE CENTIPEDE TO BE EXCITED, ***BUT:*** NO REACTION AT ALL. GUY WAITS. AFTER A MINUTE, HE REPEATS--
"WANT TO GO TO THE PARK?"
NOTHING. OUR GUY IS GETTING FRUSTRATED.
FINALLY HE YELLS, ***"DO YOU WANT TO GO TO THE PARK?"***, AND THE CENTIPEDE LOOKS UP AT HIM AND SAYS--
ARCHIE!
GOTTAGO.
ARCHIE!
HEYYY.
WILL YOU PUT THIS UP FOR MY PARTY? IT HAS TO BE DONE BEFORE THE WEEKEND SO THE ***CATERERS*** CAN SET UP.
150 person TENT
Uhh...ISN'T THIS A HUGE ESTATE FULL OF PEOPLE WHO ***WORK*** FOR YOU?
DADDY SAYS I CAN'T USE THEM. HE SAYS I CHANGE MY MIND TOO MUCH, AND IT'LL TAKE THEM FOREVER, AND SOME OF THEM WILL QUIT.
BUT ***YOU*** WON'T QUIT, WILL YOU, ARCHIEKINS?

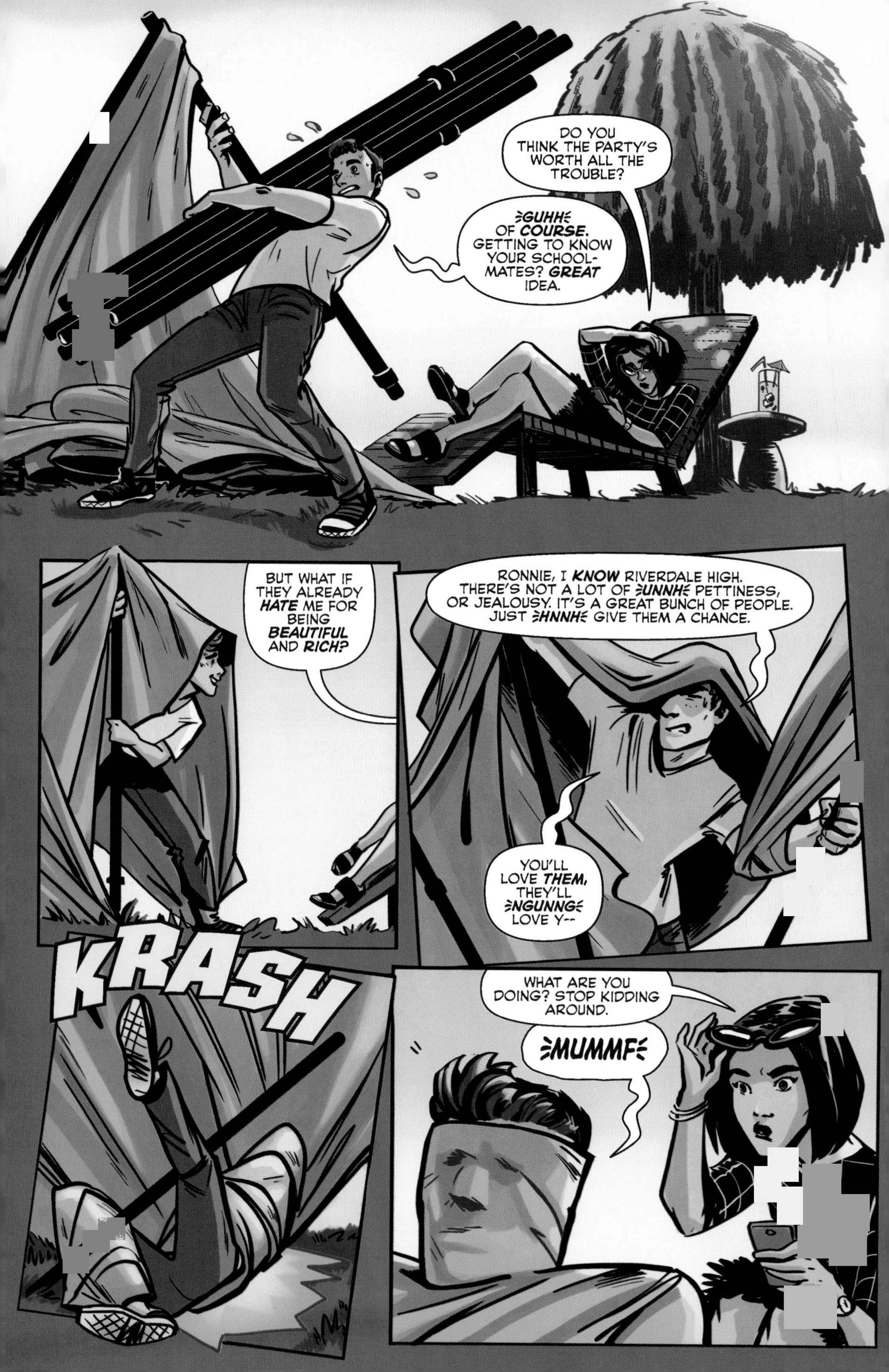
DO YOU THINK THE PARTY'S WORTH ALL THE TROUBLE?
≶GUHH≷ OF COURSE. GETTING TO KNOW YOUR SCHOOL-MATES? GREAT IDEA.
BUT WHAT IF THEY ALREADY HATE ME FOR BEING BEAUTIFUL AND RICH?
RONNIE, I KNOW RIVERDALE HIGH. THERE'S NOT A LOT OF ≶UNNH≷ PETTINESS, OR JEALOUSY. IT'S A GREAT BUNCH OF PEOPLE. JUST ≶HNNH≷ GIVE THEM A CHANCE.
YOU'LL LOVE THEM, THEY'LL ≶NGUNNG≷ LOVE Y--
KRASH
WHAT ARE YOU DOING? STOP KIDDING AROUND.
≶MUMMF≷

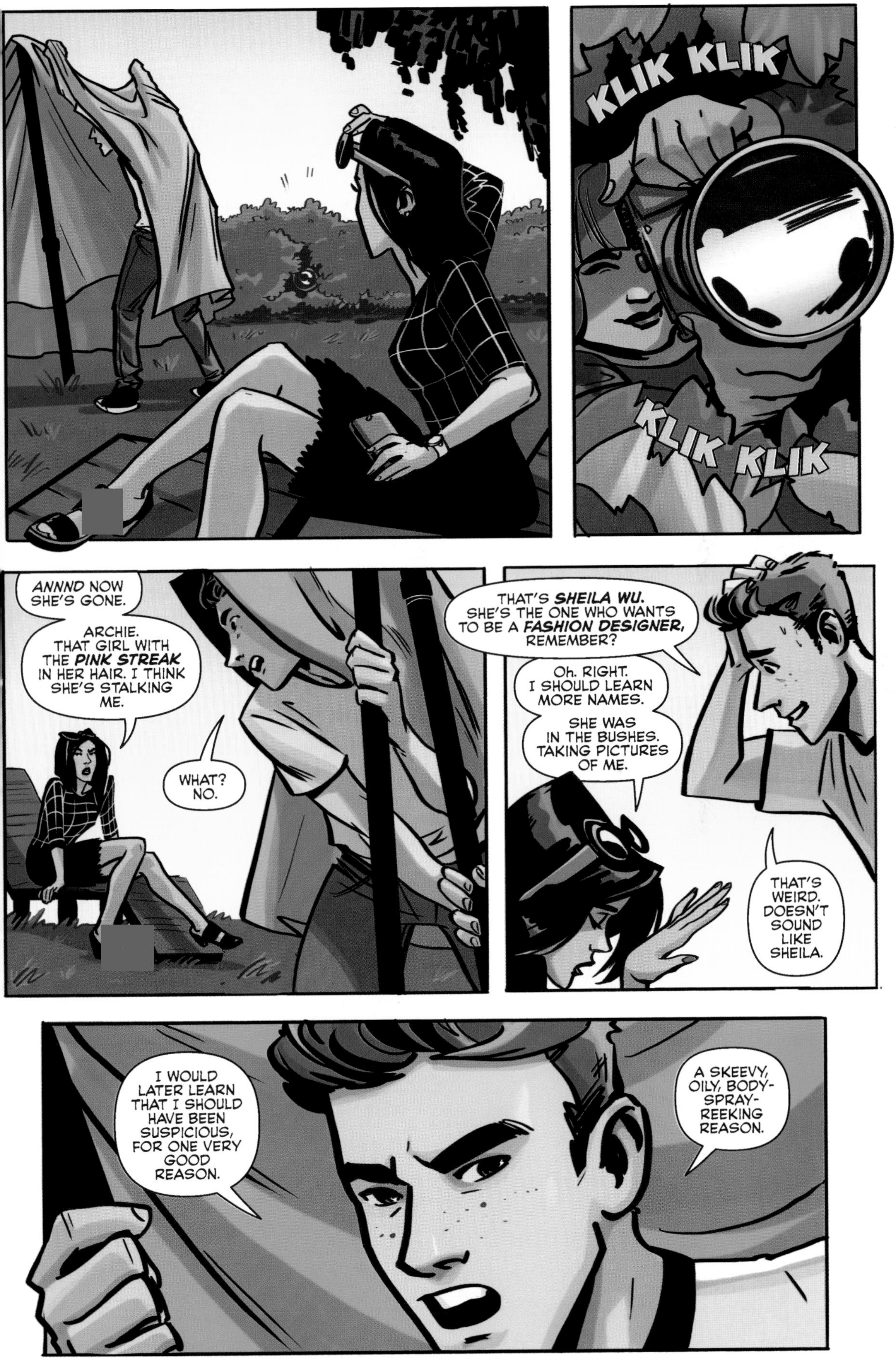
KLIK KLIK
KLIK KLIK
ANNND NOW SHE'S GONE.
ARCHIE. THAT GIRL WITH THE PINK STREAK IN HER HAIR. I THINK SHE'S STALKING ME.
WHAT? NO.
THAT'S SHEILA WU. SHE'S THE ONE WHO WANTS TO BE A FASHION DESIGNER, REMEMBER?
Oh. RIGHT. I SHOULD LEARN MORE NAMES.
SHE WAS IN THE BUSHES. TAKING PICTURES OF ME.
THAT'S WEIRD. DOESN'T SOUND LIKE SHEILA.
I WOULD LATER LEARN THAT I SHOULD HAVE BEEN SUSPICIOUS, FOR ONE VERY GOOD REASON.
A SKEEVY, OILY, BODY-SPRAY-REEKING REASON.

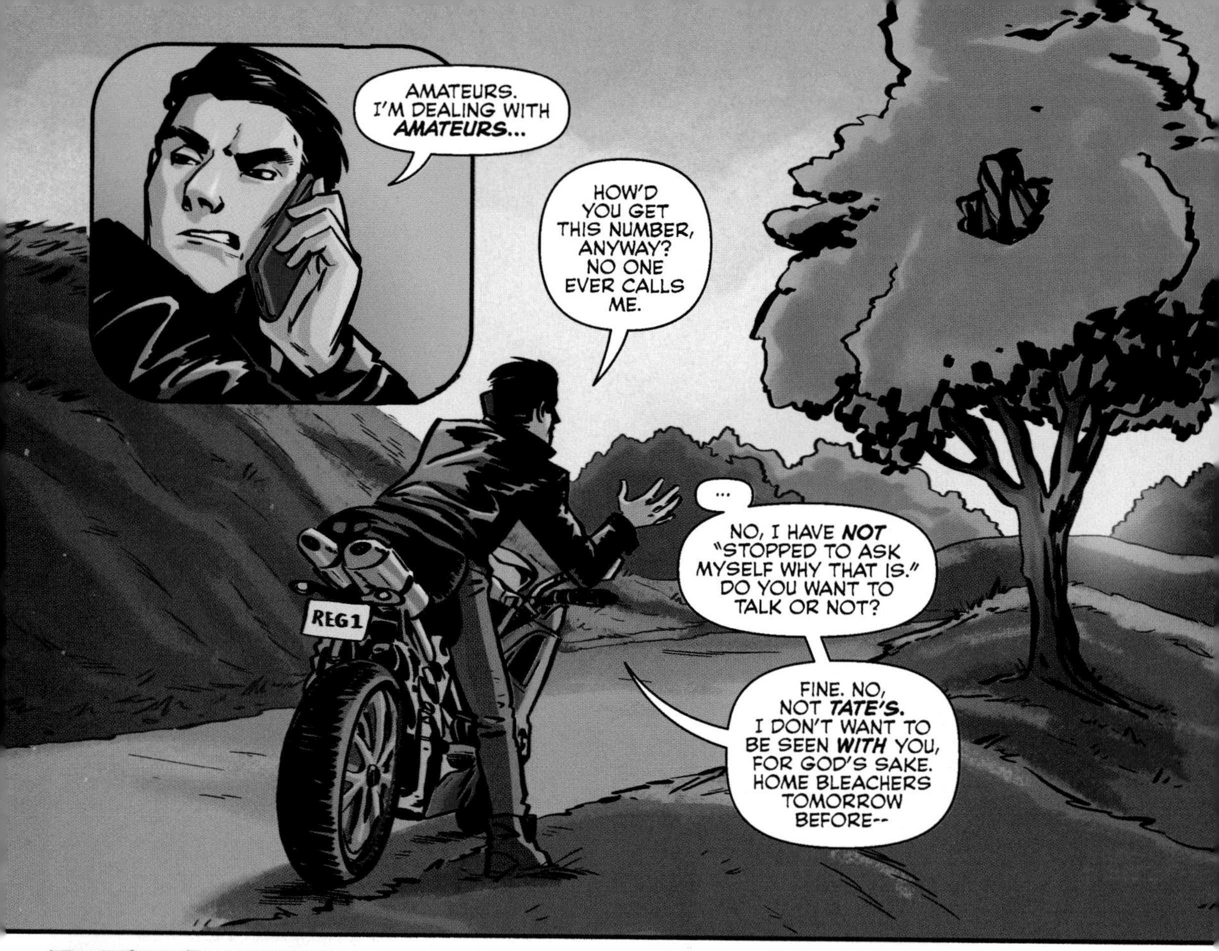
AMATEURS. I'M DEALING WITH **AMATEURS...**
HOW'D YOU GET THIS NUMBER, ANYWAY? NO ONE EVER CALLS ME.
...
NO, I HAVE **NOT** "STOPPED TO ASK MYSELF WHY THAT IS." DO YOU WANT TO TALK OR NOT?
FINE. NO, NOT **TATE'S.** I DON'T WANT TO BE SEEN **WITH** YOU, FOR GOD'S SAKE. HOME BLEACHERS TOMORROW BEFORE--
REG1

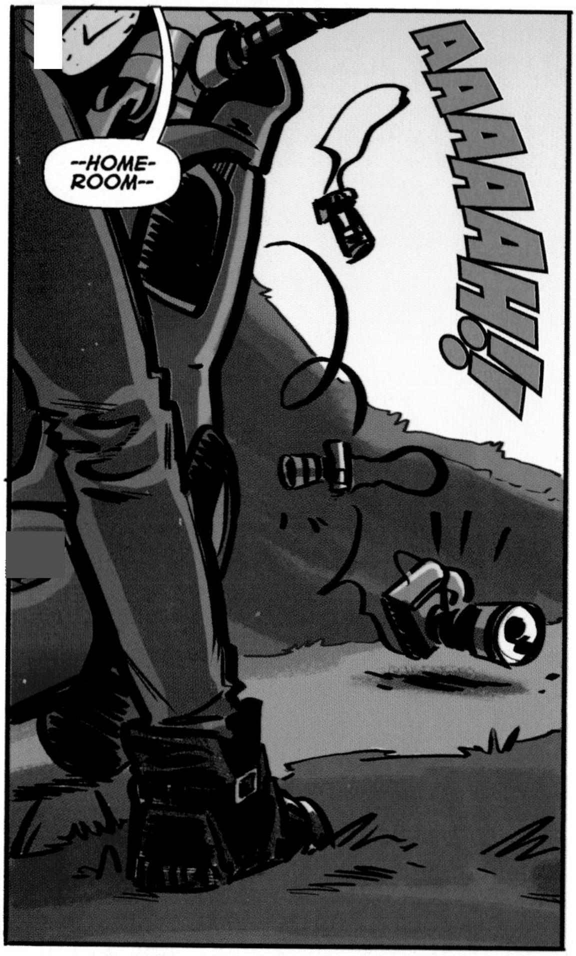
--HOME-ROOM--
AAAAAH!!

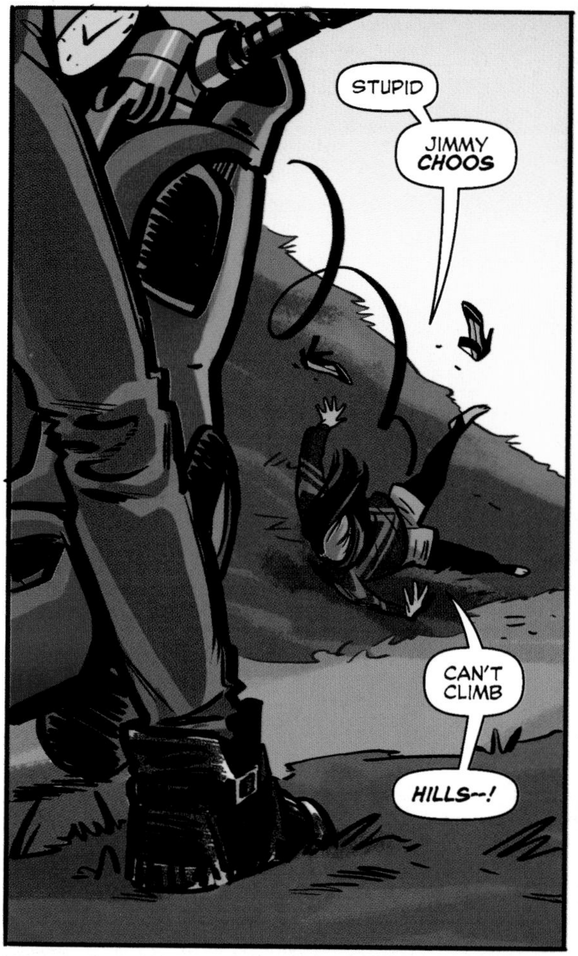
STUPID
JIMMY **CHOOS**
CAN'T CLIMB
HILLS--!

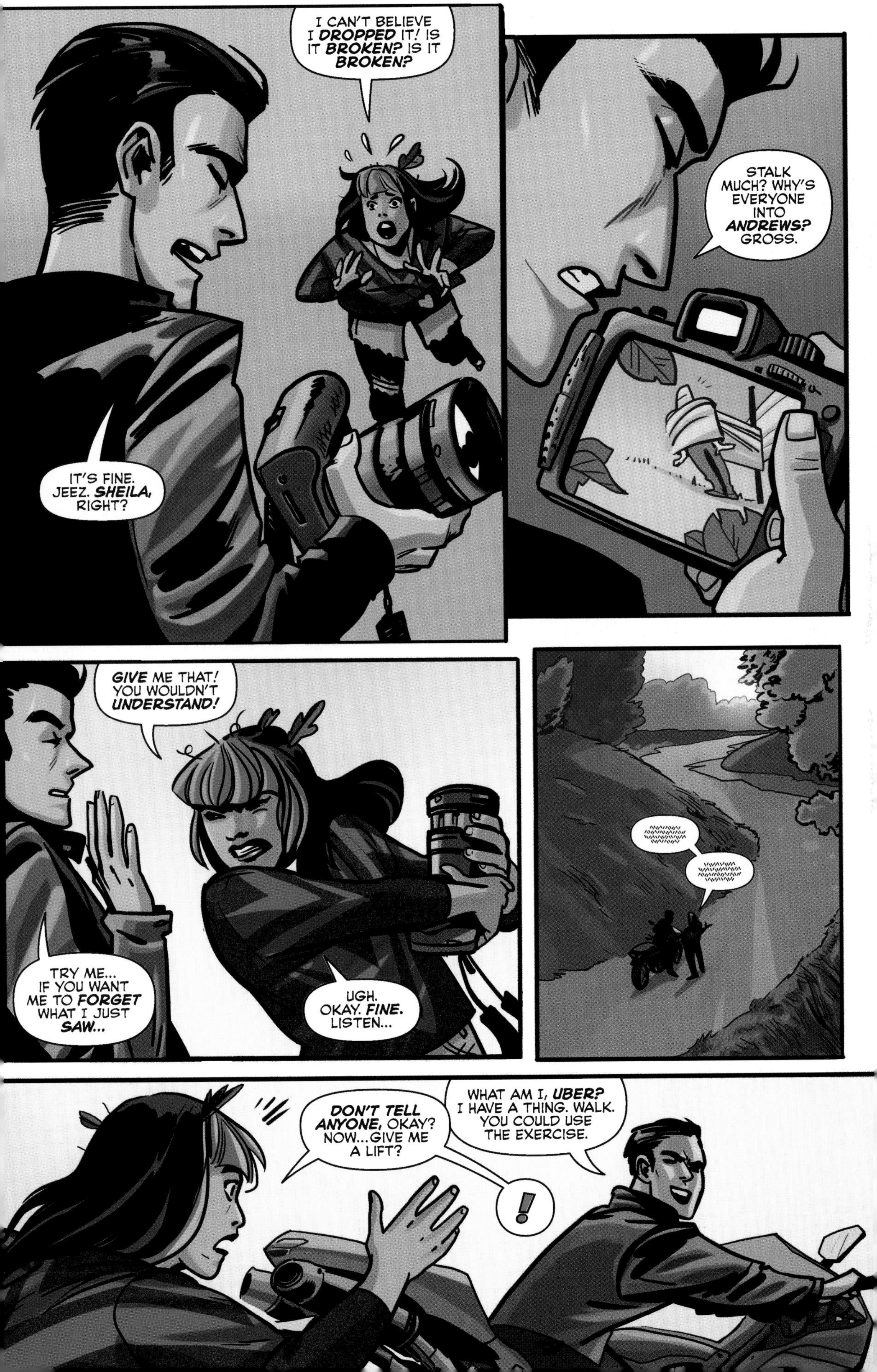
I CAN'T BELIEVE I DROPPED IT! IS IT BROKEN? IS IT BROKEN?
IT'S FINE. JEEZ. SHEILA, RIGHT?
STALK MUCH? WHY'S EVERYONE INTO ANDREWS? GROSS.
GIVE ME THAT! YOU WOULDN'T UNDERSTAND!
TRY ME... IF YOU WANT ME TO FORGET WHAT I JUST SAW...
UGH. OKAY. FINE. LISTEN...
DON'T TELL ANYONE, OKAY? NOW...GIVE ME A LIFT?
WHAT AM I, UBER? I HAVE A THING. WALK. YOU COULD USE THE EXERCISE.
!

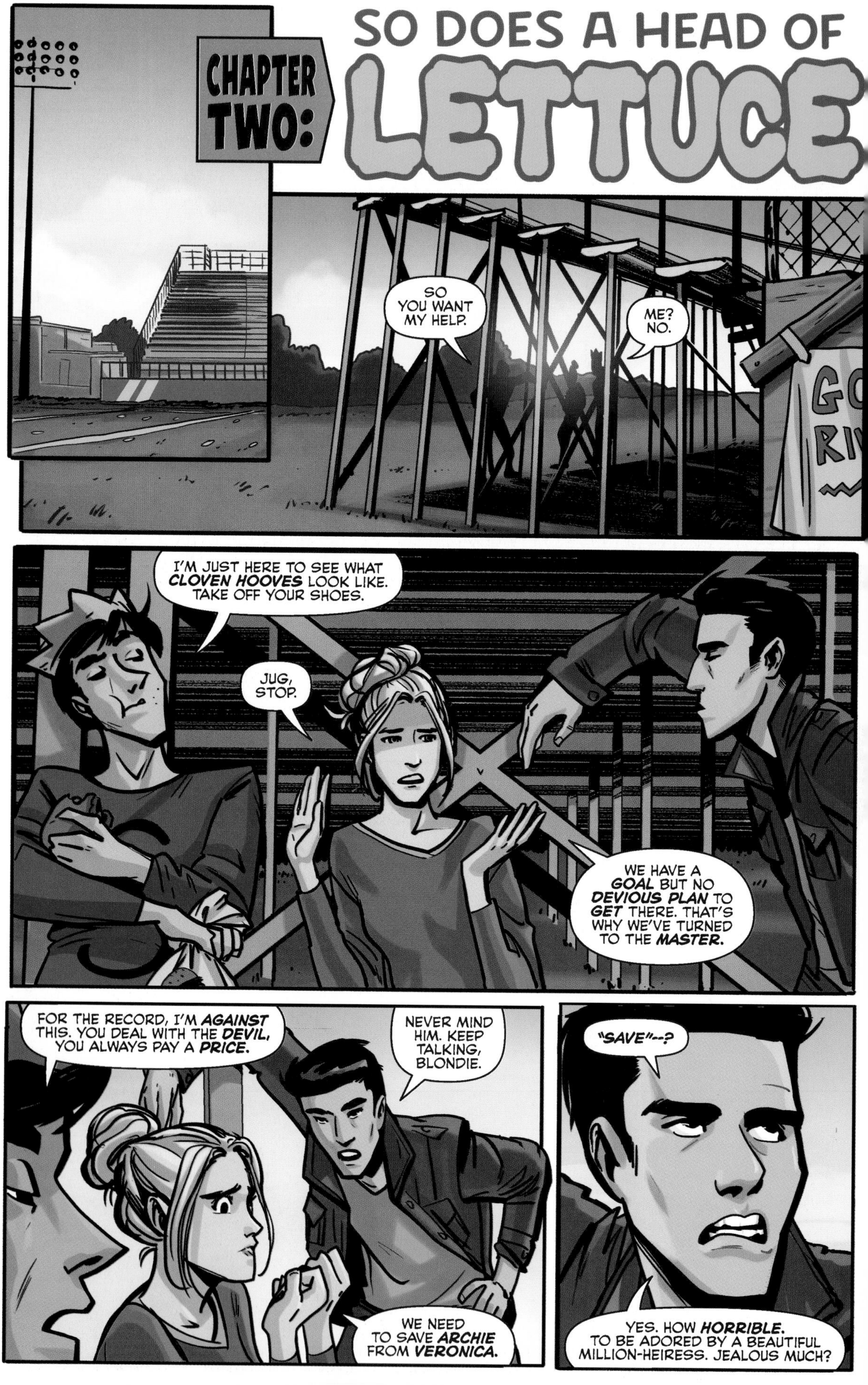
CHAPTER TWO:
SO DOES A HEAD OF
LETTUCE
SO YOU WANT MY HELP.
ME? NO.
GO RIV
I'M JUST HERE TO SEE WHAT CLOVEN HOOVES LOOK LIKE. TAKE OFF YOUR SHOES.
JUG, STOP.
WE HAVE A GOAL BUT NO DEVIOUS PLAN TO GET THERE. THAT'S WHY WE'VE TURNED TO THE MASTER.
FOR THE RECORD, I'M AGAINST THIS. YOU DEAL WITH THE DEVIL, YOU ALWAYS PAY A PRICE.
NEVER MIND HIM. KEEP TALKING, BLONDIE.
WE NEED TO SAVE ARCHIE FROM VERONICA.
"SAVE"--?
YES. HOW HORRIBLE. TO BE ADORED BY A BEAUTIFUL MILLION-HEIRESS. JEALOUS MUCH?

I'M NOT--

THAT IS *NOT* WHAT THIS IS ABOUT! WE BROKE UP *MONTHS* AGO! I DON'T *CARE* THAT WAY! BUT I DO *CARE*! WE *BOTH* DO!

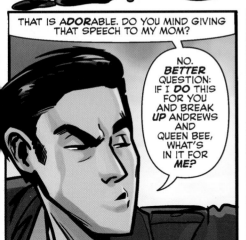

HE'S OUR *FRIEND* AND HE DESERVES SOMEONE WHO WILL *RESPECT* HIM!

THAT IS *ADORABLE.* DO YOU MIND GIVING THAT SPEECH TO MY MOM?

NO. *BETTER* QUESTION: IF I *DO* THIS FOR YOU AND BREAK *UP* ANDREWS AND QUEEN BEE, WHAT'S IN IT FOR *ME?*

A CLEAR SHOT AT THE *QUEEN BEE.*

PLEASE. THAT'S MINE TO *TAKE,* NOT YOURS TO *GIVE.* YOU WANT A FOOLPROOF PLAN, THEN GET ME A *FAKE I.D.*

AREN'T *YOU* THE GO-TO FOR THOSE?

MY SOURCE TAPPED OUT. I NEED A GOOD ONE. DON'T CARE WHERE YOU GET IT. WE ON?

I DON'T KNOW.

SOME FRIEND YOU ARE.

JERK.

ALL RIGHT. DEAL. WHAT NOW? WHAT'S YOUR PLAN?

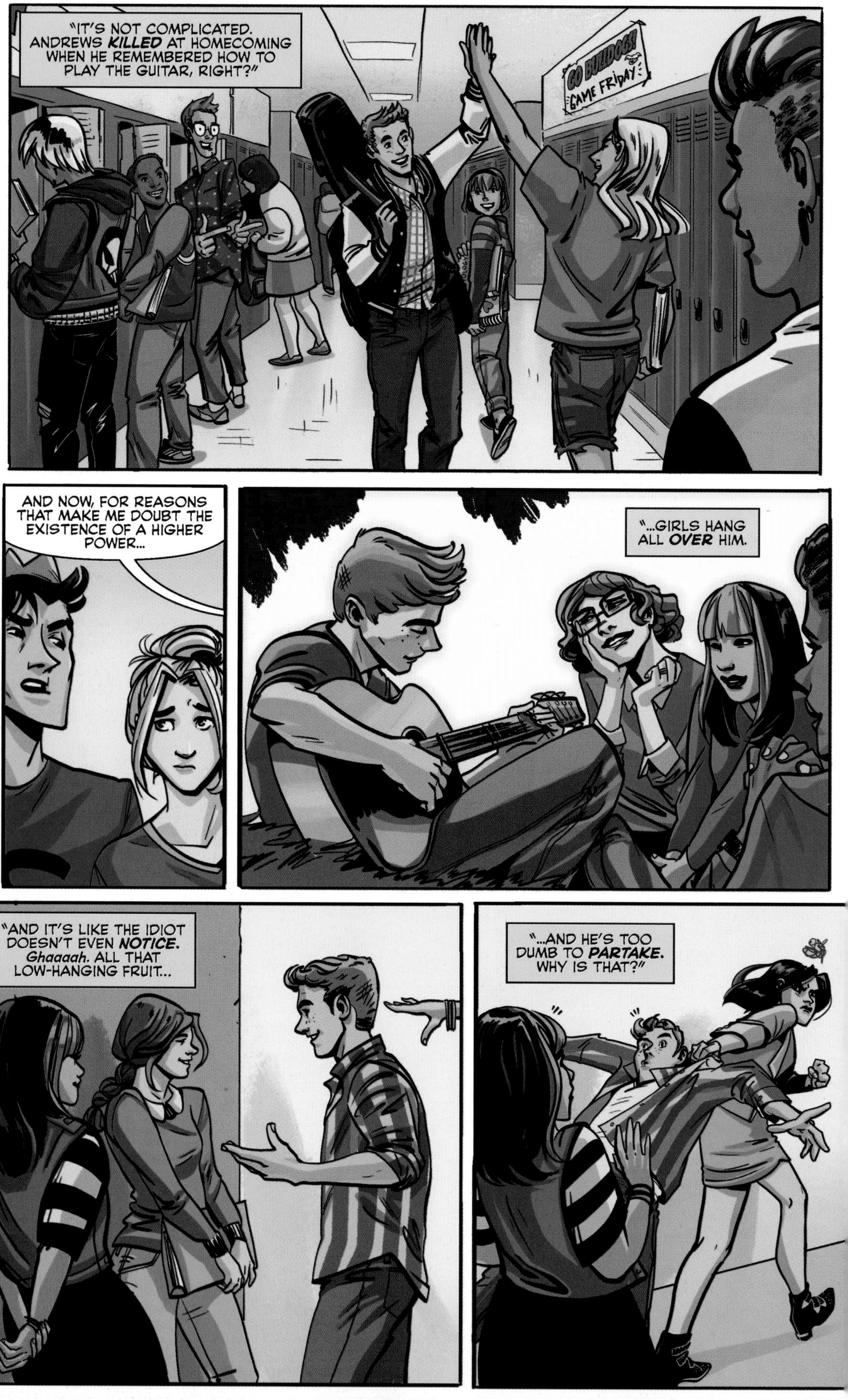
"IT'S NOT COMPLICATED. ANDREWS KILLED AT HOMECOMING WHEN HE REMEMBERED HOW TO PLAY THE GUITAR, RIGHT?"
GO BULLDOGS! GAME FRIDAY
AND NOW, FOR REASONS THAT MAKE ME DOUBT THE EXISTENCE OF A HIGHER POWER...
"...GIRLS HANG ALL OVER HIM.
"AND IT'S LIKE THE IDIOT DOESN'T EVEN NOTICE. Ghaaaah. ALL THAT LOW-HANGING FRUIT...
"...AND HE'S TOO DUMB TO PARTAKE. WHY IS THAT?"

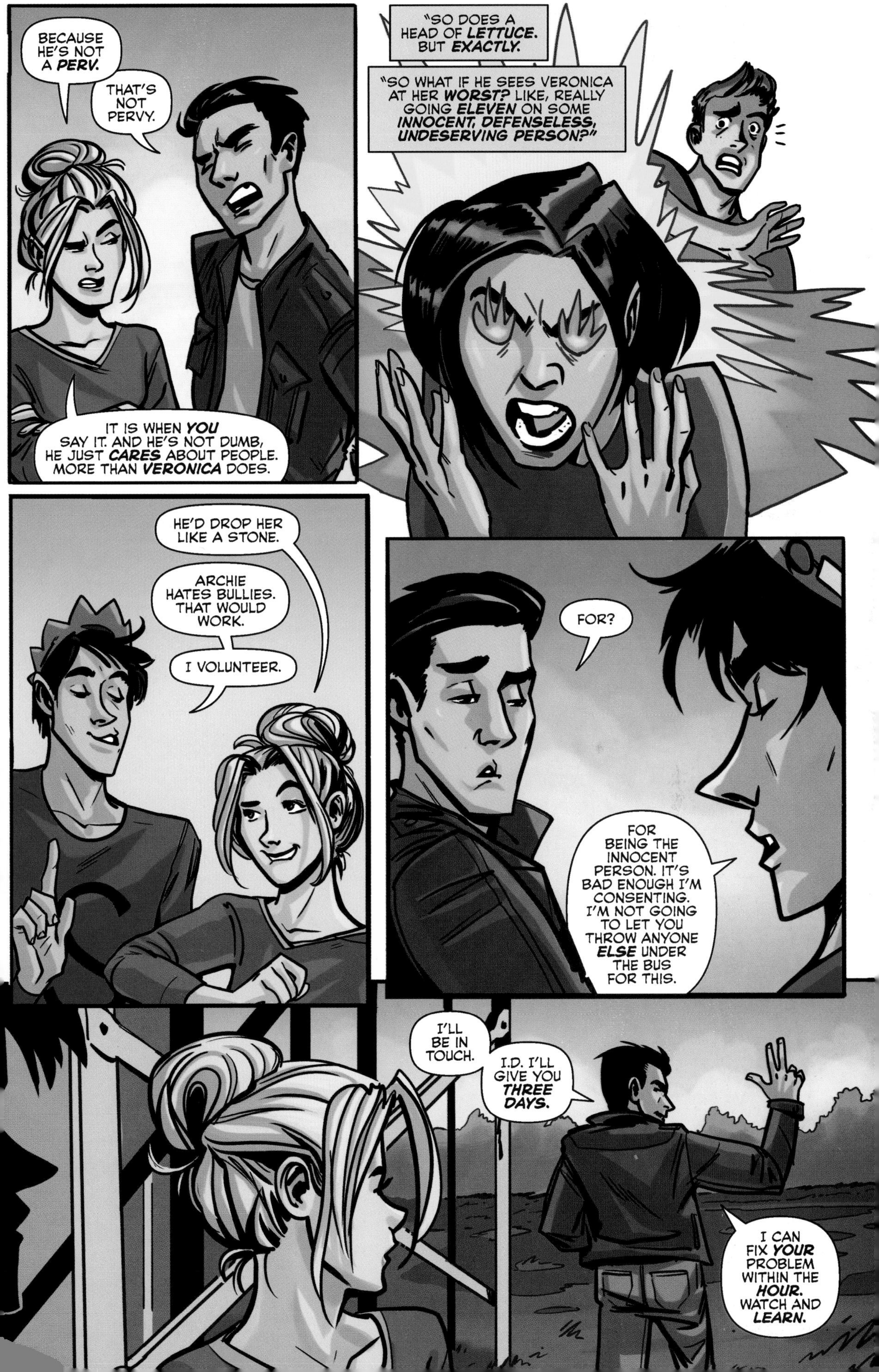
BECAUSE HE'S NOT A PERV.
THAT'S NOT PERVY.
IT IS WHEN YOU SAY IT. AND HE'S NOT DUMB, HE JUST CARES ABOUT PEOPLE. MORE THAN VERONICA DOES.
"SO DOES A HEAD OF LETTUCE. BUT EXACTLY.
"SO WHAT IF HE SEES VERONICA AT HER WORST? LIKE, REALLY GOING ELEVEN ON SOME INNOCENT, DEFENSELESS, UNDESERVING PERSON?"
HE'D DROP HER LIKE A STONE.
ARCHIE HATES BULLIES. THAT WOULD WORK.
I VOLUNTEER.
FOR?
FOR BEING THE INNOCENT PERSON. IT'S BAD ENOUGH I'M CONSENTING. I'M NOT GOING TO LET YOU THROW ANYONE ELSE UNDER THE BUS FOR THIS.
I'LL BE IN TOUCH.
I.D. I'LL GIVE YOU THREE DAYS.
I CAN FIX YOUR PROBLEM WITHIN THE HOUR. WATCH AND LEARN.

CHAPTER THREE: This could get MESSY

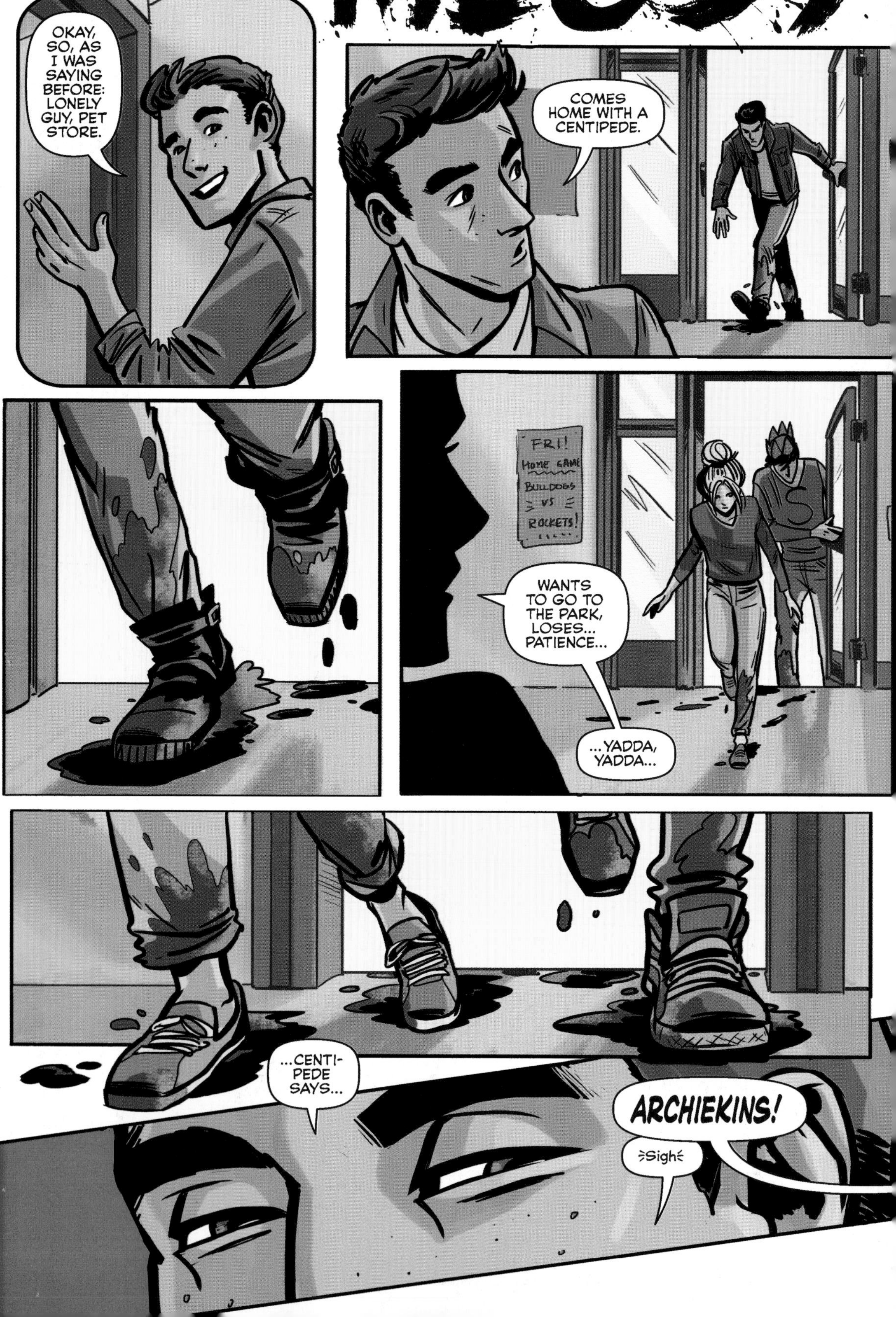

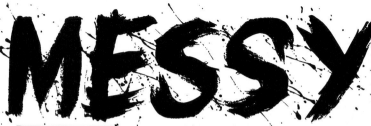

OKAY, SO, AS I WAS SAYING BEFORE: LONELY GUY, PET STORE.
COMES HOME WITH A CENTIPEDE.
FRI! HOME GAME BULLDOGS VS ROCKETS!
WANTS TO GO TO THE PARK, LOSES... PATIENCE...
...YADDA, YADDA...
...CENTI-PEDE SAYS...
ARCHIEKINS!
Sigh

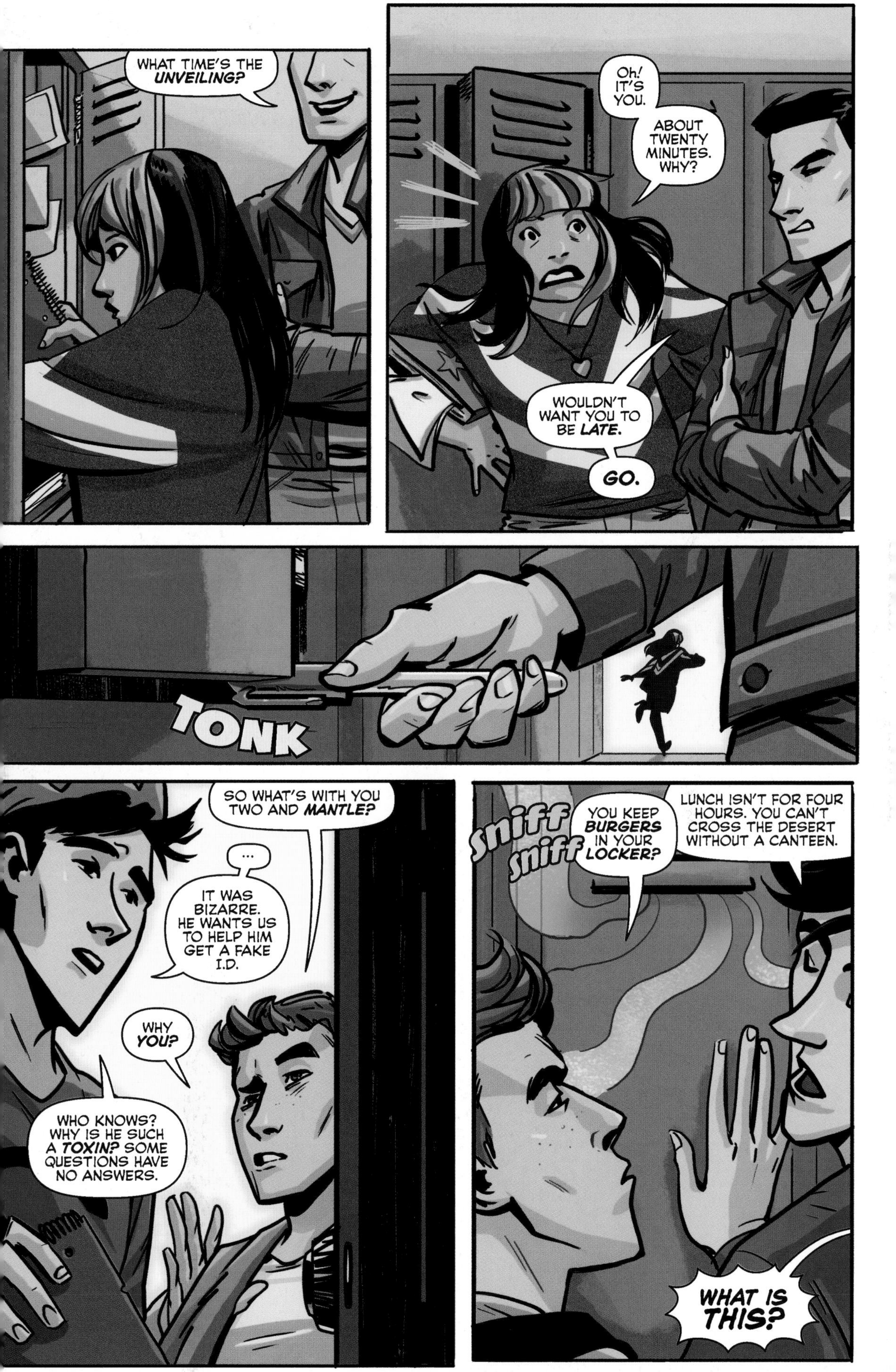
WHAT TIME'S THE **UNVEILING?**
Oh! IT'S YOU.
ABOUT TWENTY MINUTES. WHY?
WOULDN'T WANT YOU TO BE **LATE.**
GO.
TONK
SO WHAT'S WITH YOU TWO AND **MANTLE?**
...
IT WAS BIZARRE. HE WANTS US TO HELP HIM GET A FAKE I.D.
WHY **YOU?**
WHO KNOWS? WHY IS HE SUCH A **TOXIN?** SOME QUESTIONS HAVE NO ANSWERS.
Sniff Sniff
YOU KEEP **BURGERS** IN YOUR **LOCKER?**
LUNCH ISN'T FOR FOUR HOURS. YOU CAN'T CROSS THE DESERT WITHOUT A CANTEEN.
WHAT IS THIS?

SHEILA'S REALLY GOT A **RAGE ON** FOR **RED**. THOUGHT YOU SHOULD KNOW. HOPE SHE DOESN'T **STEAL** HIM FROM Y--

NO ONE.

STEALS.

FROM A **LODGE**.

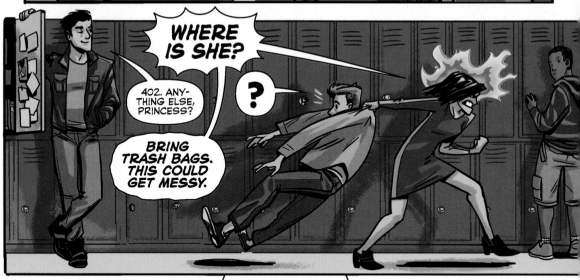

WHERE IS SHE?

402. ANYTHING ELSE, PRINCESS?

?

BRING TRASH BAGS. THIS COULD GET MESSY.

I **TOLD** YOU THIS WAS A BAD IDEA, COOPER...

WHAT DID YOU **DO**? WE SAID **I** WAS GOING TO BE THE TARGET OF **HURRICANE NARCISSUS**!

YOU SAID. THIS IS **BETTER**. YOU WANT **RESULTS**...

...DON'T **SPOIL** THIS!

WE HAVE TO GET THERE BEFORE VERONICA CAN SEE WHAT'S **REALLY** GOING ON!

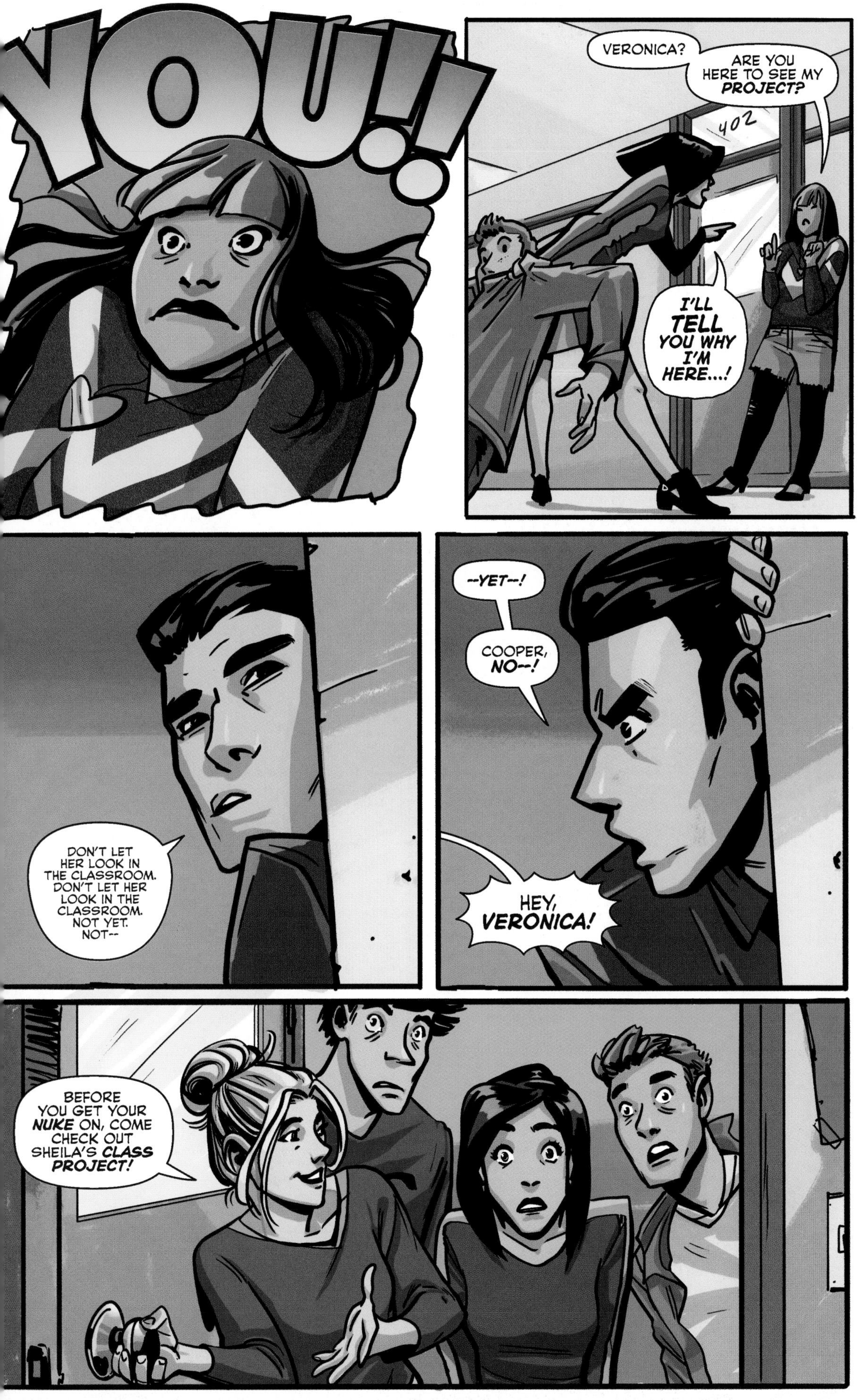
YOU!!
VERONICA?
ARE YOU HERE TO SEE MY PROJECT?
I'LL TELL YOU WHY I'M HERE...!
DON'T LET HER LOOK IN THE CLASSROOM. DON'T LET HER LOOK IN THE CLASSROOM. NOT YET. NOT--
--YET--!
COOPER, NO--!
HEY, VERONICA!
BEFORE YOU GET YOUR NUKE ON, COME CHECK OUT SHEILA'S CLASS PROJECT!

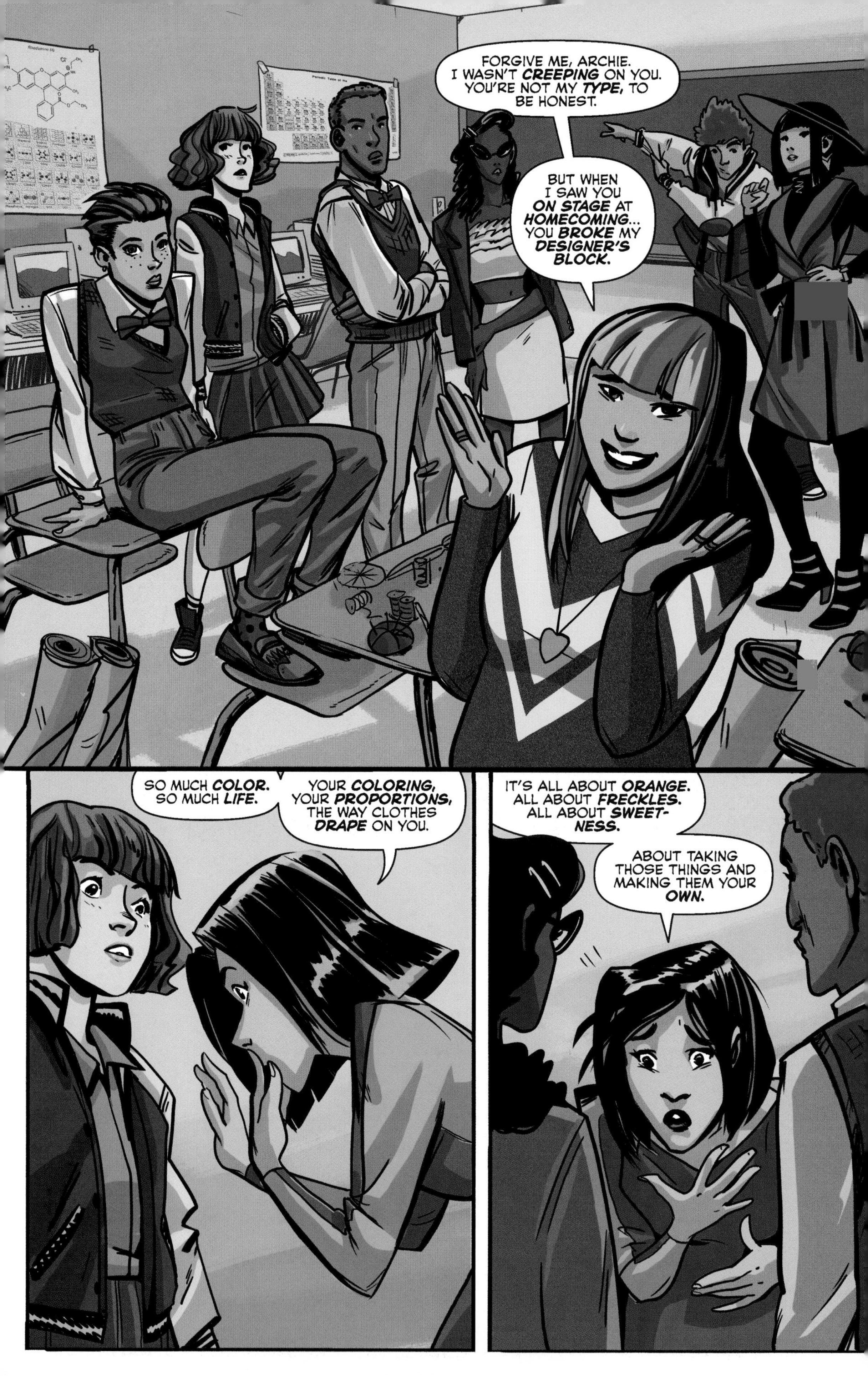
FORGIVE ME, ARCHIE. I WASN'T **CREEPING** ON YOU. YOU'RE NOT MY **TYPE**, TO BE HONEST.
BUT WHEN I SAW YOU **ON STAGE** AT **HOMECOMING**... YOU **BROKE** MY **DESIGNER'S BLOCK.**
SO MUCH **COLOR.** SO MUCH **LIFE.**
YOUR **COLORING,** YOUR **PROPORTIONS,** THE WAY CLOTHES **DRAPE** ON YOU.
IT'S ALL ABOUT **ORANGE.** ALL ABOUT **FRECKLES.** ALL ABOUT **SWEET-NESS.**
ABOUT TAKING THOSE THINGS AND MAKING THEM YOUR **OWN.**

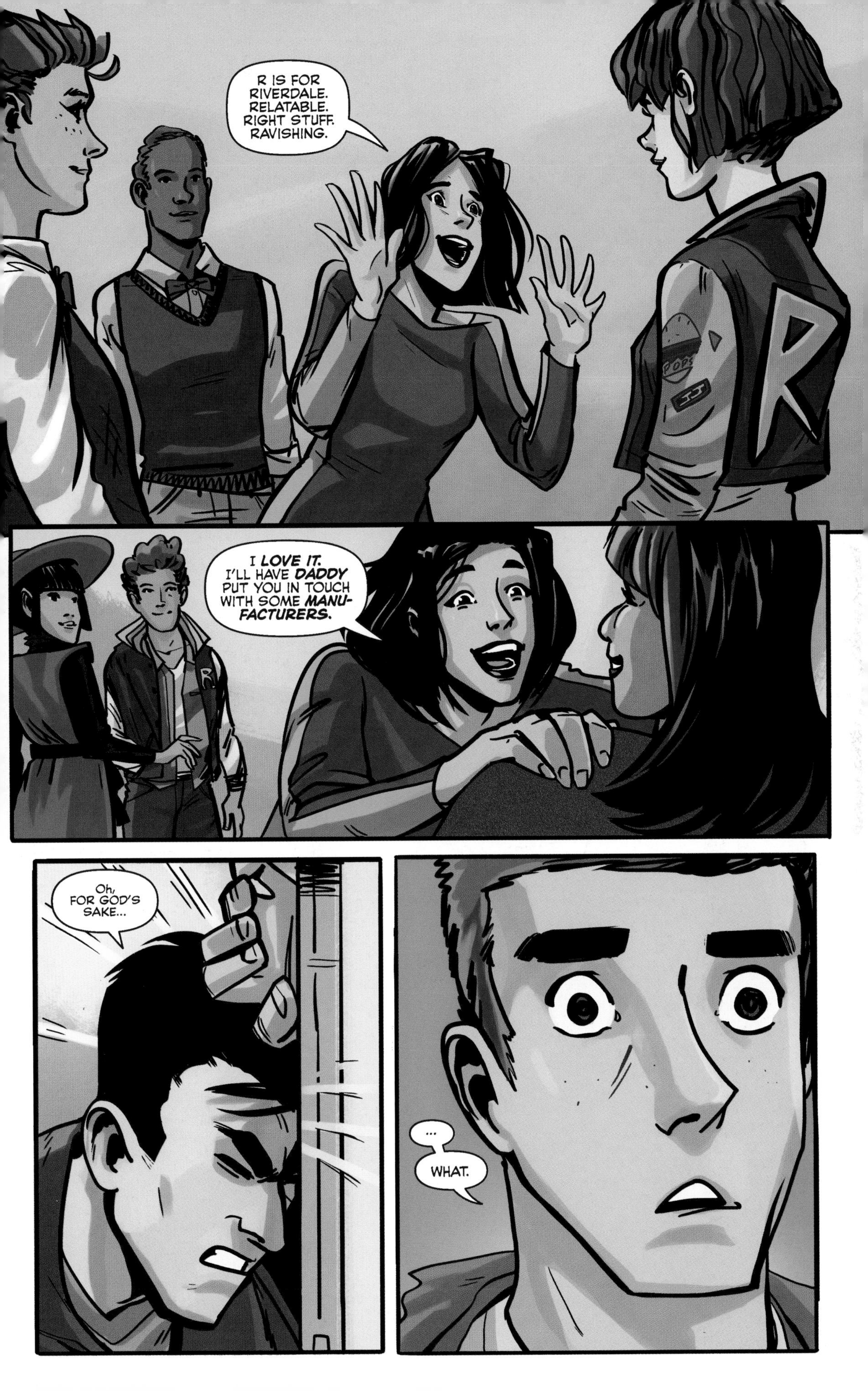
R IS FOR RIVERDALE. RELATABLE. RIGHT STUFF. RAVISHING.
I **LOVE IT.** I'LL HAVE **DADDY** PUT YOU IN TOUCH WITH SOME **MANU-FACTURERS.**
Oh, FOR GOD'S SAKE...
...
WHAT.

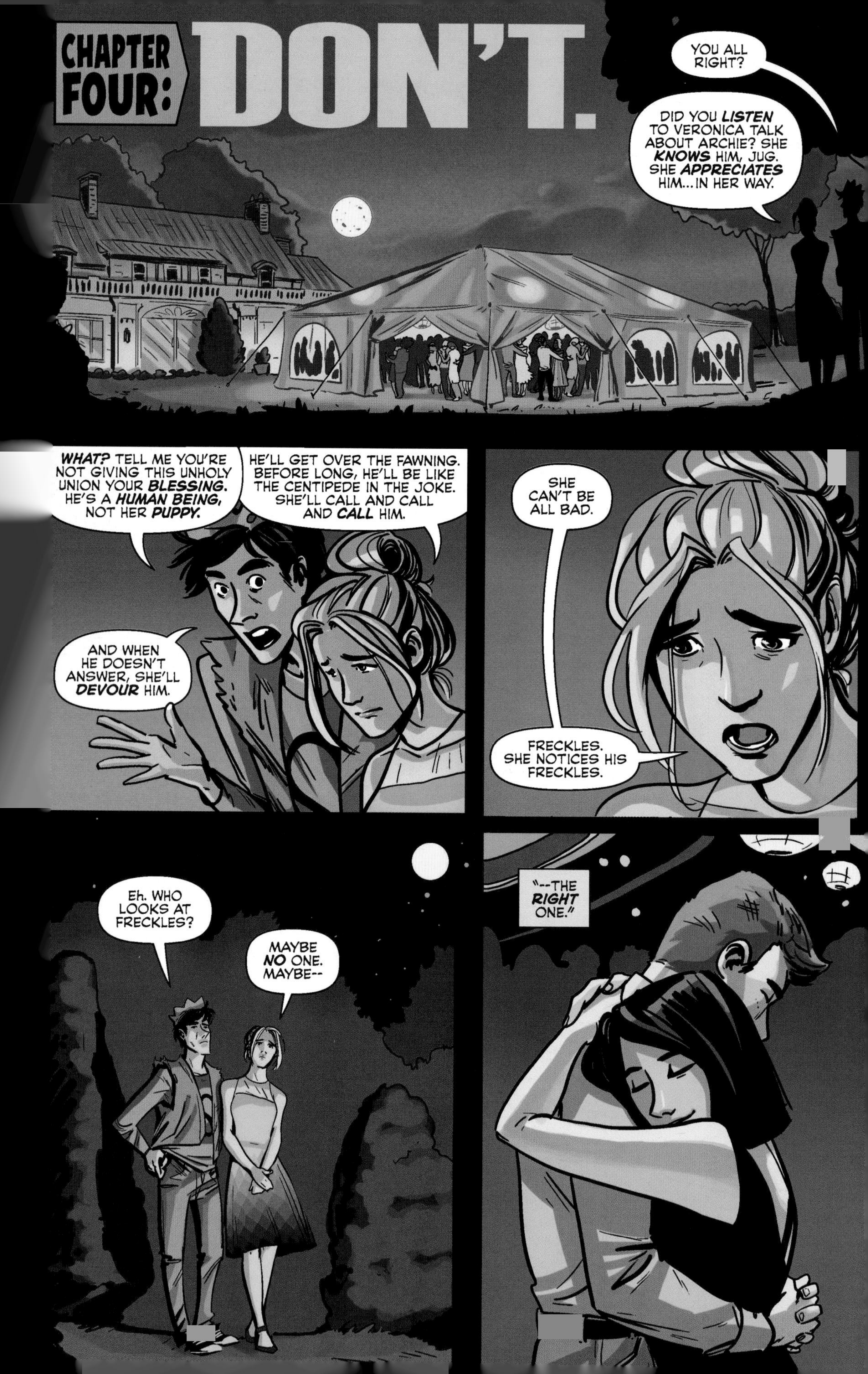
CHAPTER FOUR: DON'T.
YOU ALL RIGHT?
DID YOU LISTEN TO VERONICA TALK ABOUT ARCHIE? SHE KNOWS HIM, JUG. SHE APPRECIATES HIM...IN HER WAY.
WHAT? TELL ME YOU'RE NOT GIVING THIS UNHOLY UNION YOUR BLESSING. HE'S A HUMAN BEING, NOT HER PUPPY.
HE'LL GET OVER THE FAWNING. BEFORE LONG, HE'LL BE LIKE THE CENTIPEDE IN THE JOKE. SHE'LL CALL AND CALL AND CALL HIM.
AND WHEN HE DOESN'T ANSWER, SHE'LL DEVOUR HIM.
SHE CAN'T BE ALL BAD.
FRECKLES. SHE NOTICES HIS FRECKLES.
Eh. WHO LOOKS AT FRECKLES?
MAYBE NO ONE. MAYBE--
"--THE RIGHT ONE."

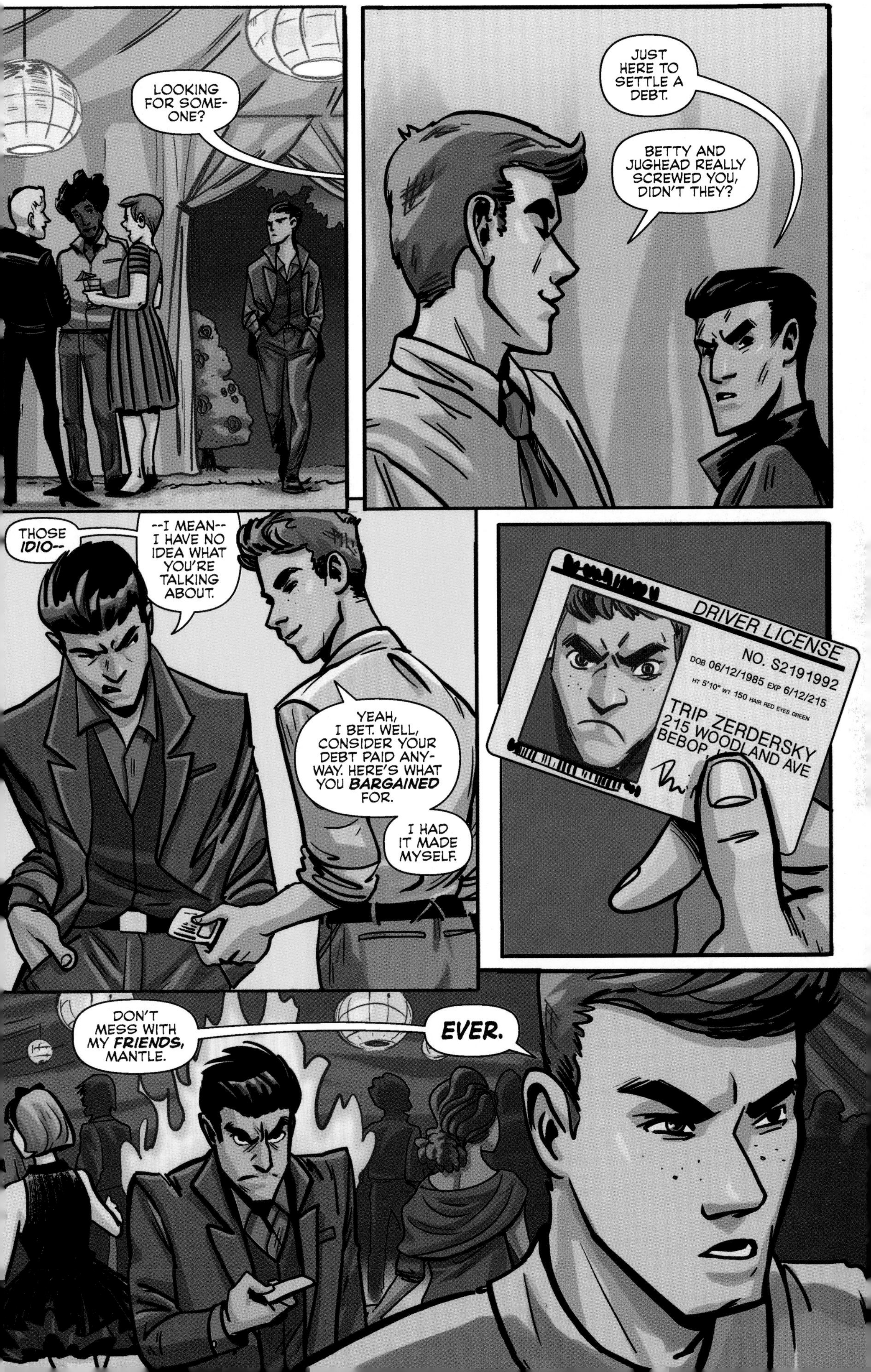

LOOKING FOR SOME-ONE?
JUST HERE TO SETTLE A DEBT.
BETTY AND JUGHEAD REALLY SCREWED YOU, DIDN'T THEY?
THOSE *IDIO--*
--I MEAN-- I HAVE NO IDEA WHAT YOU'RE TALKING ABOUT.
YEAH, I BET. WELL, CONSIDER YOUR DEBT PAID ANY-WAY. HERE'S WHAT YOU ***BARGAINED*** FOR.
I HAD IT MADE MYSELF.
DRIVER LICENSE
NO. S2191992
DOB 06/12/1985 EXP 6/12/215
HT 5'10" WT 150 HAIR RED EYES GREEN
TRIP ZERDERSKY
215 WOODLAND AVE
BEBOP
DON'T MESS WITH MY ***FRIENDS,*** MANTLE.
EVER.

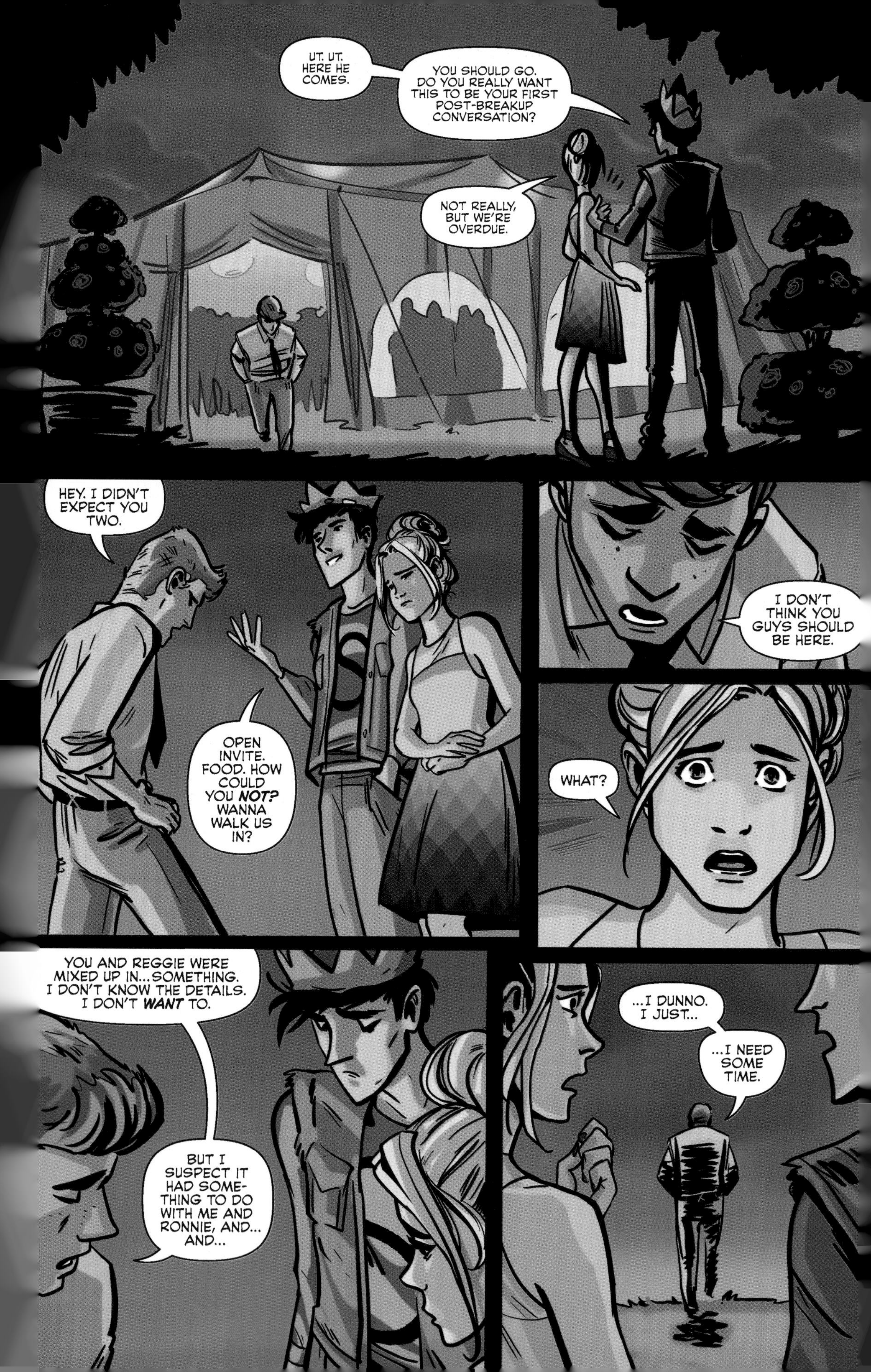
UT. UT. HERE HE COMES.
YOU SHOULD GO. DO YOU REALLY WANT THIS TO BE YOUR FIRST POST-BREAKUP CONVERSATION?
NOT REALLY, BUT WE'RE OVERDUE.
HEY. I DIDN'T EXPECT YOU TWO.
OPEN INVITE. FOOD. HOW COULD YOU NOT? WANNA WALK US IN?
I DON'T THINK YOU GUYS SHOULD BE HERE.
WHAT?
YOU AND REGGIE WERE MIXED UP IN...SOMETHING. I DON'T KNOW THE DETAILS. I DON'T WANT TO.
BUT I SUSPECT IT HAD SOME-THING TO DO WITH ME AND RONNIE, AND... AND...
...I DUNNO. I JUST...
...I NEED SOME TIME.

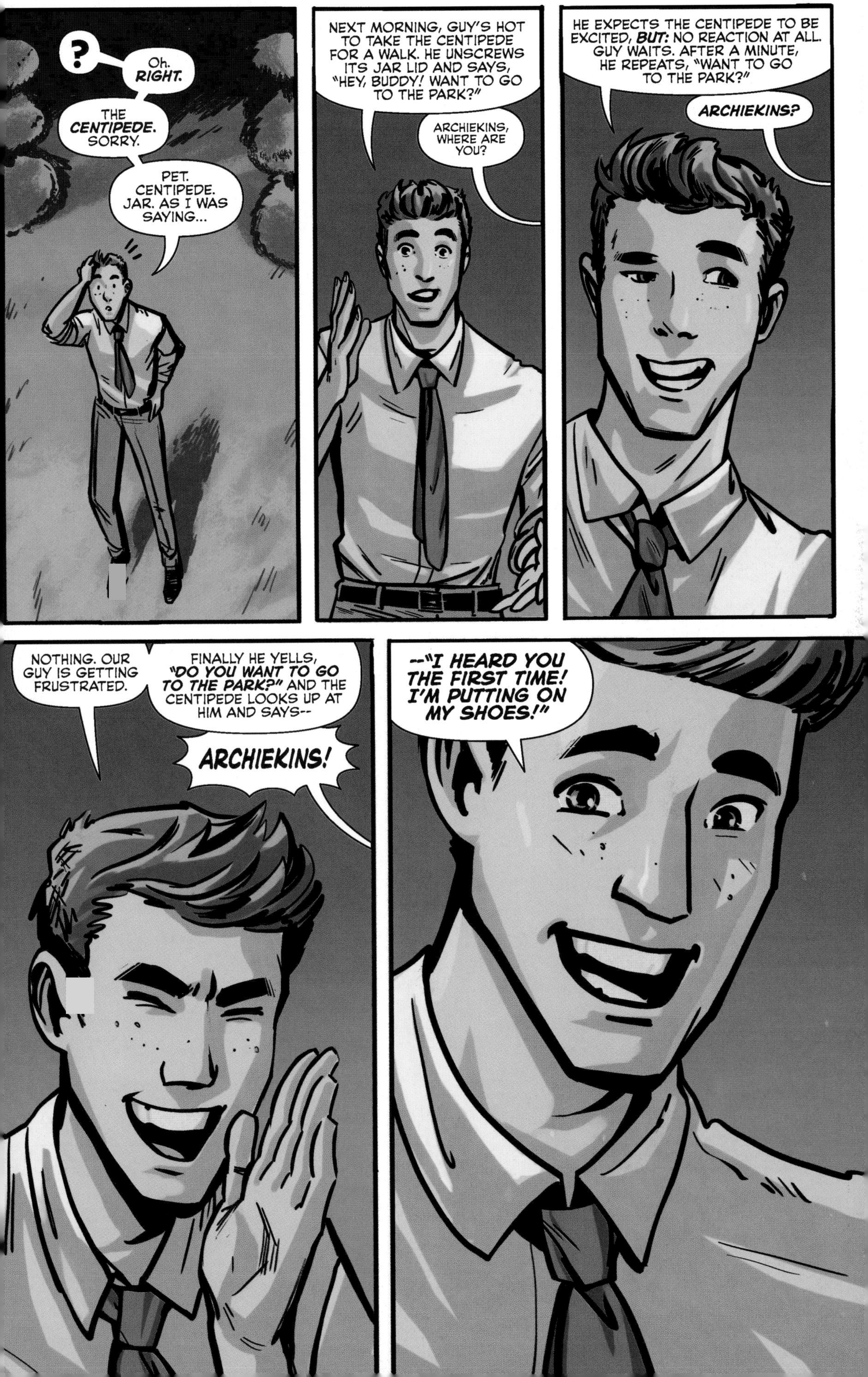
?
Oh. RIGHT.
THE CENTIPEDE. SORRY.
PET. CENTIPEDE. JAR. AS I WAS SAYING...
NEXT MORNING, GUY'S HOT TO TAKE THE CENTIPEDE FOR A WALK. HE UNSCREWS ITS JAR LID AND SAYS, "HEY, BUDDY! WANT TO GO TO THE PARK?"
ARCHIEKINS, WHERE ARE YOU?
HE EXPECTS THE CENTIPEDE TO BE EXCITED, BUT: NO REACTION AT ALL. GUY WAITS. AFTER A MINUTE, HE REPEATS, "WANT TO GO TO THE PARK?"
ARCHIEKINS?
NOTHING. OUR GUY IS GETTING FRUSTRATED.
FINALLY HE YELLS, "DO YOU WANT TO GO TO THE PARK?" AND THE CENTIPEDE LOOKS UP AT HIM AND SAYS--
ARCHIEKINS!
--"I HEARD YOU THE FIRST TIME! I'M PUTTING ON MY SHOES!"

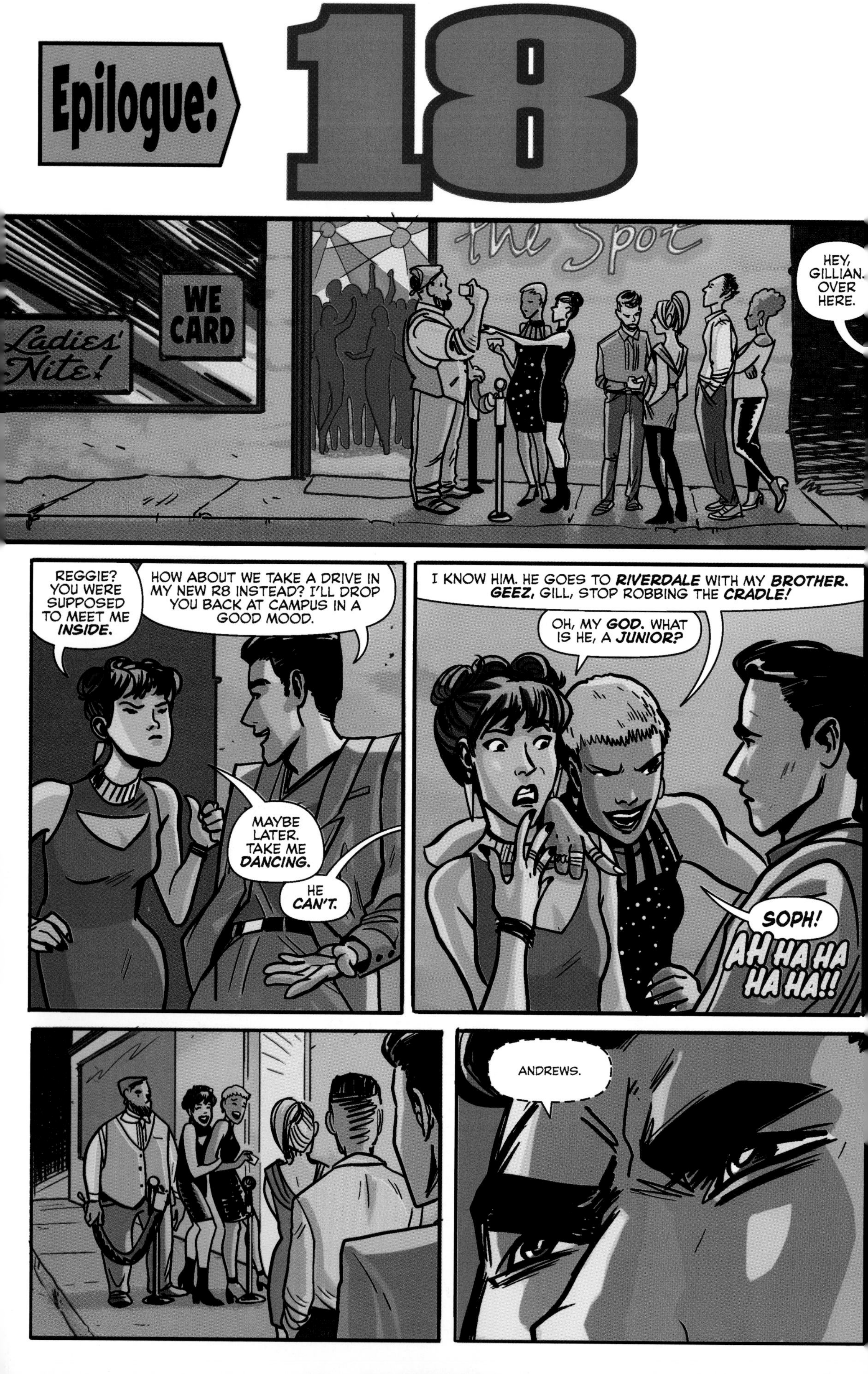
Epilogue:
18
Ladies' Nite!
WE CARD
the Spot
HEY, GILLIAN. OVER HERE.
REGGIE? YOU WERE SUPPOSED TO MEET ME INSIDE.
HOW ABOUT WE TAKE A DRIVE IN MY NEW R8 INSTEAD? I'LL DROP YOU BACK AT CAMPUS IN A GOOD MOOD.
MAYBE LATER. TAKE ME DANCING.
HE CAN'T.
I KNOW HIM. HE GOES TO RIVERDALE WITH MY BROTHER. GEEZ, GILL, STOP ROBBING THE CRADLE!
OH, MY GOD. WHAT IS HE, A JUNIOR?
SOPH!
AH HA HA HA HA!!
ANDREWS.

TO BE CONTINUED...

ISSUE SIX

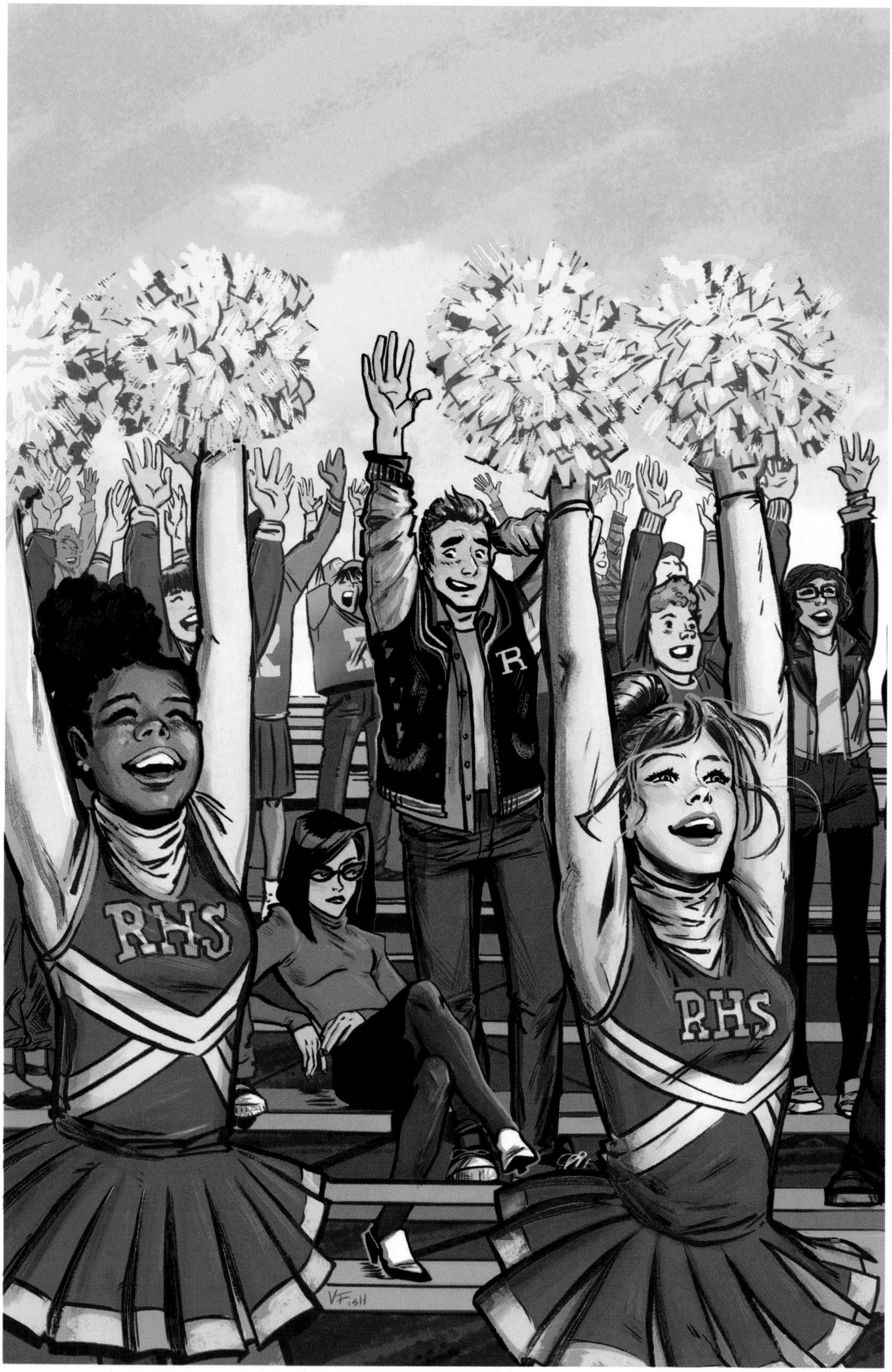
RHS
RHS

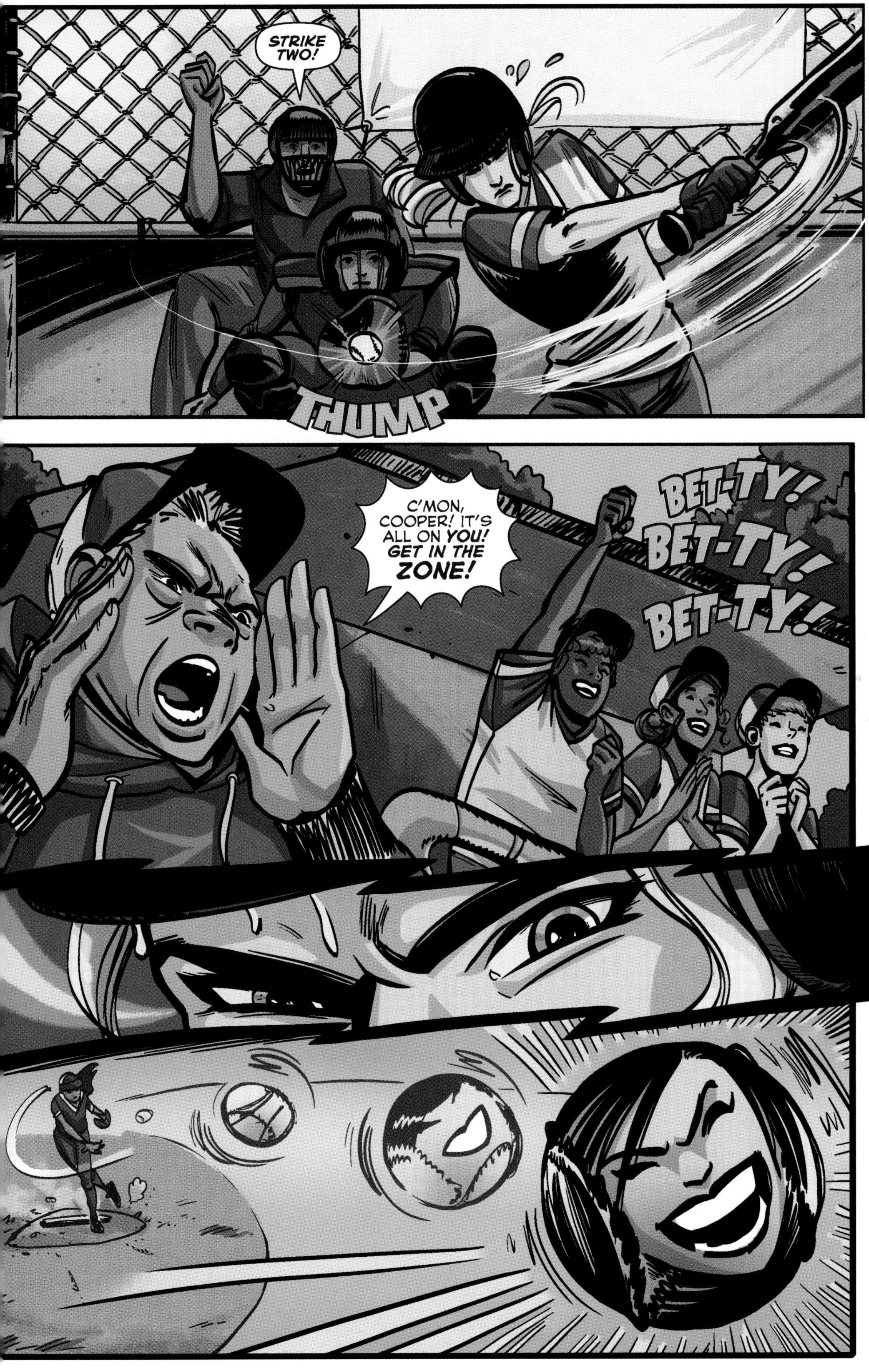
STRIKE TWO!
THUMP
C'MON, COOPER! IT'S ALL ON YOU! GET IN THE ZONE!
BET-TY! BET-TY! BET-TY!

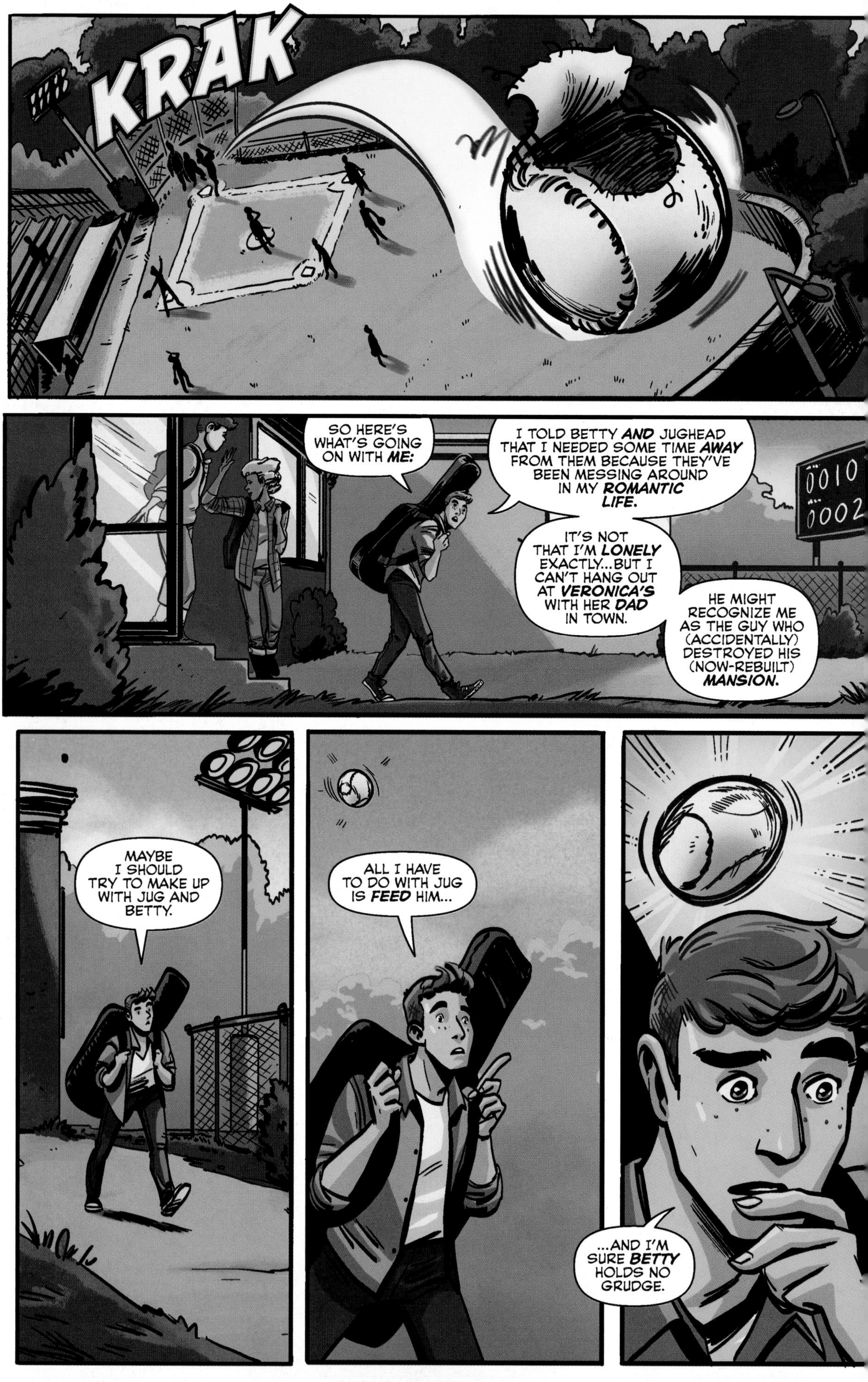
KRAK
SO HERE'S WHAT'S GOING ON WITH ME:
I TOLD BETTY AND JUGHEAD THAT I NEEDED SOME TIME AWAY FROM THEM BECAUSE THEY'VE BEEN MESSING AROUND IN MY ROMANTIC LIFE.
IT'S NOT THAT I'M LONELY EXACTLY...BUT I CAN'T HANG OUT AT VERONICA'S WITH HER DAD IN TOWN.
HE MIGHT RECOGNIZE ME AS THE GUY WHO (ACCIDENTALLY) DESTROYED HIS (NOW-REBUILT) MANSION.
MAYBE I SHOULD TRY TO MAKE UP WITH JUG AND BETTY.
ALL I HAVE TO DO WITH JUG IS FEED HIM...
...AND I'M SURE BETTY HOLDS NO GRUDGE.

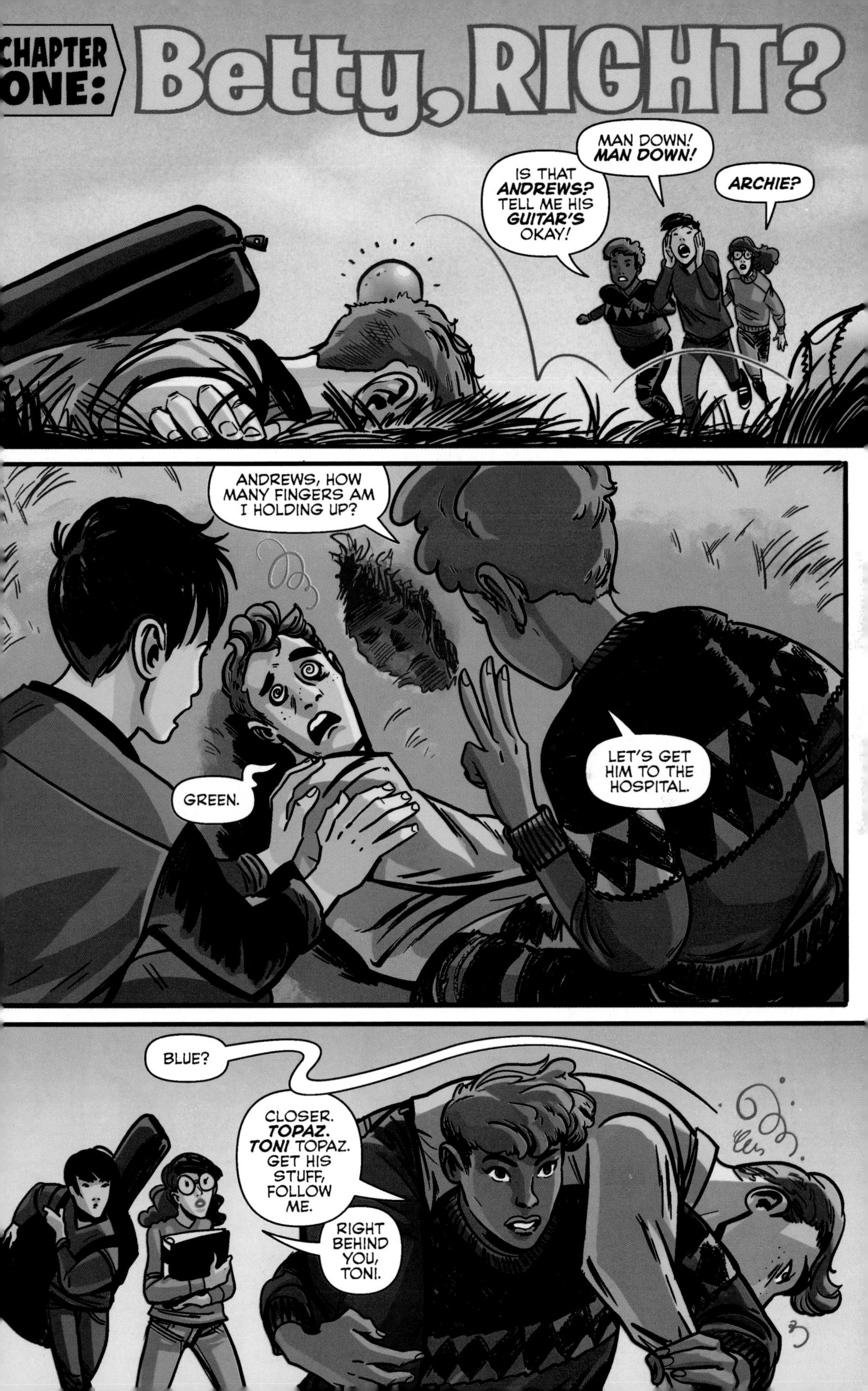
CHAPTER ONE: Betty, RIGHT?
IS THAT ANDREWS? TELL ME HIS GUITAR'S OKAY!
MAN DOWN! MAN DOWN!
ARCHIE?
ANDREWS, HOW MANY FINGERS AM I HOLDING UP?
GREEN.
LET'S GET HIM TO THE HOSPITAL.
BLUE?
CLOSER. TOPAZ. TONI TOPAZ. GET HIS STUFF, FOLLOW ME.
RIGHT BEHIND YOU, TONI.

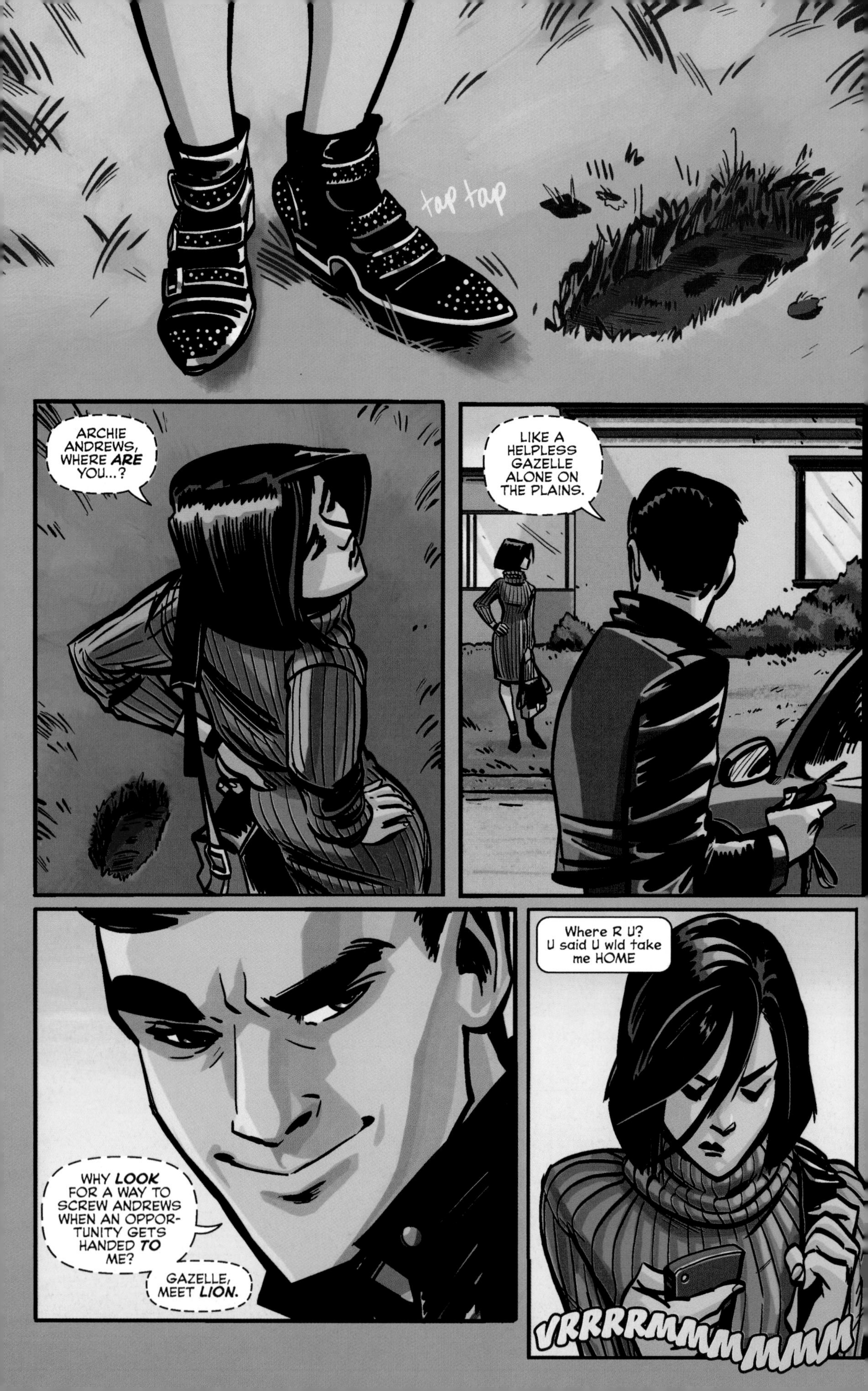
tap tap
ARCHIE ANDREWS, WHERE **ARE** YOU...?
LIKE A HELPLESS GAZELLE ALONE ON THE PLAINS.
WHY **LOOK** FOR A WAY TO SCREW ANDREWS WHEN AN OPPORTUNITY GETS HANDED **TO** ME?
GAZELLE, MEET **LION**.
Where R U? U said U wld take me HOME
VRRRRMMMMMMMM

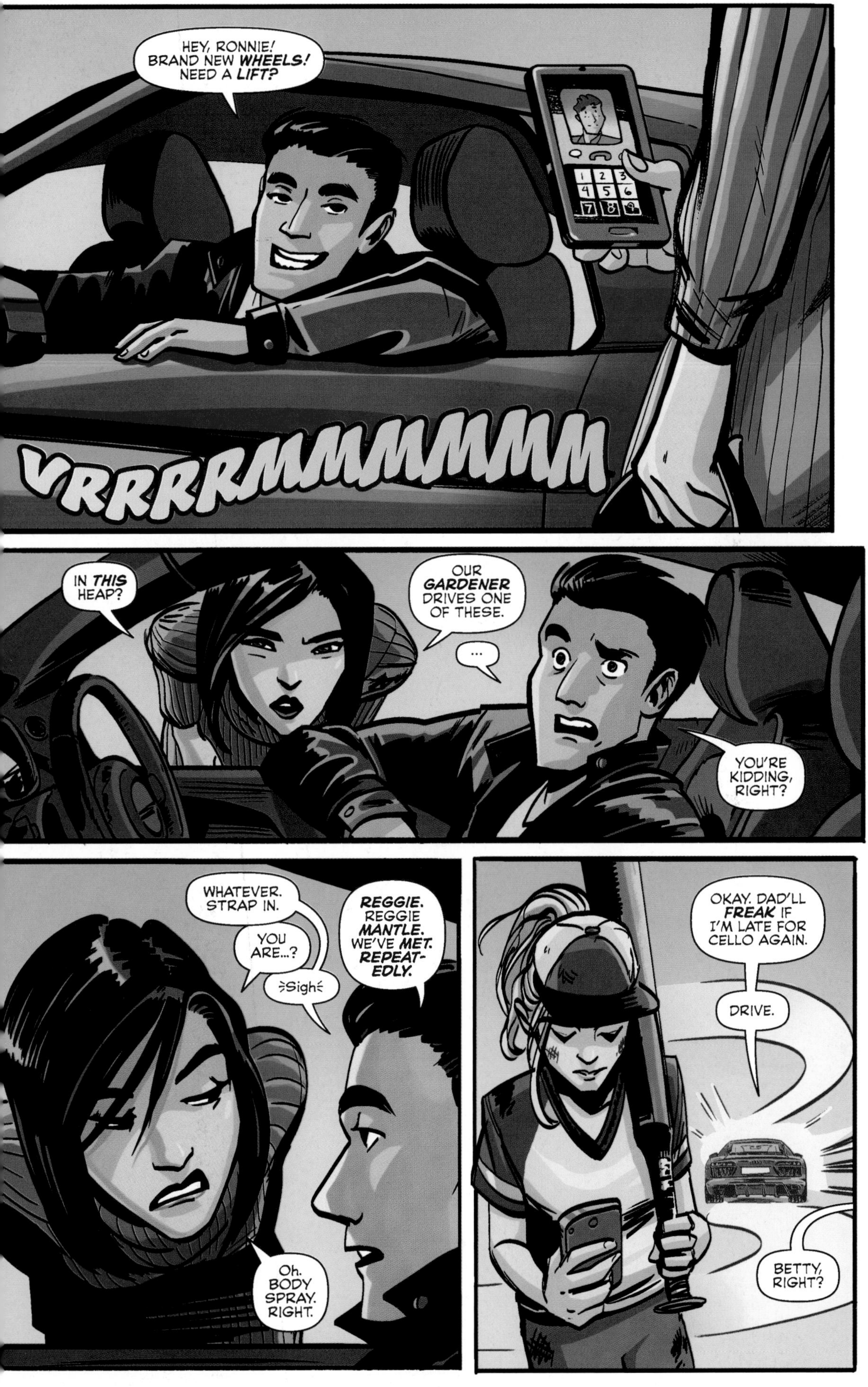
HEY, RONNIE! BRAND NEW WHEELS! NEED A LIFT?
VRRRRMMMMMMM
IN THIS HEAP?
OUR GARDENER DRIVES ONE OF THESE.
...
YOU'RE KIDDING, RIGHT?
WHATEVER. STRAP IN.
YOU ARE...?
Sigh
REGGIE. REGGIE MANTLE. WE'VE MET. REPEAT-EDLY.
Oh. BODY SPRAY. RIGHT.
OKAY. DAD'LL FREAK IF I'M LATE FOR CELLO AGAIN.
DRIVE.
BETTY, RIGHT?

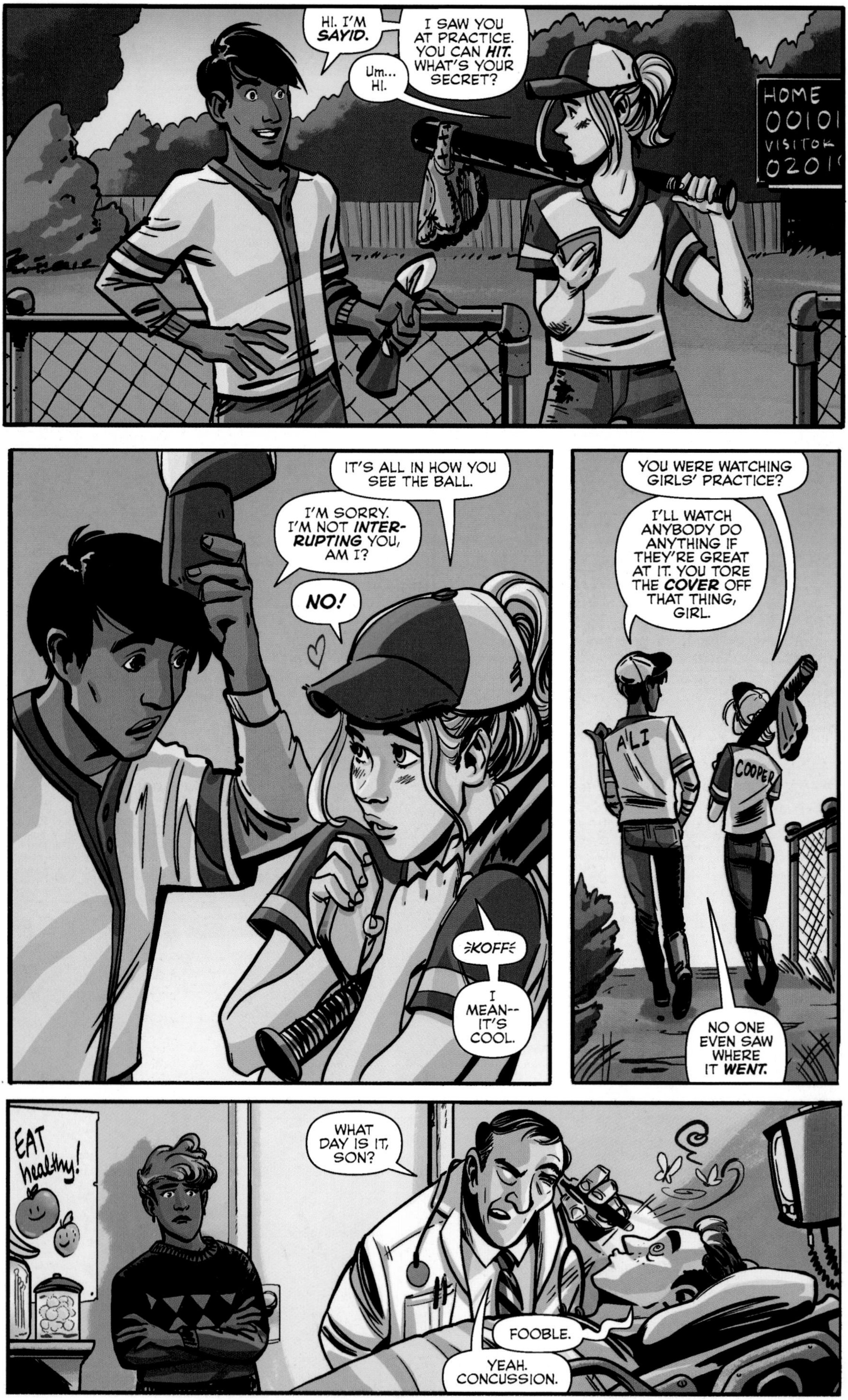

HI. I'M SAYID.
Um... HI.
I SAW YOU AT PRACTICE. YOU CAN HIT. WHAT'S YOUR SECRET?
HOME
00101
VISITOR
0201
IT'S ALL IN HOW YOU SEE THE BALL.
I'M SORRY. I'M NOT INTERRUPTING YOU, AM I?
NO!
KOFF
I MEAN-- IT'S COOL.
YOU WERE WATCHING GIRLS' PRACTICE?
I'LL WATCH ANYBODY DO ANYTHING IF THEY'RE GREAT AT IT. YOU TORE THE COVER OFF THAT THING, GIRL.
ALI
COOPER
NO ONE EVEN SAW WHERE IT WENT.
EAT healthy!
WHAT DAY IS IT, SON?
FOOBLE.
YEAH. CONCUSSION.

CHAPTER TWO: KIND OF A BIG DEAL

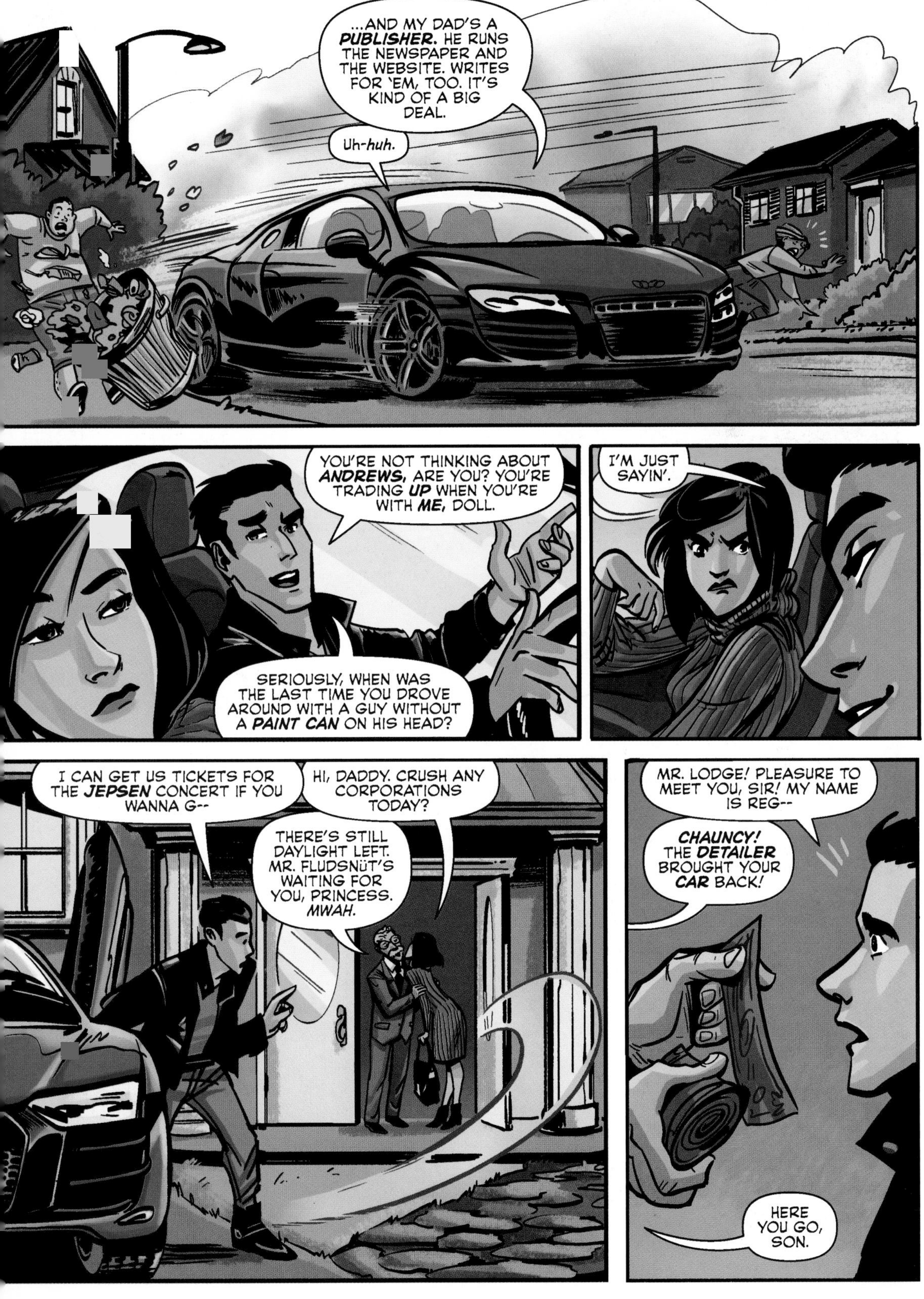

...AND MY DAD'S A PUBLISHER. HE RUNS THE NEWSPAPER AND THE WEBSITE. WRITES FOR 'EM, TOO. IT'S KIND OF A BIG DEAL.
Uh-huh.
YOU'RE NOT THINKING ABOUT ANDREWS, ARE YOU? YOU'RE TRADING UP WHEN YOU'RE WITH ME, DOLL.
SERIOUSLY, WHEN WAS THE LAST TIME YOU DROVE AROUND WITH A GUY WITHOUT A PAINT CAN ON HIS HEAD?
I'M JUST SAYIN'.
I CAN GET US TICKETS FOR THE JEPSEN CONCERT IF YOU WANNA G--
HI, DADDY. CRUSH ANY CORPORATIONS TODAY?
THERE'S STILL DAYLIGHT LEFT. MR. FLUDSNÜT'S WAITING FOR YOU, PRINCESS. MWAH.
MR. LODGE! PLEASURE TO MEET YOU, SIR! MY NAME IS REG--
CHAUNCY! THE DETAILER BROUGHT YOUR CAR BACK!
HERE YOU GO, SON.

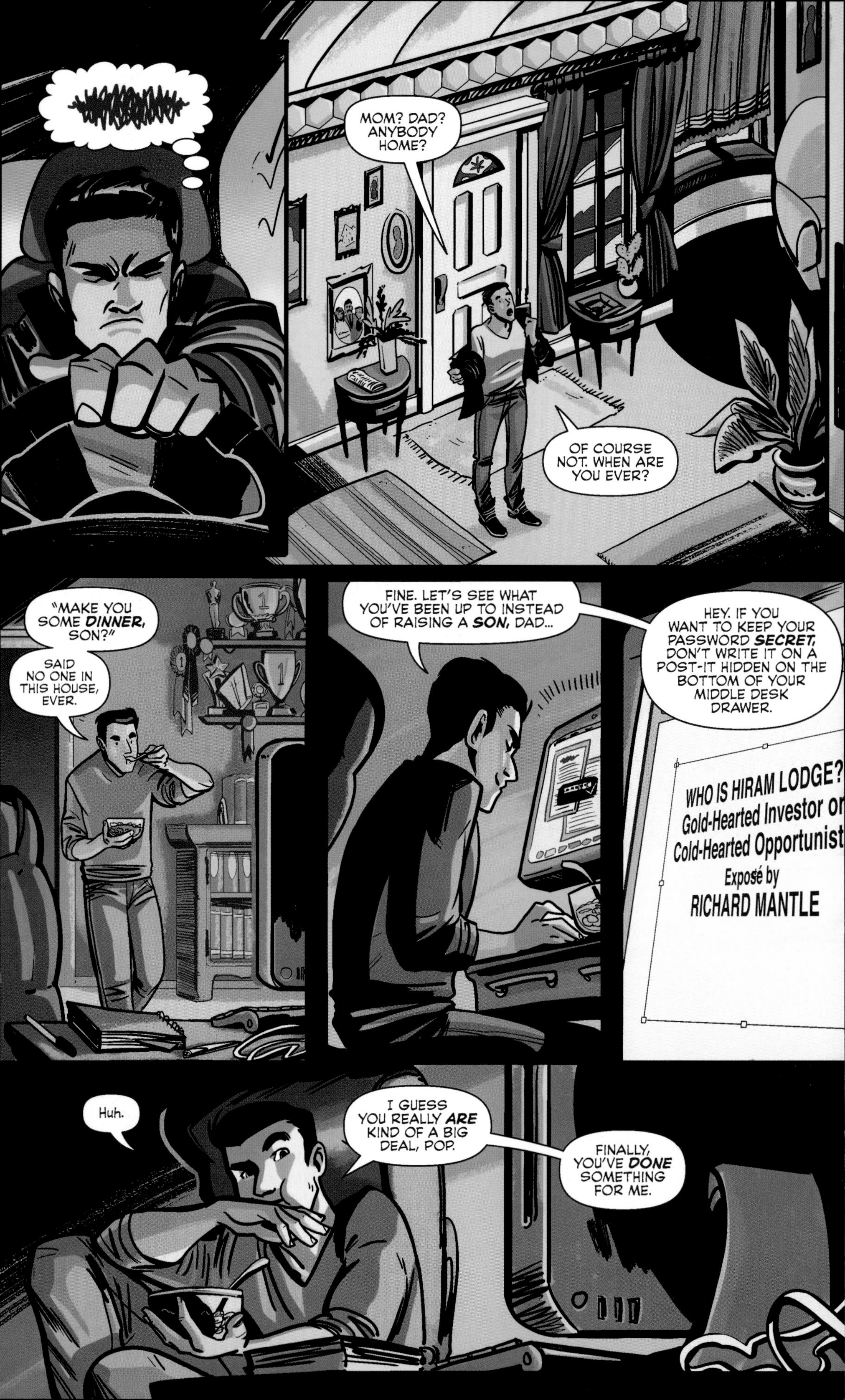

MOM? DAD? ANYBODY HOME?
OF COURSE NOT. WHEN ARE YOU EVER?
"MAKE YOU SOME DINNER, SON?"
SAID NO ONE IN THIS HOUSE, EVER.
FINE. LET'S SEE WHAT YOU'VE BEEN UP TO INSTEAD OF RAISING A SON, DAD...
HEY. IF YOU WANT TO KEEP YOUR PASSWORD SECRET, DON'T WRITE IT ON A POST-IT HIDDEN ON THE BOTTOM OF YOUR MIDDLE DESK DRAWER.
WHO IS HIRAM LODGE?
Gold-Hearted Investor or
Cold-Hearted Opportunist
Exposé by
RICHARD MANTLE
Huh.
I GUESS YOU REALLY ARE KIND OF A BIG DEAL, POP.
FINALLY, YOU'VE DONE SOMETHING FOR ME.

CHAPTER THREE: ARE YOU STILL HERE?

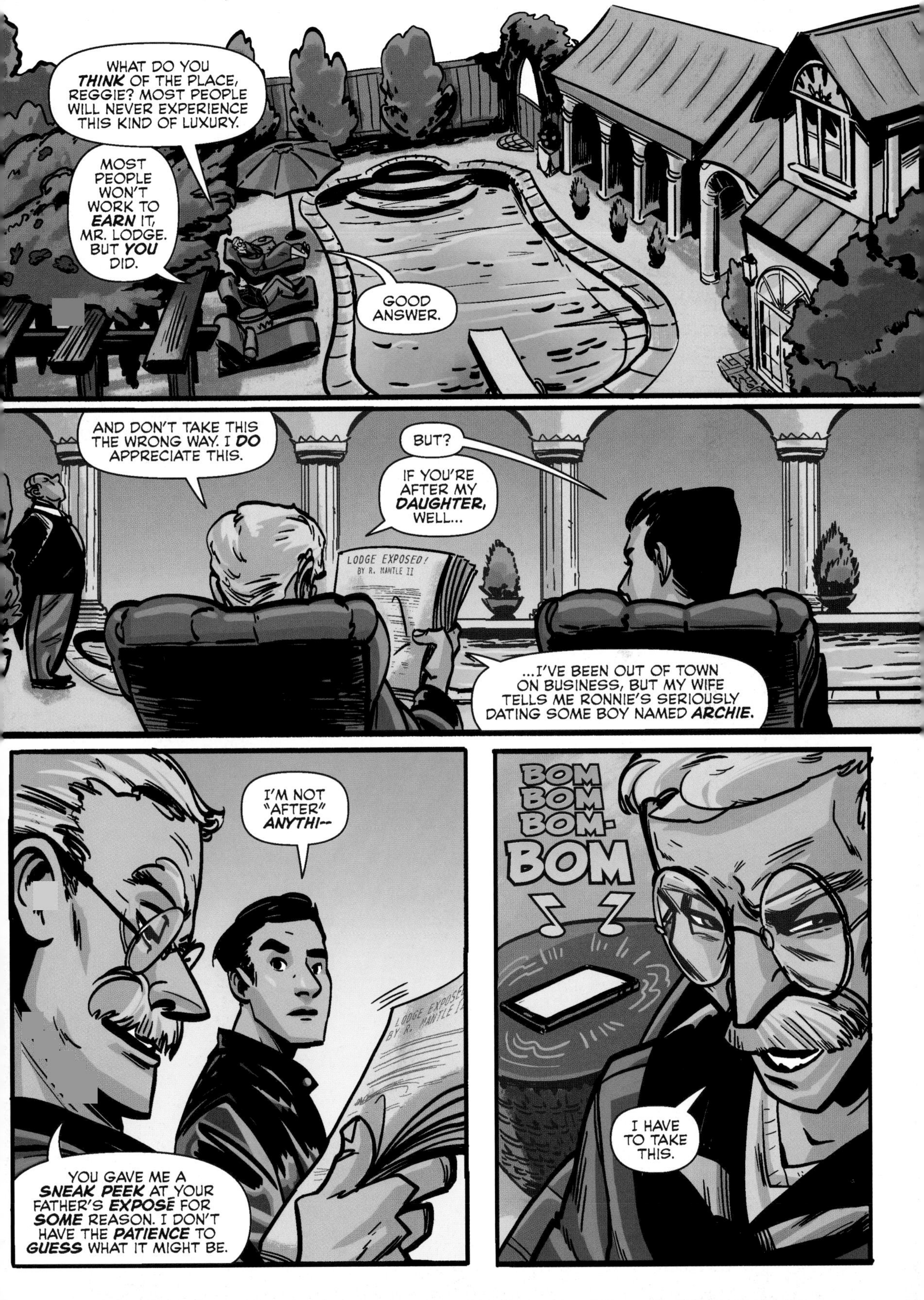
WHAT DO YOU THINK OF THE PLACE, REGGIE? MOST PEOPLE WILL NEVER EXPERIENCE THIS KIND OF LUXURY.
MOST PEOPLE WON'T WORK TO EARN IT, MR. LODGE. BUT YOU DID.
GOOD ANSWER.
AND DON'T TAKE THIS THE WRONG WAY. I DO APPRECIATE THIS.
BUT?
IF YOU'RE AFTER MY DAUGHTER, WELL...
LODGE EXPOSED! BY R. MANTLE II
...I'VE BEEN OUT OF TOWN ON BUSINESS, BUT MY WIFE TELLS ME RONNIE'S SERIOUSLY DATING SOME BOY NAMED ARCHIE.
I'M NOT "AFTER" ANYTHI--
LODGE EXPOSED BY R. MANTLE II
YOU GAVE ME A SNEAK PEEK AT YOUR FATHER'S EXPOSÉ FOR SOME REASON. I DON'T HAVE THE PATIENCE TO GUESS WHAT IT MIGHT BE.
BOM BOM BOM-BOM
I HAVE TO TAKE THIS.

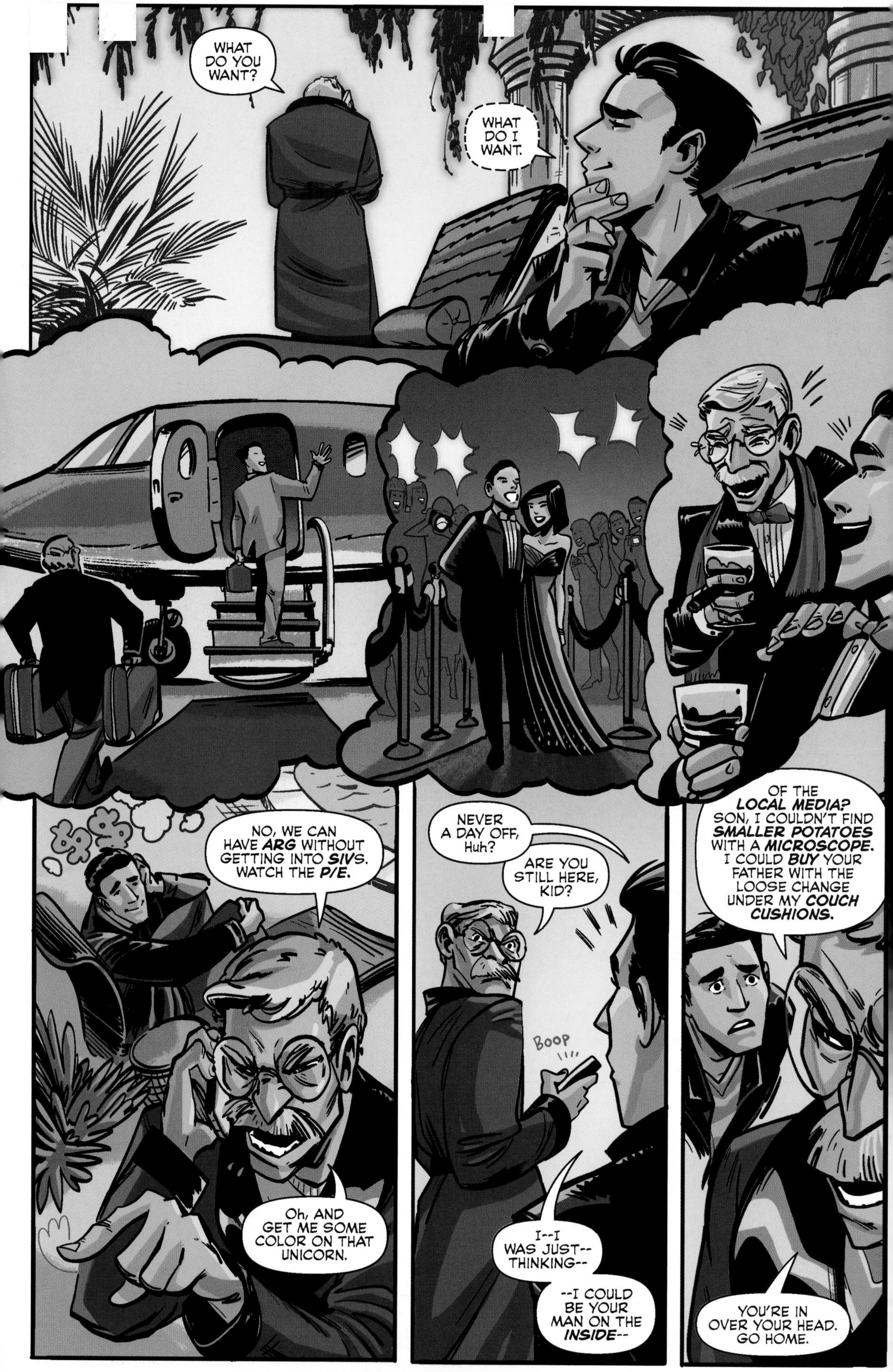
WHAT DO YOU WANT?
WHAT DO I WANT.
NO, WE CAN HAVE ARG WITHOUT GETTING INTO SIVS. WATCH THE P/E.
Oh, AND GET ME SOME COLOR ON THAT UNICORN.
NEVER A DAY OFF, Huh?
ARE YOU STILL HERE, KID?
BOOP
I--I WAS JUST-- THINKING--
--I COULD BE YOUR MAN ON THE INSIDE--
OF THE LOCAL MEDIA? SON, I COULDN'T FIND SMALLER POTATOES WITH A MICROSCOPE. I COULD BUY YOUR FATHER WITH THE LOOSE CHANGE UNDER MY COUCH CUSHIONS.
YOU'RE IN OVER YOUR HEAD. GO HOME.

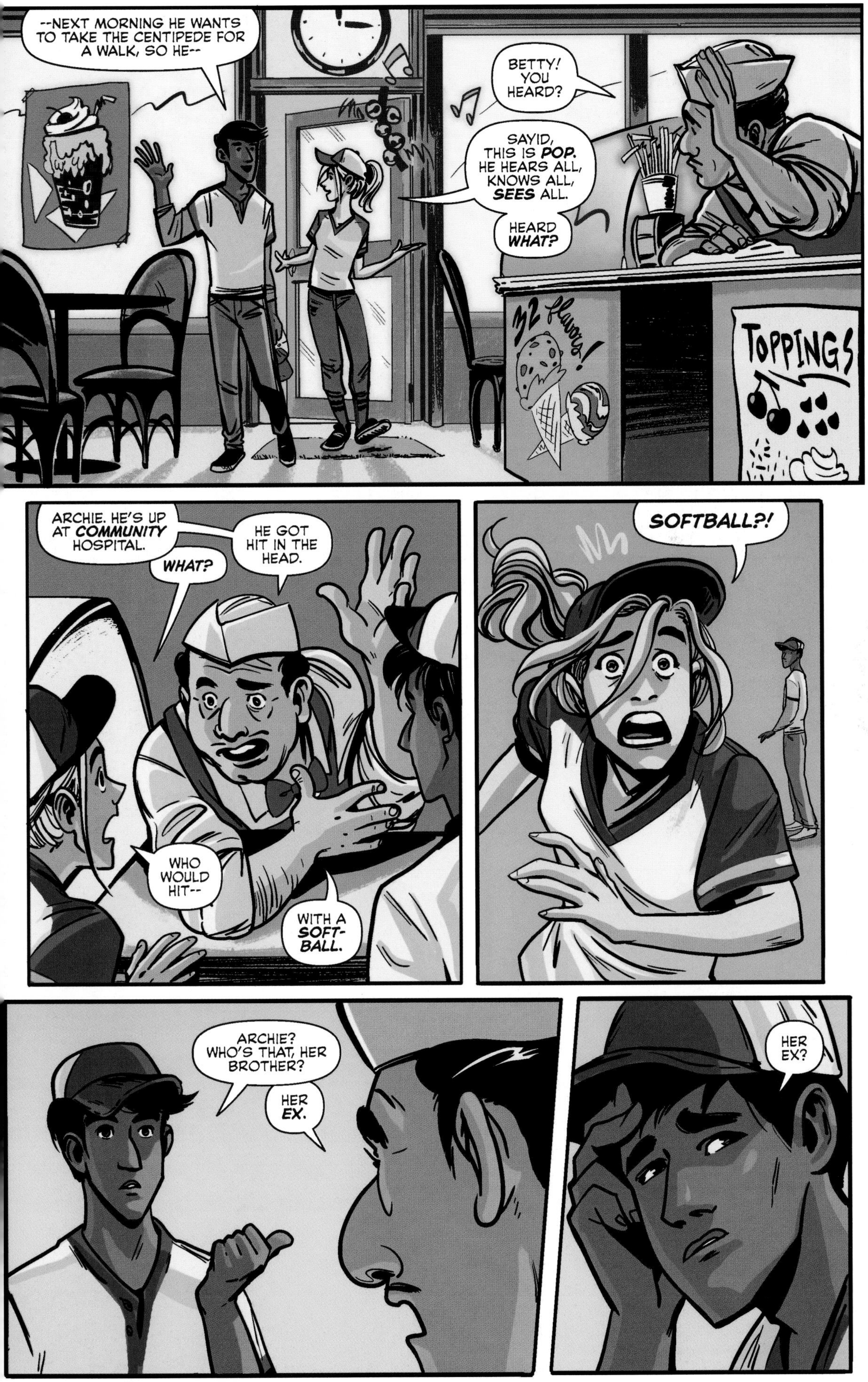
--NEXT MORNING HE WANTS TO TAKE THE CENTIPEDE FOR A WALK, SO HE--
BETTY! YOU HEARD?
SAYID, THIS IS POP. HE HEARS ALL, KNOWS ALL, SEES ALL.
HEARD WHAT?
TOPPINGS
32 flavors!
ARCHIE. HE'S UP AT COMMUNITY HOSPITAL.
WHAT?
HE GOT HIT IN THE HEAD.
WHO WOULD HIT--
WITH A SOFT-BALL.
SOFTBALL?!
ARCHIE? WHO'S THAT, HER BROTHER?
HER EX.
HER EX?

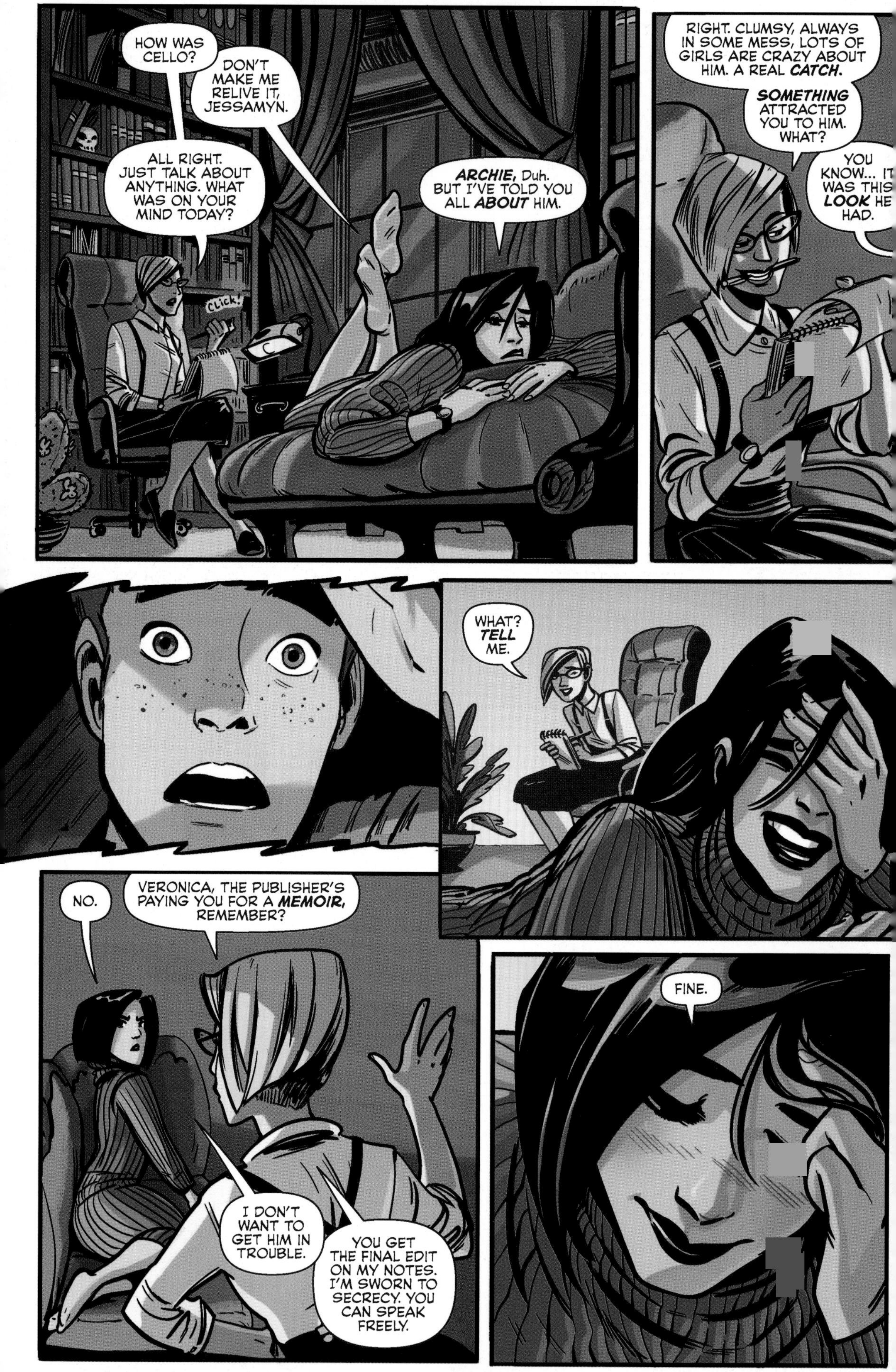
HOW WAS CELLO?
DON'T MAKE ME RELIVE IT, JESSAMYN.
ALL RIGHT. JUST TALK ABOUT ANYTHING. WHAT WAS ON YOUR MIND TODAY?
CLICK!
ARCHIE, Duh. BUT I'VE TOLD YOU ALL ABOUT HIM.
RIGHT. CLUMSY, ALWAYS IN SOME MESS, LOTS OF GIRLS ARE CRAZY ABOUT HIM. A REAL CATCH.
SOMETHING ATTRACTED YOU TO HIM. WHAT?
YOU KNOW... IT WAS THIS LOOK HE HAD.
WHAT? TELL ME.
NO.
VERONICA, THE PUBLISHER'S PAYING YOU FOR A MEMOIR, REMEMBER?
I DON'T WANT TO GET HIM IN TROUBLE.
YOU GET THE FINAL EDIT ON MY NOTES. I'M SWORN TO SECRECY. YOU CAN SPEAK FREELY.
FINE.

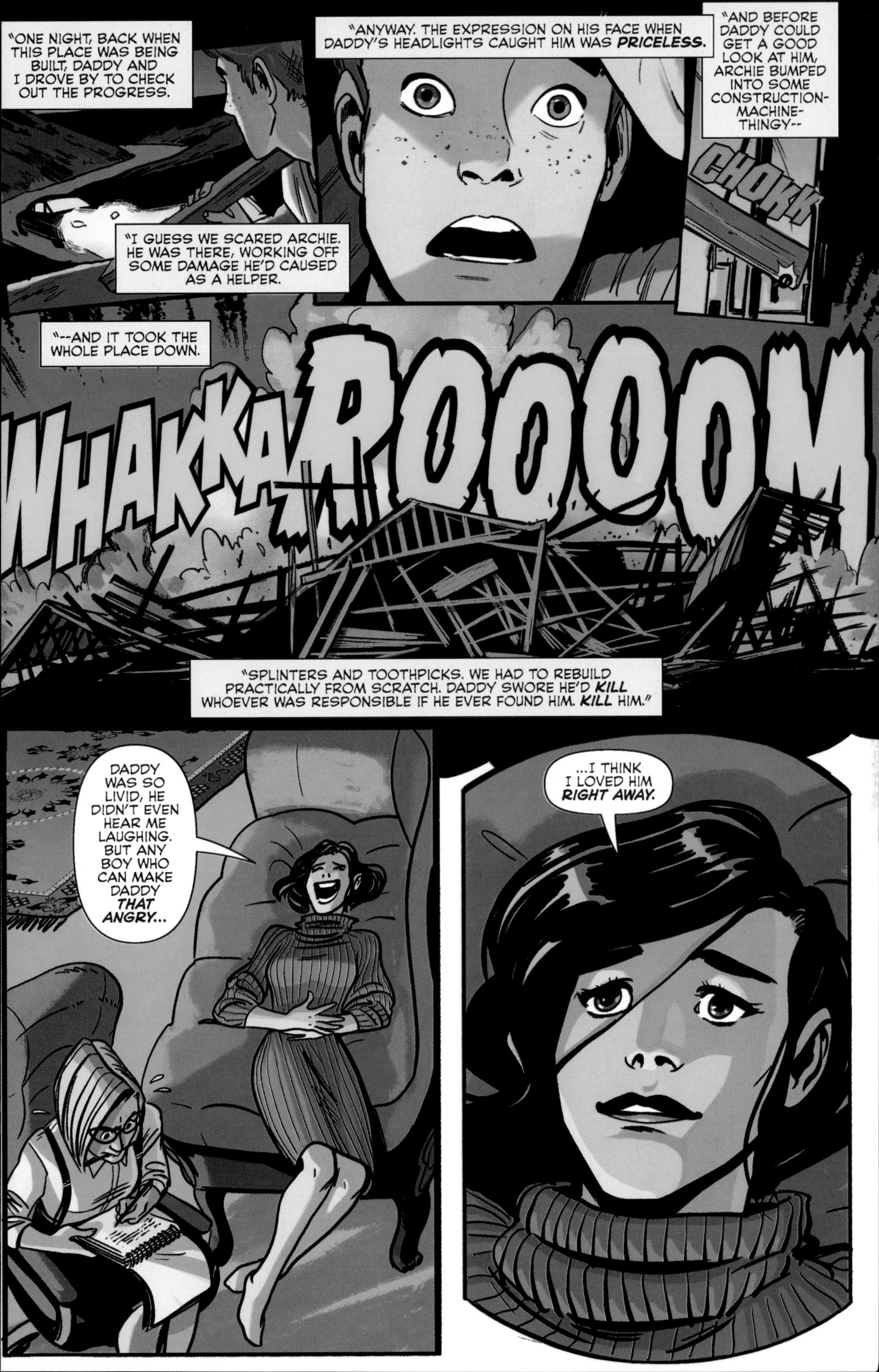

"ONE NIGHT, BACK WHEN THIS PLACE WAS BEING BUILT, DADDY AND I DROVE BY TO CHECK OUT THE PROGRESS.
"I GUESS WE SCARED ARCHIE. HE WAS THERE, WORKING OFF SOME DAMAGE HE'D CAUSED AS A HELPER.
"ANYWAY. THE EXPRESSION ON HIS FACE WHEN DADDY'S HEADLIGHTS CAUGHT HIM WAS PRICELESS.
"AND BEFORE DADDY COULD GET A GOOD LOOK AT HIM, ARCHIE BUMPED INTO SOME CONSTRUCTION-MACHINE-THINGY--
CHOKK
"--AND IT TOOK THE WHOLE PLACE DOWN.
WHAKKAROOOOM
"SPLINTERS AND TOOTHPICKS. WE HAD TO REBUILD PRACTICALLY FROM SCRATCH. DADDY SWORE HE'D KILL WHOEVER WAS RESPONSIBLE IF HE EVER FOUND HIM. KILL HIM."
DADDY WAS SO LIVID, HE DIDN'T EVEN HEAR ME LAUGHING. BUT ANY BOY WHO CAN MAKE DADDY THAT ANGRY...
...I THINK I LOVED HIM RIGHT AWAY.

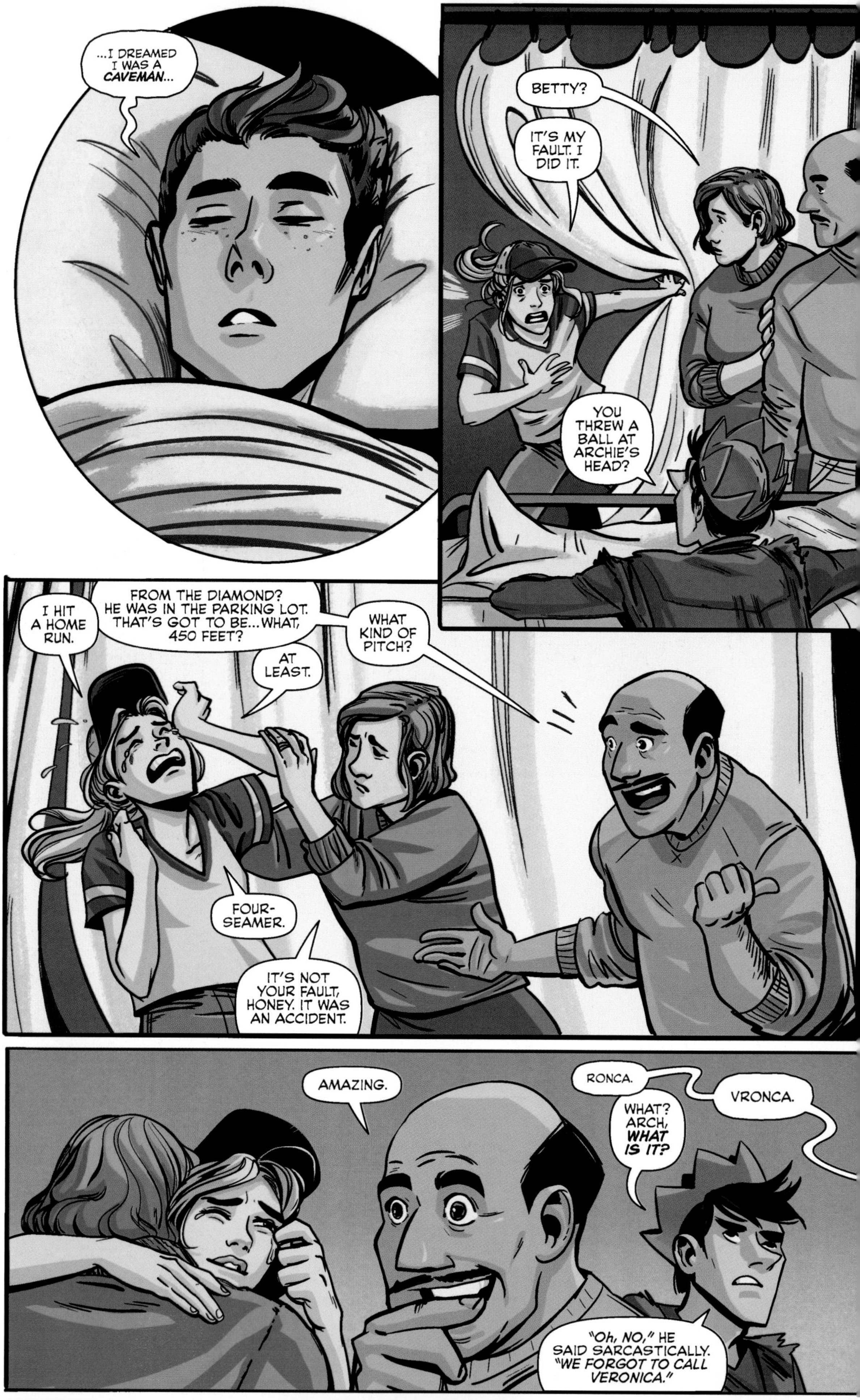

...I DREAMED I WAS A *CAVEMAN*...
BETTY?
IT'S MY FAULT. I DID IT.
YOU THREW A BALL AT ARCHIE'S HEAD?
I HIT A HOME RUN.
FROM THE DIAMOND? HE WAS IN THE PARKING LOT. THAT'S GOT TO BE...WHAT, 450 FEET?
AT LEAST.
WHAT KIND OF PITCH?
FOUR-SEAMER.
IT'S NOT YOUR FAULT, HONEY. IT WAS AN ACCIDENT.
AMAZING.
RONCA.
VRONCA.
WHAT? ARCH, *WHAT IS IT?*
"Oh, NO," HE SAID SARCASTICALLY. *"WE FORGOT TO CALL VERONICA."*

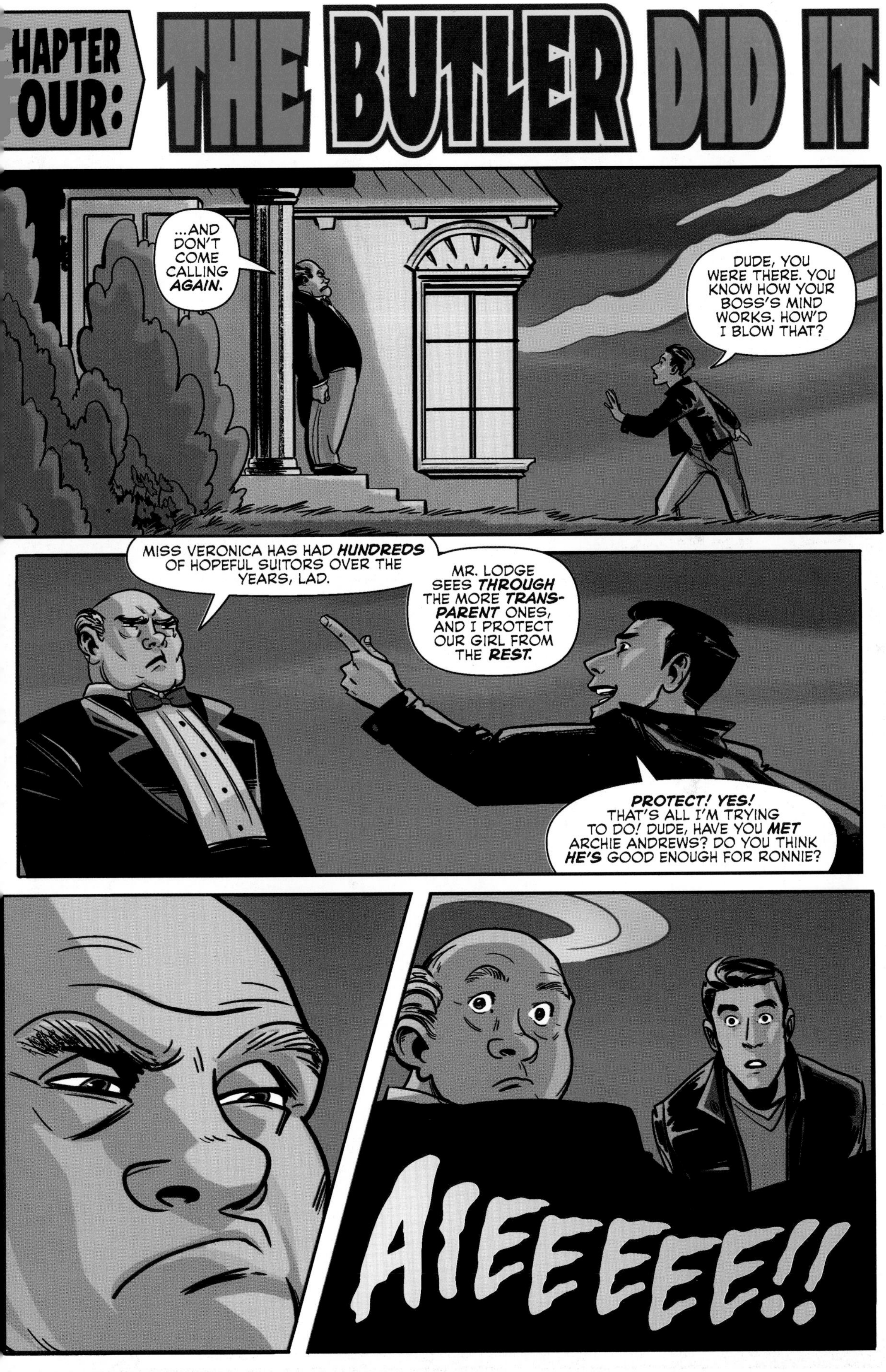
HAPTER OUR: THE BUTLER DID IT
...AND DON'T COME CALLING AGAIN.
DUDE, YOU WERE THERE. YOU KNOW HOW YOUR BOSS'S MIND WORKS. HOW'D I BLOW THAT?
MISS VERONICA HAS HAD HUNDREDS OF HOPEFUL SUITORS OVER THE YEARS, LAD.
MR. LODGE SEES THROUGH THE MORE TRANS-PARENT ONES, AND I PROTECT OUR GIRL FROM THE REST.
PROTECT! YES! THAT'S ALL I'M TRYING TO DO! DUDE, HAVE YOU MET ARCHIE ANDREWS? DO YOU THINK HE'S GOOD ENOUGH FOR RONNIE?
AIEEEEEE!!

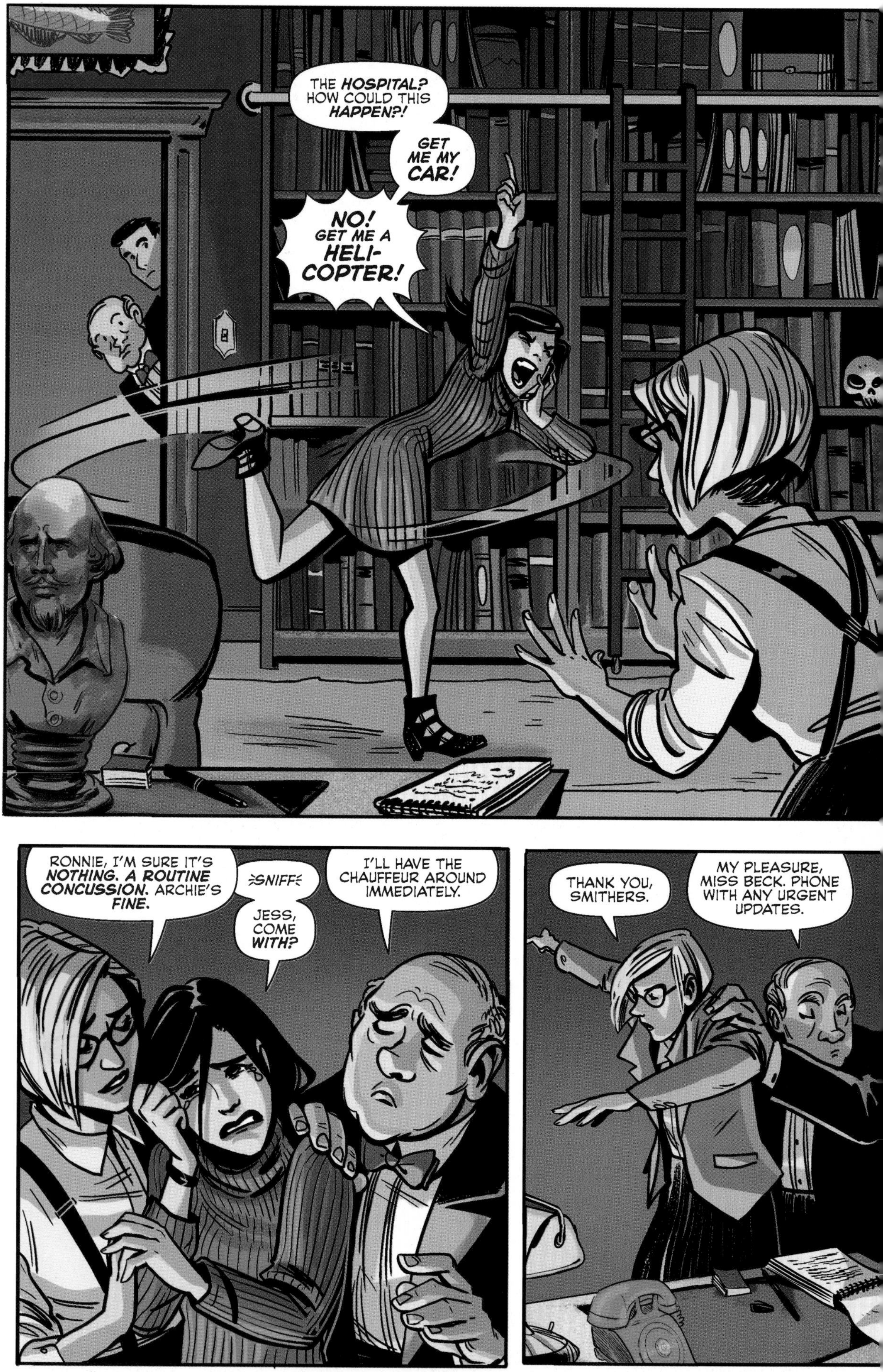
THE HOSPITAL? HOW COULD THIS HAPPEN?!
GET ME MY CAR!
NO! GET ME A HELI-COPTER!
RONNIE, I'M SURE IT'S NOTHING. A ROUTINE CONCUSSION. ARCHIE'S FINE.
SNIFF
JESS, COME WITH?
I'LL HAVE THE CHAUFFEUR AROUND IMMEDIATELY.
THANK YOU, SMITHERS.
MY PLEASURE, MISS BECK. PHONE WITH ANY URGENT UPDATES.

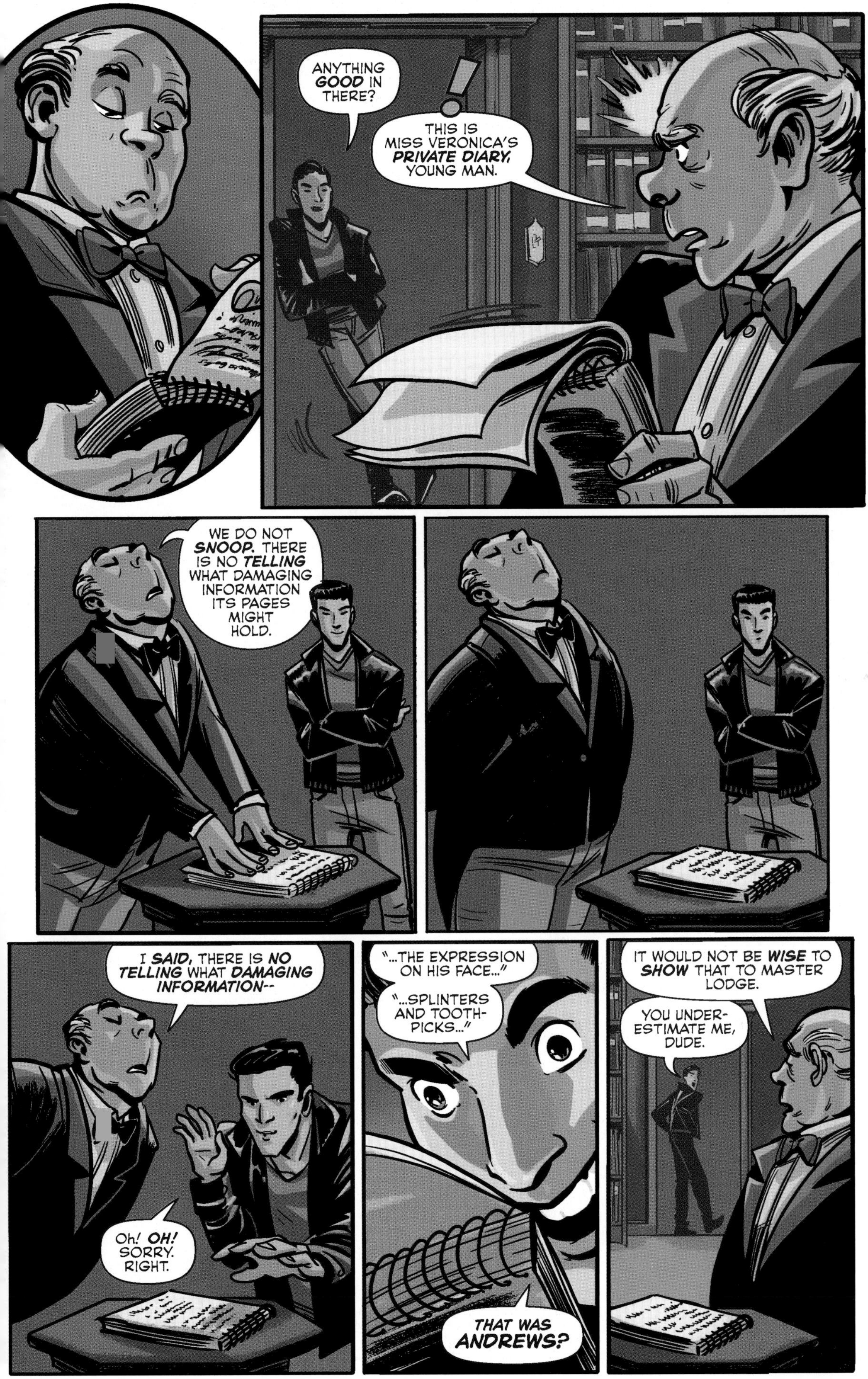

ANYTHING GOOD IN THERE?
!
THIS IS MISS VERONICA'S PRIVATE DIARY, YOUNG MAN.
WE DO NOT SNOOP. THERE IS NO TELLING WHAT DAMAGING INFORMATION ITS PAGES MIGHT HOLD.
I SAID, THERE IS NO TELLING WHAT DAMAGING INFORMATION--
Oh! OH! SORRY. RIGHT.
"...THE EXPRESSION ON HIS FACE..."
"...SPLINTERS AND TOOTH-PICKS..."
THAT WAS ANDREWS?
IT WOULD NOT BE WISE TO SHOW THAT TO MASTER LODGE.
YOU UNDER-ESTIMATE ME, DUDE.

CHAPTER FIVE: KLIK

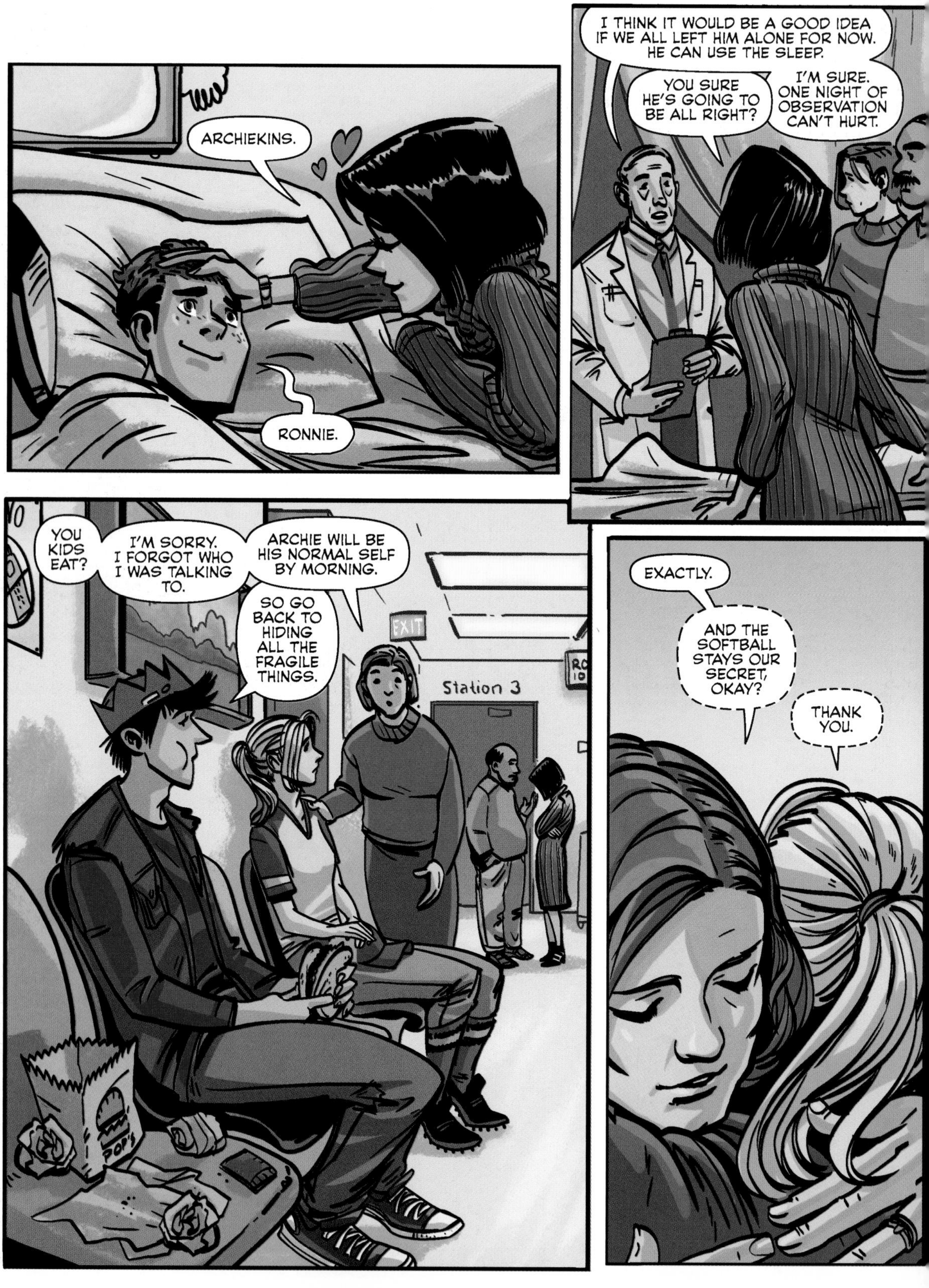
ARCHIEKINS.
RONNIE.
I THINK IT WOULD BE A GOOD IDEA IF WE ALL LEFT HIM ALONE FOR NOW. HE CAN USE THE SLEEP.
YOU SURE HE'S GOING TO BE ALL RIGHT?
I'M SURE. ONE NIGHT OF OBSERVATION CAN'T HURT.
YOU KIDS EAT?
I'M SORRY. I FORGOT WHO I WAS TALKING TO.
ARCHIE WILL BE HIS NORMAL SELF BY MORNING.
SO GO BACK TO HIDING ALL THE FRAGILE THINGS.
EXIT
Station 3
POP'S
EXACTLY.
AND THE SOFTBALL STAYS OUR SECRET, OKAY?
THANK YOU.

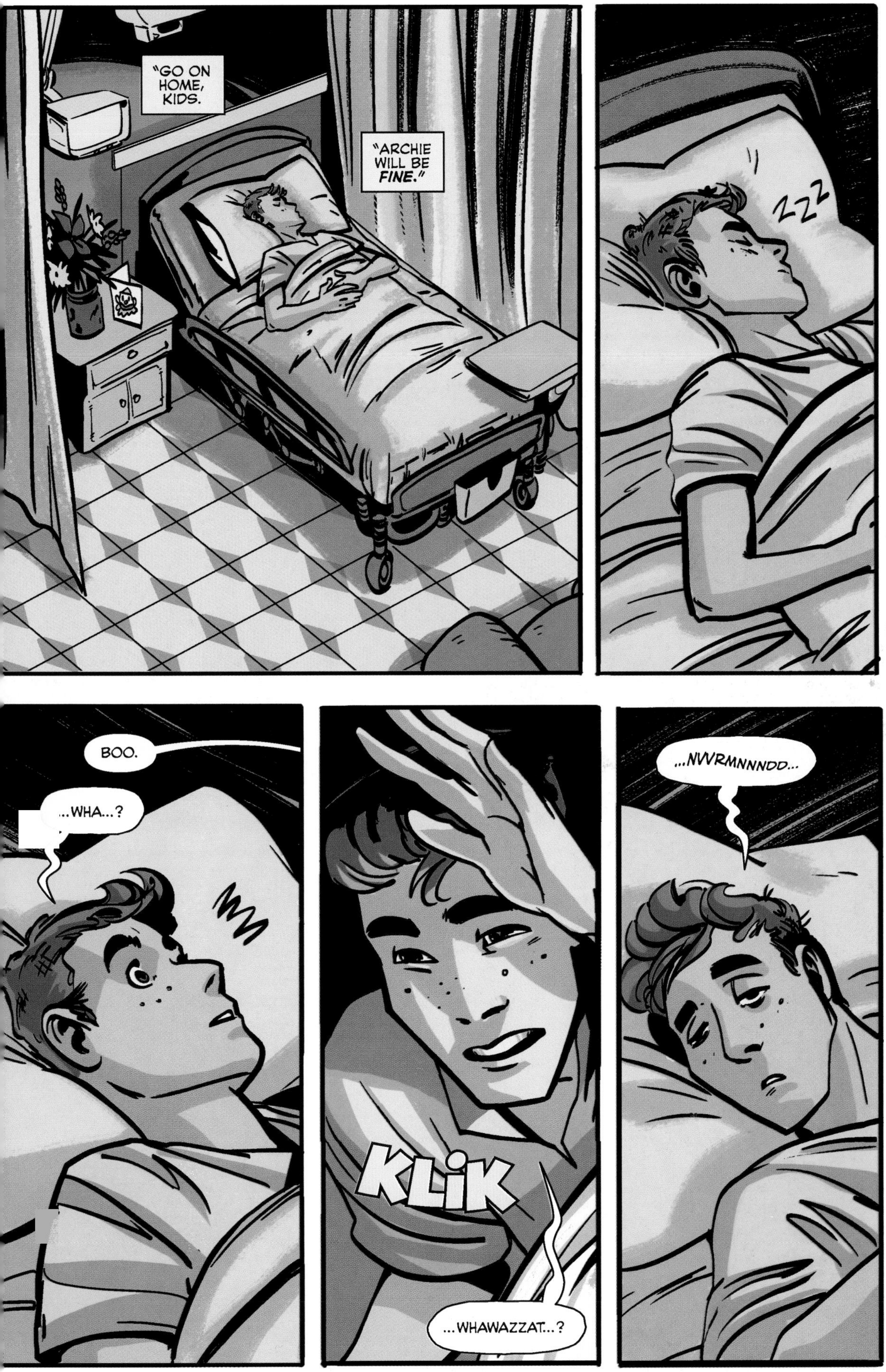
"GO ON HOME, KIDS.
"ARCHIE WILL BE *FINE.*"
ZZZ
BOO.
...WHA...?
KLIK
...WHAWAZZAT...?
...NVVRMNNNDD...

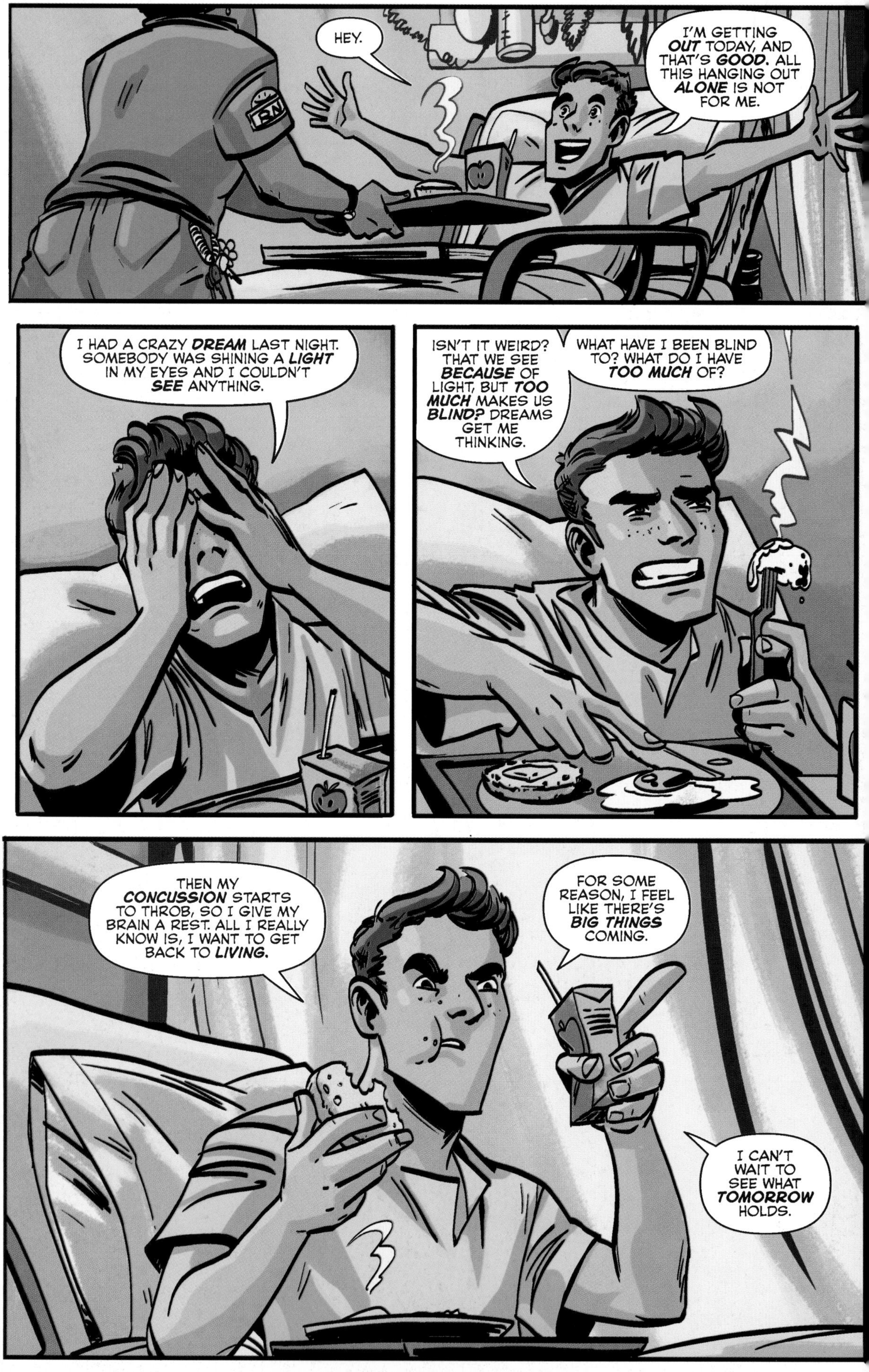
HEY.
I'M GETTING OUT TODAY, AND THAT'S GOOD. ALL THIS HANGING OUT ALONE IS NOT FOR ME.
I HAD A CRAZY DREAM LAST NIGHT. SOMEBODY WAS SHINING A LIGHT IN MY EYES AND I COULDN'T SEE ANYTHING.
ISN'T IT WEIRD? THAT WE SEE BECAUSE OF LIGHT, BUT TOO MUCH MAKES US BLIND? DREAMS GET ME THINKING.
WHAT HAVE I BEEN BLIND TO? WHAT DO I HAVE TOO MUCH OF?
THEN MY CONCUSSION STARTS TO THROB, SO I GIVE MY BRAIN A REST. ALL I REALLY KNOW IS, I WANT TO GET BACK TO LIVING.
FOR SOME REASON, I FEEL LIKE THERE'S BIG THINGS COMING.
I CAN'T WAIT TO SEE WHAT TOMORROW HOLDS.

MR. LODGE! WAIT!

Ah. THE *FAMILY TURNCOAT.*

DRIVER, CALL *SECURITY--*

NO! I JUST NEED *ONE SECOND* TO *APOLOGIZE!*

MR. LODGE, SIR, I WAS LESS THAN HONEST. I *DO* WANT SOMETHING FROM YOU.

A PLACE IN YOUR ORBIT. I DON'T MEAN AN IMPORTANT ONE. I JUST WANT TO *BE* SOMEBODY.

TO BE A PART OF ALL ...*THIS.*

I SEE. AND WHAT COULD YOU *POSSIBLY* OFFER ME IN *RETURN?*

A LITTLE INTEL ON THIS *"ARCHIE"* YOUR DAUGHTER IS DATING.

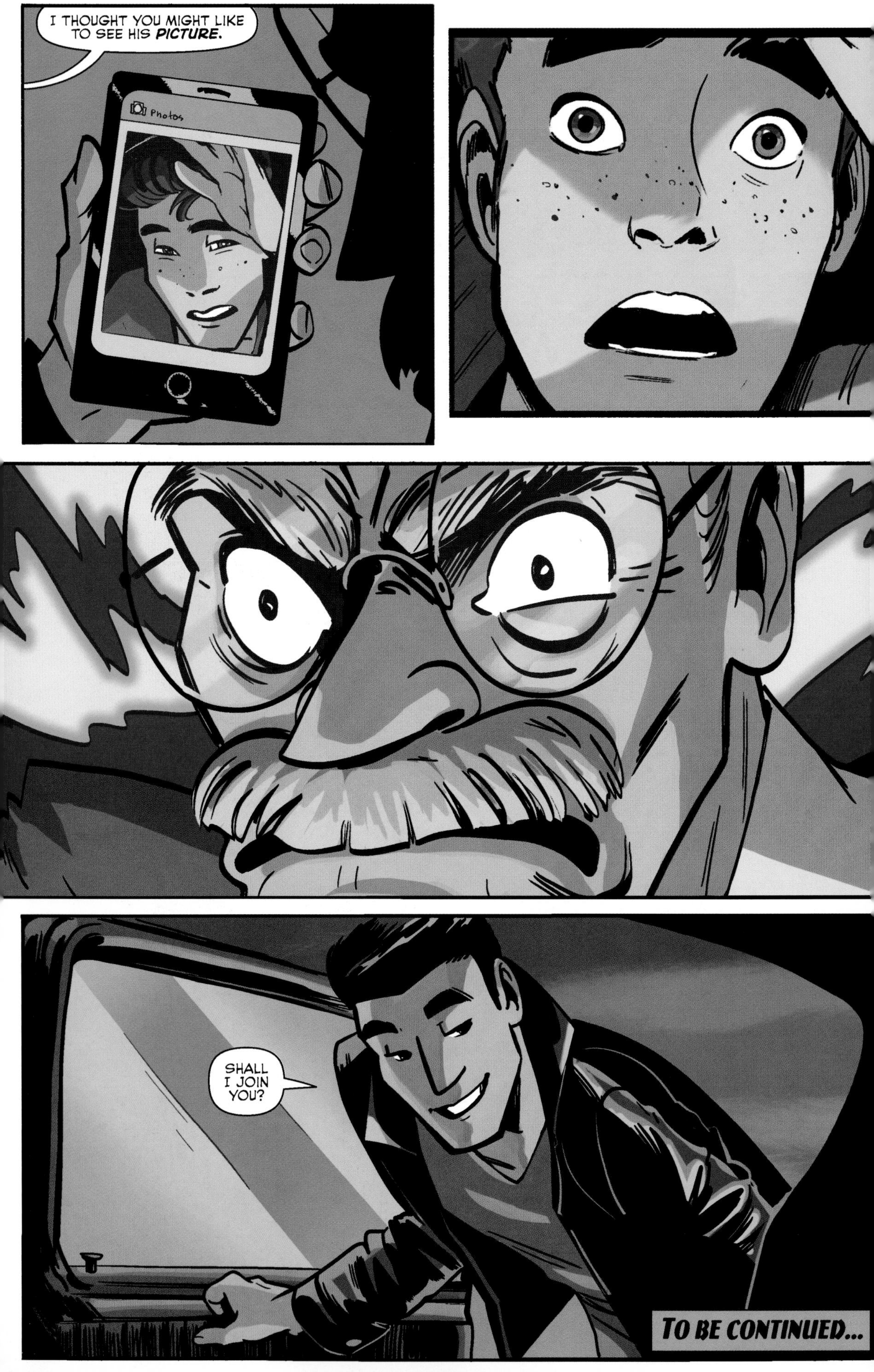
I THOUGHT YOU MIGHT LIKE TO SEE HIS ***PICTURE.***
Photos
SHALL I JOIN YOU?
TO BE CONTINUED...

ARCHIE®

SPECIAL FEATURES

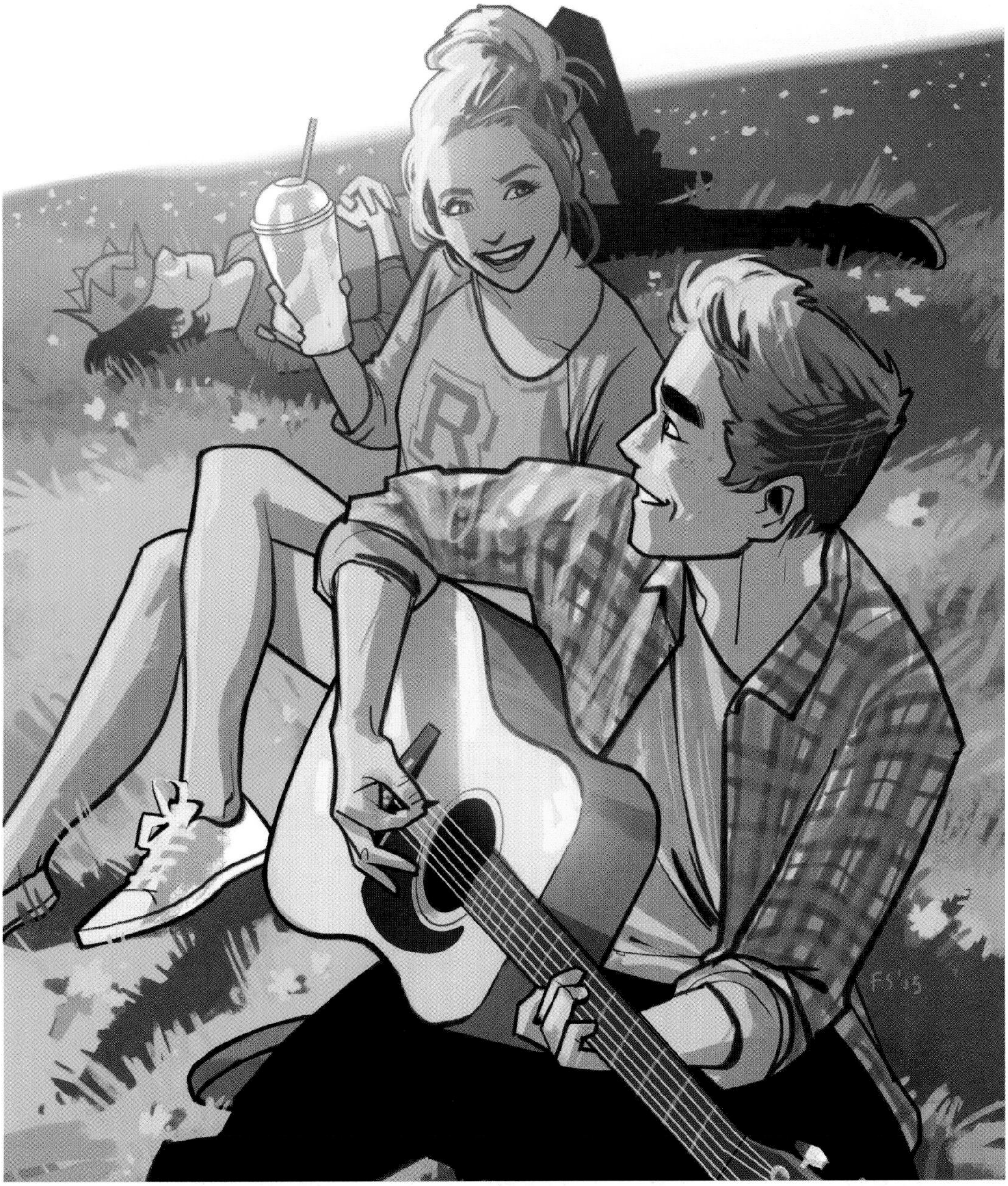
FS '15

COVER GALLERY

ARCHIE®

ISSUE ONE

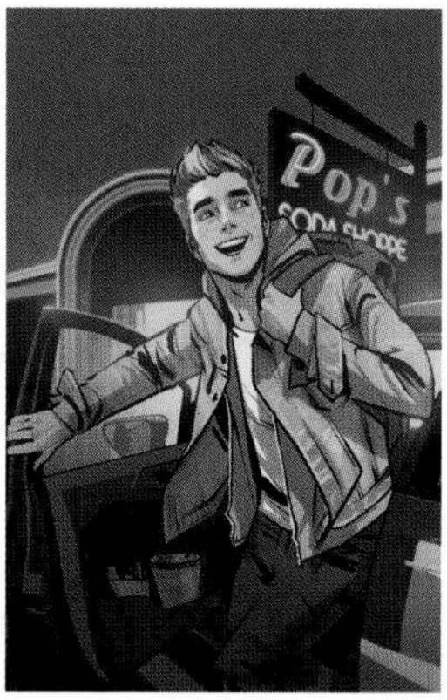
Pop's
SODA SHOPPE

FIONA STAPLES

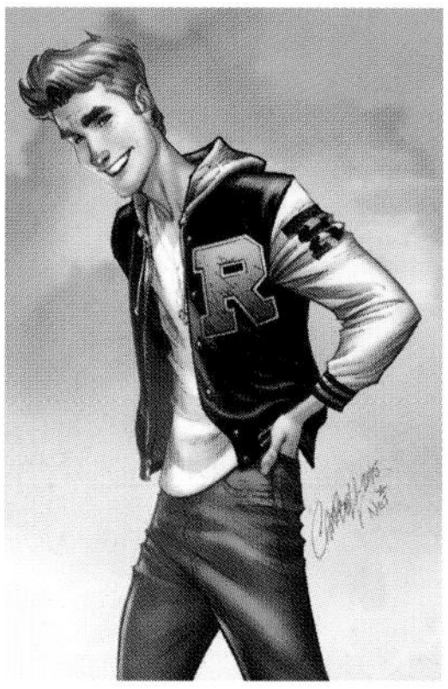

J. SCOTT CAMPBELL

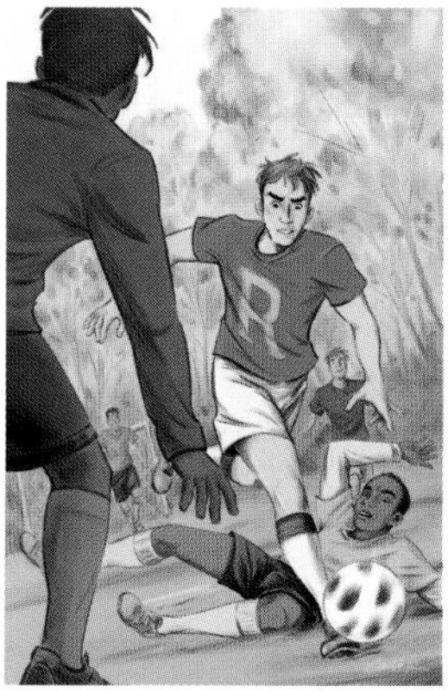

COLLEEN COOVER

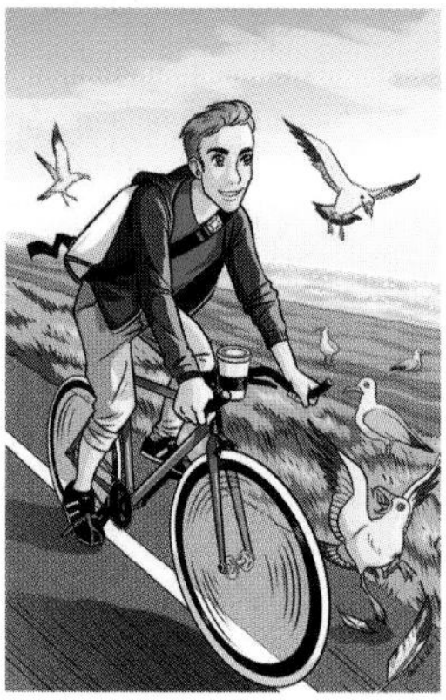

TANIA DEL RIO

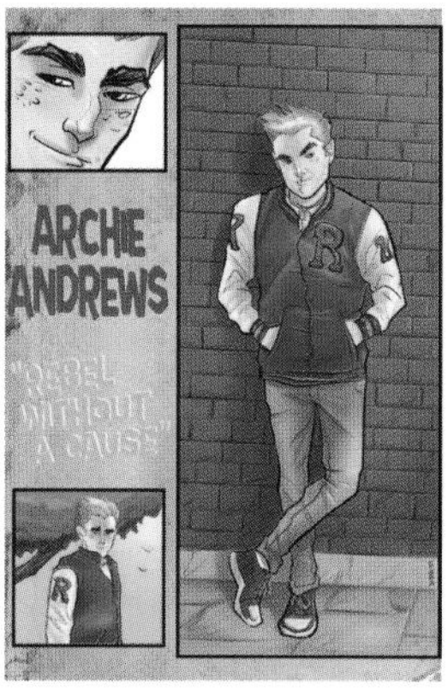
ARCHIE ANDREWS
"REBEL WITHOUT A CAUSE"

JOE EISMA

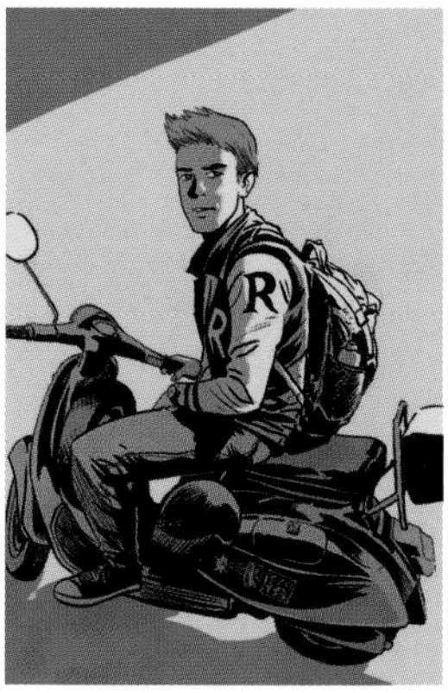

FRANCESCO FRANCAVILLA

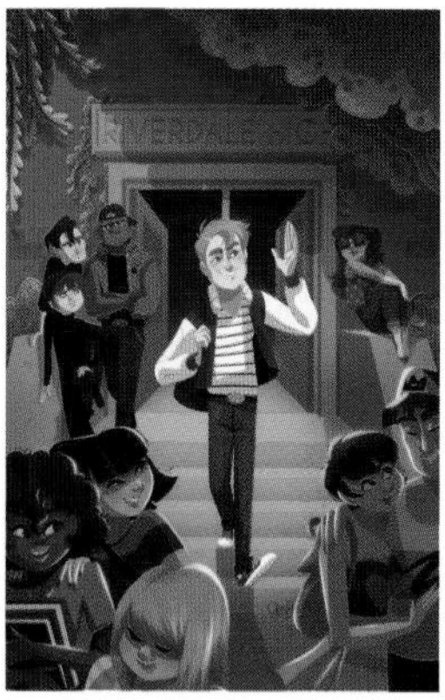

GENEVIEVE F.T.

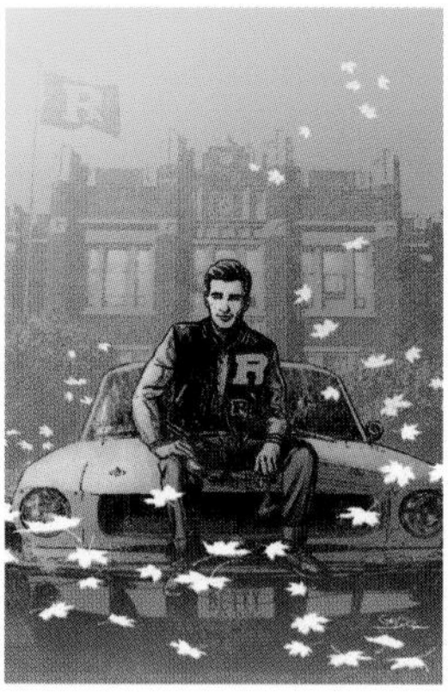

MICHAEL GAYDOS

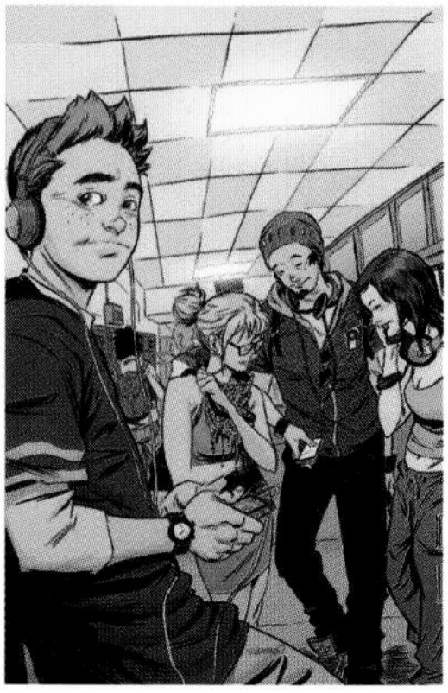

SANFORD GREENE

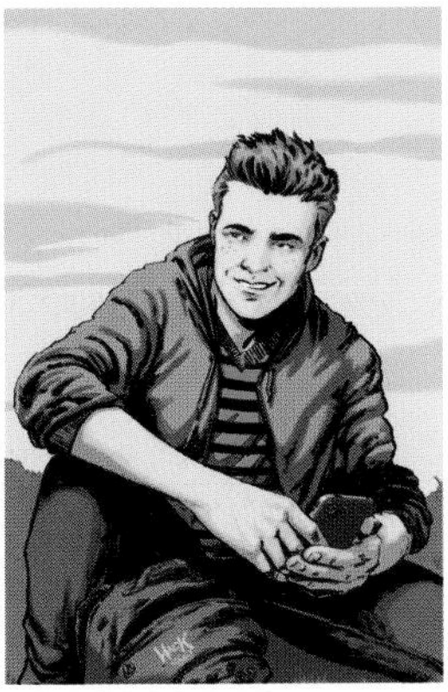
ROBERT HACK

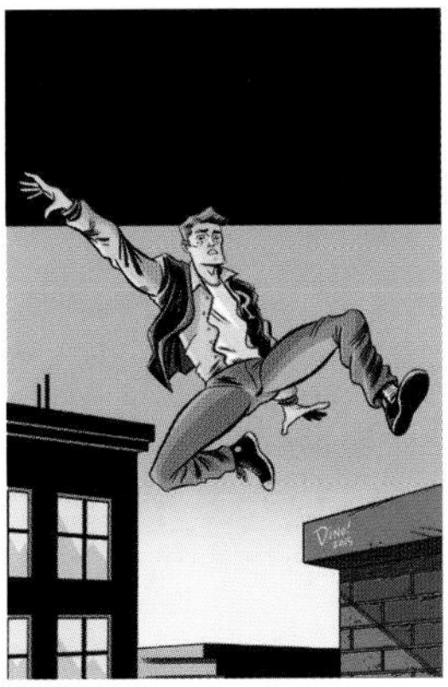
DEAN HASPIEL

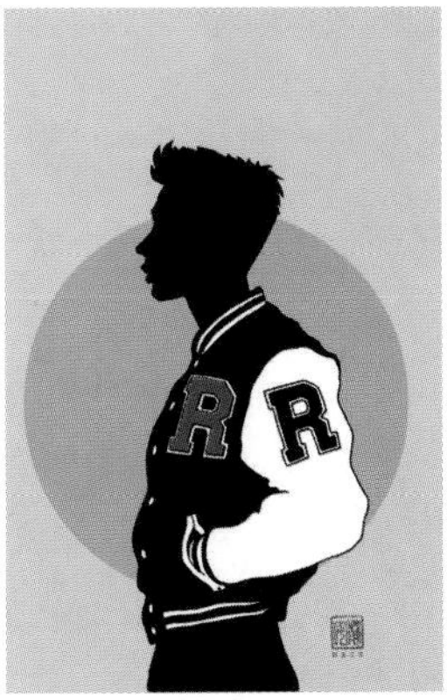
R
R
DAVID MACK

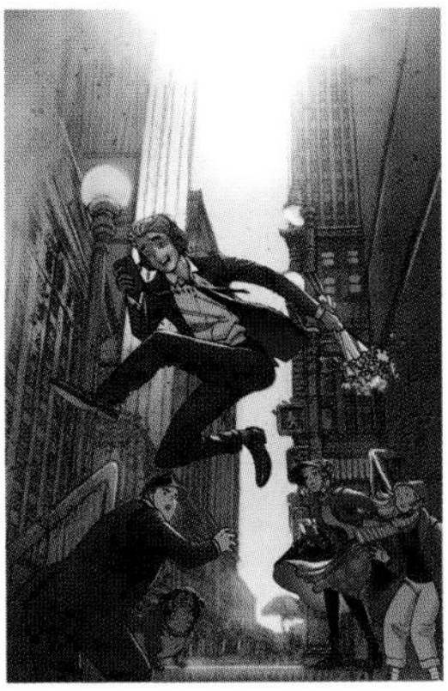
MORITAT

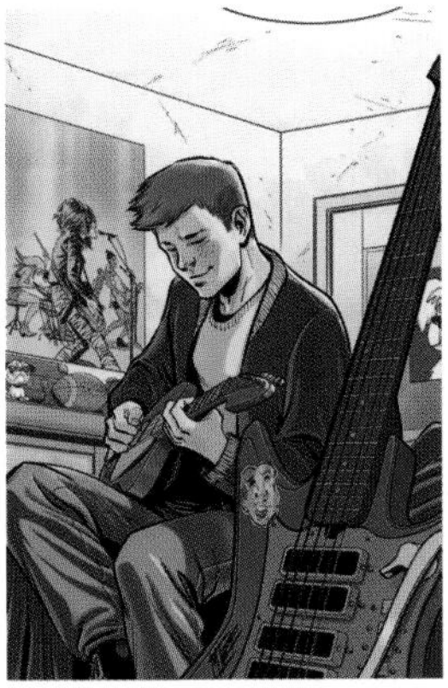
MIKE NORTON

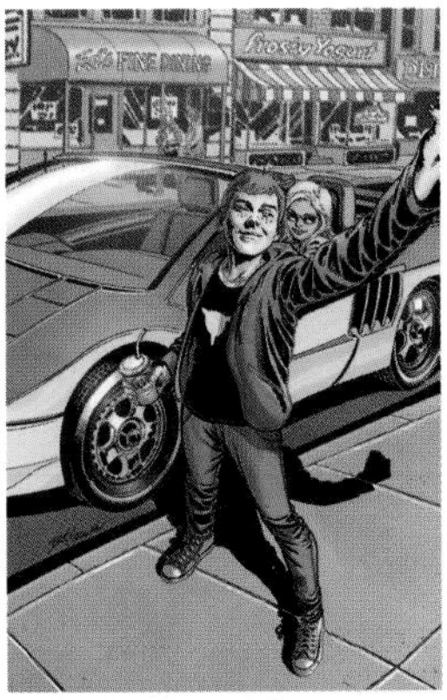
FINE DINING
Frosty Yogurt
JERRY ORDWAY

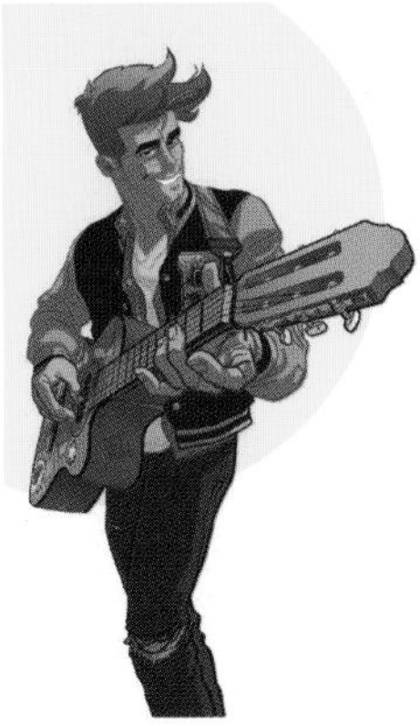
RAMON PEREZ

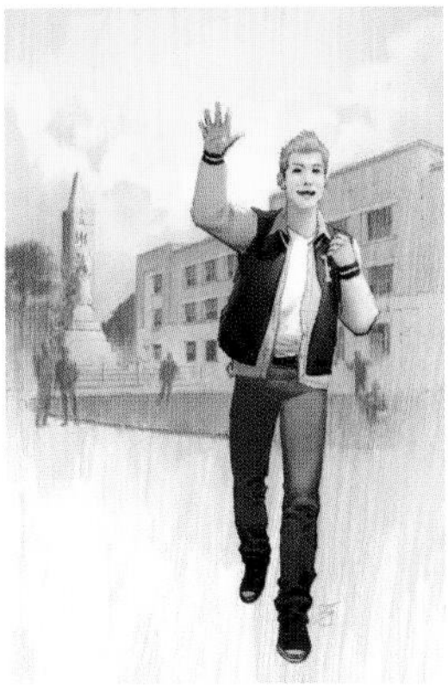
RON SALAS

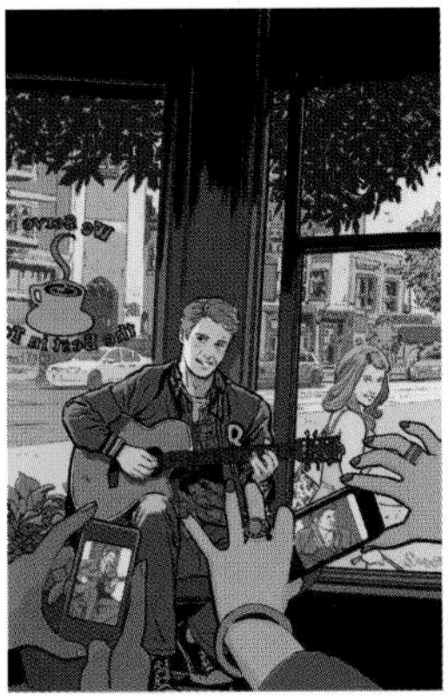
GREG SCOTT

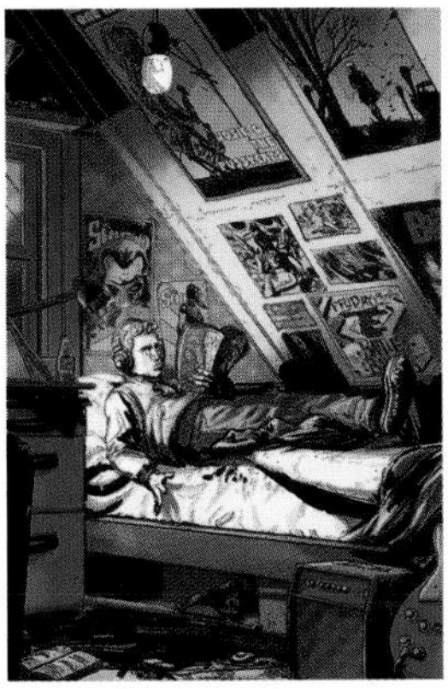
T-REX

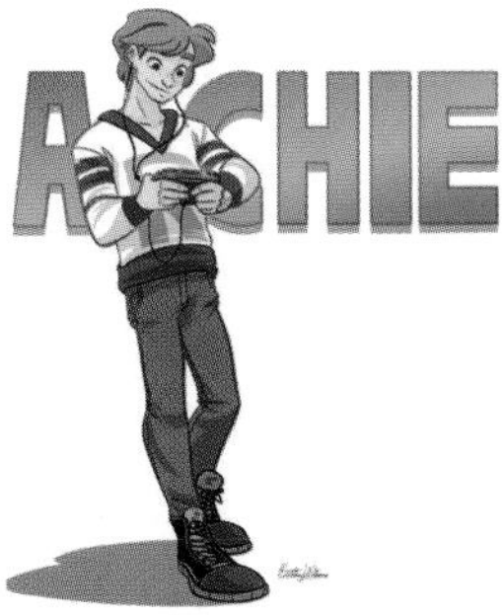
BRITTNEY WILLIAMS

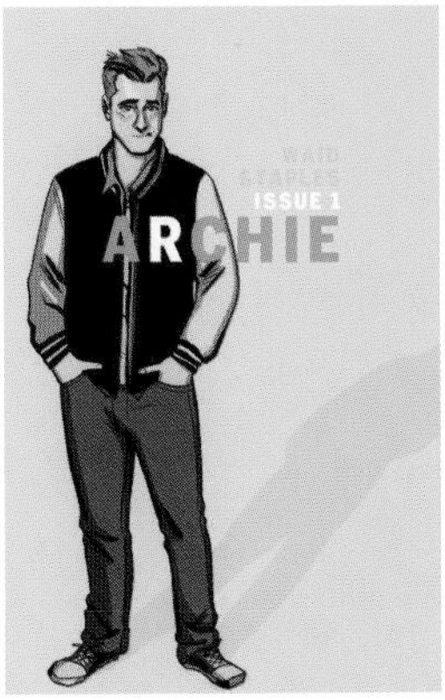
WAID
STAPLES
ISSUE 1
CHIP ZDARSKY

ISSUE TWO

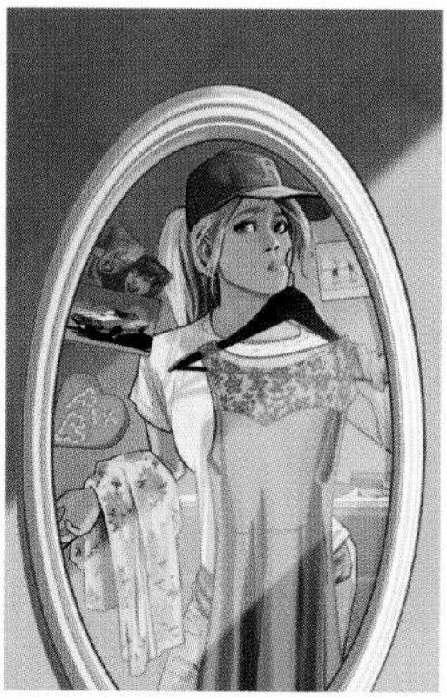

FIONA STAPLES

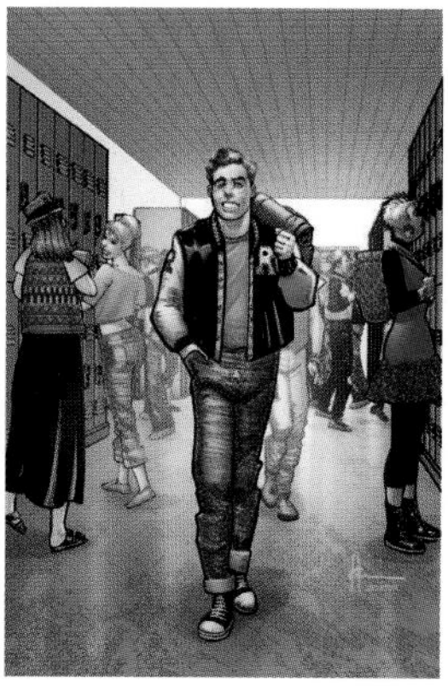

HOWARD CHAYKIN

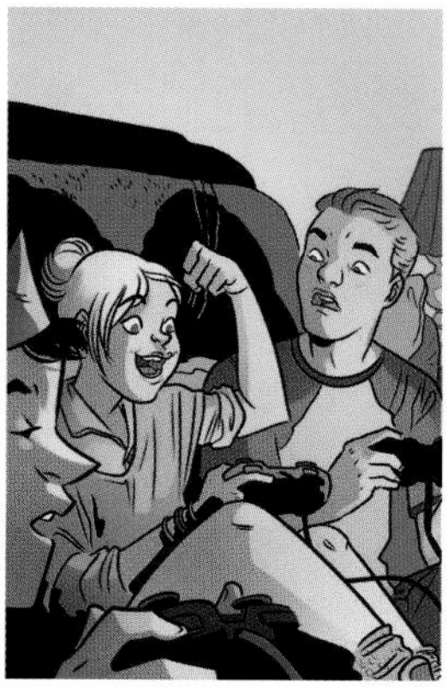

ERICA HENDERSON

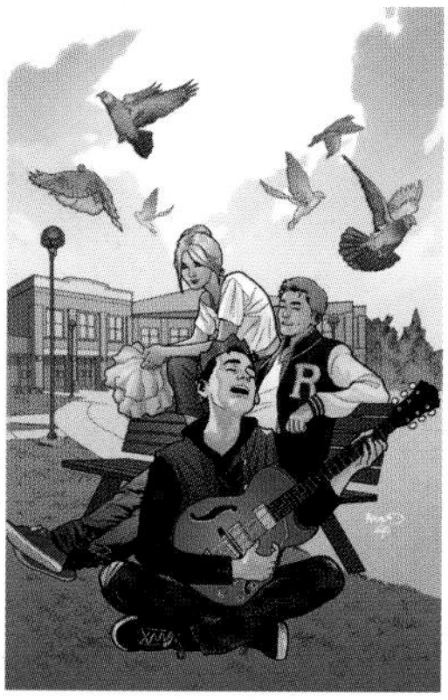

PAUL RENAUD

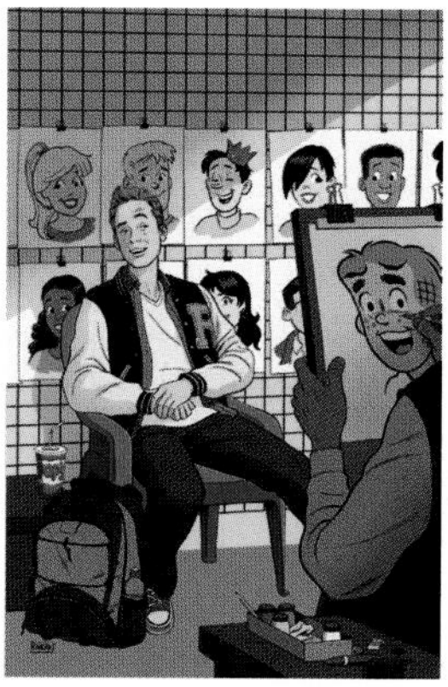

PAOLO RIVERA

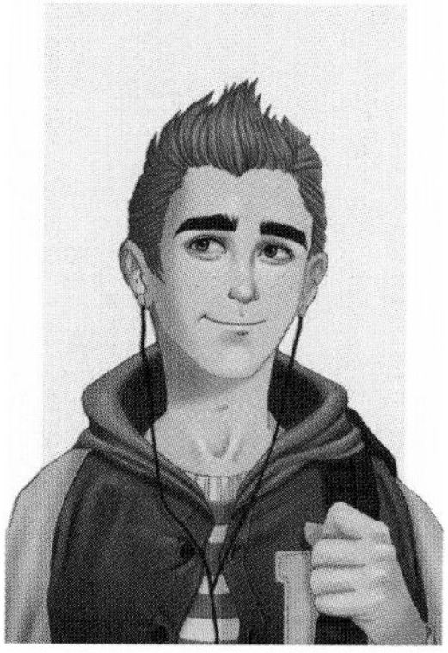

CHRISSIE ZULLO

ISSUE THREE

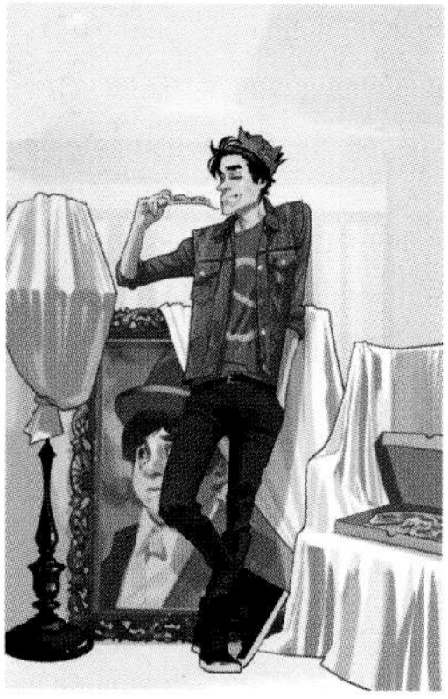

FIONA STAPLES

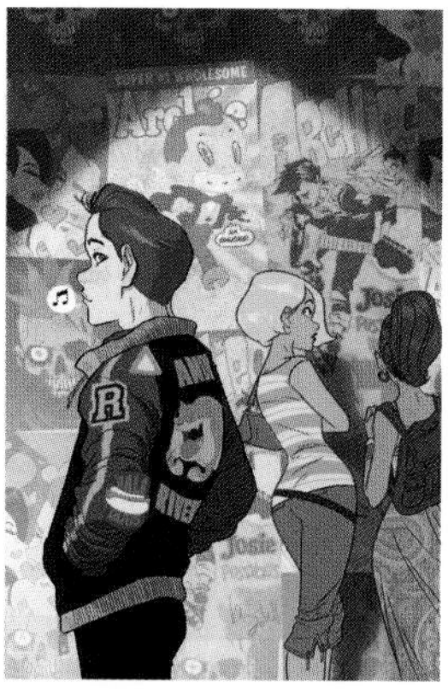

BEN CALDWELL

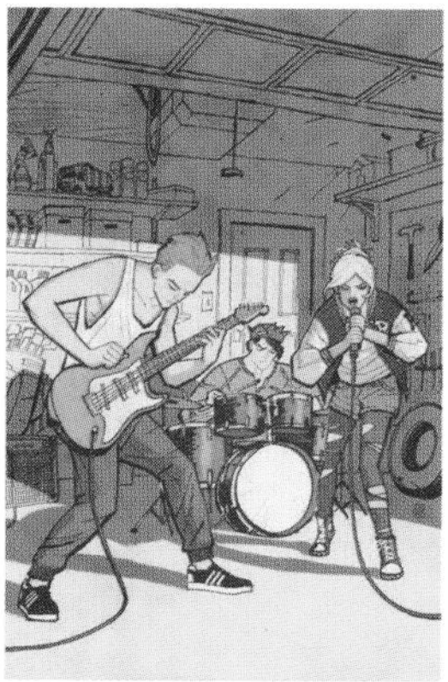

CLIFF CHIANG

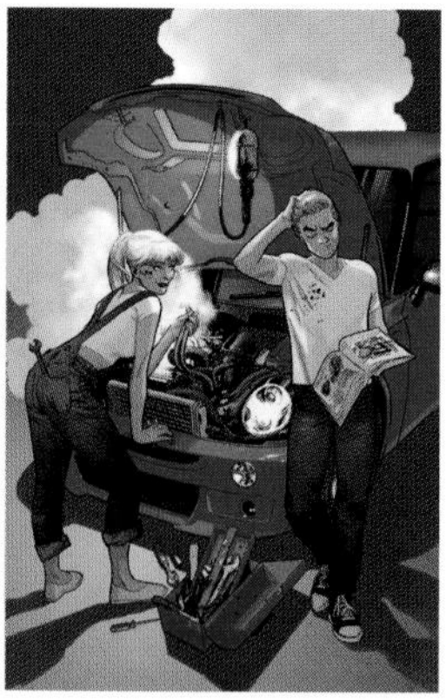

STUART IMMONEN

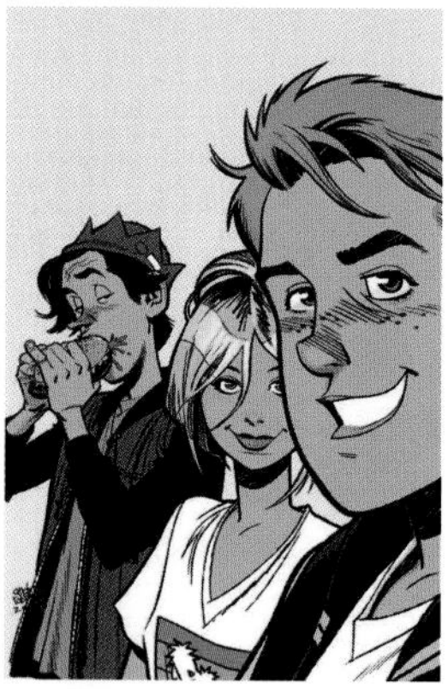

ANDREW ROBINSON

ISSUE FOUR

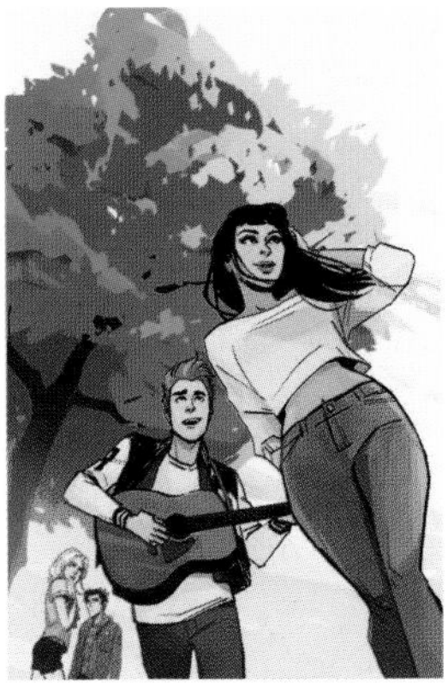

ANNIE WU

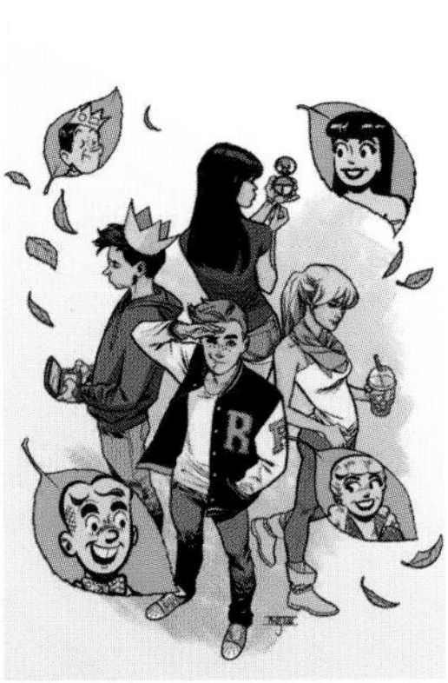

MAHMUD ASRAR

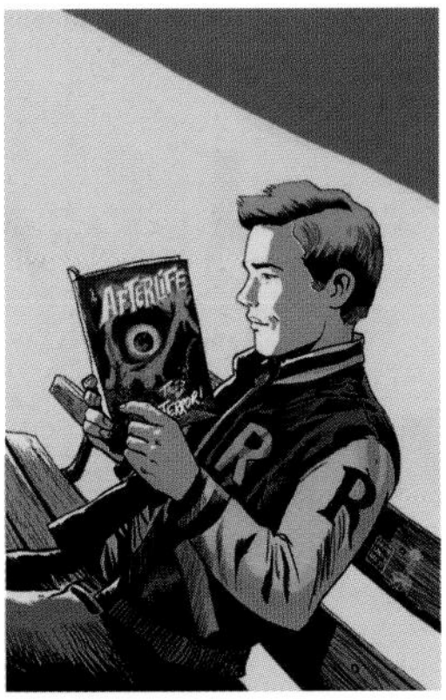
AFTERLIFE

FRANCESCO FRANCAVILLA

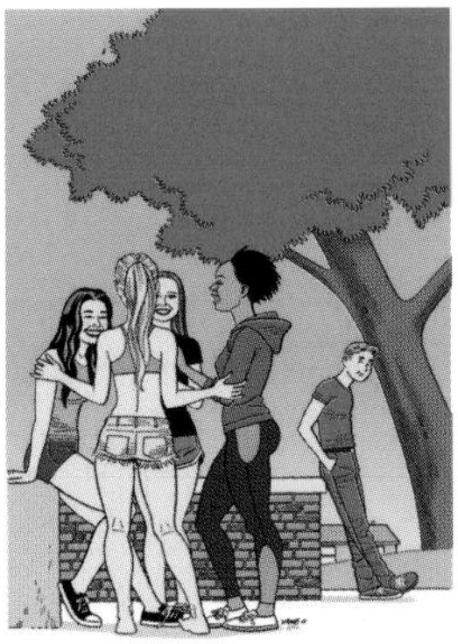

JAIME HERNANDEZ

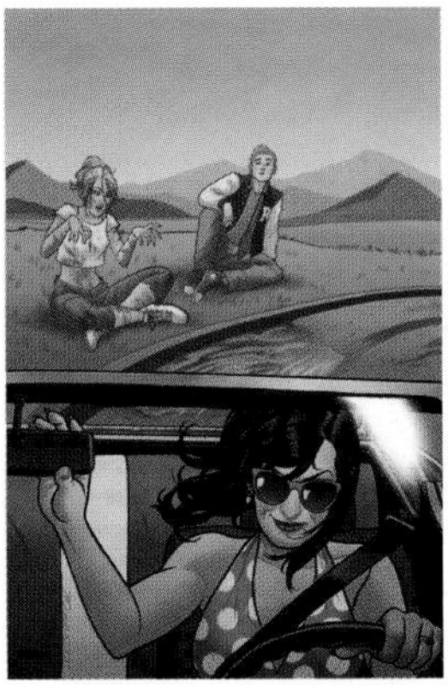

JOE QUINONES

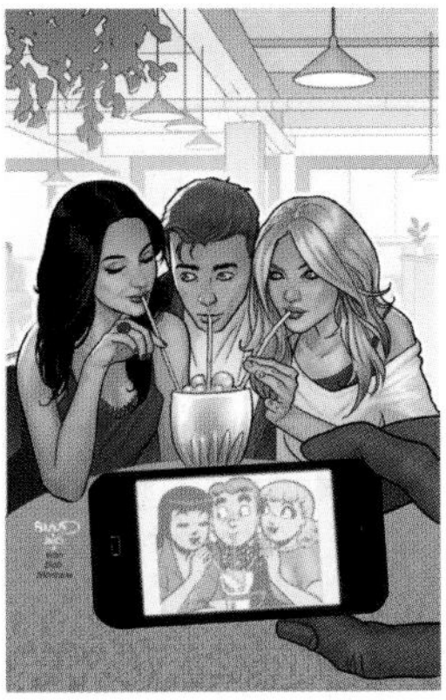

PAUL RENAUD

ISSUE FIVE

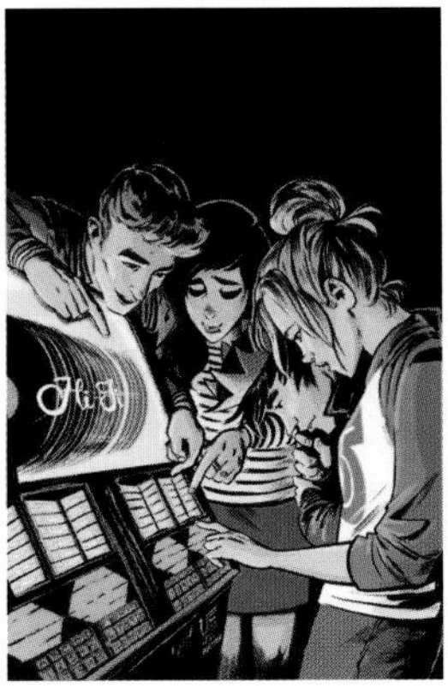

VERONICA FISH

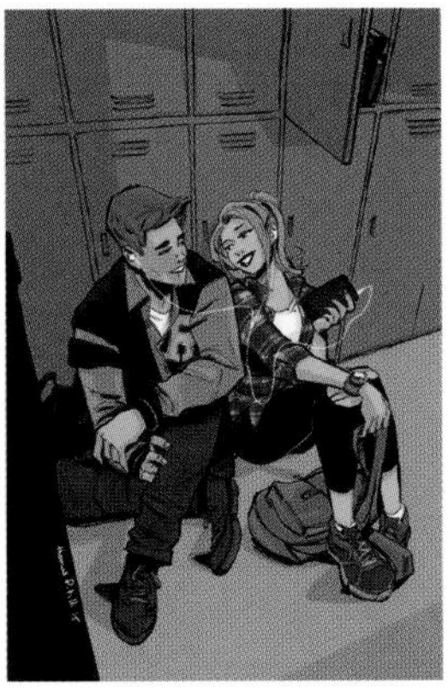

THOMAS PITILLI

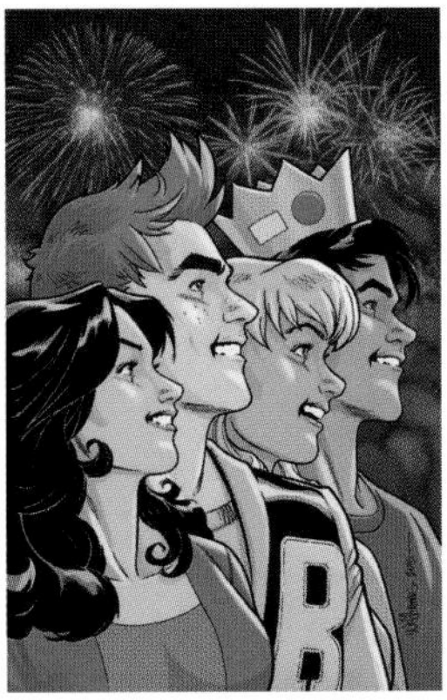

DAVID WILLIAMS

ISSUE SIX

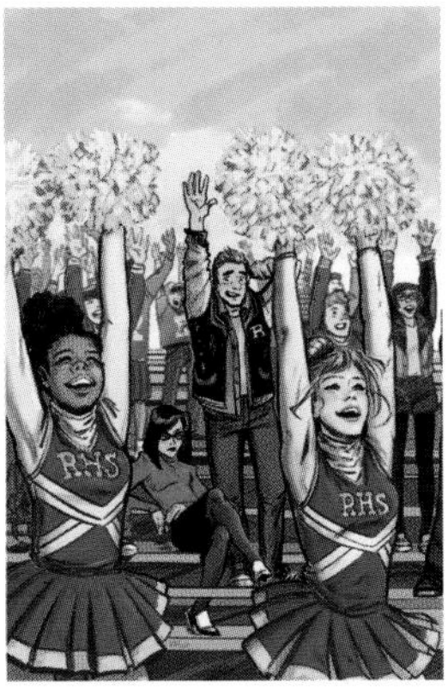

VERONICA FISH

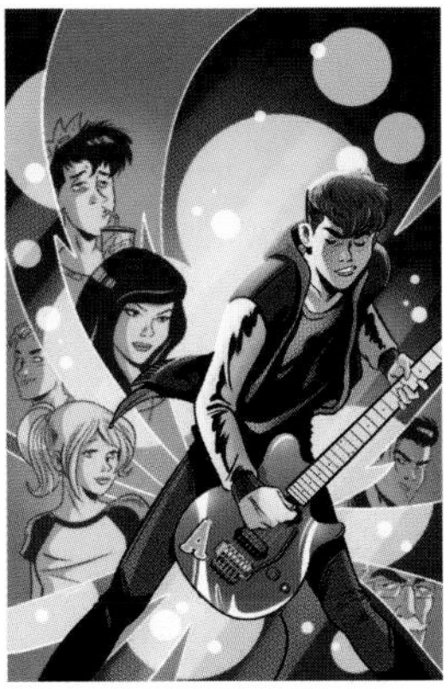

DEREK CHARM

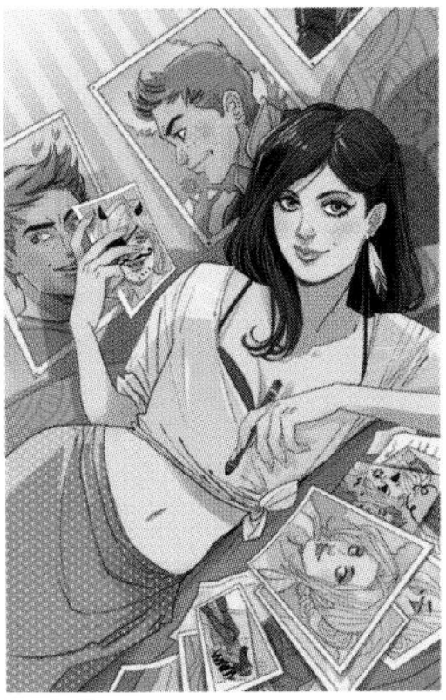

MARGUERITE SAUVAGE

HOW IT'S MADE

ARCHIE®

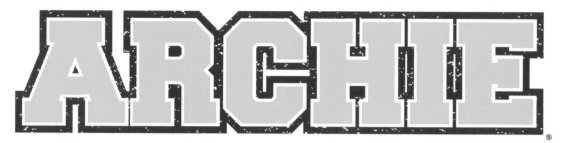

Get an inside look at the artistic process behind the historic relaunch of ARCHIE starting from the minds of MARK WAID and FIONA STAPLES. While the structure for all issues follow these same basic steps, different artists all bring their own creative spins on their ways of handling the process!

SCRIPT

It all starts with a script from writer MARK WAID, which is then looked over by President/Editor MIKE PELLERITO and Editor-in-Chief VICTOR GORELICK for any feedback. MARK will make any changes to the script requested, and then will send a finalized script back to the Archie offices to begin the art process.

ARCHIE #1/Script/FOURTH DRAFT/Ms. Page 2 **MARK WAID**

PAGE TWO

PANEL ONE/PAGE-WIDE: OPEN FOR TYPE.

1 TYPE: CHAPTER 1:
THERE IS THIS GIRL

PANEL TWO: ARCHIE WALKS DOWN THE HALLWAY AMONG THE STUDENTS. HE SEEMS IN GOOD SPIRITS--NEITHER TOO BLUE NOR TOO CHEERFUL.

2 ARCHIE: Don't pay too much attention to me. I'm not exactly the most interesting guy in town.

PANEL THREE: HE PASSES DILTON AND RAJ (FILMING SOMETHING WITH HIS SMARTPHONE) AND TREV.

3 ARCHIE: I'm not super-smart, like Dilton.

4 ARCHIE: Or an aspiring filmmaker, like Raj.

5 ARCHIE: I don't have an American Idol-winning sister like Trev does.

PANEL FOUR: AS ARCHIE LEAVES THOSE THREE IN THE BACKGROUND, THEY STARE AFTER HIM AND WHISPER TO EACH OTHER.

6 ARCHIE: All I am is the guy everybody's TALKING about today. Y'see...

7 DILTON/small: Did you HEAR?

8 RAJ/small: Do we know WHY? They BELONG together. This is UNREAL.

9 TREV/small: It's like up is DOWN. Right is LEFT. Dilton is MOOSE.

PANEL FIVE: ARCHIE, HAVING TURNED THE CORNER, LEANS MOPILY AGAINST THE WALL AND LOOKS AT BETTY COOPER RUMMAGING THROUGH HER LOCKER OR, REALLY, DOING ANYTHING SO LONG AS SHE'S NOT NOTICING ARCHIE.

10 ARCHIE: ...there is this GIRL.

11 ARCHIE: ...

Chapter 1 (p.1-6): D.O.S. 3/20/15 Code No. B-34 Computer Code #8247
Chapter 2 (p.7-11): D.O.S. 3/20/15 Code No. B-35 Computer Code #8248
Chapter 3 (p.12-22): D.O.S. 3/20/15 Code No. B-36 Computer Code #8249

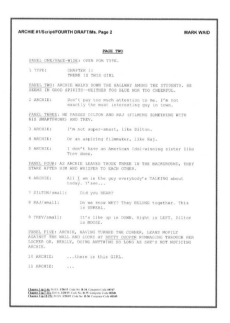

THUMBNAILS

Once artist FIONA STAPLES receives the script from MARK WAID and the team at Archie, she begins by penciling thumbnail sketches of all the pages of the script, creating a storyboard. These are rough images that are used for layout purposes, to see how each scene will play out and where word balloons can be placed.

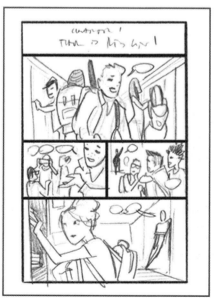

PENCILS & INKS

FIONA STAPLES then pencils more polished and refined versions of the thumbnail pages, capturing the characters' features, clothing and backgrounds. She then digitally inks the artwork. From there the pages are sent to letterer JACK MORELLI.

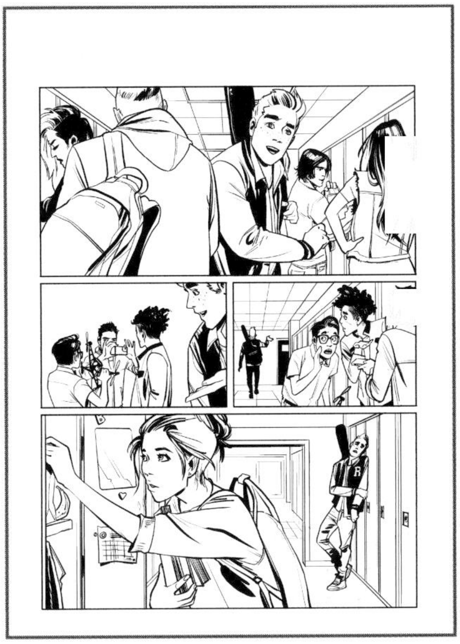

LETTERS

JACK MORELLI uses the script to guide him in adding word balloons, captions and sound effects to the art, which are then sent back to the Archie offices for early proofreading. JACK then makes any changes if needed, and sends them off to the colorists ANDRE SZYMANOWICZ and JEN VAUGHN.

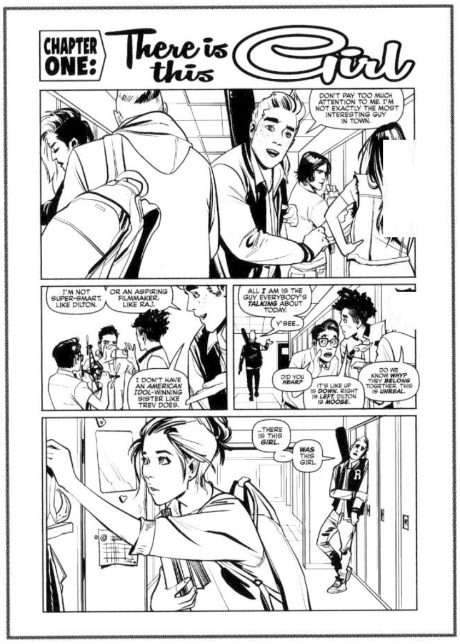
CHAPTER ONE: There is this Girl
DON'T PAY TOO MUCH ATTENTION TO ME. I'M NOT EXACTLY THE MOST INTERESTING GUY IN TOWN.
I'M NOT SUPER-SMART, LIKE DILTON.
OR AN ASPIRING FILMMAKER, LIKE RAJ.
I DON'T HAVE AN AMERICAN IDOL-WINNING SISTER LIKE TREV DOES.
ALL I AM IS THE GUY EVERYBODY'S TALKING ABOUT TODAY.
Y'SEE...
DID YOU HEAR?
IT'S LIKE UP IS DOWN, RIGHT IS LEFT, DILTON IS MOOSE.
DO WE KNOW WHY? THEY BELONG TOGETHER. THIS IS UNREAL.
...THERE IS THIS GIRL.
...
WAS THIS GIRL.

COLORS

Next ANDRE SZYMANOWICZ and JEN VAUGHN flat color and render all of the pages, and then combine the lettering with the final colored pages. The files are then sent back to the Archie offices where they are placed into the publishing software InDesign, which are then proofread one final time, and routed around to the Editor, Editor-in-Chief, and then to Publisher/Co-CEO JON GOLDWATER for final approval. Once this is done, the digital files are sent to the printer.

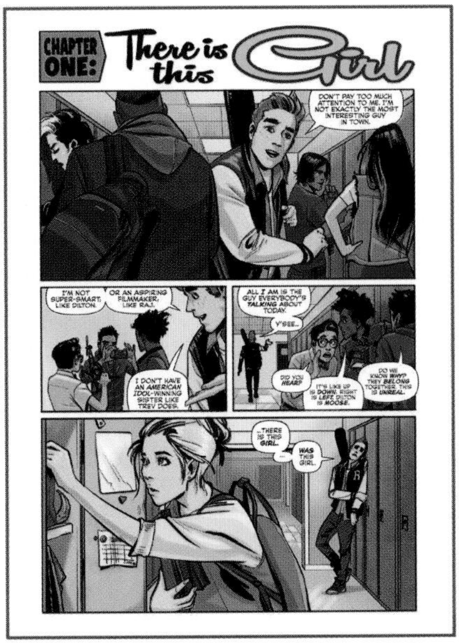
CHAPTER ONE: There is this Girl
DON'T PAY TOO MUCH ATTENTION TO ME. I'M NOT EXACTLY THE MOST INTERESTING GUY IN TOWN.
I'M NOT SUPER-SMART, LIKE DILTON.
OR AN ASPIRING FILMMAKER, LIKE RAJ.
I DON'T HAVE AN AMERICAN IDOL-WINNING SISTER LIKE TREV DOES.
ALL I AM IS THE GUY EVERYBODY'S TALKING ABOUT TODAY.
Y'SEE...
DID YOU HEAR?
IT'S LIKE UP IS DOWN, RIGHT IS LEFT, DILTON IS MOOSE.
DO WE KNOW WHY? THEY BELONG TOGETHER. THIS IS UNREAL.
...THERE IS THIS GIRL.
...
WAS THIS GIRL.

AFTERWORD

by MARK WAID

FIRST, DO NO HARM

That headline? Those were the first words I typed back in late 2014 when I wrote up my pitch for the Archie reboot you just read. I'm a big believer in the Hippocratic Oath when it comes to reinventing characters who've been around since before you or I were born.

Yes, there was a general feeling among everyone involved with the relaunch that Riverdale could stand a little bit of updating, but no one took that to mean "Betty fails a pregnancy test" or "Archie flips off Mr. Weatherbee." First off, a character created for an all-ages audience should stay exactly that. Writing for irony-starved hipsters is no challenge. Second, any chimpanzee can type the words, "Page One, Panel One: Establishing shot, Jughead's meth lab" and get a laugh (and a Million-Mom March), but– not to sound preachy– that's a gross betrayal of who and what Archie's gang has come to mean to generations of readers.

All the term "updating" meant to me, to us, was digging a little more deeply into the kids and their personalities. It meant allowing actual, permanent conflict between them so that there's a greater, more dramatic sense of consequence to their interactions and their choices. It meant never ignoring an opportunity for Archie to get a paint can stuck on his head. It's still comedy, people.

Whatever support and cooperation I'd hoped we'd get from publisher Jon Goldwater and his staff, we got ten times that. Better, they found me the perfect launch partner in Fiona Staples, one of the best comics artists of our time and one who loves the Archie universe like Jughead loves burgers. She can bring the serious, she can bring the funny, and her work's never looked more spectacular than when colored by Andre Szymanowicz and Jen Vaughn and lettered by Jack Morelli.

If you liked what you've just read, come back for more; you can find Archie in all good comics shops and on the web. We promise you'll have a great time in Riverdale.

SPECIAL PREVIEW

Jughead®

ISSUE ONE

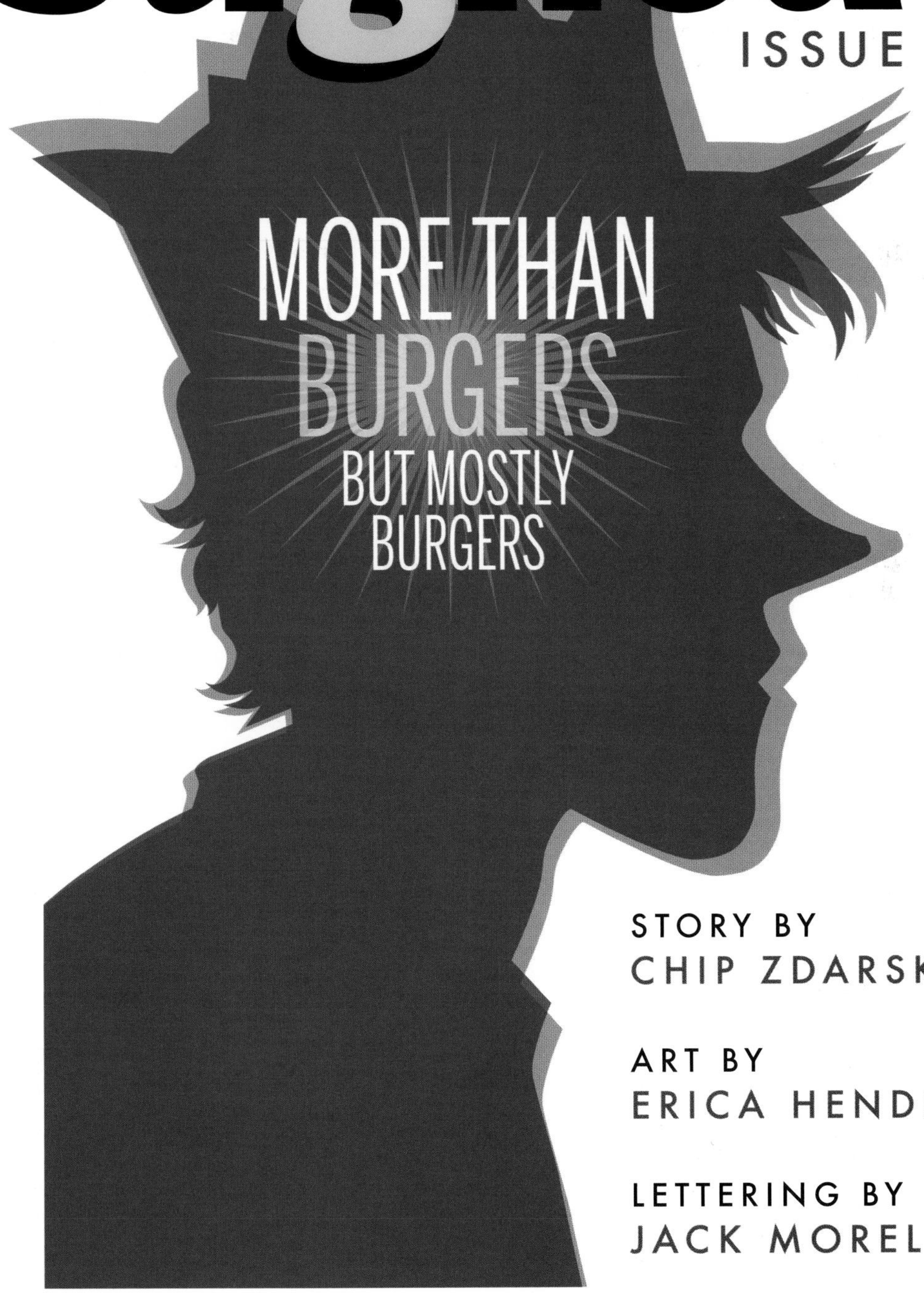
MORE THAN
BURGERS
BUT MOSTLY
BURGERS

STORY BY
CHIP ZDARSKY

ART BY
ERICA HENDERSON

LETTERING BY
JACK MORELLI

ISSUE ONE

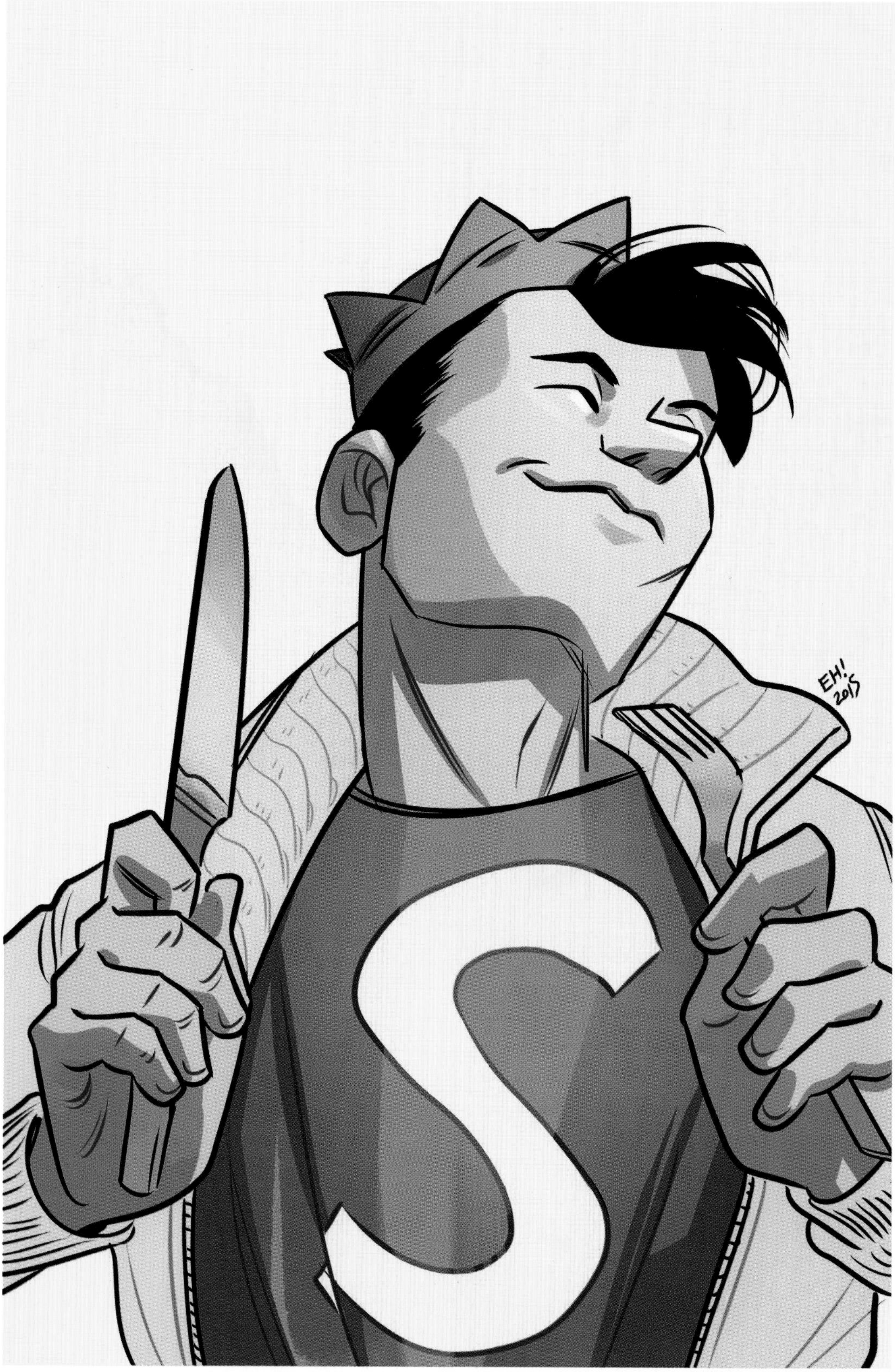
EH! 2015

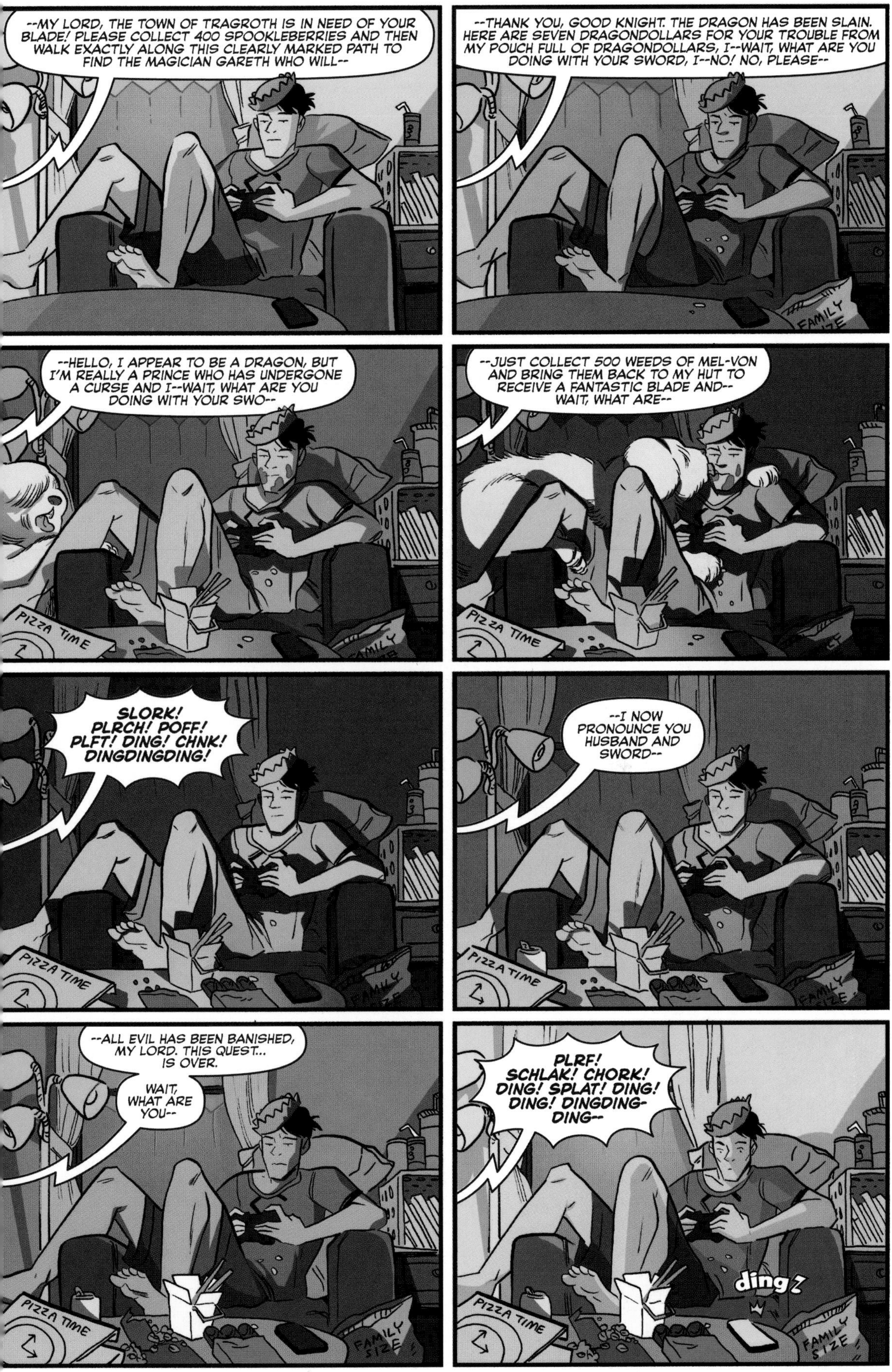
--MY LORD, THE TOWN OF TRAGROTH IS IN NEED OF YOUR BLADE! PLEASE COLLECT 400 SPOOKLEBERRIES AND THEN WALK EXACTLY ALONG THIS CLEARLY MARKED PATH TO FIND THE MAGICIAN GARETH WHO WILL--
--THANK YOU, GOOD KNIGHT. THE DRAGON HAS BEEN SLAIN. HERE ARE SEVEN DRAGONDOLLARS FOR YOUR TROUBLE FROM MY POUCH FULL OF DRAGONDOLLARS, I--WAIT, WHAT ARE YOU DOING WITH YOUR SWORD, I--NO! NO, PLEASE--
FAMILY SIZE
--HELLO, I APPEAR TO BE A DRAGON, BUT I'M REALLY A PRINCE WHO HAS UNDERGONE A CURSE AND I--WAIT, WHAT ARE YOU DOING WITH YOUR SWO--
PIZZA TIME
FAMILY SIZE
--JUST COLLECT 500 WEEDS OF MEL-VON AND BRING THEM BACK TO MY HUT TO RECEIVE A FANTASTIC BLADE AND-- WAIT, WHAT ARE--
PIZZA TIME
SLORK! PLRCH! POFF! PLFT! DING! CHNK! DINGDINGDING!
PIZZA TIME
--I NOW PRONOUNCE YOU HUSBAND AND SWORD--
PIZZA TIME
--ALL EVIL HAS BEEN BANISHED, MY LORD. THIS QUEST... IS OVER.
WAIT, WHAT ARE YOU--
PIZZA TIME
FAMILY SIZE
PLRF! SCHLAK! CHORK! DING! SPLAT! DING! DING! DINGDING-DING--
ding
PIZZA TIME
FAMILY SIZE

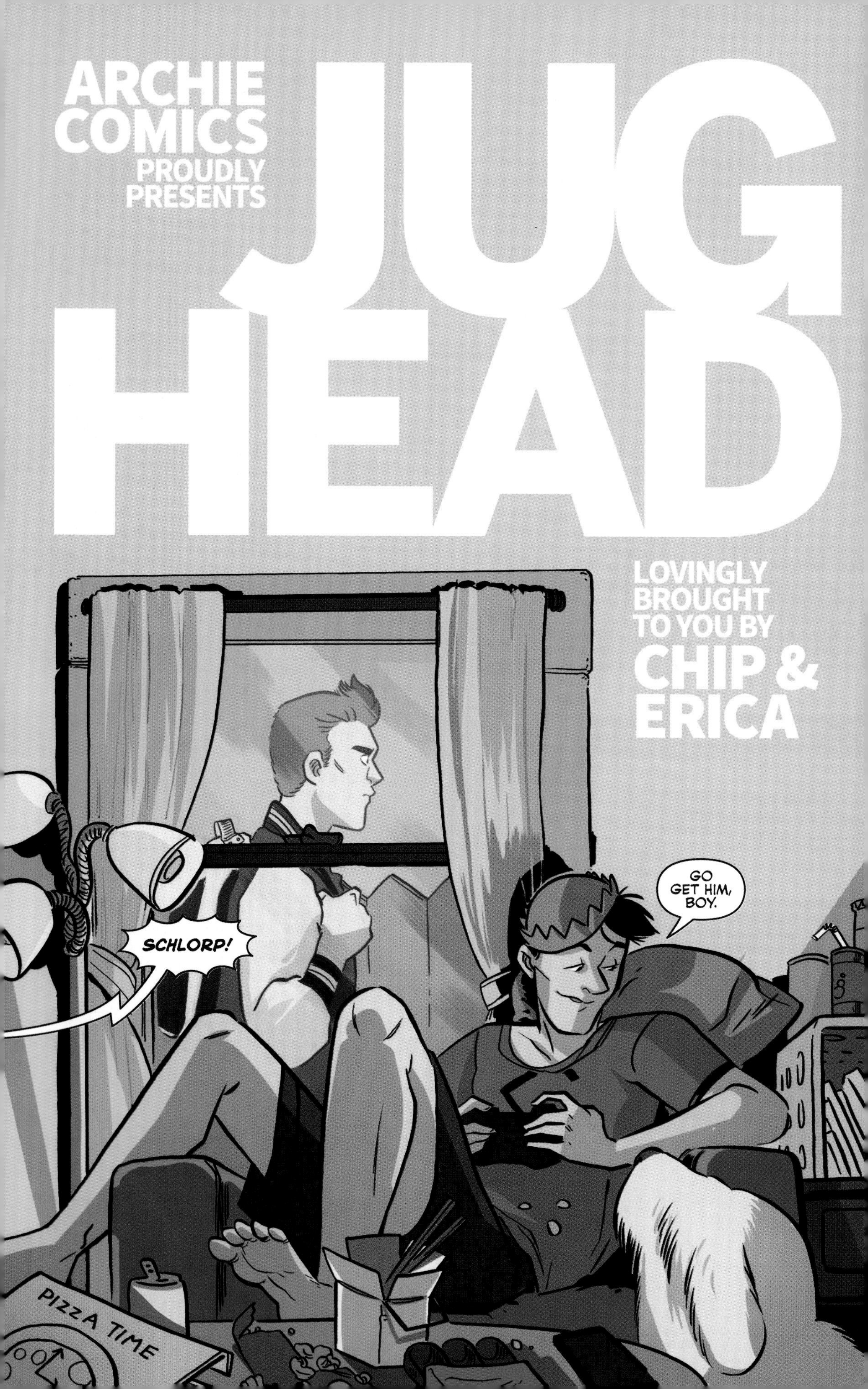
ARCHIE COMICS PROUDLY PRESENTS
JUG HEAD
LOVINGLY BROUGHT TO YOU BY CHIP & ERICA
GO GET HIM, BOY.
SCHLORP!
PIZZA TIME

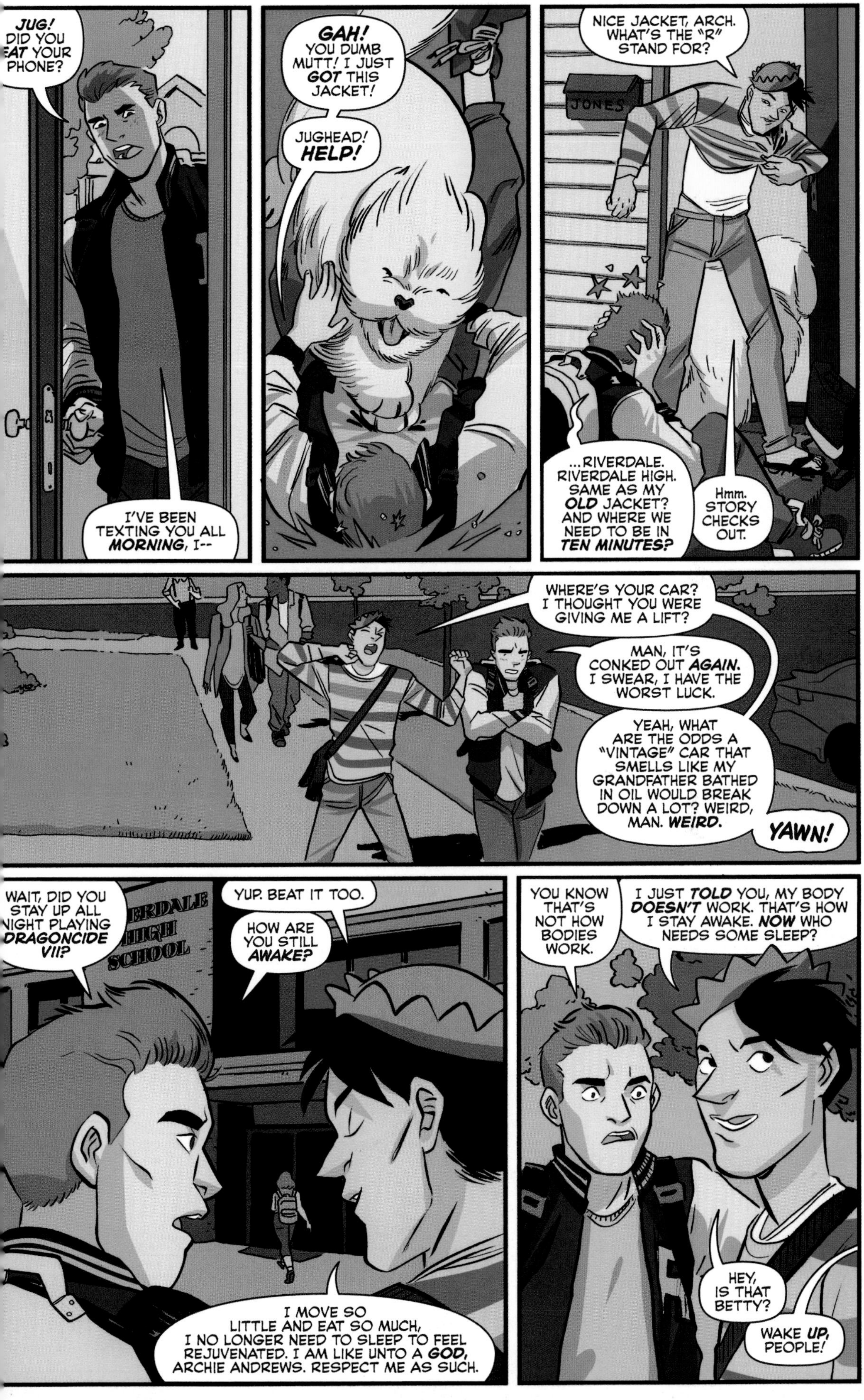
JUG! DID YOU EAT YOUR PHONE?
I'VE BEEN TEXTING YOU ALL MORNING, I--
GAH! YOU DUMB MUTT! I JUST GOT THIS JACKET!
JUGHEAD! HELP!
NICE JACKET, ARCH. WHAT'S THE "R" STAND FOR?
JONES
...RIVERDALE. RIVERDALE HIGH. SAME AS MY OLD JACKET? AND WHERE WE NEED TO BE IN TEN MINUTES?
Hmm. STORY CHECKS OUT.
WHERE'S YOUR CAR? I THOUGHT YOU WERE GIVING ME A LIFT?
MAN, IT'S CONKED OUT AGAIN. I SWEAR, I HAVE THE WORST LUCK.
YEAH, WHAT ARE THE ODDS A "VINTAGE" CAR THAT SMELLS LIKE MY GRANDFATHER BATHED IN OIL WOULD BREAK DOWN A LOT? WEIRD, MAN. WEIRD.
YAWN!
WAIT, DID YOU STAY UP ALL NIGHT PLAYING DRAGONCIDE VII?
ERDALE HIGH SCHOOL
YUP. BEAT IT TOO.
HOW ARE YOU STILL AWAKE?
I MOVE SO LITTLE AND EAT SO MUCH, I NO LONGER NEED TO SLEEP TO FEEL REJUVENATED. I AM LIKE UNTO A GOD, ARCHIE ANDREWS. RESPECT ME AS SUCH.
YOU KNOW THAT'S NOT HOW BODIES WORK.
I JUST TOLD YOU, MY BODY DOESN'T WORK. THAT'S HOW I STAY AWAKE. NOW WHO NEEDS SOME SLEEP?
HEY, IS THAT BETTY?
WAKE UP, PEOPLE!

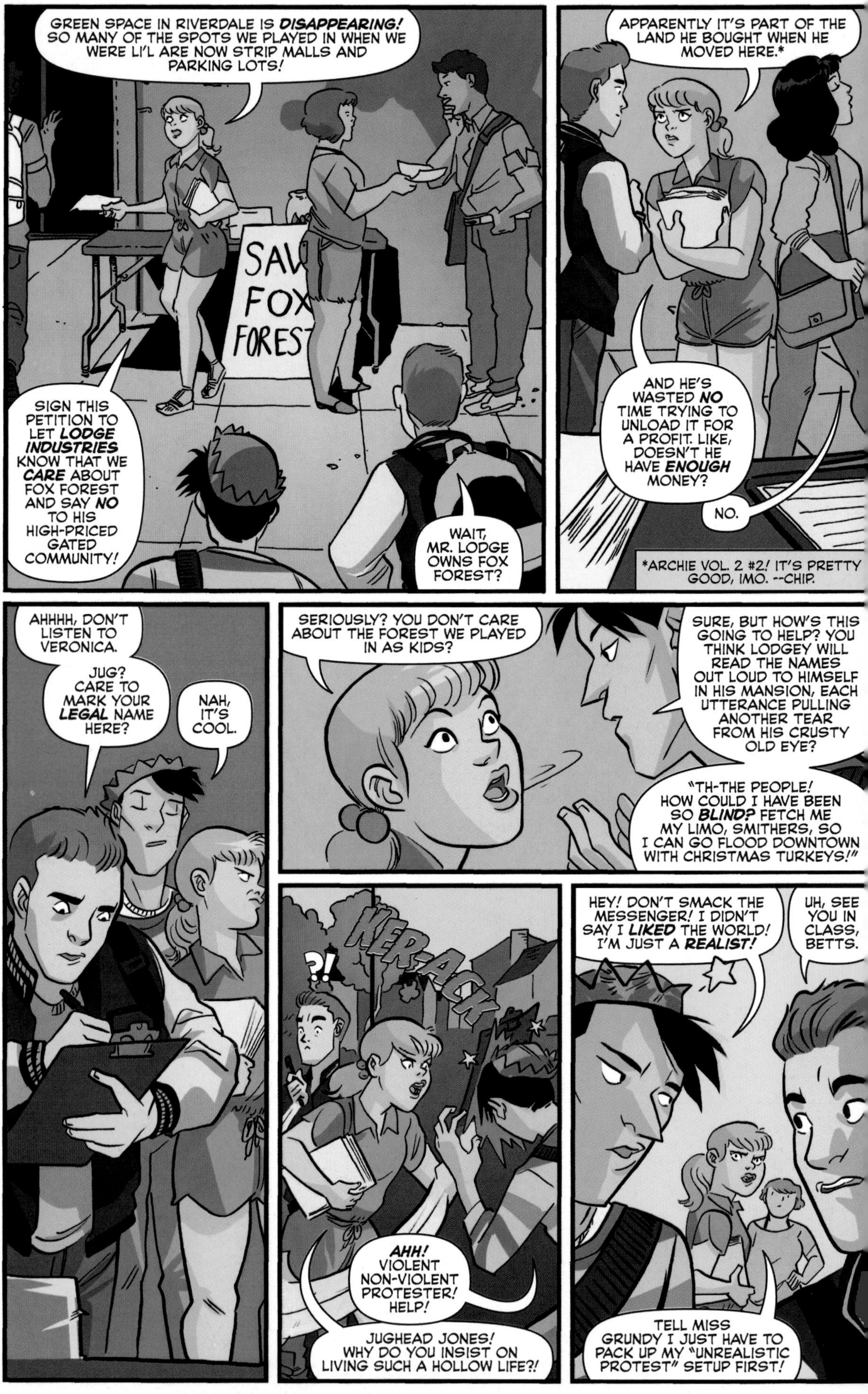
GREEN SPACE IN RIVERDALE IS DISAPPEARING! SO MANY OF THE SPOTS WE PLAYED IN WHEN WE WERE LI'L ARE NOW STRIP MALLS AND PARKING LOTS!
SAV FOX FOREST
SIGN THIS PETITION TO LET LODGE INDUSTRIES KNOW THAT WE CARE ABOUT FOX FOREST AND SAY NO TO HIS HIGH-PRICED GATED COMMUNITY!
WAIT, MR. LODGE OWNS FOX FOREST?
APPARENTLY IT'S PART OF THE LAND HE BOUGHT WHEN HE MOVED HERE.*
AND HE'S WASTED NO TIME TRYING TO UNLOAD IT FOR A PROFIT. LIKE, DOESN'T HE HAVE ENOUGH MONEY?
NO.
*ARCHIE VOL. 2 #2! IT'S PRETTY GOOD, IMO. --CHIP.
AHHHH, DON'T LISTEN TO VERONICA.
JUG? CARE TO MARK YOUR LEGAL NAME HERE?
NAH, IT'S COOL.
SERIOUSLY? YOU DON'T CARE ABOUT THE FOREST WE PLAYED IN AS KIDS?
SURE, BUT HOW'S THIS GOING TO HELP? YOU THINK LODGEY WILL READ THE NAMES OUT LOUD TO HIMSELF IN HIS MANSION, EACH UTTERANCE PULLING ANOTHER TEAR FROM HIS CRUSTY OLD EYE?
"TH-THE PEOPLE! HOW COULD I HAVE BEEN SO BLIND? FETCH ME MY LIMO, SMITHERS, SO I CAN GO FLOOD DOWNTOWN WITH CHRISTMAS TURKEYS!"
KER-ACK
?!
AHH! VIOLENT NON-VIOLENT PROTESTER! HELP!
JUGHEAD JONES! WHY DO YOU INSIST ON LIVING SUCH A HOLLOW LIFE?!
HEY! DON'T SMACK THE MESSENGER! I DIDN'T SAY I LIKED THE WORLD! I'M JUST A REALIST!
UH, SEE YOU IN CLASS, BETTS.
TELL MISS GRUNDY I JUST HAVE TO PACK UP MY "UNREALISTIC PROTEST" SETUP FIRST!

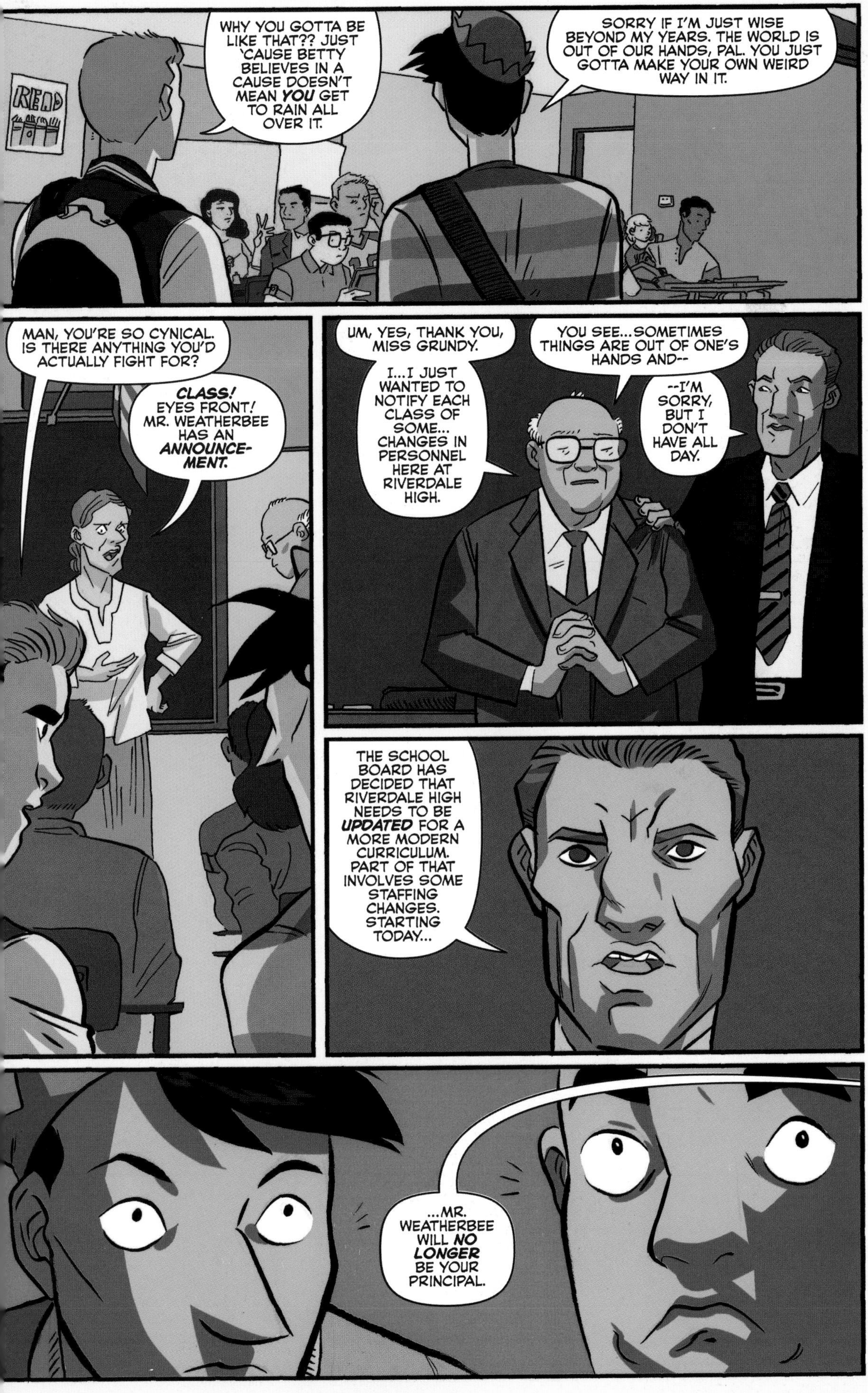
READ
WHY YOU GOTTA BE LIKE THAT?? JUST 'CAUSE BETTY BELIEVES IN A CAUSE DOESN'T MEAN **YOU** GET TO RAIN ALL OVER IT.
SORRY IF I'M JUST WISE BEYOND MY YEARS. THE WORLD IS OUT OF OUR HANDS, PAL. YOU JUST GOTTA MAKE YOUR OWN WEIRD WAY IN IT.
MAN, YOU'RE SO CYNICAL. IS THERE ANYTHING YOU'D ACTUALLY FIGHT FOR?
CLASS! EYES FRONT! MR. WEATHERBEE HAS AN ***ANNOUNCE-MENT.***
UM, YES, THANK YOU, MISS GRUNDY.
I...I JUST WANTED TO NOTIFY EACH CLASS OF SOME... CHANGES IN PERSONNEL HERE AT RIVERDALE HIGH.
YOU SEE...SOMETIMES THINGS ARE OUT OF ONE'S HANDS AND--
--I'M SORRY, BUT I DON'T HAVE ALL DAY.
THE SCHOOL BOARD HAS DECIDED THAT RIVERDALE HIGH NEEDS TO BE ***UPDATED*** FOR A MORE MODERN CURRICULUM. PART OF THAT INVOLVES SOME STAFFING CHANGES. STARTING TODAY...
...MR. WEATHERBEE WILL ***NO LONGER*** BE YOUR PRINCIPAL.

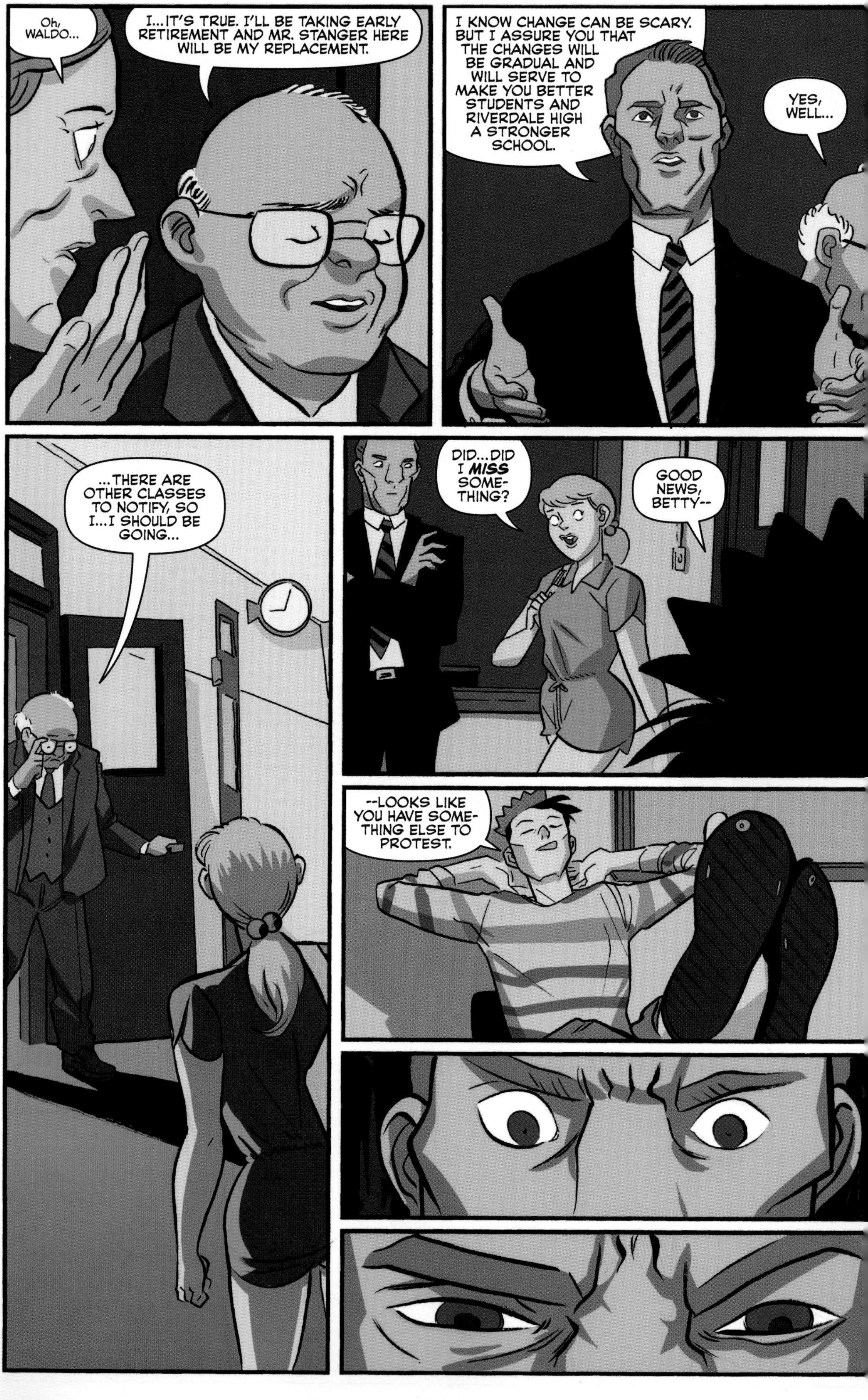

Oh, WALDO...
I...IT'S TRUE. I'LL BE TAKING EARLY RETIREMENT AND MR. STANGER HERE WILL BE MY REPLACEMENT.
I KNOW CHANGE CAN BE SCARY. BUT I ASSURE YOU THAT THE CHANGES WILL BE GRADUAL AND WILL SERVE TO MAKE YOU BETTER STUDENTS AND RIVERDALE HIGH A STRONGER SCHOOL.
YES, WELL...
...THERE ARE OTHER CLASSES TO NOTIFY, SO I...I SHOULD BE GOING...
DID...DID I MISS SOMETHING?
GOOD NEWS, BETTY--
--LOOKS LIKE YOU HAVE SOMETHING ELSE TO PROTEST.

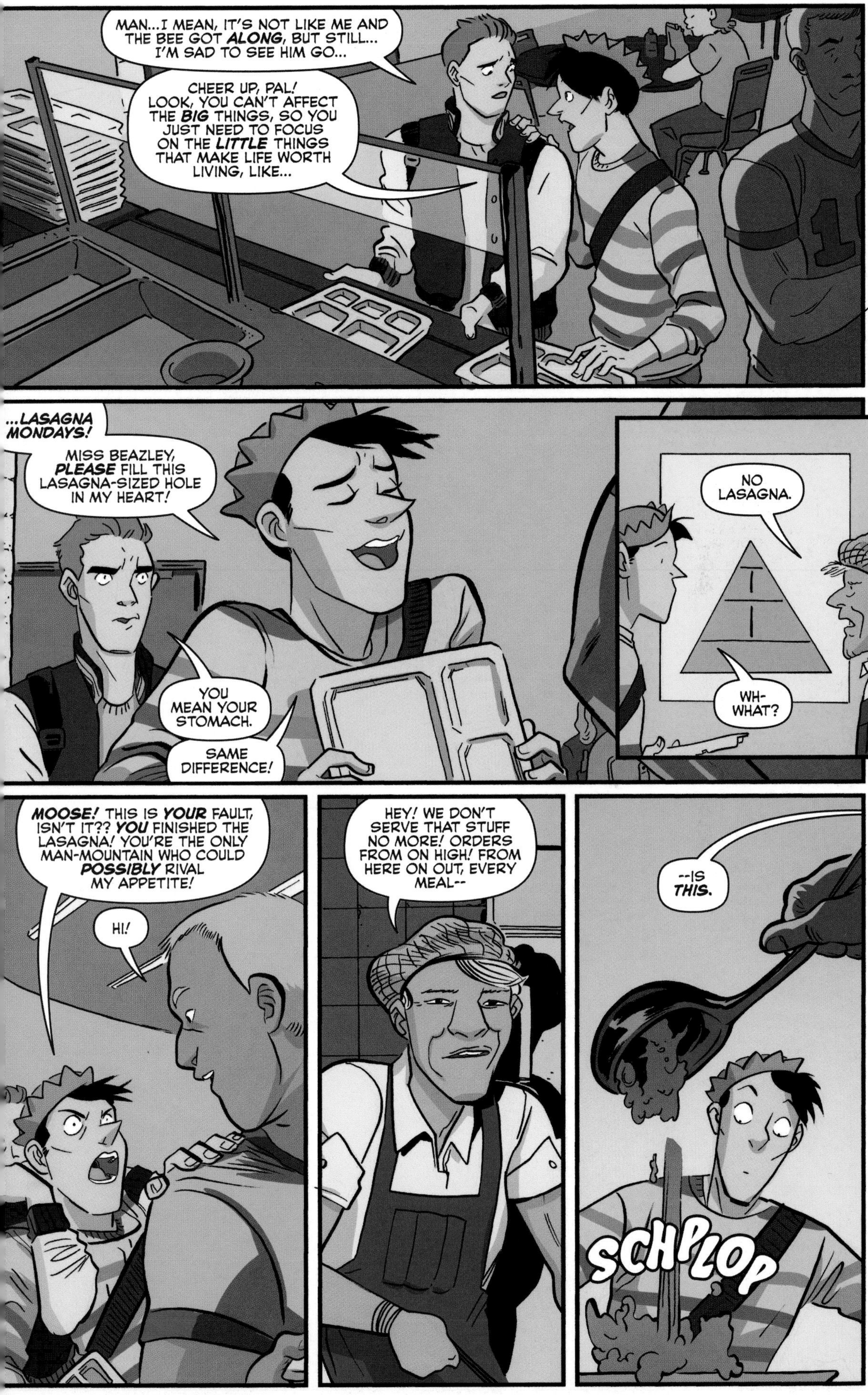
MAN...I MEAN, IT'S NOT LIKE ME AND THE BEE GOT ALONG, BUT STILL... I'M SAD TO SEE HIM GO...
CHEER UP, PAL! LOOK, YOU CAN'T AFFECT THE BIG THINGS, SO YOU JUST NEED TO FOCUS ON THE LITTLE THINGS THAT MAKE LIFE WORTH LIVING, LIKE...
...LASAGNA MONDAYS!
MISS BEAZLEY, PLEASE FILL THIS LASAGNA-SIZED HOLE IN MY HEART!
YOU MEAN YOUR STOMACH.
SAME DIFFERENCE!
NO LASAGNA.
WH-WHAT?
MOOSE! THIS IS YOUR FAULT, ISN'T IT?? YOU FINISHED THE LASAGNA! YOU'RE THE ONLY MAN-MOUNTAIN WHO COULD POSSIBLY RIVAL MY APPETITE!
HI!
HEY! WE DON'T SERVE THAT STUFF NO MORE! ORDERS FROM ON HIGH! FROM HERE ON OUT, EVERY MEAL--
--IS THIS.
SCHPLOP

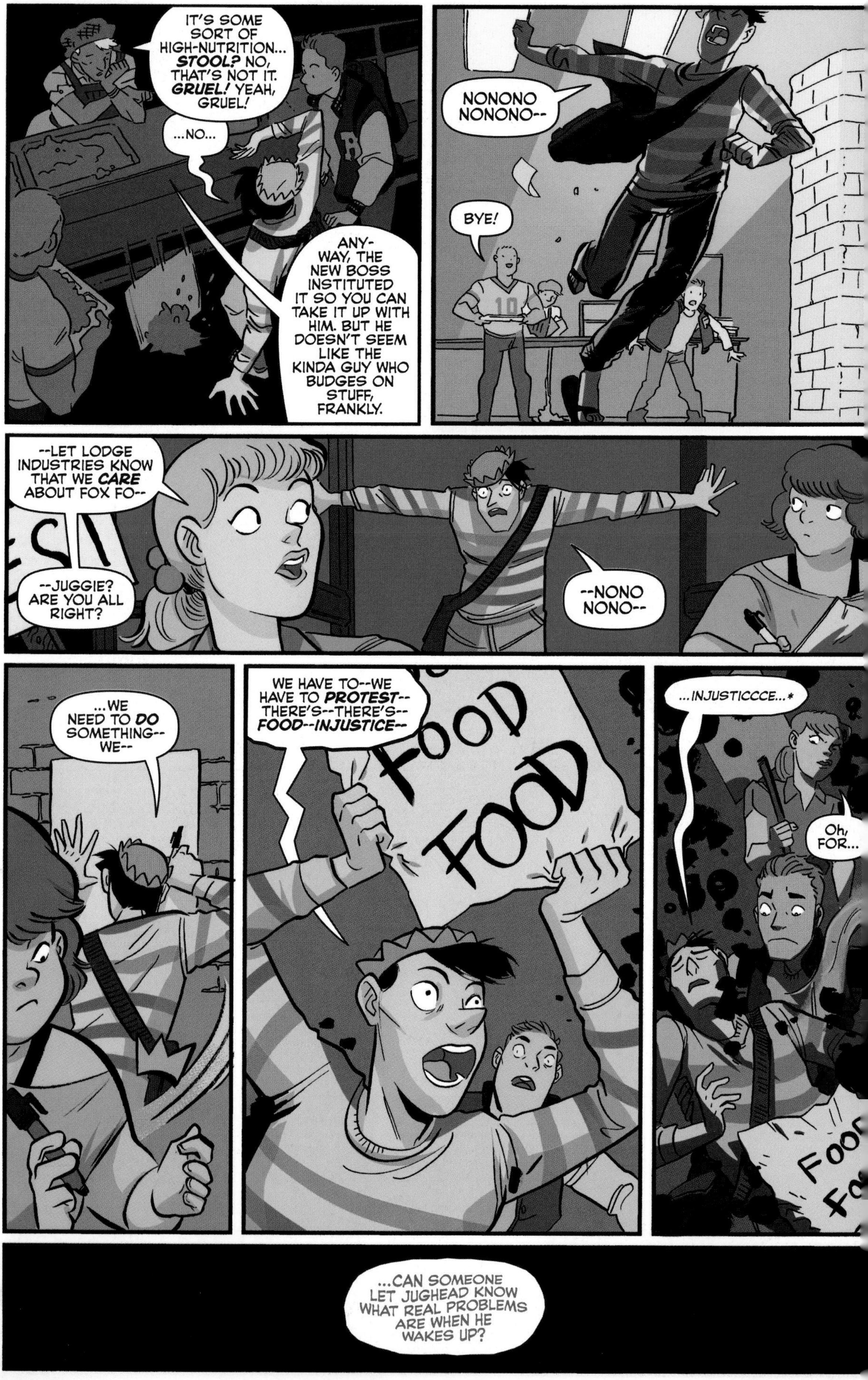
IT'S SOME SORT OF HIGH-NUTRITION... STOOL? NO, THAT'S NOT IT. GRUEL! YEAH, GRUEL!
...NO...
ANY-WAY, THE NEW BOSS INSTITUTED IT SO YOU CAN TAKE IT UP WITH HIM. BUT HE DOESN'T SEEM LIKE THE KINDA GUY WHO BUDGES ON STUFF, FRANKLY.
NONONO NONONO--
BYE!
--LET LODGE INDUSTRIES KNOW THAT WE CARE ABOUT FOX FO--
--JUGGIE? ARE YOU ALL RIGHT?
--NONO NONO--
...WE NEED TO DO SOMETHING-- WE--
WE HAVE TO--WE HAVE TO PROTEST-- THERE'S--THERE'S-- FOOD--INJUSTICE--
FOOD
FOOD
...INJUSTICCCE...*
Oh, FOR...
...CAN SOMEONE LET JUGHEAD KNOW WHAT REAL PROBLEMS ARE WHEN HE WAKES UP?

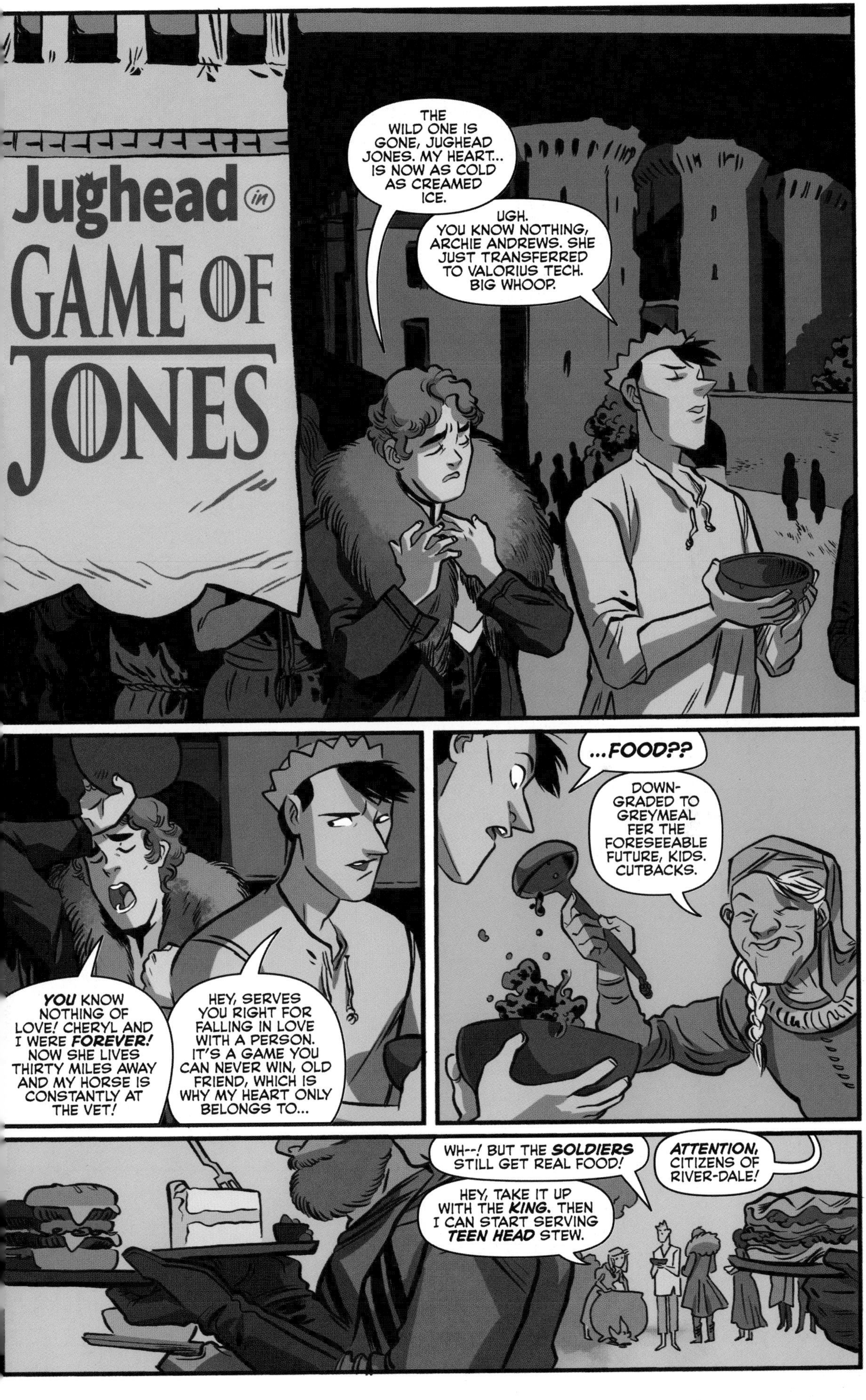
Jughead in
GAME OF JONES
THE WILD ONE IS GONE, JUGHEAD JONES. MY HEART... IS NOW AS COLD AS CREAMED ICE.
UGH. YOU KNOW NOTHING, ARCHIE ANDREWS. SHE JUST TRANSFERRED TO VALORIUS TECH. BIG WHOOP.
YOU KNOW NOTHING OF LOVE! CHERYL AND I WERE FOREVER! NOW SHE LIVES THIRTY MILES AWAY AND MY HORSE IS CONSTANTLY AT THE VET!
HEY, SERVES YOU RIGHT FOR FALLING IN LOVE WITH A PERSON. IT'S A GAME YOU CAN NEVER WIN, OLD FRIEND, WHICH IS WHY MY HEART ONLY BELONGS TO...
...FOOD??
DOWN-GRADED TO GREYMEAL FER THE FORESEEABLE FUTURE, KIDS. CUTBACKS.
WH--! BUT THE SOLDIERS STILL GET REAL FOOD!
HEY, TAKE IT UP WITH THE KING. THEN I CAN START SERVING TEEN HEAD STEW.
ATTENTION, CITIZENS OF RIVER-DALE!

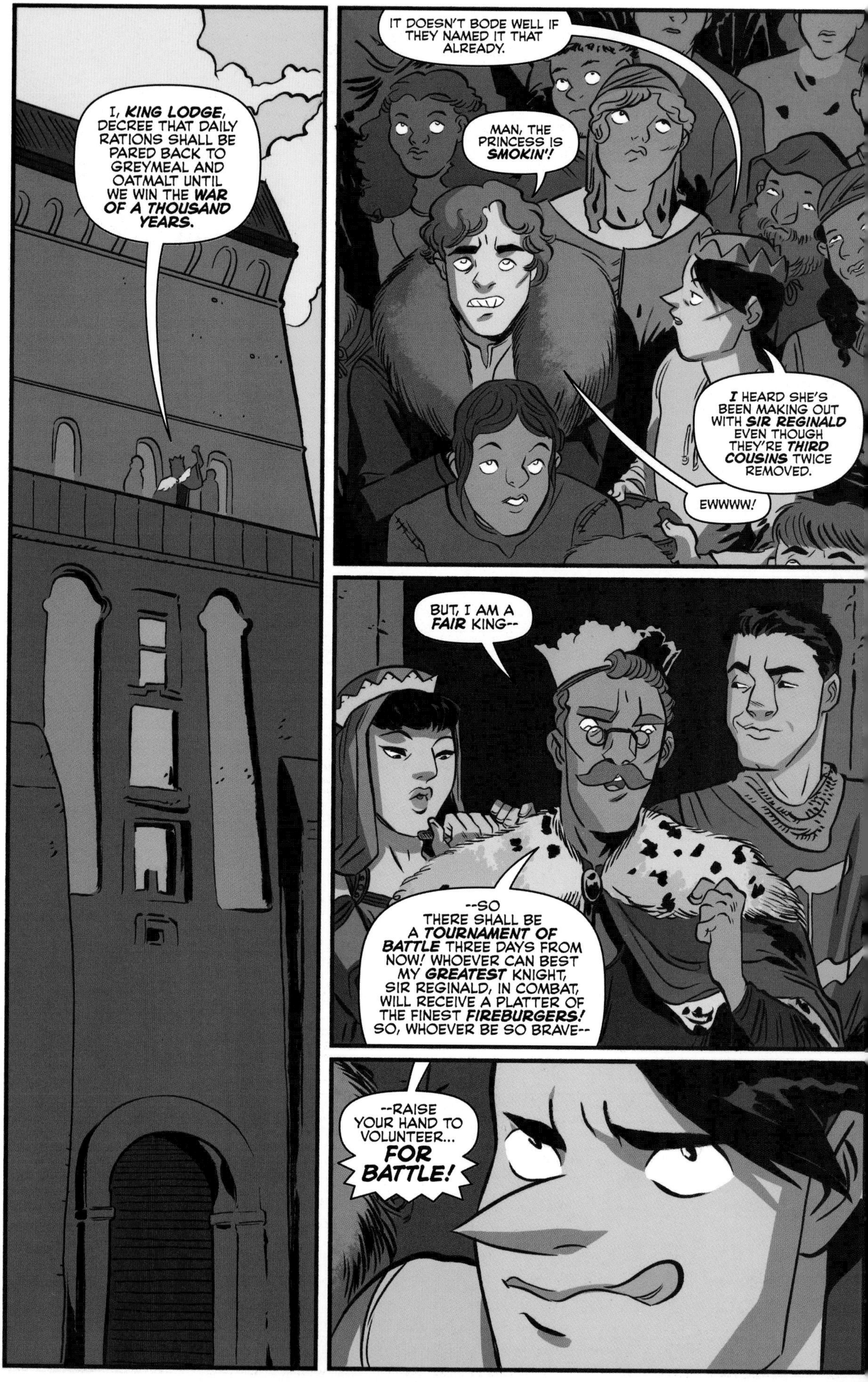
I, KING LODGE, DECREE THAT DAILY RATIONS SHALL BE PARED BACK TO GREYMEAL AND OATMALT UNTIL WE WIN THE WAR OF A THOUSAND YEARS.
IT DOESN'T BODE WELL IF THEY NAMED IT THAT ALREADY.
MAN, THE PRINCESS IS SMOKIN'!
I HEARD SHE'S BEEN MAKING OUT WITH SIR REGINALD EVEN THOUGH THEY'RE THIRD COUSINS TWICE REMOVED.
EWWWW!
BUT, I AM A FAIR KING--
--SO THERE SHALL BE A TOURNAMENT OF BATTLE THREE DAYS FROM NOW! WHOEVER CAN BEST MY GREATEST KNIGHT, SIR REGINALD, IN COMBAT, WILL RECEIVE A PLATTER OF THE FINEST FIREBURGERS! SO, WHOEVER BE SO BRAVE--
--RAISE YOUR HAND TO VOLUNTEER... FOR BATTLE!

MAN, I **TOTALLY** THOUGHT YOU WERE GOING TO RAISE YOUR HAND.

I'M FOOD-CRAZY, NOT DEATH-CRAZY.

WHERE AM I GOING TO GET GRUB THAT LIVES UP TO MY HIGH STANDARDS OF BEING NOT-GARBAGE?

GENTLEMEN...

OH, HEY, DILTON. HEY, MOOSE.

MOOSE.

UH, YEAH. MOOSE.

I THINK I KNOW WHAT COULD SATE MR. JONES HERE.

IN OUR TRAVELS WE'VE HEARD TALES OF **THE DRAGON BURGER**--

--A HAMBURGER SO POWERFUL THAT IT CONTAINS AN INFINITE NUMBER OF HAMBURGERS.

MOOSE.

...YES, MOOSE IS CORRECT. THE LOCATION IS UNKNOWN TO US, SADLY.

BUT NOT TO **ME.**

AHH! MR. WEATHERBEE!

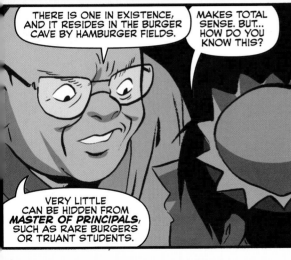

THERE IS ONE IN EXISTENCE, AND IT RESIDES IN THE BURGER CAVE BY HAMBURGER FIELDS.

MAKES TOTAL SENSE. BUT... HOW DO YOU KNOW THIS?

VERY LITTLE CAN BE HIDDEN FROM **MASTER OF PRINCIPALS,** SUCH AS RARE BURGERS OR TRUANT STUDENTS.

...WE'RE LATE FOR CLASS, AREN'T WE?...

YES.

MOOSE.

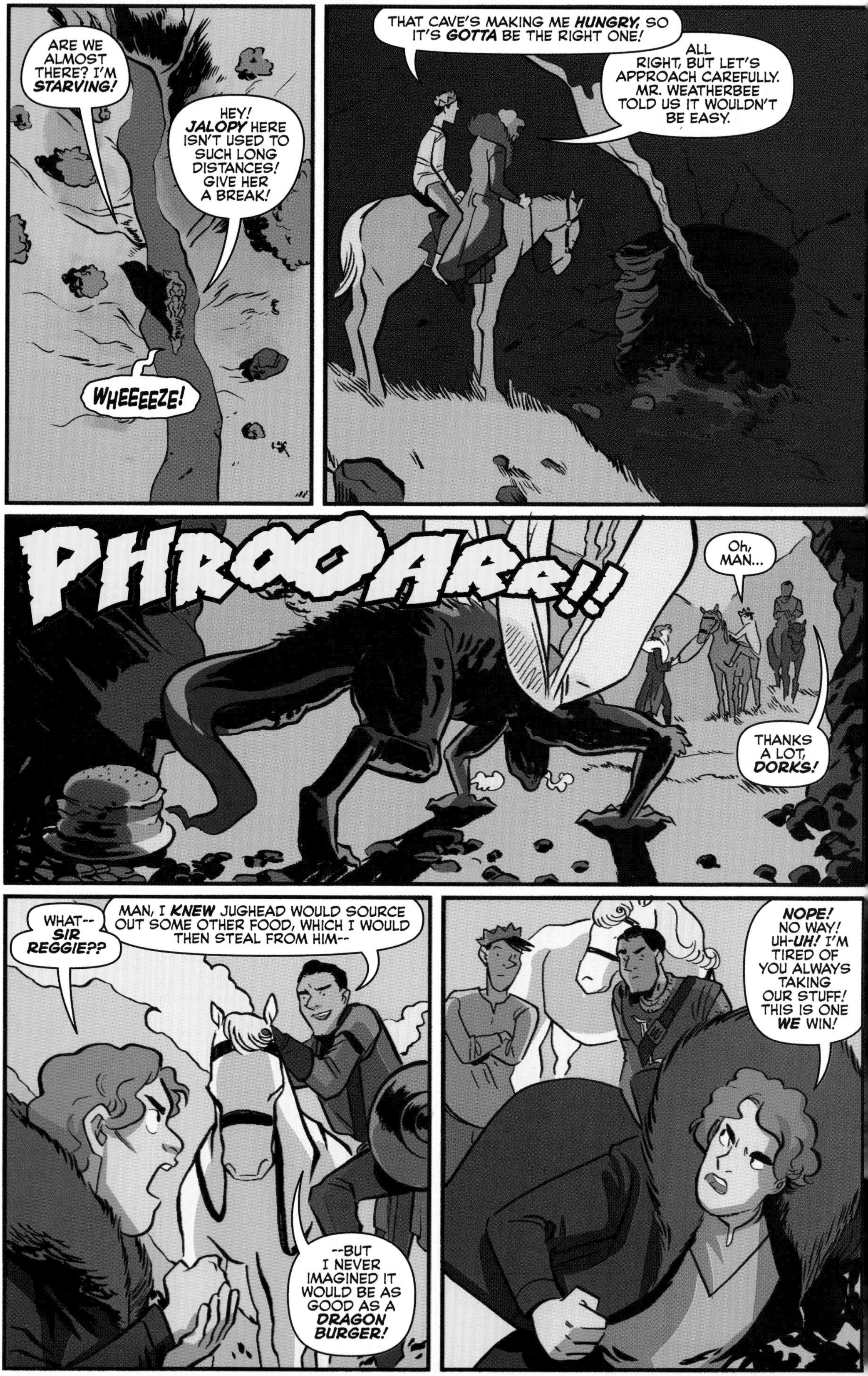
ARE WE ALMOST THERE? I'M STARVING!
HEY! JALOPY HERE ISN'T USED TO SUCH LONG DISTANCES! GIVE HER A BREAK!
WHEEEEZE!
THAT CAVE'S MAKING ME HUNGRY, SO IT'S GOTTA BE THE RIGHT ONE!
ALL RIGHT, BUT LET'S APPROACH CAREFULLY. MR. WEATHERBEE TOLD US IT WOULDN'T BE EASY.
PHROOARR!!
Oh, MAN...
THANKS A LOT, DORKS!
WHAT-- SIR REGGIE??
MAN, I KNEW JUGHEAD WOULD SOURCE OUT SOME OTHER FOOD, WHICH I WOULD THEN STEAL FROM HIM--
--BUT I NEVER IMAGINED IT WOULD BE AS GOOD AS A DRAGON BURGER!
NOPE! NO WAY! UH-UH! I'M TIRED OF YOU ALWAYS TAKING OUR STUFF! THIS IS ONE WE WIN!

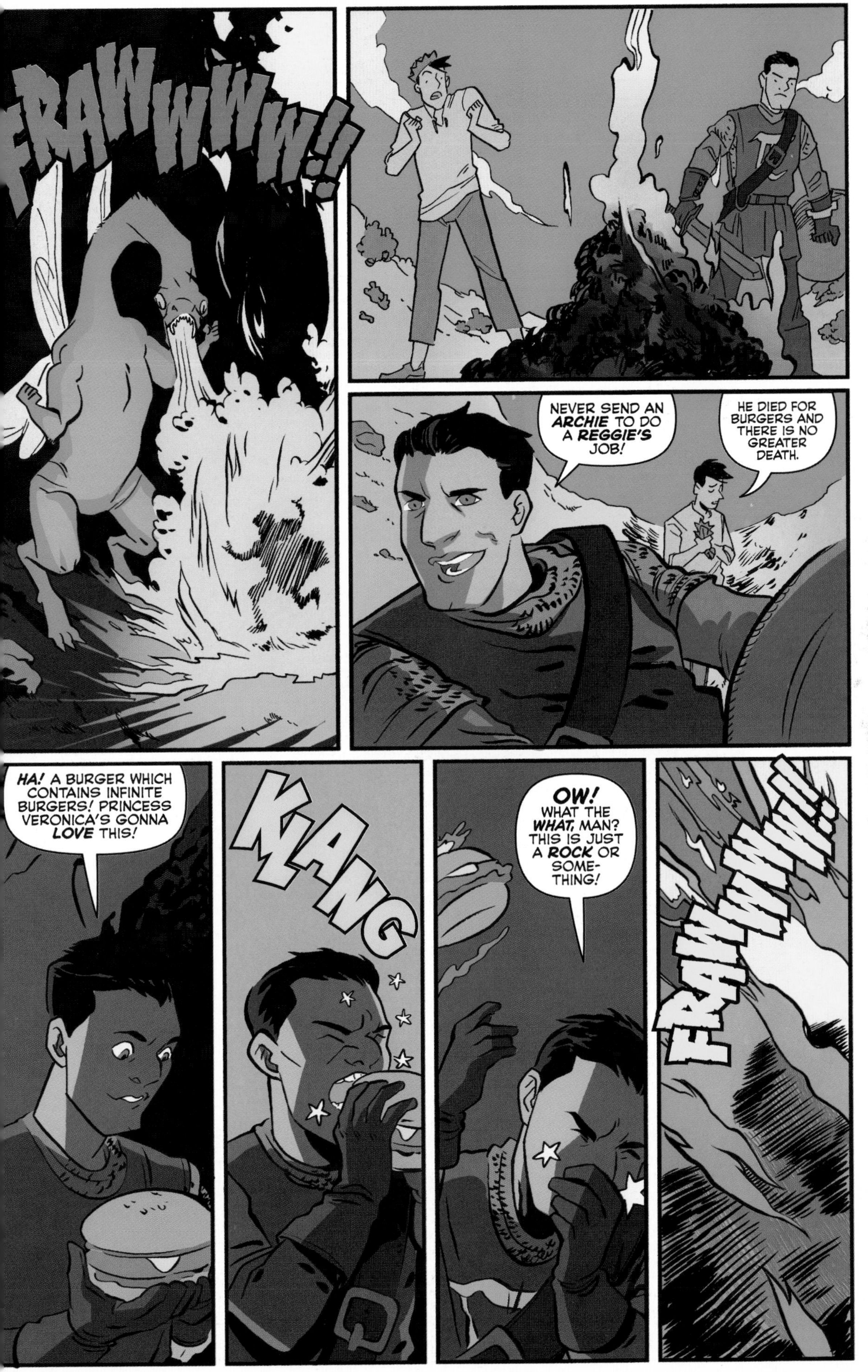
FRAWWWW!!
NEVER SEND AN ARCHIE TO DO A REGGIE'S JOB!
HE DIED FOR BURGERS AND THERE IS NO GREATER DEATH.
HA! A BURGER WHICH CONTAINS INFINITE BURGERS! PRINCESS VERONICA'S GONNA LOVE THIS!
KLANG
OW! WHAT THE WHAT, MAN? THIS IS JUST A ROCK OR SOME-THING!
FRAWWWW!!

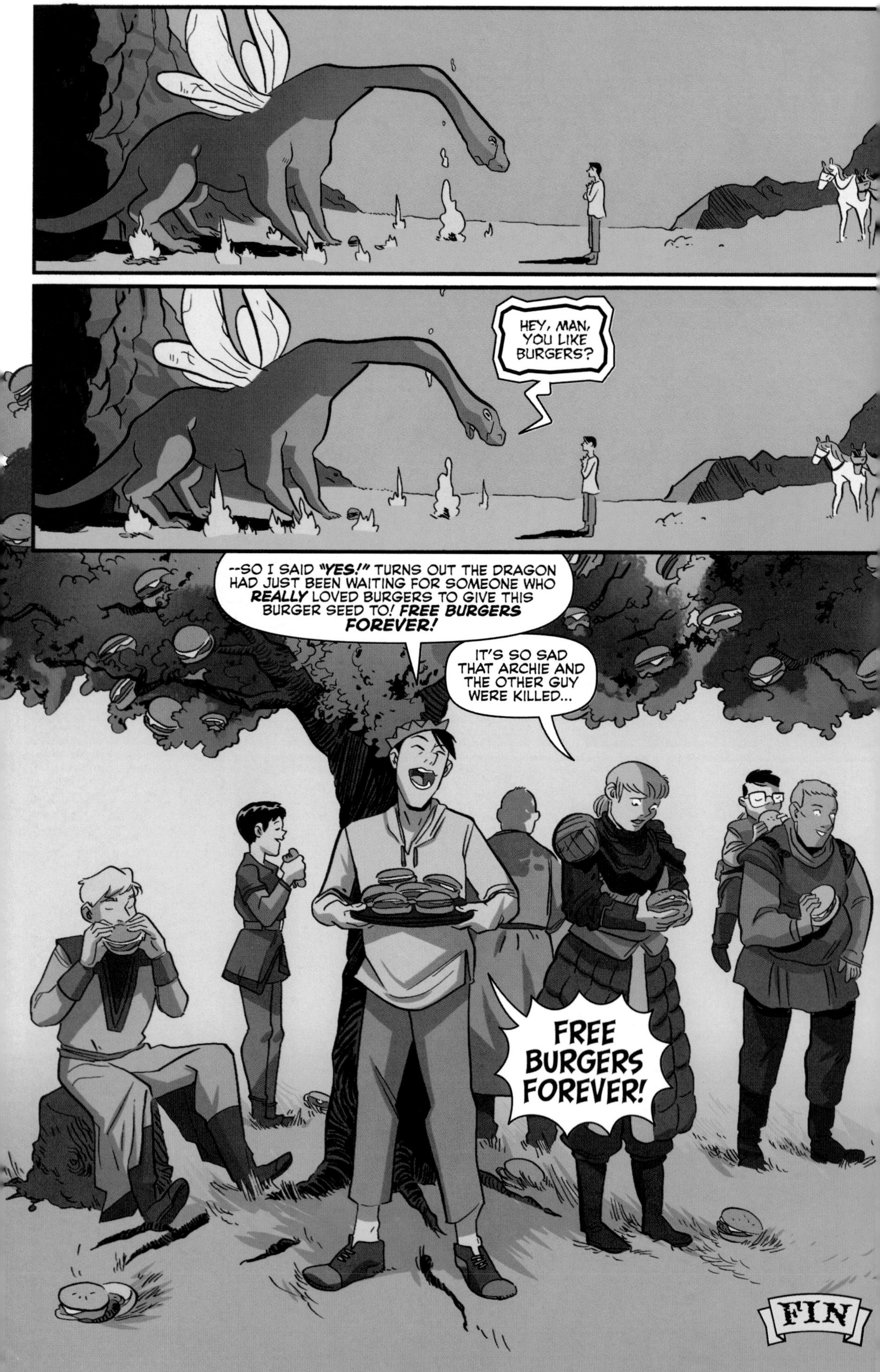
HEY, MAN, YOU LIKE BURGERS?
--SO I SAID "YES!" TURNS OUT THE DRAGON HAD JUST BEEN WAITING FOR SOMEONE WHO REALLY LOVED BURGERS TO GIVE THIS BURGER SEED TO! FREE BURGERS FOREVER!
IT'S SO SAD THAT ARCHIE AND THE OTHER GUY WERE KILLED...
FREE BURGERS FOREVER!
FIN

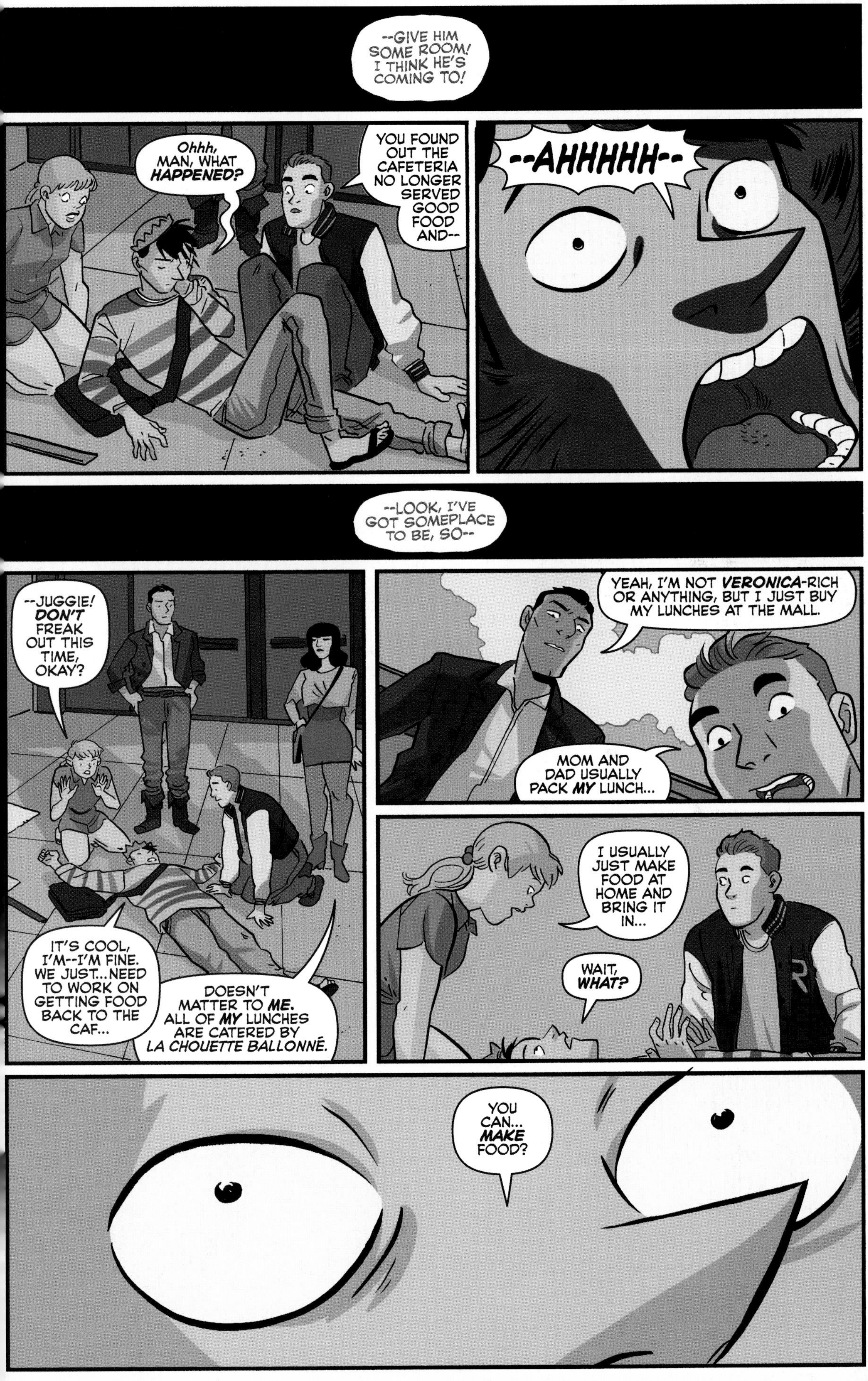
--GIVE HIM SOME ROOM! I THINK HE'S COMING TO!
Ohhh, MAN, WHAT HAPPENED?
YOU FOUND OUT THE CAFETERIA NO LONGER SERVED GOOD FOOD AND--
--AHHHHH--
--LOOK, I'VE GOT SOMEPLACE TO BE, SO--
--JUGGIE! DON'T FREAK OUT THIS TIME, OKAY?
IT'S COOL, I'M--I'M FINE. WE JUST...NEED TO WORK ON GETTING FOOD BACK TO THE CAF...
DOESN'T MATTER TO ME. ALL OF MY LUNCHES ARE CATERED BY LA CHOUETTE BALLONNÉ.
YEAH, I'M NOT VERONICA-RICH OR ANYTHING, BUT I JUST BUY MY LUNCHES AT THE MALL.
MOM AND DAD USUALLY PACK MY LUNCH...
I USUALLY JUST MAKE FOOD AT HOME AND BRING IT IN...
WAIT, WHAT?
YOU CAN... MAKE FOOD?

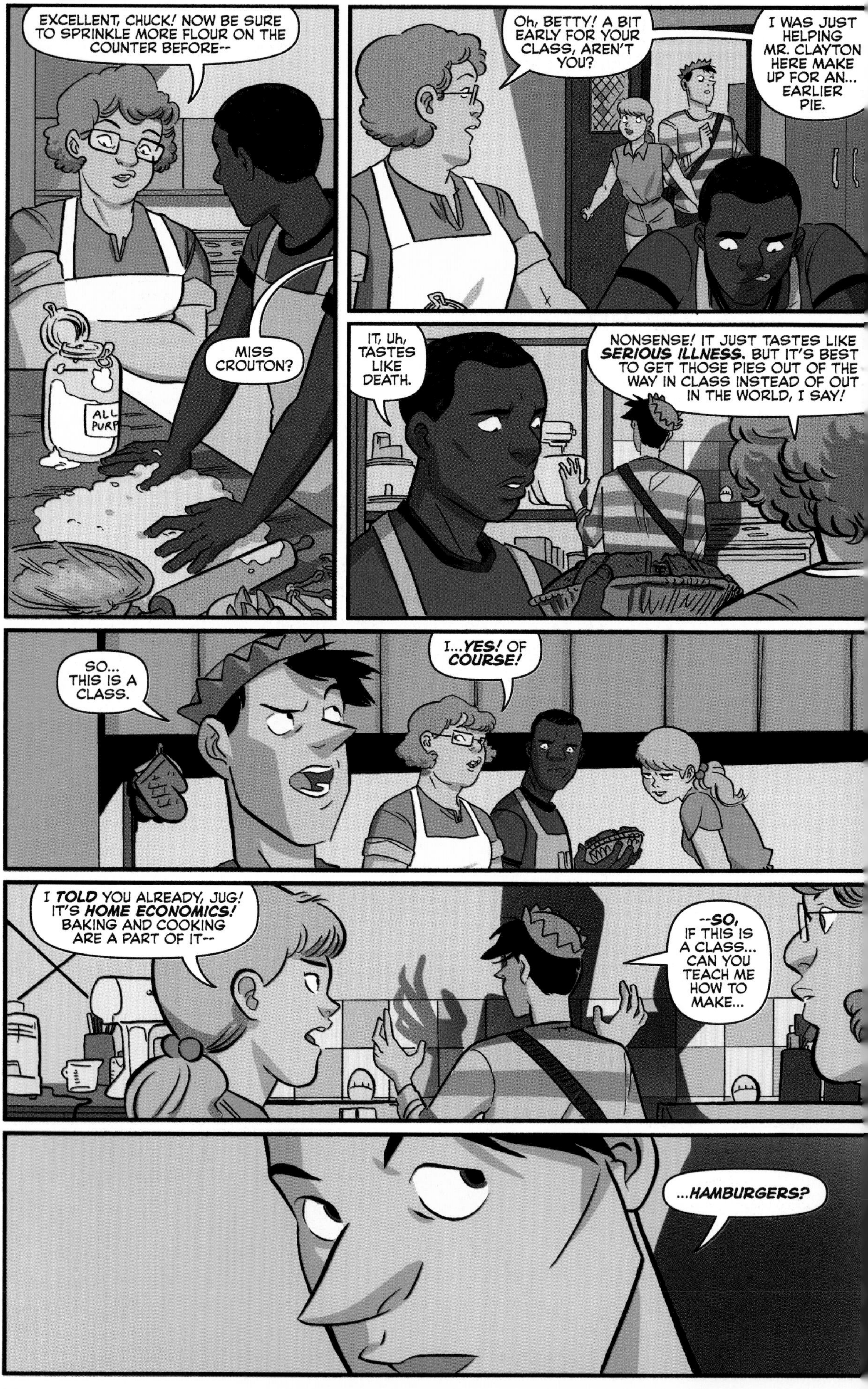
EXCELLENT, CHUCK! NOW BE SURE TO SPRINKLE MORE FLOUR ON THE COUNTER BEFORE--
MISS CROUTON?
Oh, BETTY! A BIT EARLY FOR YOUR CLASS, AREN'T YOU?
I WAS JUST HELPING MR. CLAYTON HERE MAKE UP FOR AN... EARLIER PIE.
IT, Uh, TASTES LIKE DEATH.
NONSENSE! IT JUST TASTES LIKE SERIOUS ILLNESS. BUT IT'S BEST TO GET THOSE PIES OUT OF THE WAY IN CLASS INSTEAD OF OUT IN THE WORLD, I SAY!
SO... THIS IS A CLASS.
I...YES! OF COURSE!
I TOLD YOU ALREADY, JUG! IT'S HOME ECONOMICS! BAKING AND COOKING ARE A PART OF IT--
--SO, IF THIS IS A CLASS... CAN YOU TEACH ME HOW TO MAKE...
...HAMBURGERS?

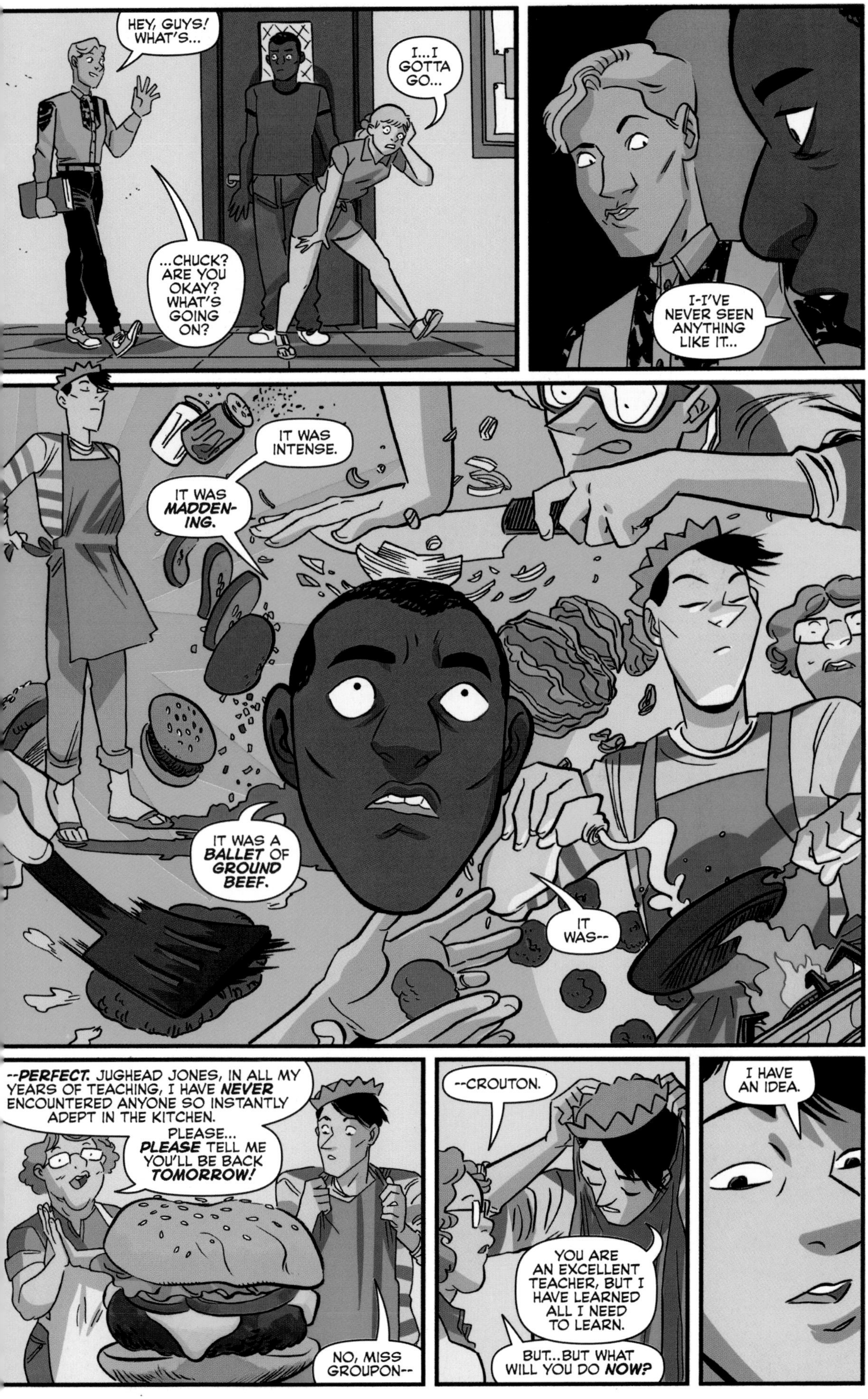

HEY, GUYS! WHAT'S...
I...I GOTTA GO...
...CHUCK? ARE YOU OKAY? WHAT'S GOING ON?
I-I'VE NEVER SEEN ANYTHING LIKE IT...
IT WAS INTENSE.
IT WAS MADDENING.
IT WAS A BALLET OF GROUND BEEF.
IT WAS--
--PERFECT. JUGHEAD JONES, IN ALL MY YEARS OF TEACHING, I HAVE NEVER ENCOUNTERED ANYONE SO INSTANTLY ADEPT IN THE KITCHEN.
PLEASE... PLEASE TELL ME YOU'LL BE BACK TOMORROW!
NO, MISS GROUPON--
--CROUTON.
YOU ARE AN EXCELLENT TEACHER, BUT I HAVE LEARNED ALL I NEED TO LEARN.
BUT...BUT WHAT WILL YOU DO NOW?
I HAVE AN IDEA.

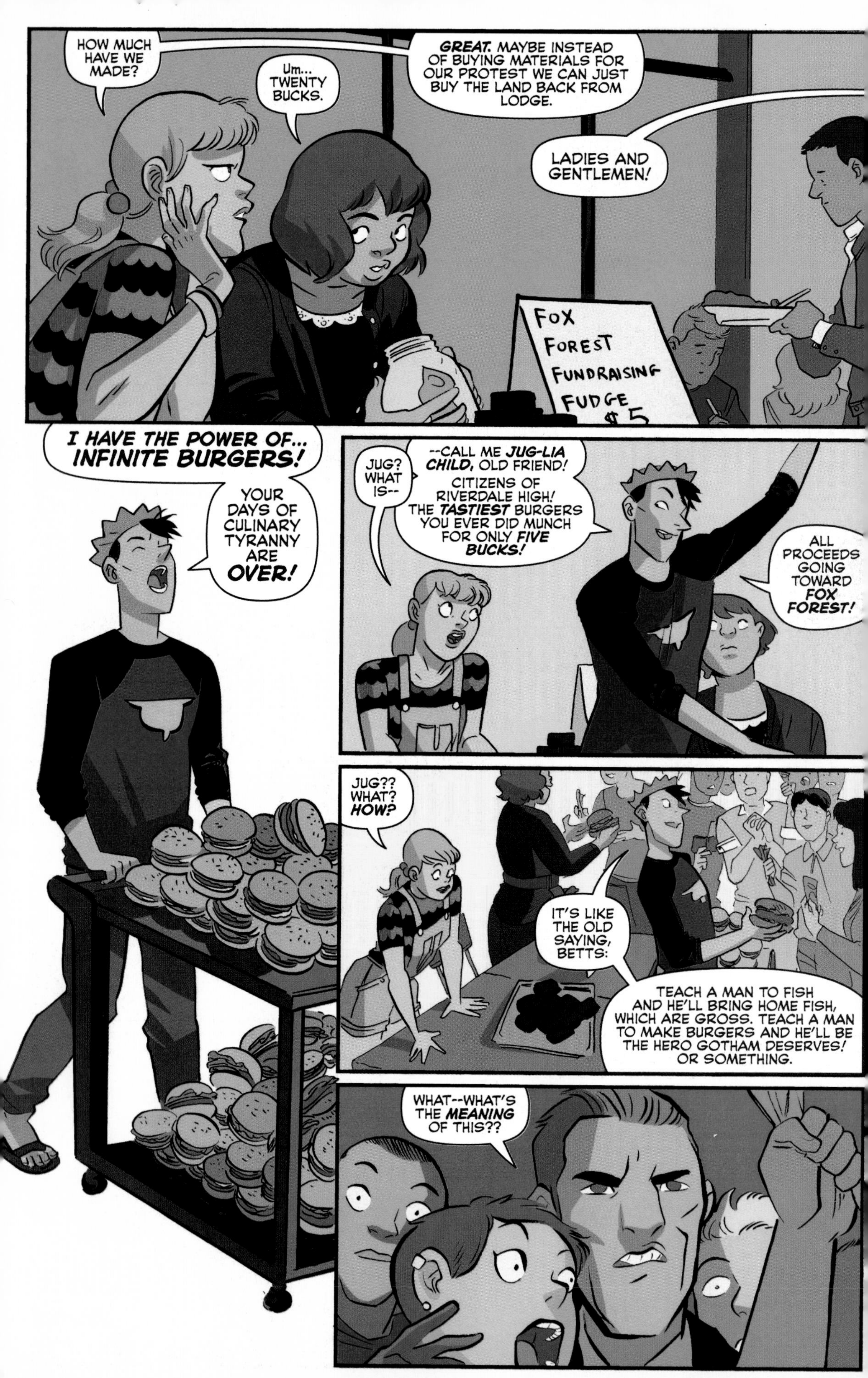

HOW MUCH HAVE WE MADE?
Um... TWENTY BUCKS.
GREAT. MAYBE INSTEAD OF BUYING MATERIALS FOR OUR PROTEST WE CAN JUST BUY THE LAND BACK FROM LODGE.
LADIES AND GENTLEMEN!
FOX FOREST FUNDRAISING FUDGE $5
I HAVE THE POWER OF... INFINITE BURGERS!
YOUR DAYS OF CULINARY TYRANNY ARE OVER!
JUG? WHAT IS--
--CALL ME JUG-LIA CHILD, OLD FRIEND!
CITIZENS OF RIVERDALE HIGH! THE TASTIEST BURGERS YOU EVER DID MUNCH FOR ONLY FIVE BUCKS!
ALL PROCEEDS GOING TOWARD FOX FOREST!
JUG?? WHAT? HOW?
IT'S LIKE THE OLD SAYING, BETTS:
TEACH A MAN TO FISH AND HE'LL BRING HOME FISH, WHICH ARE GROSS. TEACH A MAN TO MAKE BURGERS AND HE'LL BE THE HERO GOTHAM DESERVES! OR SOMETHING.
WHAT--WHAT'S THE MEANING OF THIS??

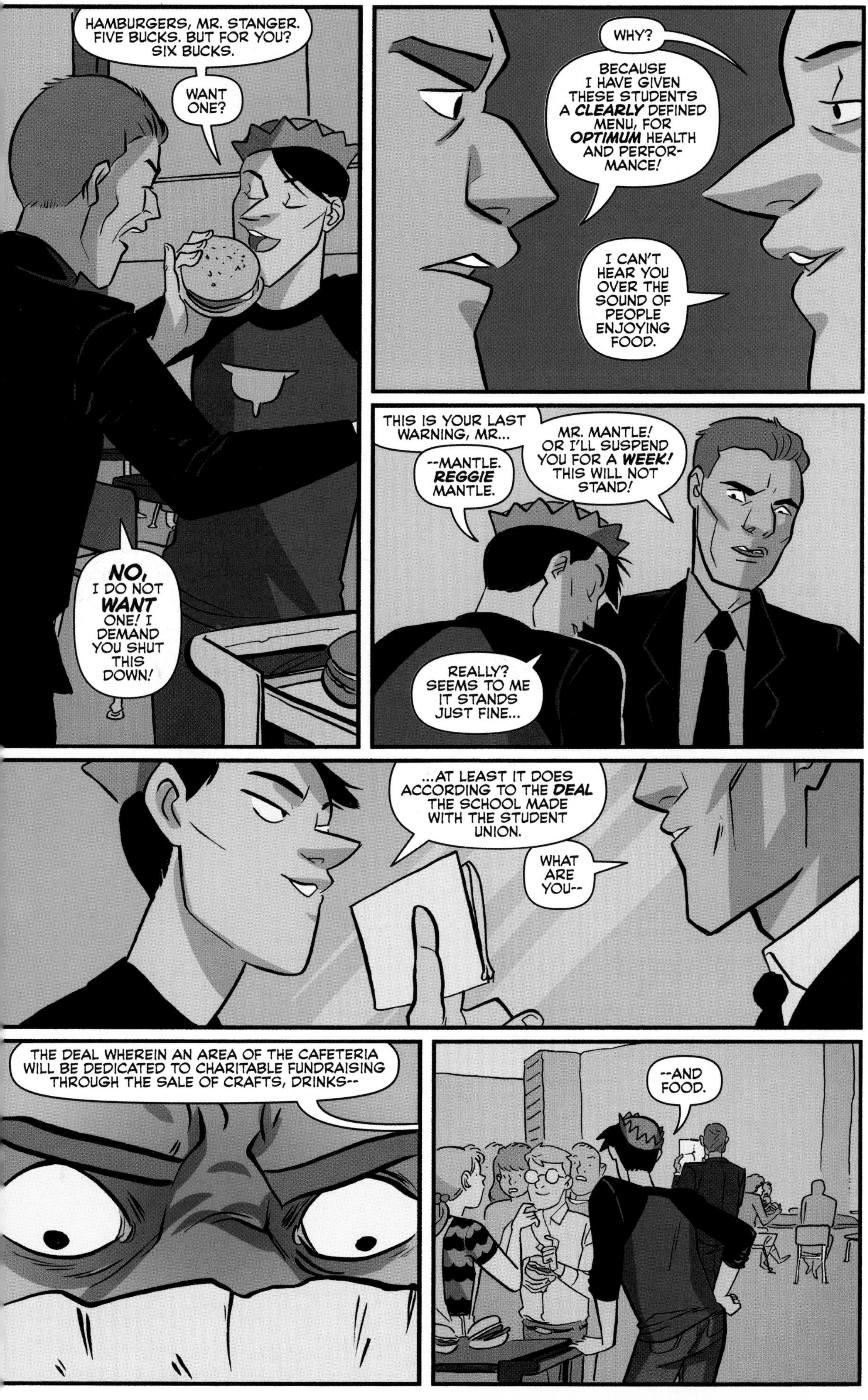
HAMBURGERS, MR. STANGER. FIVE BUCKS. BUT FOR YOU? SIX BUCKS.
WANT ONE?
NO, I DO NOT WANT ONE! I DEMAND YOU SHUT THIS DOWN!
WHY?
BECAUSE I HAVE GIVEN THESE STUDENTS A CLEARLY DEFINED MENU, FOR OPTIMUM HEALTH AND PERFORMANCE!
I CAN'T HEAR YOU OVER THE SOUND OF PEOPLE ENJOYING FOOD.
THIS IS YOUR LAST WARNING, MR...
--MANTLE. REGGIE MANTLE.
MR. MANTLE! OR I'LL SUSPEND YOU FOR A WEEK! THIS WILL NOT STAND!
REALLY? SEEMS TO ME IT STANDS JUST FINE...
...AT LEAST IT DOES ACCORDING TO THE DEAL THE SCHOOL MADE WITH THE STUDENT UNION.
WHAT ARE YOU--
THE DEAL WHEREIN AN AREA OF THE CAFETERIA WILL BE DEDICATED TO CHARITABLE FUNDRAISING THROUGH THE SALE OF CRAFTS, DRINKS--
--AND FOOD.

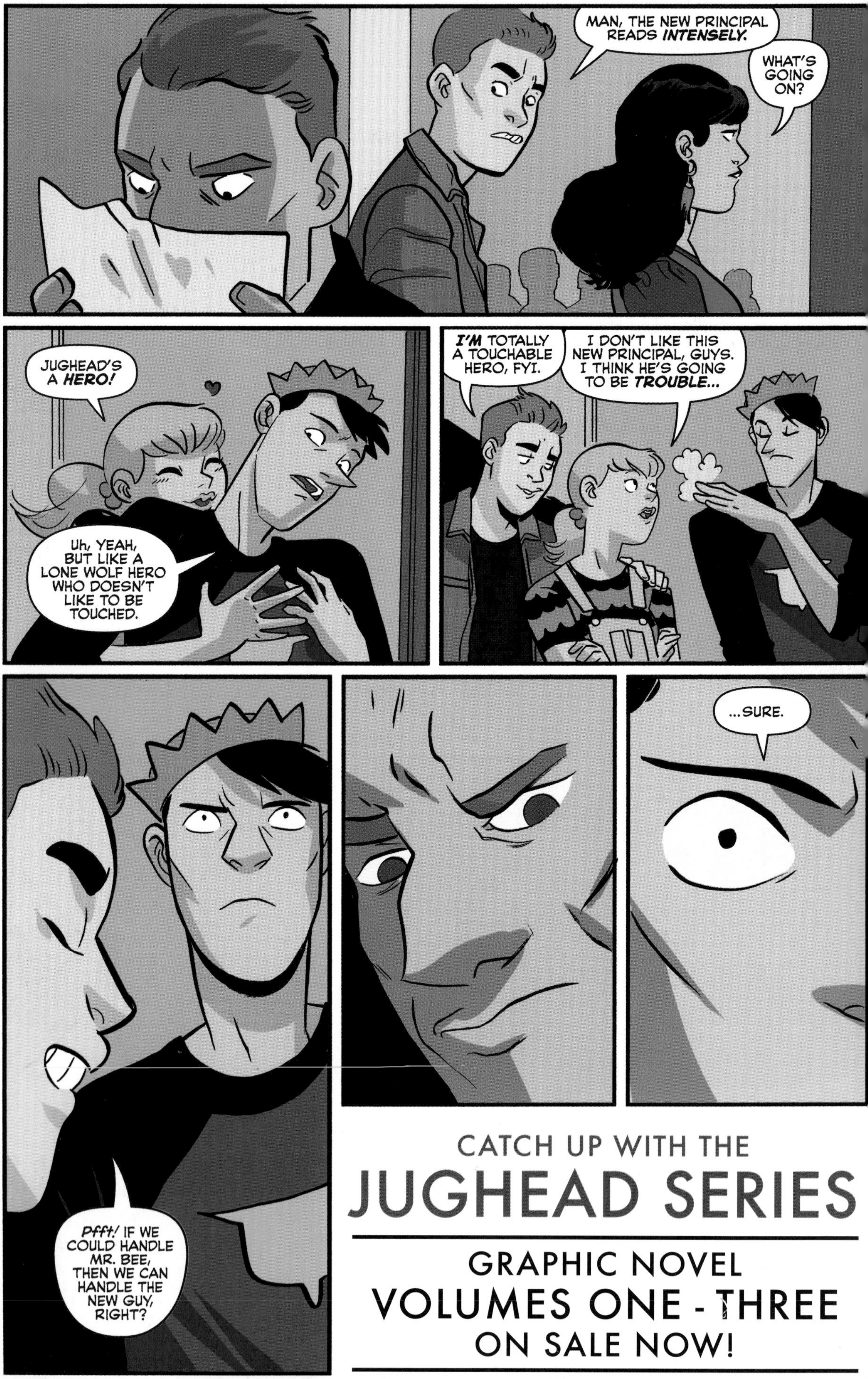
MAN, THE NEW PRINCIPAL READS INTENSELY.
WHAT'S GOING ON?
JUGHEAD'S A HERO!
Uh, YEAH, BUT LIKE A LONE WOLF HERO WHO DOESN'T LIKE TO BE TOUCHED.
I'M TOTALLY A TOUCHABLE HERO, FYI.
I DON'T LIKE THIS NEW PRINCIPAL, GUYS. I THINK HE'S GOING TO BE TROUBLE...
Pfft! IF WE COULD HANDLE MR. BEE, THEN WE CAN HANDLE THE NEW GUY, RIGHT?
...SURE.